CW00924535

Grigori Grabovoi

# The Resurrection of People and Eternal Life From Now On Is Our Reality!

Translation from Russian into English by
EHL Development Kft.

Self-Publishing

2014

**Grigori Grabovoi**

The Resurrection of People and Eternal Life From Now On Is Our Reality! –
2014. – 536 p.

The work "The Resurrection of People and Eternal Life From Now On Is Our
Reality!" was created by Grigori Petrovich Grabovoi in Russian in the period from
2000 till February 2001, on the basis of his early manuscripts.

GRIGORI GRABOVOI®
© Г.П. Грабовой, 2001
© Grabovoi G.P., English translation, 2013

ISBN-13: 978-495476679
ISBN-10: 1495476677

# TABLE OF CONTENTS

# INTRODUCTION

In this book I will tell you about my practical work on the resurrection of people. We can speak about the resurrection or the regeneration of not only people but animals, plants and any other objects as well; however, in this book I will speak primarily of the resurrection of people.

For many people resurrection is something symbolic, though everyone at soul level perceives resurrection as the reality of the World existent at any time. However, many people have yet to grow spiritually to be able to perceive the World at soul level, and therefore, they so far do not perceive the word "resurrection" in its direct meaning, the way it is really meant to be perceived. Having this level of understanding, a person has to make an effort in order to comprehend how someone who is gone can indeed suddenly come back.

The matter is that there are people who do not purposefully ponder on how the World is organized, what its laws are, what life is. Therefore besides resurrection, many other facts may be perceived with wonder as well, for example, cures performed by me without touch and on distance of aides and cancer in their terminal stages, weather control, precise detection of malfunctions and defects of technical equipment of any level of complexity, including equipment on space objects, materialization and dematerialization of different things; computer management on distance by the power of thought; changing the past, the present and the future; understanding a conversation among people no matter the distance, no matter the language, and so on. All these facts have been confirmed by the official documentation and already add up to several volumes. Many of these facts may be perceived as a miracle, however the following needs to be kept in mind: it is known that a miracle doesn't conflict with the laws of Nature, a miracle conflicts with our idea of Nature's laws.

The time has come to change conventional views about the world around us and its organization. All the more reasons for doing this on the eve of the new millennium. And this is necessary for the World's salvation.

This book is part of the book series, devoted to the exposition of the true and real

World view.

We are witnessing a rapid advancement of science and technology, and this advancement is occurring at ever accelerating pace. But let us ask ourselves: what is happening to man himself? Is he evolving? And if yes, then in which respect? What should generally man's growth, his progress, his evolution be attributed to? In actuality the development of man, his improvement involves the evolution of his consciousness. At the present stage of development, a person usually is in one of the two states of consciousness: either in the sleeping state or in the state of being awake. Everybody is well familiar with these states. Here I am not talking about prophetic dreams, because a prophetic dream means exactly entering other states of consciousness. Here I am talking about a regular sleep.

So, the most part of his life man spends in two states of consciousness: the state of being asleep and the state of being awake. While in the state of wakefulness man can move around, reason, make decisions and generally many things are accessible to him that are beyond his reach during the sleep state. Well, it turns out that there are higher states of consciousness, compared to which an ordinary state of wakefulness is similar to a deep sleep.

Let's see how man's perception of the world changes as the state of his consciousness changes. During regular sleep the perception of the world is transformed. During the state of wakefulness man perceives the world through the prism of a three-dimensional space and a one-dimensional time. Here we can make such a comparison. Suppose that at birth contact lenses of a definite color were put into a person's eyes, but he is not aware of the fact. After that he perceives everything in this color. And since he sees the world this way from the very birth, he, naturally, has no doubt that the world is the way he sees it. But the contact lenses can be taken out and then the world will appear as entirely different, in the whole gamut of splendid colors. In the same way if we eliminate the limitations of ordinary wakeful consciousness together with the three-dimensional perception of the world and time that goes with it - that is, if we shift to a higher state of consciousness - the world will appear as utterly different.

This truth has been known from times immemorial. Let's see what Apostle Paul says about space in his epistle to Ephesians (3.18):

"… So that you being rooted and established in love, may have the power together with all the saints to grasp what the width, and the length, and the depth, and the height are."

Four dimensions of space are listed there. It means that as a result of a certain work and under certain conditions, and, above all, as stated by Apostle Paul, upon condition of "being rooted and established in love", man will be able to start perceiving four dimensions of space. And I will add on what will happen due to the change of the state of consciousness. In reality, as the state of his consciousness changes, man may begin to perceive spaces of any number of dimensions.

And what does in actual fact the ability to be able to perceive four dimensions of space mean? To clear up the situation let's make use of an acquainted demonstrative example. Let's think of a straight line. If we mark some dot on the line, the dot will divide the straight line into two parts. If we now consider this dot as a partition, it then divides the straight line into two parts, and now because of the partition, from the position of the dots of one half the dots of the other half can't be seen (the same as in your apartment, where, because of the wall, you can't see what's behind it). But a straight line from the mathematical standpoint can be considered as the space of one dimension. If we can enter the space of two dimensions, that is, a plane, then we will be able to see our straight line <u>on one side</u> and thus we will be able to see both halves of the straight line <u>simultaneously</u>.

Now let's examine a plane, no matter which, for instance, a surface of a table. We now draw a circumference on the plane. The circumference divides the entire plane into two parts: it separates what is inside from what is outside of the circumference. But if we enter the space of three-dimensions, that is, in this case, rise above the table, we will then be able to look at the table's surface from above and <u>simultaneously</u> see what's inside the circumference and what is outside of it.

We have, finally, come to an instance of a three-dimensional space. Let us take a sphere. It divides the entire space into two parts: what lies within the sphere and what is outside of it. But if you have acquired an ability to perceive four dimensions of space, you then will be able to <u>simultaneously</u> see what is inside the circumference and what is outside of it. You will be able to see simultaneously what is, let's say, inside the house and outside of it.

Let's go back to the example with the surface of the table. In our example with the circumference on the plane you may take an object, no matter which, for example, a coin, from the inside and transfer it by air to the outside. By doing so you won't cross the circumference, that is, the line that divides the two parts of the plane. You will be able to move an object from the interior region of a two-dimensional space into the exterior domain, without crossing the boundaries, because you use the entrance into a three-dimensional space, that is, into the space of a larger number of dimensions.

In much the same way in a three-dimensional world you will be able to go from one room into another without using a door, as if going through a wall, but in fact using the fourth dimension. For the inhabitants of the rooms it will be a miracle, and they may start calling a newspaper office to tell them about an absolutely incredible incident.

We have discussed a space aspect. Let's hear now what it says about time in "Revelation of St. John the Divine" (10, 6): "And he swore... there would be no time."

Presenting both this utterance about time and Apostle Paul's utterance about space, we can see that there has always been an understanding of the fact that the perception of the world through the prism of three-dimensional space and time appears to be narrow and that this narrow world perception is related to the level of man's state of consciousness at this stage of his evolution.

This situation can be changed. The two quoted statements taken from the canonical texts speak of the feasibility of going beyond the bounds of ordinary perception.

In actual fact the laws of Nature based on the concepts of three-dimensional space and time, are but a superficial description of this World. In reality there is a deeper, more fundamental interconnection of the world structures, in virtue of which the changes in this World can be caused simply by a specific act of volition.

In order to be able to make such changes one has to possess a higher state of consciousness or, at least, to be in such a state at the moment of performing a volitional act, necessary to achieve the result wanted.

Everybody is well familiar with the Gospels. But let's ask ourselves, which word, which term is the key one in them? If we read the Gospels carefully, it will become clear that the key word in them is the term "the Kingdom of God" ("the Kingdom of Heaven"). Jesus Christ using different allegories calls again and again to abandon everything for the sake of attainment of the Kingdom of God, explaining, that if someone has been able to attain the Kingdom of God, then the rest will come to him of itself.

So, the Kingdom of God, first of all, **is** a higher state of consciousness. And the ascension to still higher and higher states of consciousness – **is**, virtually, a way to God.

And then the meaning of the phrase "the Kingdom of God is inside us" becomes clear. It is because the Kingdom of God is a higher state of consciousness that is why it is inside us.

And when Jesus says again and again "Wake up!", he means the proper sense of the word, because compared to higher states of consciousness, an ordinary state of wakefulness represents a deep sleep, nearly the same as our ordinary sleep is, compared to the state of wakefulness.

And if the Kingdom of God has been attained, the rest will come, because a person who has a higher state of consciousness is free from the limitations of a three-dimensional space and time model, which is a way of perceiving the World, characteristic of ordinary wakeful consciousness; and thus man will be able to start perceiving the fundamental reality.

In this higher state of consciousness a person becomes capable of performing acts which in terms of ordinary wakeful consciousness seem impossible, unreal. Well, for example, such as communication with the gone ones. It is possible to acquire the ability to see the gone ones, and to communicate with them. And it is possible to help them come back here. For the matter is that only few of them manage to return back to our world on their own.

As a matter of fact, it should be noted that those, who we call the gone ones have gone only from the perspective of ordinary wakeful consciousness.

As a certain analogy we may cite such an example. Let's imagine that we conduct the following experiment at home. Let's take a piece of ice and put it on a plate. At the moment it is a solid substance: we can hold it in the hand, estimate its weight. However, if this piece of ice stays in the room for some time, we will find out that now there is only the water on the plate. As physicists say, a phase transition took place: the substance has passed from its solid into the liquid phase. Let's leave the water on the plate and see, what happens. The water will start evaporating and after a while there will be nothing left on the plate. Another phase transition occurred: the substance has passed from the liquid into the gaseous state. If we look around, we won't find the water that has just been on the plate. However, if in your apartment you have a cold water-supply pipe, then in winter sometimes, when the water, running through the pipe, is especially cold, you can see droplets of water on the pipe. It is the water vapor from the air that got condensed on the surface of the cold pipe. If we collect some of this water and put it into a refrigerator, we will have ice again.

I gave this example in order to state the following. It turns out that the transition from the state of life to the state in which the gone ones are is in the nature of a phase transition. When water turns into vapor, it is near us, around us, though we do not see it. The same is true about the gone ones: they are near us. Let's call to mind the stories of those, who experienced clinical death. These people saw, from somewhere under the ceiling, the doctors being busy with their bodies, heard what they were saying, and later, after the resuscitation, often, to the doctors' great amazement, would give detailed accounts of what they had seen and heard.

Of course, the analogy between the turning of ice into invisible vapor and the subsequent reverse passage, as any analogy, can't be complete. During dying and then during subsequent coming back to life shifts to other spaces are used; we will talk about them later. But an amazing, we may say, improbable, unbelievable fact is, that in reality, essentially, there is no fundamental difference between these two states, the state of life and the state of the gone ones; and that is why it is always possible to bring people back to the state of life. Thereby it would be generally better to even use a different language and to speak not of the living or the gone but of those who are called the living or those who are called the gone. For, in actual fact, the one and the other is just a state of consciousness, only in different manifestations (as in our example with ice – water – water vapor, where all of these are $H_2O$). In this context we may say that from a certain perspective resurrection is a standard procedure, which expands the state of consciousness to the level when coming back to life is possible. And that's precisely why resurrection can be taught, just as any other standard procedure can.

In the books of this series we examine how the past, the present and the future can be changed based on the knowledge of the fundamental laws of the World organization and in accordance with the task of attaining eternal life. In reality, this is only from the perspective of ordinary wakeful consciousness, that is, I will repeat, of consciousness, which uses a three-dimensional space and time model, only from the viewpoint of such consciousness the past lives were in the past, or the past events of this life were in the past, the present exists in the present, and the future will exist in the future. But in actual fact, or, better to say, for someone having a higher state of consciousness, all of these: the past, the present and the future exist simultaneously, or, in other words, they are in a static state. (Let's recall: "And he swore… there would be no time"). This is precisely why it is possible to move a person from "the past" into "the present", that is, someone who has gone can be brought back again into our world. When he does come back, he does not regard his return as something extraordinary or, all the more, improbable. All this is natural to him. He perceives this transition the same way someone in everyday life perceives the transition to his normal condition of health after he has recovered from the cold or the flu. You can assure yourself, if you talk to one of those who came back. At present they are increasingly growing in numbers.

A few words need to be said about the difference between two approaches towards comprehension of the World: one of them is the approach of a scientist; the other is the approach of someone, who develops a harmonious spiritual control of reality, which can be characterized as inner seeing.

Everybody is well familiar with the first approach. Based on their observations and experiments scientists try to see what isolated phenomena which sometimes at first seem unrelated, have in common that unites them together. And in case of success they make a law where a single formula unites different phenomena. We all know from school about Newton's laws, which allow calculating movements of a football as well as a plane flight and the Solar system planetary motion. In their work scientists use devices, created in laboratories and plants. And improvement of the devices enables to obtain new information.

The second approach to the World understanding is completely different. In this case a person in his work instead of using devices made either in laboratories or plants, that is, devices artificially created, utilizes the device created by the Creator – his own body. It is this "device" that does the work. And we may say at once that all the books of this series are based on this second approach. And as we shall see later, this particular approach should be the first and the main one.

However, even now we may say that the necessity to prevent the existing threat of global destruction and to establish a spiritual control over the technological expansion is the evidence of it. For it is clear that continuous accumulative advancement of technical systems can become dangerous, if they are not based on control through human consciousness. As it is consciousness that develops harmoniously concurrently with the development of the entire World.

Scientists, who work at the forefront of science, understand perfectly well, that in order to explain the phenomena of this world, it is necessary to create theories which use multidimensional spaces, that is, the spaces of more number of dimensions than three. And not only the scientists realize that, but they do so. However, if they are not able to perceive such spaces, it will at once limit them dramatically. That is why here, as everywhere else, the objective is to somehow overcome the limitations of our present perception.

But the question is how it can be done. This question is facing every person, no matter his occupation. This is always one of the key questions. I have already stated above that the change of the state of consciousness and the ascension to ever higher states of consciousness – **is** the most important task facing man.

What specifically needs to be done for man's growth and first of all for the evolution of his consciousness is a big separate subject, and it will find its place in this series of books. But in order for you even now to begin altering your body and to start harmonizing its function with the pulse of the Universe, at the end of the book, in the Appendix, there are exercises for every day of the month. They may only take several minutes a day, but their effect will be tangible, because for every particular day of the month they suggest practice most suitable for that very day. And thus the exercises ensure maximum efficacy while requiring minimum efforts and time.

In life we come up against the importance of the matter of changing the state of our consciousness at every step. Again and again life challenges us with this question. Imagine you are in a park and suddenly see a blossoming rose. You see the amazing colors of its tender petals, feel its delicate aroma and, perhaps, a water droplet on its petal is sparkling in the sun after the rain. You are contemplating this heavenly beauty, and the beauty and the fragrance fascinate you. You feel the presence of a different kind of life beside you. You would like to understand it. But how can it be done?

You feel that the answer is somewhere near. You feel it with the very core of your being. But at the same time you feel as if something were lacking. The flower is here, it's in front of you, but as if an invisible barrier separated you from it. The answer is coming to you, you feel it, but as if it were in an unknown language. You feel as if you couldn't break through something. And the question remains: how could one learn what a rose is?

Let's turn to science. Science can, among other things, perform a chemical analysis of a flower, determine the percentage of certain chemical elements in it, study the processes proceeding in the flower tissues, but the knowledge of all these percentage ratios and types of processes won't help us very much to find out, to understand, to feel what a lovely fragrant natural flower really is.

And thus the question arises again: how in the world can it be done? How to find out what a rose is? And is it at all possible? It turns out that it is. But there is only one way to do it. And it is as follows.

To find out what a rose is, one has to become a rose. One has to become one with it. Even if for a moment. And this **is** possible, but only, of course, when in a higher state of consciousness.

And this **is** the way to comprehend the World, which is the main way. Must be the main one.

Please notice: in order to gather knowledge following this path there is no need to cut a flower, no need to destroy it. This is a principally different technology of gaining knowledge. This is gaining knowledge without destruction.

We shall have a short digression. We've just talked that in a higher state of consciousness the world may be perceived in a fundamentally different way. It should, however, be borne in mind that the state, in which we ordinary are, does not always remain the same. Just a simple self-observation reveals it almost immediately. Recall your perception of some repetitive event; try to remember your sensations. You will recall that your perception wasn't always one and the same. Your impressions varied. We all experienced that. Sometimes the perception is as if in a fog, but sometimes the fog seems to clear away, and the perception becomes clearer, sharper; we notice that this time, today, we suddenly care much more about a given event or a given person.

All this to a large extent is due to the fact that we in actual fact are never in one and the same state of consciousness; it constantly fluctuates within certain limits commensurate with the level of our development at the moment.

And when at times we experience particular states, states of elation, sense of living a full life, of being filled with joy and happiness – then all these are the exact indications of a higher state of consciousness compared to our ordinary state. And these are often the very moments that stay in our memory, sometimes for life.

It may, of course, happen that even from our ordinary state a sudden shift to a relatively high state of consciousness occurs, and then a person experiences something similar to an illumination, bliss, overwhelming joy of being; however it is impossible to describe this state in words, one has to experience it. By proper spiritual aspiration, proper understanding, and proper regular practice you may attain the level when these higher states of consciousness are always with you.

The issues we have discussed can be viewed from a somewhat different perspective.

Imagine that in your summer house, in the storeroom or in the attic, you find a magnifying glass that you once put there. It's been there for a long time and therefore got covered with a thick layer of dust. You come out into the yard and suddenly see an ant, creeping along the path. You would like to have a better look at it, you bend over, but no use - the ant is too small. At this moment you remember of the magnifying glass that you found and now have in your hand. You bring it closer to the ant and begin to distinguish dimly some details, and yet, with no significant improvement.

We then can take a scientific approach to the matter. We can start moving the glass closer towards the ant and then away from it analyzing the changes taking place; we can start observing the ant from different angles by changing our position; we can develop more complex algorithms of our actions and include statistic database processing; in short, we can develop a strong program of scientific investigations.

But there is a different way to do it. We can get a clean piece of cloth and wipe the glass. And then without any algorithms and statistical data processing we will be able to see the ant clearly. We were able to achieve the desirable result quickly and easily, because we did the main thing: we improved the device, used in our observations.

Thus, in order to succeed on the path of true understanding of the World, it is essential first of all to improve our perception, it is essential to change the body state, for example, we need to perfect the brain functioning, though the change of even one cell can change the state of the entire body.

And a cardinal question then arises: how could such a change be made, how could it be done?

There are many ways to achieve this objective, but one of the easiest and at the same time the most effective methods is meditation. As a result of a regular meditation practice a fundamental change in the brain functioning takes place: gradually more and more parts of the brain begin to work in alignment. This is confirmed by a scientific research, conducted using encephalograms. By means of electroencephalograms the effect of meditation on the character of brain waves in different parts of the brain was studied. The research have shown that as one becomes more experienced in meditation practice, more and more segments of the brain begin to function in accord. And, when a person has fully mastered the practice, his entire brain starts functioning concordantly. In terms of physics, it is possible to say that the human brain has begun to function coherently.

Everybody knows what a revolution the creation of the laser has made in science and technology. The research in this field has been honored with the Noble Prize in physics. The point of this work is that for the first time it was possible to create coherent radiation and to determine the principles of its generation. And it is laser coherence that explains all its unique amazing qualities.

Similarly, when due to a certain practice a person has attained a coherent functioning of his brain, he gets a qualitatively different instrument into his hands. And as with the laser, it is the coherent operation of man's brain functioning that brings his principally new abilities and potential into existence.

We will make an important remark. The purpose of the aforementioned experiments was to determine the effect of meditation on the brain function in particular; that is why we have talked about it earlier. However, in actual fact, not only functioning of the brain, but functioning of the entire body, of its each and every cell becomes affected by meditation practice.

So, if we draw an analogy with a laser and take into account that a laser is compared to a living body, then we can understand that though there is an immense difference between the properties of laser radiation and ordinary light sources radiation, still, the difference in the way the body functions before and after mastering meditation is immeasurably greater.

As a matter of fact the difference is so great that a person actually moves to another level of existence. For it should be borne in mind that a human body is a system, capable of infinite self-improvement. And it is hard even to imagine an overall potential of this system.

And one more remark. When I say that one of the methods of changing the state of the body is meditation, it should be noted that meditation itself can be very diverse. There are many kinds of meditation. A prayer, for instance, is, in fact, a form of meditation. At the same time, of course, a prayer, like any true meditation, must be spiritual. In the Christian tradition, there is, among other prayers, a so called Prayer of a Single Thought, Jesus Prayer, the prayer of a high spiritual level, during which consciousness stays in the region of the heart, and which is very effective for entering higher states of consciousness.

Fast transitions into higher states of consciousness can be accomplished by means of different concentrations. In practicing concentrations, meditations can be a constituent part of the process.

In order to know the condition of a patient's internal organs, health professionals use units and thus send a patient, for example, to take an X-ray or for diagnostic ultrasound. But a person with developed inner seeing acts differently. He uses his own body as a unit. He shifts his body into the required mode of operation and now can see all the patient's internal organs by means of clairvoyance. By using clairvoyance it is possible not only to see a patient's internal organs but to know their function, as well as methods for their restoration.

Moreover, through clairvoyance an answer to a question is received instantaneously. Here we don't need, as in the scientific approach, to conduct experiments, accumulate any data, analyze it, and search for regularities and so on. All these actions, as a matter of fact, are performed in order to obtain an answer. But the answer in actuality already exists somewhere; we only have to take it. Indeed, suppose, for example, we are interested in such an organ as the appendix and we would like to know what its purpose is. It is clear that its purpose is known to Nature. So the answer already exists. We need only to stretch out a hand and take it. And it can be done by the use of clairvoyance.

Clairvoyance is a universal method of accessing information. What could such acquisition of information be compared with? In fact, we already have something like that in our modern life. It is a global net – Internet. By dint of this net we can obtain any information within the net from any spot of the Earth. So, turns out, there is some sort of Cosmic Net, the Net of the Universe, which holds the data about absolutely everything. A person in this case can be compared to an operator. Then for the operator clairvoyance is a way to enter the Cosmic Net with an inquiry. And the speed-in-action there is so immense, that the answer is given instantaneously. I will note that instead of Cosmic Net it is rather be called a universal informational field.

This brings up an interesting question: how are discoveries made? The discoveries, and sometimes outstanding, are made in different areas of life. First and foremost it can be seen by the example of science, but in other fields they are, naturally, made too, for example, a certain change in a technological process at a plant or in society, this is generally one of the occurrences of our life, though science, perhaps, is the most obvious example in terms of making discoveries.

Now, the question that arises is: what can be said from the perspective being considered about the discoveries made by people who do not have clairvoyance?

When someone has a brilliant idea, and makes a discovery, this idea, this answer to his search, comes, of course, from the same database, from the Cosmic Net database. And in a sense it is no coincidence that this answer comes to him, no coincidence in the sense that it is often obtained as a result of long years of search and hard work. But one can never say when the answer will come, and if it will come at all. So it must be admitted that this breakthrough to the database is, none the less, unfortunately, accidental, for it is not controllable, it is not manageable.

We can make such a comparison. Assume there are two people who need water. One of them puts his palms together, outstretches his arms waiting, when it will start raining in order to get some water. The other one knows about the existence of a water supply system. Furthermore, he knows how to use it. That is why when he needs water, he just comes up to a tap and turns it on. And he fills either a glass, or a bucket, or an entire tank with water - as needed.

So one has to know and understand the standard procedure of accessing information. The fact of the matter is, there are a great many questions, but there are too few accidental breakthroughs to the answers. If we consider, for example, the question, mentioned above, of the purpose of the appendix, up to now there has been no such breakthrough yet, just as in a countless number of other cases.

An important remark must be made to what has been said. For clarity I have compared the use of clairvoyance with entry into the Cosmic Net, where there is an answer to any question. This comparison reflects more the facade of the phenomenon, it does not reflect its intrinsic profundity, its multiversion, and thus certain clarifications need to be made. Namely, as it has been said, it is, of course, possible to enter into the universal Cosmic Net with an inquiry in order to access the information. But it can be done differently. The information can be taken directly from the place, where the transmitter, supplying the information is. In fact, and this is very important, the information exists already in the status of the one, asking a question, that is, as direct knowledge, when the information, still not being decoded, that is, not having yet been brought to a person's conscious awareness, already determines his behavior. In order for it to be recognized immediately and used by the person consciously to determine his line of behavior, a high level of consciousness is required, and this is just the goal I have already spoken about.

Above I have mentioned the problem of the appendix. As an example let's examine this question in greater detail. Contemporary science, I will repeat, has not yet, as a matter of fact, found out, what the appendix is and what it is for. But by use of clairvoyance it is possible to learn everything about the appendix. Turns out, it is an important organ. It has several functions. One of them is the following. The appendix reflects the projection of the left hemisphere on the right hemisphere through the immune system of the body. And one of the purposes of the appendix is to support the balance of these systems. If the appendix has been taken out, the function of reserve restoration of the immune system weakens. In this case for its rehabilitation the immune system has, instead, to be reflected within either the left or the right hemisphere, which causes stress on the brain, leads to an increase of intracranial pressure, and other undesirable consequences. Thus we now see the appendix in a completely different light. In fact, we discover it for the first time. Amazing things can be told about other organs as well. Look at the hypophysis alone!

In Chapter IV we will talk about new medicine, the medicine of the future and already of the present. This medicine is based on the practice of resurrection. It is the practice of resurrection which determines the principles of new medicine, and, above all, the principle of full matter regeneration, re-creation. This new medicine has already set about solving its main goal. The goal is non-dying of the living.

In one of the books of this series we will also speak about numerology - a symbolic numeration. The matter is, this science may be used for the analysis of specific situations and for forecasting. For instance, when I, by use of clairvoyance, give my conclusion on a plane's maintenance status based on its tail number, I can see that numbers are linked to specific malfunctions. That is why numerology permits one to analyze a situation.

Someone, who has not specially studied numerology, does not see, how common numbers he has known from school arithmetic, can be related to the events of real life.

It is a mystery to him. He cannot see the connection. We will gain insight into what the connection is and how numerology can be used in everyday life.

Another interesting subject is the life of animals and birds. Since childhood we've been observing the birds flit from branch to branch, from tree to tree. We admire their ease. As well as the way they hover high in the sky.

However, there are a lot of surprises in birds' flight. Science, for example, hasn't yet learnt that birds' ability to fly only partially attributes to their wing beats. In their flight antigravity, created by them, plays an essential role. For example, gravity in a pigeon's head is ten times less than it is on the tip of its tail, that is, it is able to distribute gravity and due to this can change flight dynamics. Different kinds of birds have different ways of changing gravity and its distribution throughout the body. And even the flight may be based on a different principle: for example, the principle of flight of the owl, a nocturnal bird, differs from the daylight birds' principle of flight. The most interesting is the case of the eagle. It has the ability to create antigravity too, but in addition, it has the ability to dematerialize. If we watch an eagle when it makes an attack, it looks like a small round flying ball. One may think it became so small because it had shrunk into itself so much. We, however, need to consider the fact, that the eagle is capable of making his body size several times bigger or smaller. So, it is not shrinkage, though shrinkage, of course, is present too, but most of that reduction in size is due to dematerialization of some parts of its body. The eagle is also capable of altering its body shape depending on the task it faces. In terms of abilities only the falcon can be partially compared to the eagle. The eagle possesses other amazing abilities as well, of which we will talk in the proper book. This is no mere chance that primitive peoples of the entire world used to associate the eagle with the Creator. It is no mere coincidence either that the eagle is seen on the coats of arms of a number of states. We can see the eagle on the coat of arms of Russia as well. In this case it is a double-headed eagle. The eagle with two heads is an indication of a stable and happy future.

In the books to come we will also discuss such phenomena as levitation, materialization and dematerialization, telepathy, telekinesis, teleportation, etc. These phenomena have remained a puzzle for a long time. The time has come to unravel that puzzle.

The humanity in fact has come up to a qualitatively new period in its development: on the agenda are non-dying of the living and the resurrection of those who have gone. And it is no longer a question of theory, but of practice. Now it is, finally, a living reality; the living reality of actual salvation of all.

And note that the facts of resurrection prove the ability of matter to be restored, regenerated, which in its turn bears evidence of non-expediency and illogic of any destruction.

In our age of accumulation of weapons of mass destruction, the practice of resurrection is a method of salvation. It shows an alternative development of civilization.

The development of regeneration mechanisms, of restoration mechanisms will allow one to set about the task of creation without destruction. The principle of restoration, of regeneration can be easily applied to the entire range of human activity. It can also provide the basis for the development of creative thinking of the generations to come.

With this approach any so called aggressive environments can be transformed, and, in a transformed form they can now act as a non-aggressive element of primary medium. As a result, an effective behavior strategy may be determined, that makes it possible to avoid any ecological disaster and ensure further development without any environmental damage. For it should be kept in mind that resurrection is in fact the control of the entire external space.

Greater harmony with the environment can be assured by creating, for example, materials which won't wear out, or machines which, when in operation, won't require substantial additional resources. And all this is absolutely real. Just as real as resurrection is. And all this is in our hands.

And a very simple truth to be always remembered: a man is born for joy, happiness and for living a full productive infinite life.

# CHAPTER I
## CONCRETE FACTS OF THE RESURRECTION OF PEOPLE

In this chapter we will examine several concrete facts of resurrection. All these facts have been documented. Documents are given in the APPENDIX A.

Actually, by now the facts of resurrection are very many. It's just that out of the abundance of the facts available now, several facts, representing different cases, have been selected. The matter is that the requests for resurrection come to me sometimes immediately after the occurrence of biological death, but sometimes a long time after it happened, for which reason the four cases, analyzed below, differ from one another in the time it took for the resurrection to take place after the occurrence of biological death. The facts presented are as such: the resurrection that occurred several hours after biological death (case 4), several weeks after (case 3), several months after (case 1), and several years after (case 2). Cases (1) and (2) are concerned with the resurrection of men; two other cases - with the resurrection of women.

## 1

So, we now proceed to consideration of the first case. The texts of the two statements cited here are taken from the book by Grigori Grabovoi. "The Practice of Control. The Way of Salvation", volume 3, pp. 756-757, 758-759. The books were published in Moscow by the publishing house «Soprichastnost» in 1998. Cited statements are given in the APPENDIX A.

The statement of Rusanova Emily Alexandrovna dated 27.05.1996.
APPENDIX A, p. 309,310
"On September 25, 1995 during my personal meeting with Grabovoi Grigori Petrovich I asked him for a complete regeneration, restoration of my son, Rusanov A.E., born on August 22, 1950, who passed away on June 16, 1995. My son was born in Moscow and passed away also in Moscow. Before I asked Grabovoi G.P. for help, I'd been in total despair, had a heart attack. After my turning to Grabovoi G.P. somewhere around early October 1995 hope sprang within me of my son's coming

back, I started feeling his presence (spiritual) within the house. I went to the cemetery and, upon approaching my son's grave saw a deep crack going across the entire surface of the grave, in the middle of which a dimple had formed as if the soil had been pushed out from the inside.

Somewhere around midnight I vividly saw (with my eyes shut) two white cords stretching out from my chest over to my son's grave, to the dimple in the middle, and then I sort of pulled these cords, feeling heavy weight as I pulled. It all lasted a few seconds. My son was buried in the Vostryakovskoye cemetery in Moscow, but my vision of his grave was at the level of my apartment window, which is on the 7th floor.

When I turned to Grabovoi G.P. asking for my son, Rusanov A.E.'s regeneration, I shared the information with my son's former wife, Kozlova Tatyana Ivanovna, with whom after their divorce I kept a warm relationship; she attended his funeral, Kozlova Tatyana Ivanovna. Afterwards during our conversations within the period from the month of October through February Kozlova T.I. told me several times that she was often meeting people, resembling my son, Rusanov A.E., in the streets of Kaliningrad and Moscow. Early February 1996 she was on the train "Yantar" going from Moscow to Kaliningrad Baltic, and she happened to share a compartment with a man, who resembled my son, Rusanov A.E., very closely. He was of similar appearance, had similar manners, behavior, gestures, glance, but seemed somewhat detached, lost. He was travelling with a man, who was sort of accompanying him, handling him, but who never called him by name. Kozlova T.I. was surprised, when my son, Rusanov A.E. at the sight of the money (one thousand roubles of new tenor) showed apparent lack of recognition of this money."

The statement of Kozlova Tatyana Ivanovna, dated 27.05, 1996.

(Grigori Grabovoi "The practice of control. The Way of Salvation", p. 758. In this work - APPENDIX A, pp.313, 314

"From December 1975 till October 1982 I was married to Rusanov A.E. After I had divorced Rusanov A.E., I remained friends with his mother, Rusanova Emily Alexandrovna, born on June 20, 1927 in Moscow Region. During our meeting on September 26, 1995 she told me that she had turned to Grabovoi Grigori Petrovich asking him to regenerate her son Rusanov A.E., born on August 22, 1950 in Moscow. Rusanov A.E., according to his death certificate, passed away on June 16, 1995 in Moscow. Afterwards, knowing that Grabovoi Grigori Petrovich had been working on Rusanov A.E.'s regeneration, I, within the period from October 1995 till February 1996, when outside, started seeing people, resembling Rusanov A.E., and during my travel to Kaliningrad, Kaliningrad region, I happened to share a compartment with a man, on looking at whom one would think he had been pulled out from the other side. The man, who had entered the compartment, matched Rusanov A.E., born in 1950, in the following criteria: hair color, eye colors, general appearance and shape of the face.

The man's pattern of conduct precisely matched the one of Rusanov A.E.. And his personality traits did too. He had the same habits (taciturnity, predilection for reading, for the most part he was reading a newspaper). The man, accompanying him, was of average height, who never during the entire travel called him by name. And when that man showed money, the person, who matched Rusanov, on seeing a new sample 1000 roubles, showed surprise, to which the man, accompanying him, explained that this was new tenor. I had the impression that he (the one being accompanied by the man) had been out-of-touch with reality for some time. Though he, probably, retained his professional skills, as the man, accompanying him, said they moved vehicles.

The encounter described above happened on February 2, 1996 in the train "Yantar" during my travel on the route Moscow - Kaliningrad."

Such is the description of this case, as presented by the direct participants of these events. These descriptions reflect a number of important instances, which will be examined in more detail. We begin the consideration with the statement of Emily Alexandrovna, the mother of the gone.

In fact in the very beginning of her statement Emily Alexandrovna says that after I had begun working on her son's regeneration, she started experiencing his spiritual presence within the house.

The matter is, that even when a person experiences biological death and goes through a burial phase and occupies a certain grave, his consciousness still retains all the knowledge previously acquired, and this consciousness is aware of its connection with the body, in which by now there is no life, or rather, what is usually called life. And thereby the body, even without any life processes in it, in this case the son's body, when the mother focuses her consciousness on it, responds adequately to the touch of external consciousness, to the information, contained in the external consciousness impulse, and thus, accordingly, gives an adequate response. It follows from here that, by visualizing a body, one can communicate the knowledge of resurrection to its soul.

Later on, after the resurrection had taken place, when questioning the resurrected one, it turned out that he, at the moment of contact made by external consciousness, was perceiving it all in real time, and was associating his physical body with his own "I", though his physical body was in the grave, and thus, was, naturally, restricted in its capabilities in many ways. What is more, the returned one says, and this is a well-known fact, that his being at the universal information level was an indication that his physical body continued to exist and had all necessary qualities to continue to be part of general socium, part of the society, and it is important to note, that this knowledge contained both previous information, associated with the former functions of this physical body, and new information, associated with his biological death.

Let's continue reading the statement. When Emily Alexandrovna came to the cemetery and approached her son's grave, she saw "a deep crack going across the entire surface of the grave, in the middle of which a dimple had formed as if the soil had been pushed out from the inside."

The explanation of this is as follows. The mentioned release from the inside should be considered as initial materialization of consciousness, the consciousness that was in the physical body. After I had begun my work on the resurrection, there was initial materialization of this consciousness as a spherical shape and its entering the information frame of the planet. After that follows the stage of creating a material structure around the soul, the structure that we usually see, when looking at people. We may say that both, theoretically and practically, man can be viewed as a structure of consciousness, having a given physical form.

Here I will make an offhand remark. I have told you about the initial materialization of consciousness as a spherical shape. So, after this sphere has passed the informational frame of the planet, it may be projected either into another foetus (and then of a child will be born) or it may be projected into the structure of resurrection. In this case, due to control, the projection into the structure of resurrection was carried out. That is, the same body was re-created, the same person. Thus here the same was done what Jesus Christ had done by resurrecting Lazar. The only difference being that in this case not several days, but several months passed after biological death.

Further Emily Alexandrovna writes that one day around midnight she clearly saw with her eyes shut two white cords stretching out from her chest towards her son's grave, towards the dimple that had been formed in it, then she sort of pulled these cords towards herself, feeling heavy weight as she pulled. It all lasted several seconds. From further description it follows that Rusanova's son was buried in the Vostryakovskoye cemetery in Moscow, but her vision of his grave was at the level of her apartment window, which is on the 7th floor.

The two cords described above indicate a transitional phase. The first cord appeared when mother was giving birth to a child, this is her son's birth structure. The second cord is a structure of a possible prolongation, of extension, of continuation of his consciousness or his essence. I have already mentioned above that after biological death of a person there are two possible alternatives: either a birth as a different child and, therefore, realization of reincarnation, or resurrection, and, therefore, re-creation of the same body, and not only re-creation of former matter, but also of any structures of consciousness. In this case due to external control the variant of resurrection was carried out.

The appearance of two connecting cords and perception at the same level of the son's grave and the apartment, located on the seventh floor, means connection of structures of her son's consciousness and outside environment.

In the practice of resurrection there is a fairly unique aspect, which is characterized by a body being tied to the structure, to the place, where the body happens to be after its biological death. That is, the place, where the body is put, is the place of its tie. The primary tie is within the radius of about two meters away from the physical body. The entire tie area is approximately within the radius of 50 meters from the grave, and farther is the exit to the informational frame of the outside world. Knowing about the tie and the aspects related to it is important for the resurrection procedure, since transition back through biological death in actuality includes the transition through the tie structure as well. And the one being resurrected, naturally, should be aimed at leaving this tie. By the way, if the description of the vision, given by Emily Alexandrovna, is viewed from this perspective, then we can say that the shape of the grave she saw is a tie variant of a biological body to a fixed place.

Further the text of Rusanova E.A.'s statement is based on the information she received from Kozlova T.I. (so we can use both descriptions of further events). It becomes clear from the text that after Emily Alexandrovna had turned to me asking for her son's resurrection and shared the information with her son's former wife Kozlova, Kozlova started seeing people in the streets of Kaliningrad and Moscow, who resembled her former husband Rusanov. And later, when travelling from Moscow to Kaliningrad by the train "Yantar", she met a man, who had all Rusanov's characteristics, that time close to her, right in her compartment.

Having read the description of this meeting, given by Kozlova, one might think that she was too passive. But just imagine that it's you who are in a train, and in the compartment of the carriage you suddenly see a man, who is an express image of your relative, who you buried a few months ago. In addition this man does not take any notice of you. Do you think, you would come up to him saying "Hi! Don't you recognize me?" Or, rather, you would freeze at gaze, utterly speechless, unable to stir a foot, because your legs would suddenly become wobbly? And though Tatiana Ivanovna does not describe her feelings during the meeting, one can imagine an emotional chute-the-chute she was seized with: amazement, and embarrassment, and perplexity, and a sudden realization of the fact that the resurrection had really took place, against all odds. Against all odds because at present resurrection is still perceived by many as a miracle; because there are still people, who have no genuine understanding of the fact that in actuality resurrection is a standard procedure, and soon resurrection will be in the nature of things, it will become a norm of life.

But so far someone, who all of a sudden in the compartment of the train sees a relative, who was buried, beside him, can't reach any conclusion, for he either denies a possible miracle from the start or has a fear that he might do something wrong. So when reading the statement a person's state in a situation like this has to be considered. This is the book to direct one towards awareness of true reality and to help understand how one should respond in the circumstances. At the very first meeting with a resurrected one of prime importance is starting a conversation with him and offering him help.

We now turn back to Rusanova's description, to where she says that at first Kozlova, when outside, started encountering people resembling Rusanov, and then during her trip from Moscow to Kaliningrad she encountered a man, who had all Rusanov's characteristics, that time close to her, right in her compartment.

In connection with this narrative it should be said that the gone ones, or in this case it is better to say the returning ones, feel very well the state of the people, to whom they are returning, and by no means they would subject them to unnecessary stress. That is why at first Rusanov would appear at a distance from his former wife, gradually leading her up to the acceptance of the possibility of his return, especially as Kozlova had already known that the resurrection process was underway.

So when she writes that she was observing people who looked like her former husband, in reality she saw Rusanov who by that time had been resurrected in actual fact.

It may be clarified that the resurrected ones are so considerate and understanding because the elements of resurrection have been communicated to their consciousness. And due to the fact that they have been communicated these elements, they now have a different psychic structure of perception of reality. They, for example, consider life to be eternal, which has been proved by their personal experience. They now have a particular understanding of the laws of macrocosm. Many of the laws are absolute for them, and they never overstep them.

They also know about the existence of a fifty-meter tie, and on their return to the physical level they for some time stay outside those fifty-meters, away from the people to whom they are returning.

After the first stage of the contact, at which the returning one is perceived at sensation level, the transition to the second stage, the stage of visualization, takes place, when the resurrected begins making closer contacts with the living. We can see that Rusanov appears now in close proximity from his former wife, in the compartment of the train.

Notice that here the resurrected one exhibits his mastery of control technique, in this case control of the situation. This technique is given to the one being resurrected during his resurrection. As a result he now can find, as well as create, on his own, the situations, needed for establishing a contact with those, who knew him and to whom he is returning.

That's what Emily Alexandrovna writes: about the impression, made by her son on his former wife in the compartment of the carriage "He was of similar appearance, had similar manners, behavior, gestures, look, but seemed somewhat detached, lost. He was travelling with a man, who was sort of accompanying him, handling him, but who never called him by name."

Here in the actions of the resurrected one we see another element of knowledge, namely, his empathy towards the person, who knows him. If he had appeared alone, on his own, the attention concentration on him by his former wife could've been so high that it would have complicated his smooth adaptation and could've changed the expected course of events.

That is why an element, partially distracting Kozlova's attention is introduced into the situation: a man, accompanying the resurrected one. And this second person does not necessarily have to be a real human-being in the ordinary sense, in actual fact he may only look like human, that is, only look human, but, in this book, for now, I will put these technical details aside.

Earlier I have spoken about the existence of a primary tie within the radius of about two meters from the physical body. So, a partial or significant focus on the second person, if we view these events in terms of the subtle plane, means, untie from the primary zone, that is, from the zone of the grave itself, and transfer of this zone to the accompanying person. I will note that it may not necessarily be a human-being, it may be just a thing, for example, a car, which a resurrected one is riding, or something else. It is the principle itself which is important, which is the principle of untie of the resurrected one from the primary zone.

Now, the fact that the man accompanying Rusanov never called him by name in

Kozlova's presence, tells us that in that situation it could have brought Kozlova to a state of shock, and thus to some cell breakdown as a consequence. But I have already said that a resurrected one is well attuned to a situation and the state of the person he is dealing with; he has gone through deeper stages of restructuring and then structuring of his consciousness. That is why when moving forward, he acts with great discretion.

We may mention the following fundamental point in Emily Alexandrovna's statement. After the aforementioned sentence she writes: "Kozlova T.I. was surprised, when my son, Rusanov A.E. …". Rusanova doesn't talk about someone resembling her son, no, she says, "when my son…". Here we can see that after Kozlova's accounts of her encounter with her son in the compartment of the train, Rusanova had a just identification of the resurrected one precisely with her son, who had been dead before, and then appeared alive. I will note that later on this was fully confirmed, and the story described ended happily.

It must be emphasized that spiritual identification is the key factor that the resurrection of that particular person has taken place.

The next sentence in the statement: "At the sight of the money (1000 roubles of new tenor) he showed apparent lack of recognition of this money."

In which case may an ordinary living person have such kind of response? In a situation when he at the time when the new money was introduced was, for example, abroad. Then he would show similar surprise, having encountered a new reality. As for Rusanov, he, during the period, when the new money was being introduced, was in the closed space of his grave; his consciousness, which was by his physical body, was also limited by the confines of this space. Hence the consciousness of the gone ones, that is, of those who went through biological death, this consciousness is practically the same as the consciousness of those, who are in the state that is usually called life. That is why the reaction to one and the same situation is the same too.

From the given exposition one should not conclude that the described scheme of resurrection is a standard one. For the time being it is indeed rather typical, due to the current perception of the resurrection phenomenon by society. In essence, it reflects real laws of resurrection. In actuality it all to a great extent depends on the degree of readiness of the living to the return of their relatives and friends. The entire process of resurrection does not necessarily have to take a long time. And in the not distant future, when at least a part of society will realize, that the process of resurrection is a normal standard procedure, resurrection will be occurring faster due to society's readiness to accept this phenomenon.

I have selected the testimonials of the resurrections in such a way that the scheme of the resurrections should allow one to learn how to resurrect through a generalized analysis of the facts.

Chapter II tells also about the possibility of virtually instantaneous resurrection, but in order for that to happen the person, performing resurrection, must possess a very high level of spiritual development.

# 2

We now proceed to the examination of the second case of the resurrection.

The statement of K. S. A. dated Jan. 01, 1999. APPENDIX A p.313-316

"It being the case that on 24.12,1998 (Dec. 24, 1998) I turned to Grabovoi Grigori Petrovich concerning the resurrection of my murdered son V., 26 years of age, I state that Grabovoi Grigori Petrovich really has the ability to resurrect murdered people.

After seeing Grigori Petrovich Grabovoi and his agreeing to resurrect my son V., born in 1967 and murdered in 1993, I started studying hard his doctoral thesis paper and a three-volume edition of "The Practice of Control. The Way of Salvation". The more I progressed the more questions I had. At times my lack of knowledge of where the formulas come from and my inability to comprehend the laconic phrases of the thesis drove me to despair. After each new reading the paper seemed different, something would change in it somehow.

And suddenly on 10.01.1999 (Jan. 1, 1999), at around 11 pm, after yet another attempt to understand what I was failing to grasp, in annoyance I, in my mind, asked Grigori Petrovich for help. And after a while all the confusion and whatever I had failed to grasp, left me. Perfectly clear and intelligible definitions of the cubic form of time and the laws of the World organization formed in my mind. I was filled with joy and happiness. For several days I was tormented by the question: "Who is Grigori Petrovich Grabovoi?"

On January 13, 1999 on the old New Year's Eve, having laid the table for the relatives, I felt an irresistible urge to come to the window. Standing by the window I admired a beautiful winter scene, glittering blue snow. It was 10:40 – 10:50 pm. And again the question arose in my mind: "Still, who is Grigori Petrovich Grabovoi?" And immediately instead of the snow huge black digits: 14111963 began pulsating before my eyes. Then addition symbols appeared in between the digits and all this turned into a strange equation: 1+4+1+1+1+9+6+3=8. The eight was gleaming with lilac-violet light. Then the eight turned and lay denoting the infinity sign ∞. I was called to the table and the digits disappeared. Only the next day did I realize that those digits were Grigori Petrovich Grabovoi's date of birth. And their sum gave 8 – the number of Jesus Christ, which by turning denoted infinity.

On 14.01.99 (Jan. 14, 1999 – tr.) my daughter K. who lives separate and who is the twin to my murdered son V., stayed overnight. At 2 am, when the entire family was already sleeping, and K. had just entered her room, I heard a kick, as if a balloon burst, and a little later rustling of the foil, which lay in the armchair in one of the rooms. Immediately K. came out of her room and said that literally before her very eyes the box from the machine was flying as if someone invisible had kicked it. I said I'd heard that kick and also heard the rustling of the foil in the armchair. We went to have a look at the armchair and saw that the foil had been sort of pressed down and had an imprint of an adult human hand on it. And after this incident somebody's presence was constantly felt within the house. There would be sudden rustles, the curtains would start moving, and the floor would creak.

On 16.01.99 (Jan. 16, 1999) my son (D., born in1965) and my grandson (M., born in 1985) told me with one voice that on waking up in the middle of the night, my son D. saw V., alive, on the wall, opposite from the bed, near the huge photograph of a lion. My son D. closed his eyes and opened them again. V. was still there. Then my son woke up my grandson M. and made sure that my grandson was also seeing V. Though prior to that my son, when told, had been very skeptical of the possibility of V's resurrection. Now he is absolutely sure of it. I would like to add that at the time of my visit to Grigori Grabovoi he gave me an audiocassette with his recorded voice, where he explained to me what the criteria was and why space was secondary in relation to consciousness, but the movement interval was primary. After I had realized that, the cassette disappeared, that is to say, it dematerialized."

So, K.S.A. turned to me asking to resurrect her son. Her son V., born in 1967, was murdered in 1993. She requested his resurrection only in 1998. Thus, based on the dates, in fact more than five years passed, it was the sixth year, since he had been murdered.

Generally, resurrection requires equal effort, regardless of whether a person died recently or a long time ago. However, time difference may have the following effect. The more time has passed since the day of biological death, in this case as a result of murder, the more likely becomes the fact that the factors that led to death (murder) soften, mitigate or totally disappear. This circumstance simplifies the resurrection procedure and can expedite it. Therefore, in resurrection it is often important to understand the cause of the event, for it expedites resurrection itself.

Now we begin the analysis of the statement.

K. S. A. writes that she was studying my work "Application Structures of Creating Information Area" and a three-volume edition of "The Practice of Control. The Way of Salvation", containing concrete facts from my practice, including the resurrection facts. At the same time for several days her mind was totally occupied with, or, as she writes, even "tormented", by the question, who I am.

Probably, her focus on that thought was so deep, that one day, standing by the window and admiring a winter scene, K. S. A. received a symbolized answer to her question.

It happened in the evening, on the New Year's Eve in the old style. She writes: "…I felt an irresistible urge to come to the window. Standing by the window I admired a beautiful winter scene, glittering blue snow. It was 10:40 – 10:50 pm. And again the question arose in my mind: "Still, who is Grigori Petrovich Grabovoi?" And immediately instead of the snow huge black digits 14111963 began pulsating before my eyes. Then addition symbols appeared in between the digits and all this turned into a strange equation: $1+4+1+1+1+9+6+3=8$. The eight was gleaming with lilac-violet light. Then the eight turned and lay denoting the infinity sign $\infty$. I was called to the table and the digits disappeared. Only the next day did I realize that those digits were

Grigori Petrovich Grabovoi's date of birth. And their sum gave 8 – the number of Jesus Christ, which by turning denoted the infinity.

The first comment to this fragment. The date 14.11.1963 is the date of my birth.

And the second comment. In the text the numbers were added according to the rule, used in numerology: numbers are being added up until a one-digit number is obtained. In this case we have 1+4+1+1+1+9+6+3=26, 2+6=8.

We now continue the analysis of the statement. There is information that during the Last Supper Jesus Christ gave his disciples an eight sign, with the eight is slightly tilted, being at the same time the number eight and the infinity sigh. This was the symbol of his level; he was holding it in his hands and then passed it to the disciples.

If eight is vertical, then it is an ordinary eight, but if it is positioned horizontally, it is then the infinity sign. An ordinary eight is a number, it's just eight units added up together, and that is to say, it is represented by the finite number of elements.

A horizontally positioned eight is a completely different eight, it is now the infinity symbol, and it is a symbol of infinite number of elements, a symbol of infinite number of connections.

Jesus had a tilted eight, that is, it had an intermediate position between two extreme, vertical and horizontal, positions. The eight tilted this way is an iconic symbol, corresponding to conversion of infinity to a finite number. It corresponds to the base, master structure that connects infinitude of phenomena with a single concrete phenomenon, it means the projection of all the diversity of the World specifically on what we see, feel, sense now.

This sign symbolizes the principle of connection between the spiritual and the material. It, virtually, means the act of creation.

Until recently this knowledge has been concealed, I'm now revealing the features of this sign for the first time.

As for K. S. A., she, seized by a passionate desire to get to the core of what was taking place, to understand it on her own, she for some time had been in a constant state of a particular strain, and as a result the knowledge, she writes about, came to her as a revelation. "Seek and you shall find!" Only, of course, if one seeks wholeheartedly.

We now continue reading the statement:

"On 14.01.1999 my daughter K., who lives separate and who is the twin to my murdered son V., stayed overnight. At 2 am, when the entire family was already sleeping, and K. had just entered her room, I heard a kick, as if a balloon burst, and a little later rustling of the foil, which lay in the armchair in one of the rooms. Immediately K. came out of her room and said that literally before her very eyes the box from the machine was flying as if someone invisible had kicked it. I said I'd heard that kick and also heard the rustling of the foil in the armchair. We went to have a look at the armchair and saw that the foil had been sort of pressed down and had an imprint of an adult human hand on it. And after this incident somebody's presence was constantly felt within the house. There would be sudden rustles, the curtains would start moving, and the floor would creak."

Here we must make an important point. When a resurrected one approaches a living relative, the latter may experience a reaction of the hypophysis. A relative, with a certain degree of reaction, can see the resurrected one, but perceives what is taking place in a state of expanding consciousness. This happens when the living is not quite ready for the direct meeting with the resurrected one, and for that reason, for him, the meeting occurs in a somewhat sparing mode.

When experiencing a different degree of reaction of the hypophysis, a relative may not see the resurrected one at all, though other people may see him as well as register his presence by means of devices. In this case due to the reaction of the hypophysis V.'s relatives were not able to perceive him.

There is another point of interest in the text. V. and K. were twins, and a twin in terms of information is an informational reflection and thus is the most propitious channel for the first level of resurrection.

Resurrection is a multilevel system, we are going to discuss it now, but first I will make the following point.

There is a principle of resurrection, which is: the more people wish for resurrection, the easier the access to the person being resurrected is. This proposition is called the principle of signal parallelization. This implies that in order for resurrection to occur, it is necessary that as many people as possible wish for it, preferably close relatives, for then it is easier to access the world of the living, and the access through the twin is particularly propitious. That is why K. provided the most favourable channel for the first level of resurrection. And now we will talk about the levels of resurrection.

LEVELS OF RESURRECTION

The first level is the mere fact of resurrection.

The second level is the level of harmonization, harmonization with two kinds of reality. One of them is the reality of the gone; the other is the reality of the living. This harmonization is that for some time the resurrected one has to be present at these two levels of reality simultaneously, besides, there is also, of course, something intermediate in between, which exists during the entire period, while the transition from one level to the other takes place.

The time during registration, when, for example, the tissue analysis is performed, can be considered to a greater extent as leaving the level of the gone ones.

The third level. At the third level the connection with the gone ones is such that a resurrected one is no longer part of the structure of the gone, he now belongs to the structure of the living; the process of stabilization of his physical body is under way, but he still has a so called balance body. This is the body, which the material body shifts (flows) into whenever necessary. When this happens the shift of the material body into the balance body occurs on account of the flow of the matter into the latter in just about the same way the liquid in communicating vessels flows from one vessel into the other. That is how this mechanism works.

Imagine that a resurrected one encountered one of the living, one of those, who is not yet ready for the meeting. The soul of the resurrected one absorbs this information, and then the resurrected one in order not to traumatize the person, forms the reaction of the person's hypophysis in such a way, that the person begins to perceive the occurring events in a state of expanding consciousness, in the meantime the balance body is shifting (flowing) the matter to a different place of space-time. For it should be kept in mind that the soul, controlling the entire process, is largeness, it is an infinite structure in terms of size. So the resurrected one finds himself in an entirely different place. The presence of this ability helps to harmonize an adaptation process of the resurrected to the living.

The phenomenon described resembles teleportation; however, it is not teleportation. The difference between them is as follows.

For a living, the one, who did not experience death, in order to teleport knowing exact teleportation location coordinates is required, it is necessary to possess highly developed control structures, that is, a highly evolved soul level. But it is easier to do in case when a returning one begins shifting (flowing) the matter to a different location of space-time, as a place has already been ready for him.

There is another distinction. This distinction is captured by the camera in these two cases. From the footage it is seen that at teleportation parts of the body appear as discrete movements, while when shifting (flowing) the matter into the balance body, which is in a different location of space-time, all the movements are very smooth, as if the matter really flows out of one place and appears in another, in the place of registration.

The fourth level. At the fourth level the balance body is virtually no longer needed, because by now the contacts have been established with many people, whom the resurrected one used to know before, by now he has the official documents.

The fifth level. At the fifth level the resurrected one functions just as any ordinary person does, now he is virtually no different from the living.

We need to say that the resurrected one may choose, whether he will be staying with his relatives or his former friends or not. The matter is that some of them after his resurrection, when meeting him, may not react the way the resurrected one would like them to. So the resurrected one has a choice. And when he has made his choice and decided upon his place of residence, then now this is the fifth level. And it means that now he does not need to have the second, the balance, body, because there is no need for him to hide any more.

It should be noted though that lately the shift (the flow) into the balance body occurs practically less and less frequently. This is due to the fact that in our more enlightened time it is often sufficient to just explain the fact of resurrection.

We now continue reading the statement.

"On 16.01.1999 my son (D., born in1965) and my grandson (M., born in 1985) told me with one voice that on waking up in the middle of the night, my son D. saw

V., alive, on the wall, opposite from the bed, near the huge photograph of a lion. My son D. closed his eyes and opened them again. V. was still there. Then my son woke up my grandson M. and made sure that my grandson was also seeing V."

It follows from general principles of resurrection, that if resurrection occurs in the presence of close relatives, in this case D. and M., it expedites resurrection, and it is easier to access the entry area of those, being resurrected. The resurrection took place in the presence of these two witnesses; they saw living V. near the big photograph of a lion.

Of no small importance here is the presence in the resurrection area of a photograph of the animal world representative, but instead of a photograph it could be a living cat or a dog, or a plant. I have already touched upon this subject when examining the previous case of the resurrection. The presence of an additional object distracts a person's attention and, therefore, reduces his stress, thus accelerating resurrection.

Thus the following rules can be stated:

Firstly, in order for resurrection to occur faster, there need to be more people wishing for the resurrection of a given person.

Secondly, it is better, if they are his relatives.

And, finally, thirdly, it is very good if there is a representative of the animal world, even if only a photograph, as in this case, of a lion.

It must be said that the presence of a lion in particular, had here an additional interesting feature, which allows one to see the connection between the person being resurrected and the surrounding world. In this regard I will tell you about the informational capabilities of the lion and the eagle.

The matter is that, unlike other animals, a lion moves around with prior knowledge of what he is approximately to expect, what may happen to it in the nearest time interval, roughly somewhere within an hour. In order to better understand what is taking place here, let us turn to a more familiar phenomenon. In big modern airports planes sometimes land every minute. To ensure safety of flights flight dispatchers have to see the motion of all the aircrafts that are up on their radar screens in order to direct their flights and landings. Let's briefly see, how the radar or, in other words, a radar station, works.

The radar radiates a short electromagnetic pulse in a certain direction. If there is an aircraft flying in this direction, the pulse, having reached the aircraft, gets reflected from it and returns back: a point of light appears in that spot on the radar screen. The distance to the plane is determined by the length of time it takes the reflected signal to come back. The next instant a pulse is sent in a slightly different direction, then the direction changes a little again; all this happens exceedingly fast and as a result the air area is monitored, thus the radar screen has a complete picture of aircrafts position for the given moment.

Such monitoring of air area in terms of professionals is called scanning.

So, the lion has the ability to scan space of future events for the period of up to an hour, besides, he sees the events of the future just like he sees the present events. Please note, that instead of calling it scanning of space of future events, it may be called time scanning. Such an expression may be used as well.

From time to time a lion shoots out an impulse of consciousness from its chest and, upon receiving the reflected signal, obtains preliminary knowledge of the future events.

This impulse is formed in the region of a lion's stomach, it is then reflected from the stomach walls, passes through the brain and is shot out somewhere from the level of the stomach - this is the first signal; and the second signal, made immediately after the first one, is shot out from the brain, they almost instantly blend, and the resulting impulse is used for scanning time. During the impulse formation a lion's stomach slightly contracts, becomes somewhat like a rugby ball, and the impulse comes from one of its tops.

In the context of the topic discussed, it makes sense to say a few words about the ostrich. Such an expression as "the ostrich policy" and other comments of the sort are attributable to a popular belief that in the hour of danger instead of acting an ostrich out of fear tucks its head into the sand. In reality the situation is different.

An ostrich is able to scan time up to about one minute ahead. And if it sees a real threat, it runs away. It was confirmed by the ball tossing experiments of American scientists. Even when there is a potential danger, but not yet imminent at the time, and an ostrich knows, nothing bad is going to happen to it, it tucks its head into the sand. If the threat becomes real, it none the less runs away.

I now turn back to the lion. The lion scans time approximately an hour ahead. If instead of an hour it looked into the future, let's say, an hour and twenty minutes ahead, then because of lack of mobility it would start getting out of shape, but a lion can't allow this to happen.

We must say that in one respect the lion's scanning of the future events differs essentially from scanning the air area by the radar. An impulse, sent by the radar, is a segment of an electromagnetic wave, it moves through space with the speed of light. Whereas an impulse of consciousness, sent by a lion, does not travel anywhere, it does not propagate anywhere, there is no movement. The impulse occurs at once, instantaneously at the spot (point), where a lion is planning to go. The impulse appears at the spot (point) as well as is reflected from the spot (point), having first scanned all the surrounding area.

However, for a reflected signal, as distinct from a direct signal, there is wave propagation. A reflected wave propagates at a very high speed, higher than the speed of light and returns to the original source.

Let us go back to the direct signal. In order to help understand what is taking place here, in a simplified way this process can be seen as follows. When a lion needs, for example, to pass through a certain territory, it has a thought associated with it. Let's picture it as a cylindrical column (in actual fact, we are speaking of the shape of information). When the lion has that thought in the shape of a cylindrical column, instantaneously a slightly modified cylinder, say, a cone-shaped one, appears at the spot (point), where the lion would like to be. The cone-shaped cylinder appears based on the principle of universal interconnectedness of all pieces of information. And the information in the segment the lion needs is scanned around the newly originated shape (form).

We may say that the originated cone-shaped column consists of two parts. One part consists of what is always in this segment and what is the corollary of the fundamental principle which is ALL IS PRESENT IN ALL. The second part of the cone-shaped column consists of what is reproduced by will, in this case by the lion's will. By the way, here the will could be accurately calculated, that is, the segment of spirit could be singled out.

Spiritual control is a control structure. Spirit controls consciousness. And this hierarchy, naturally, affects the decision making procedure.

When a lion receives the reflected signal, prior yet to processing it by its consciousness the first immediate decision is made by the spirit, by the spiritual control structure. For example, something wrong is ahead and the lion must spring back. Next comes the reflected signal processing, here the main load is borne by the consciousness. Based on the processing of the reflected signal by its consciousness the lion decides what to do, in this case, where to run.

If for comparison we examine the behavior of the tiger, then the situation here is different. The tiger's spiritual control is substituted by the work of developed consciousness, and that is why the tiger lags a little behind. We can see that the lion significantly surpasses the tiger, as well as other animals, in spiritual control. It is this ability that singles it out from other animals, and this is precisely why the lion is considered to be the king of beasts.

If in this connection we examine the corresponding structure of man, the following can be stated. Man has a special separate capacity of spiritual level, and spiritual control goes into the structure of contact with God. So, if desired, man can evolve very fast.

And one more remark. From the given description of the decision making process we can see, that if the system of spiritual control is highly developed, significantly more developed than the system of consciousness, and if it exercises full control over all cells and consciousness itself, then the object will become indestructible altogether. Because it is possible to create matter and, therefore, any physical body, including the one of man by means of consciousness which is based on evolved spiritual principles.

Now let us pass on to a unique representative of birds that we spoke of in the Introduction, - the eagle. In addition to the capabilities previously mentioned, the eagle also possesses a well-developed ability to scan space of future events.

His first impulse starts from the feathers, though it may seem to be a totally wrong part of the body for that purpose, as feathers may fall out, but, nevertheless, it is so.

The second impulse comes from the eyes; after that, as with the lion, these two impulses blend and the resulting complex impulse is used for scanning time. No other part of the body is practically involved in creating the impulse. But if the eagle's eyes are shut or covered, it sends the system of parallel signals and for that it actuates its body. Other birds are not capable to do this. For example, some tamable birds species such as golden eagles and falcons, if they are blindfolded they are not able to scan and thus seek not to fly.

Now pertaining to time. When scanning space of future events within an hour, an eagle sees a lot, he has a huge visual field, an eagle sees itself, sees all the processes, accurately registers interrelations, analyzes the entire situation. All this is perceived by means of clairvoyance, that is, of irrational vision. The next half an hour it still sees itself clearly as well as something of what is taking place, but the background is getting blurred. An eagle can see itself very distinctly for up to five or even seven hours. We may say that an eagle as if emanates a certain filament into space and with its help an eagle feels, for example, that there is a problem somewhere, and then it doesn't fly there.

Some species of eagles may use irrational vision just to orient themselves during the flight and in doing so they can see even sharper than with the eyes. However, they seldom exercise this ability, as such a form of orientation results in significant stress on their bone tissue.

We may add that an eagle is also an admirable master of teleportation.

When watching the birds fly, we may see them sometimes fly down and, before reaching the ground, fly up again utilizing an airlifting force. A fine example of such a flight is an albatross. As it gains speed while gliding down, before the very ground it turns against the wind and soars up.

An eagle, of course, can do it too, but we now are interested in a different maneuver it practices. It's been noticed, that sometimes an eagle swoops down at high speed, and, looking as if having hit the ground, instantaneously soars up over again at high speed. It was thought, that after touching the ground an eagle makes a powerful push off, which results in a high speed take-off. This, however, turned out not to be the case. Filming performed by Australian scientists has shown that an eagle in these cases does not touch the ground at all. This phenomenon has remained a mystery.

In actual fact, an eagle, foreseeing the future and knowing, where it would like to fly if it did push off the ground, right away teleports itself to the location, where it would be if it pushed off the ground (It just teleports while being still in the air, without ever touching the ground). So, an eagle has the ability to teleport too.

We now go back to the analysis of the statement of K. S. A., to the place, where she tells that her son and grandson saw living V. by the big photograph of a lion. Now, knowing special characteristics of this animal, we can understand that its photograph contributed to V's resurrection. For, possessing the ability to scan time, a lion may be said to shoot out the information field of the future - and then we have resurrection. Thus it contributed to the fact that, when D. opened his eyes again, he once more saw living V.

Further K. S. A. writes that she listened to the audiocassette, on which I had recorded my explanation for her of a number of fundamental provisions on the World organization. After she understood them, the cassette dematerialized.

I would like to clarify certain points. The resurrected one, having a unique experience of his own, would like to help living people to realize that resurrection is a normal natural phenomenon. The contacts of the resurrected one with living people play an important role in achieving this goal. The matter is that the contact itself with a resurrected one sends out the needed information to the entire information field, thus helping greatly resurrection become accepted as a common phenomenon by society. And of prime importance is the contact with a resurrected one of someone who never knew about his resurrection before.

After making contact with one person the resurrected comes to another place, then to the third, thus gaining experience, because he performs a mission, he must equip people with the knowledge. Besides, certain statistics of responses to the resurrected one appears; this is very useful knowledge for future resurrections.

V.'s objective was to create the system of knowledge within his family. That is why when his mother, having listened to the cassette, understood the provisions stated there, particularly, for example, the one which says that space is secondary in relation to consciousness, the cassette dematerialized.

This is the end of the analysis of the statement dated January 26, 1999. Now I proceed to examine the next statement, dated April 26, 1999.

K.S.A's statement dated 04.26.1999 (April 26, 1999). APPENDIX A, p.317-319

"I turned to Grigori Petrovich Grabovoi concerning the resurrection of my murdered son. I state that Grabovoi Grigori Petrovich is really capable of resurrecting murdered people.

On 24.12.98 (December 24, 1998) I turned to Grigori Petrovich Grabovoi with request to resurrect my murdered son V., born in1967.

On January 16, 1999 my son D. (born in 1965) and my grandson M. (born in 1985) told me with one voice that on waking up in the middle of the night, my son D. saw V., alive, near the photograph of the lion. D. closed his eyes and opened them again: V. was still there. Then my son woke up my grandson M. and made sure that my grandson was also seeing V. My daughter K. told that somewhere early in April, 1999 V. visited her and said that we were to expect big changes for the better. And with me alive V. spoke through the intercom. Moreover, K. felt him touch her. He asked her to dial a certain phone number and ask for someone. She remembers that she picked up the phone, sat up in bed, started dialing the number, but nobody was answering the phone. V. said this was not urgent, said good bye and left. On April 11, 1999, at Easter, at around 6 pm, my granddaughter M., who is V.'s (my son's) daughter (born in1990), called me, and said that V., alive, had visited her mother, G. M. (born in 1970). After this fact of V.'s meeting with his former wife G. M., the latter, together with her friend and her daughter M. went to the cemetery, to the place, where V.'s grave used to be. But they failed to find either V.'s actual, physical, grave or any records pertaining to it in the registration book."

The first part of the statement contains certain facts, described earlier in the previous statement. Let's read further:

"My daughter K. told that somewhere in early April, 1999 V. visited her and said that we were to expect big changes for the better."

This is a very important sentence. It reflects the general provision that resurrection is always a sign of future changes for the better. This is a principle. If resurrection has occurred, then the events will start to develop more harmoniously.

"Moreover, K. felt him touch her. He asked her (K.) to dial a certain phone number and ask for someone".

Here in V.'s actions we see the manifestation of another principle. After the first contact with any of the living, it can even be a resurrected one, but the one, who is already past the fifth level of resurrection; the next contact is to be made by the resurrected one indirectly, through someone, for example, through his relative - or his friend, or an acquaintance, or a UNESCO representative -who calls somebody on his behalf. In this case V. wanted to do it through K.

"She remembers that she picked up the phone, sat up in bed, started dialing the number, but nobody was answering the phone. V. said this was not urgent, said good bye and left".

After being resurrected a resurrected one has to be officially registered. There is a structure, within which the whole system for registering the resurrected ones has been established.

Special institutions are at work, with reception rooms, telephones, where a resurrected may come and be registered. Specificity of these institutions is that they have the property of, so to say, dial space: they are visible to the resurrected and to those, working with them, and not always visible to ordinary people. They can be captured by a camera though.

These institutions have not been established by people, ordinary people have nothing to do with their foundation. However, the buildings, inside which these institutions are, have the same outward appearance as everything else created by people.

Entities, who look like humans, work in these institutions, and their internal organs function just like human organs do. But they are entirely different beings, and they too, as well as their institutions possess the property of being visible to the resurrected and invisible to ordinary people.

Though sometimes there are situations, when these institutions together with their staff do become visible to ordinary people. It happens, for example, in cases, when the number of people a resurrected has been seen by or been in contact with needs to be recorded. Then such an institution comes into existence and is visible. People, passing by, naturally, do not pay much attention to it, but they bump into, come in contact with the resurrected one, standing, say, on the pavement, they may ask him something or pass round him, or he may ask them something. The pedestrians may not be aware that they are dealing with a resurrected one, in the meantime the number of people who has seen or come into contact with the resurrected one, is being recorded. So this institution is for some time as if in the open, for everybody to see, but then it again becomes invisible for ordinary people.

Once in while the material substrate of these institutions changes too, but, most importantly, they physically exist.

This whole system of registrations of the resurrected, with its special institutions, with beings – and sometimes people - working in them, - all this is only just starting to be revealed to people; I am telling about it now, but this system came into existence quite a long time ago.

In connection with the institutions just mentioned, Herbert Wells' story "The Magic Shop" comes to mind. That's how it begins.

A man and his young son are walking along the street. Suddenly the child hauls his father by the finger right up to a shop's window. The father looks up and sure enough sees in astonishment a toy shop before him. His astonishment is understandable: he passed along this street thousands of times, but there was never ever any shop there. But the child saw the shop. They went inside and there were amazing toys indeed.

This story is part of the story collection under the title "Short Fiction."

In actual fact, as we can see, our living reality, our life, seems to surpass immeasurably any fiction. And all the more so given what people are yet to learn.

So, after the resurrection a person is faced with the problem of registration. The beings we have just talked about, meet the resurrected one after his resurrection, they are aware of the situation, they have full information regarding everything, and they give the resurrected one the phone numbers of their offices as well as immediately accommodate him in case he decides to make use of the place.

A resurrected has free will, therefore he decides by himself where he will stay, whether he will stay at his relatives' or not. He makes his own choice. The choice depends largely on the relatives' actions, on their reaction to his resurrection.

It is desirable that the registration should take place not too far away from the person, who the resurrected one had his first contact with, not too far away from that person's location at the moment of the registration. Of less importance is the physical distance from the place of the first contact, though, it is better, if possible, to be registered in one of the offices close to it. Full acknowledgement of the fact of resurrection is the meeting with any of the living. But if the resurrected was only taken a picture of, without his coming into contact with any of the living, then it can only be considered to be a preliminary stage of the acknowledgement of the fact of resurrection. What makes personal, physical, contact so important is the fact that the contact with the tissue of the living is of great consequence. So it is the contact with any of the living that makes resurrection a fully acknowledged fact. This being achieved the registration process may be started.

If the resurrected one can come to one of the mentioned institutions with two accompanying people, he then can register without delay, and then, as already stated, he can either stay there or return to his relatives. If he has only one accompanying person, then first a phone call to the reception has to be made in order to be advised on how to proceed. The final stage of the registration process is the receipt of the documents. Now that he has the documents the resurrected one may continue contacts on a different level.

I must say that in the beginning the resurrected one interacts with these special-purpose organizational structures. The program is such that for some time the resurrected one participates in the overall process of salvation.

So, when V. asked K. to call, he did so because he was carrying out a certain mission entrusted to him.

Next S. A. writes that on April 11, 1999 at Easter her granddaughter M., her son V.'s daughter, called and said that V., alive, had visited them, her and her mother M., V.'s former wife. After this meeting with living V., M. together with her friend and her daughter M. went to the cemetery, to V.'s grave. During the last five years they visited the place many times and knew it well. However, they failed to find the grave at the cemetery and there was no record of V.'s burial in the registration book.

First let us count how many relatives by blood V. came into contact with. The first ones were the relatives D. and M., who saw him alive close to them in the room by the photograph of the lion. Then he spoke with his mother through the intercom.

The next direct contact was with his sister K. And finally, when he visited his former wife, he had a contact with his daughter M. too.

To sum it all up, there are total of four contacts at the level of physical vision.

Let's turn to numerology for a moment. And we will use the fact that any object always has its reflection in the area of information. Therefore, in the structure of informative control, and it is exactly control, there is always a principle of doubling. Four multiplied by two is eight.

So, eight, 8. If an eight turns, it becomes infinity, $\infty$. It means that a space-time shift occurs. The fourth contact with the relative by blood happened during the holy Easter. The holy Easter, the Resurrection of Christ, is characterized, in particular, by the fact that at that very time, at Easter, the resurrection channel (path) is simplified the most for space-time adjustment. It is at Easter that the intrinsic knowledge of the universal resurrection of the gone ones opens up the most.

Besides, that year (1999) Easter fell on April 11. If we consider the date as a number, we will have seven. That's how:

11.04.1999 = 1+1+0+4+1+9+9+ 9 = 3+4 = 7

Thus the date of the fourth contact has a vibrational structure of Christmas. That is a very strong support. Here we can clearly see immortality accomplished through the birth and the resurrection.

We see that in terms of the laws of the World organization numerology confirms seriousness of the events that took place. Disappearance of the grave and disappearance of the record of the burial in the registration book reflect the existence of one of the most fundamental laws, according to which: UNDER CERTAIN CONDITIONS AN EVENT MAY BE TAKEN OUT BEYOND THE SCOPE OF ITS OCCURANCE. That is, an event can be broken up by entering the past, and then it does not exist in the present. In this case it was possible to shift space-time into the area where V. lived peacefully in security. And it is precisely for that reason that later at the cemetery there was no grave and no record of his burial in the registration book, which is natural, since the space-time shift occurred into the area where the person was still alive, where he did not die.

Though we must say that whether the grave is present or absent to a large extend depends on what the resurrected one wishes, on whether he would like the visible information about those events to remain or not. In fact, in my practice there are already a great many cases, when all the information about the death would completely disappear. And to the extent that later none of the friends and family of the resurrected one would even remember the fact of the death.

So, V. turned out not to have experienced death. And thereby he had to go through one more registration process.

The first registration, on the physical level, stated that he had been resurrected and the second registration confirmed that he did not die.

A very important point should be made here. After the happy outcome of all these events it became clear that V. remembered his resurrection well, remembered to have gone through the registration process as a resurrected, remembered everything that was taking place before the registration of the event related to the disappearance of his grave and the record in the registration book; and concurrently he remembered all the events, that were later related to the disappearance of his grave, that is, to the registration of the fact that he did not die; remembered all those real events, stated by a large number of witnesses.

Therefore, it turned out that V. simultaneously knew perfectly well that he had gone through the resurrection ( the structure of the resurrection) as well as that he had experienced nonoccurrence (the structure of nonoccurrence) of the fact of death.

Here we see an example of practical realization of the principle, which resolves an old problem of reincarnational memory. From the perspective of certain reincarnation theories the memory of previous existences disappears so that a new experience may be gained. However, this particular fact with this resurrected one has shown that today this is not the case any longer, today an old stereotype gives way to a new one, today the memory allows to hold concurrently the fact of one's life as well as the fact of non-dying, that is, virtually, the fact of parallel life, which was possible due to the space-time shift. And this is a fundamentally new knowledge, which states that the knowledge of any number of lives may be available all at the same time. And this means that now there is no need to die any more, that is, one may live eternally. And moreover, it is possible to consciously make a better choice of life.

At the same time under any circumstances the principle of nonoccurrence of killing must always stay inviolable. And as is seen from the facts presented, any destruction is pointless, as everything can be restored to its original state.

In conclusion it may be said that later on all went well for the main character of this story. He married happily, found a good job and generally his life continued as someone's who had never died.

### 3

We now pass on to the examination of the next case.

The statement of Lubov Serafimovna Kazakova dated 01.06.1999 (June 01, 1999). APPENDIX A p.320-322

"Due to the fact that on 06.05.1999 (May 6, 1999) I turned to Grabovoi Grigori Petrovich concerning the resurrection of my mother Chigirintseva Nina Vasilievna, I state that Grabovoi Grigori Petrovich has really resurrected my mother Chigirintseva Nina Vasilievna.

I, Kazakova Lubov Serafimovna, turned to Grabovoi Grigori Petrovich concerning the resurrection of my mother Chigirintseva Nina Vasilievna, born on December 23, 1923 and deceased on April 18, 1999 in Moscow.

I went to the cemetery. On approaching the grave, I was greatly surprised to see the plastic vase, that had been dug 7-10 cm deep into the ground by my son, lying away from the grave and the flowers lying on the other side of the grave. I had the impression that the vase had been pushed out from the inside. Then I sat down by the grave and began to listen to Grigori Petrovich's lecture on my mother's resurrection. After a while the ground on the grave shook (started moving). I felt ill at ease and moved to the side, to another grave, and resumed listening to the lecture (I listened to the lecture three times), and I saw the Earth, or its large area, from the outside, it was a dark forest of brown fir-trees. After that I left right away. Upon arriving to the grave for the second time, I immediately felt that the grave was empty and there was no body in there.

Then I asked mother to give me a sigh if she thought I had been doing everything right. Suddenly I looked at the wall, there is a spoon and a fork, each 82cm long, hanging aligned on the wall; and I saw that the fork moved 61cm down and 15cm to the side, towards the spoon. Nobody entered the room during the day and could not change the fork's position, but 2-2.5 hours prior to that I had been looking at the fork and the spoon thinking of moving and hanging them in the kitchen. I was convinced that that was the sign from my mother. After my request to Grigori Petrovich Grabovoi (06.05.99) on the night of 07.05.99 (May 7, 1999) I was in contact with mother. She was displeased with me. During the contact there was physical hindrance, but it was eliminated by the touch of mother's physical hand to my cheek. I took the meeting with my physically resurrected mother in my stride, without inner turmoil".

So, let us examine sequentially what Lubov Serafimovna writes.

"On approaching the grave, I was greatly surprised to see the plastic vase that had been dug 7-10 cm deep into the ground by my son, lying away from the grave and the flowers lying on the other side of the grave. I had the impression that the vase had been pushed out from the inside".

Here we encounter the situation very similar to the one, described in the first case, in the case of Rusanov A.E. We have already discussed it. In that case there was release of a sphere. The release may happen, for example, through some small crack; generally, as a rule, a path of the least resistance is used.

It is worth noting that there is a special technology of the resurrection pertinent to burying a person into the ground. If a person is buried into the ground with beams imbedded into certain areas of the ground, then a person gets regenerated, resurrected.

In connection with this method here is some additional information. If the correct burial technology is applied, then a physical body does not decompose and may periodically get up for ingesting plant food. In case of incorruptible saints, they may ingest food much less frequently, for example, once in a hundred years.

The purpose of such a burial technology is that later, after the resurrection, it is easier to restore all the living functions of the physical body in order for a person to live a full life. In fact, in order for a physical body to have more possibilities in some graves special open spaces were provided.

Thus, in old days burial places used to be made in such a way that a person had a chance to resurrect. But speaking of resurrection, in case when a person's physical body is preserved, a somewhat different procedure of the resurrection may be applied, based on a specific orientation of the parts of the body.

The method of burying someone into the ground can be applied, among other things, also for saving people's lives from an electric shock. When applying this method the thickness of the soil layer above a person is of great importance, this is essential for the speed of the resurrection. This is due to the fact that the earth has, in particular, a shielding property, that is why depending on whether there is much or little soil above a person, entirely different processes will be taking place.

Here I will give a practical advice on how to help a person in case of an electric shock. Much, though, depends on the strength of current, but in any case it is desirable to do the following.

First. To ensure the contact of the right hand with the earth. It can be done either by directly pressing the right hand to the ground or by earthing it through the radiator or something else that has earthing.

Second. The next phase is to earth the left hand, or rather, in this case, the spot slightly above the wrist.

After that standard procedures may be applied.

The most important in case of an electric shock is to aid in the regeneration of the brain tissues. This particular function is fulfilled by these two specified procedures.

We now proceed to examine the statement.

"Then I sat down by the grave and began to listen to Grigori Petrovich's lecture on my mother's resurrection. After a while the ground on the grave shook (started moving)."

One of the possible resurrections may be like this: the resurrection takes place directly at the grave, in which case the meeting is at the grave as well. Generally, for human consciousness this option could be easier, but, of course, provided that a person is able to bear it, in order to avoid any cell deformation. As I was saying earlier resurrection should always occur in a way, that does not cause any trauma to anybody, it should be happening under the conditions that are beneficial for all.

The fact that the earth started moving indicates the beginning of the preparation process for the resurrection immediately at the grave. There are cases, when people come to visit the grave and after the resurrection take the resurrected ones with them. But in this case Lubov Serafimovna wasn't psychologically prepared for such an option. As it emerged later, she was anticipating the resurrection to take place right at home.

"I felt ill at ease and moved to the side, to another grave, and resumed listening to the lecture (I listened to the lecture three times), and I saw the Earth, or its large area, from the outside, it was a dark forest of brown fir-trees".

The process of the resurrection was under way, Lubov Serafimovna was very tense, and thus an additional element was introduced to lessen her tension by diverting her attention to a large number of brown fir-trees.

"Upon arriving to the grave for the second time, I immediately felt that the grave was empty and there was no body in there."

It needs to be said that Lubov Serafimovna possesses good extrasensory abilities, clairvoyance. She diagnosed the grave and saw that there was no presence of the physical matter there. She realized that her mother was not there any longer (and, in addition, the earth began to move during her previous visit), and that is why it became necessary for Lubov Serafimovna to draw confirmation of the fact that her mother was somewhere near and everything was getting along all right.

"Then I asked mother to give me a sigh if she thought I had been doing everything right".

As it follows further from the text, when Lubov Serafimovna looked up at the wall, where a big wooden spoon and a fork were hanging, she saw that the fork had moved downward. It may be noted that Lubov Serafimovna used very good data recording techniques. Particular measurements taken by her are given in the text. Even the photographs were taken.

By displacing the fork the mother let her daughter know that the latter was doing everything right and was not to worry. This was a transition period. Mother had left the grave and was to initiate some kind of contact with the daughter.

The described episode with the spoon and the fork was a preparatory stage for the immediate meeting with the resurrected mother, which occurred on the night of May 7.

"After my request to Grigori Petrovich Grabovoi (06.05.99) on the night of 07.05.99 (May 7, 1999) I was in contact with mother. She was displeased with me. During the contact there was physical hindrance, but it was eliminated by the touch of mother's physical hand to my cheek. I took the meeting with my physically resurrected mother in my stride, without inner turmoil".

Nina Vasilievna, Lubov Serafimovna's mother, is an enlightened person. In one of her past lives she was a yogi. She was even to a certain degree assembling her body on her own. In actual fact there was no question of her being seriously dissatisfied with her daughter. As it emerged later, she just expressed certain dissatisfaction due to the fact that her daughter, though being a clairvoyant, was not psychologically prepared for the resurrection immediately at the grave, which led to a delay in time, but overall, she was very pleased with her daughter, because her daughter acted precisely and properly.

Regarding the physical hindrance. During the first contact with the resurrected one, when a person has just been physically resurrected, the relative's stress level may be very high, due to emotional excitement the person may become extremely sensitive, specific sensations may appear, so that even slight movements of the curtains by the wind may be perceived as physical hindrance. But when the mother touched the daughter's cheek with her hand, notably, with her physical hand, the strain subsided right away. At the same time the hindrance disappeared as well.

And it is highly important that Lubov Serafimovna took their meeting with inward calm.

And all turned out well.

4

We now proceed to examine the case of the resurrection on the day of biological death. The text of the statement is taken from the book by Grigori

Grabovoi. "The practice of control. The Way of Salvation", volume 3, p. 760.

The statement of Bogomolov Lev Davidovich dated 28.01.1998 (January 28, 1998). (APPENDIX A, p.323, 324

"Due to the fact that I turned to Grabovoi Grigori Petrovich on January 7, 1998 in the city of Moscow concerning the death of O., I state, that Grabovoi Grigori Petrovich really restored O.'s living functions after I had given him the information needed within the period of time from 11:15 pm on January 7, 1998 to 4:15 pm on January 8, 1998. Her husband E.'s statement, based on the doctors' report from January 7, 1998 is the proof of O.'s death. The confirmation of the fact of O.'s vital activity restoration after Grabovoi Grigori Petrovich's remote session which lasted for 17 hours is the fact, that I personally spoke to O. at 4:15 pm on January 8, 1998 as well as the husband E.'s statement. No other methods for O.'s restoration, except for the intensive remote extrasensory influence by Grabovoi Grigori Petrovich, were applied."

In this case the resurrection occurred 17 hours after the doctors had certified biological death. When the resurrection takes place within 24 hours from the moment of biological death, the resurrected, as a rule, practically do not feel the difference between a sick condition and a condition of biological death. It proves that consciousness has the function of the body restoration no matter the degree of destruction and retains the vital activity data of the physical body for a long period of time. By telepathically communicating the principles and the methods of resurrection to the consciousness of a gone one, it is possible to develop the function of consciousness for the body restoration up to the level, when the body starts the process of restoration. The restoration (the regeneration) goes faster, if the soul has been prepared by the prior knowledge of the resurrection processes, and if as many people as possible contribute to the resurrection. Resurrection occurs based on the freedom of choice of a person's soul, of the choice of further development. The knowledge about the principles and the methods of resurrection must be disseminated everywhere so that everybody can get the knowledge of resurrection as the only way of development. Life will have developed toward its eternity. The living will turn steps toward the path of immortality. The gone ones shall resurrect. The Creator's law of eternal life will materialize.

The examination of these specific cases of resurrection allows us to make the following conclusions.

First. The resurrected one as a normal free person has a right to choose, where and with whom and for how long he will stay. This possibility is open to him, especially given that the registration takes place on the highest level and international organizations are involved, and only after that the registration takes place in the country. Although sometimes, but quite rarely, the registration first takes place in the country before it does in international organizations.

Now I am talking about ordinary organizations, that is, about organizations, created by people. But the very first registration of which I talked when analyzing the second case, the resurrected one goes through in those special structures that I spoke of. So, basically, the resurrected one goes through two different registrations: the first registration is in these special structures and the second one is in our ordinary offices.

The resurrected have equal rights with all other people, their only difference being that they have gone through resurrection (the structure of resurrection).

Second. Of great importance for expediting resurrection is the contact with the special structures, involved in the resurrection process, with the aforementioned beings, with their specific representatives, etc. For that purpose it is desirable to have any means of communication at disposal, for example, a telephone to make a call and obtain information. It is possible to do without a telephone, if one has advanced telepathic abilities. In this case the resurrected one, by focusing mentally, may send a telepathic request as well as receive a telepathic response.

Resurrection may occur even faster when one fully understands that resurrection may happen directly, that is, without any intermediaries performing the function of harmonization of the structures of a resurrected with the structures of the living. At present it happens quite often when the resurrected one appears directly before the living one; and when the living one has a prior knowledge of that, it expedites resurrection too, and the resurrected one then doesn't go through any particular stages involving the aforementioned representatives, who harmonize the resurrected with the living. Thus one should know that resurrection may happen under vastly different conditions, and in order for resurrection to occur, for example, it is not necessary to create transition structures.

Third. Resurrection always has a positive effect. This is the fundamental principle. Resurrection is always very good for everybody, because it reflects the fact that destruction is impossible. This information in itself is immensely beneficial. Resurrection always changes the situation for the better.

I have many concrete facts, which indicate that resurrection is an event, beneficial for all. For example, when after the resurrection the resurrected one would come into contact with his relatives, the relatives' illnesses would disappear, for example, malignant tumors would disappear, or the problems, unresolved issues would be resolved, there would be many positive changes in their life, their life generally would move to a qualitatively new level, the level, when all goes as it should.

Thus resurrection is highly beneficial for the living; for by the very fact of its realization it affirms the status of a completely different life, and people, by accepting this status, begin to live at a completely different level, incommensurably more beneficial, than the one, that existed before the fact of resurrection.

# CHAPTER II
## CORE PRINCIPLES OF RESURRECTION

In this chapter we will examine core principles of resurrection. All the principles are divided into four groups commensurate with the degree of their significance. The first group represents the principles of the first level, that is, the most important ones. Then follow the second, the third and the fourth levels. The definitions of the principles will be capitalized. Following each principle definition its numerical expression will be given in brackets, for example, (3.5). The figure means that this principle applies to the third level and its sequence number is five. In the end of the chapter the core principles are listed sequentially according to their level. We begin with the description of the principles of the first level.

### 1

As far back as in the Introduction it was said that man's main objective in life is raising the level of his consciousness. Raising the consciousness level is a true way to change oneself and the surrounding world.

At present there is a belief that the surrounding world exists irrespectively of us, that it exists on its own, that it exists, so to say, objectively, and all that is left for man is to study this world, to study its regularities in order for them to be used for the benefit of the people.

In reality this is not quite so.

Let's deliberate on why people have formed such a notion. Every morning man sees the Sun rise and every evening he sees the sun set, man sees a regular change of seasons, and the seasons alternate in one and the same order, the North Star and other stars can always be found on the same spots in the sky; if we let go of an object, it, like the famous Newton apple, always falls downwards. All these phenomena happen again and again and it gives man the impression that they occur irrespectively of his existence, that they represent certain objective phenomena beyond his control, that is, that he lives in an objective world, existing irrespectively of him. And this is a big misconception on the part of man.

In order to find out what the real situation is, it is necessary to introduce the concept of collective consciousness. The collective consciousness is the merged consciousness of all people. Later we will see that the collective consciousness should include consciousness of other beings, for example, animals and, on the whole, the consciousness of all that exists.

In the collective consciousness there are certain stable, persistent views. These views are stable, because they are a certain mean, that is, what we get as a result of averaging over the entire human population.

To better understand what I am referring to let's turn to specific examples. Imagine that we are tossing a coin. Is it possible to predict the exact result of the tossing: heads or tails? If it is a standard coin, then it is impossible to say in advance what it will land on. And what if we toss a coin, for example, seven times? – It'll be the same. It may be several times heads and several times tails. It may even happen that it will be heads all seven times or vice versa - all seven times it may be tails. If we form a ratio of the number of heads to the number of tails occurred, we won`t be able to predict heads to tails ratio in the above instances without applying clairvoyance, we won`t be able to say, what the ratio will be, for example, after tossing a coin seven times.

However, if we toss a coin several thousand times, then it is possible to say in advance that the ratio of the number of heads occurred to the number of tails occurred will tend to unity. If we toss a coin several million times, the ratio will virtually equal to unity. We have then that at a large number of tossing cases it is possible to predict the result. And this is not accidental. The matter is that given a large number of experiments, a large number of occurrences, there appear so called statistical regularities.

So, given a few single experiments no regularity can be traced, the result is accidental. But if the number of instances becomes very large, then the regularities, called statistical, would manifest themselves.

There are plenty of such regularities around us. Let's have a good look at a computer keyboard. We can see that the letters on the keyboard are not arranged alphabetically. They are arranged in some peculiar way, apparently according to some rule. But what rule?

In the center of the keyboard there are letters used most frequently and on the sides – the ones used less frequently. It is clear that it is easier to work with forefingers rather than with little fingers, that is exactly the reason why the most frequently used letters are placed in the center.

How can we find out which letters are used most frequently? We may, for example, charge the computer with the task of reading a lot of books and determining which letters are used most frequently, less frequently and used very rarely. For each letter the computer can calculate the probability of its appearance in the text. It is the letters with the most probability of their appearance in the text that are placed in the center of the keyboard.

Notice the following. If we become interested in the probability of the appearance of a certain letter, let`s say, the letter "A", in a word randomly taken out from a text, we will fail to get the answer to the question. But if we take a lot of books with a lot of words in them and, therefore, letters, then the statistical regularities will emerge, and thus we will be able to determine the probability of its appearance in the text.

These data may be used in printing-houses for compiling type cases. There is no need to cast all the letters of the alphabet in equal quantities. The letters may be manufactured in the quantities proportionate to the probabilities of their appearance in the text.

The same idea is used for compiling frequency dictionaries. The computer, having read a lot of books and works of classics in particular, can make a list of the words most frequently used. Such dictionaries are very useful when studying a foreign language. For example, 3000 words of the basic English language vocabulary take approximately 90% of fiction. By the way, the big Webster's dictionary contains several hundred thousand words. We can see how applying statistical regularities can expedite the study of a foreign language. The total of 3000, but most frequently used, words - and you are able to read and communicate.

We now go back to the main subject. Every person has his own beliefs, his own views regarding everything, and they may be very different from the views of another person. But if we consider all people, and this is a very large number, the averaging of these views takes place. As a result of this averaging the collective consciousness holds certain stable beliefs regarding different things. And it is this collective **belief** regarding different things that people perceive as objective reality. The illusion is created by this very persistency of the resulting belief, though it is just the mean of a large number of objects; in this case it is the mean of the beliefs existing in people's consciousness.

When I, for example, diagnose a person, who asked me for help, I can see his body state constantly changing, and often very significantly. However, if, let's say, an X-ray of his organs is performed, the X-ray screen will show a stable picture. The matter is the devices give readings, commensurate with the beliefs of the collective consciousness in regard to the given situation.

So, we now are ready to state one of the very important principles:

OUR CONSCIOUSNESS PERCEIVES WHAT EXISTS IN OUR CONSCIOUSNESS AS REALITY (1.3).

When you think, what you think about is as real for your consciousness as what happens around you, as what you see with your eyes; that is, using your ordinary, normal vision.

This principle is fundamental, for when you combine what you think about with what happens in the external, supposedly objective reality, when you combine this at action level you can materialize objects, you can resurrect.

There are as if two realities: the reality in the mental sphere of consciousness - this is one thing, and the reality of consciousness in the area of perception of the physical world, which is a different thing, which is what is perceived as something stable, persistent.

And we have to understand that all the objects of the surrounding world, say, a table, a chair, a car; - all these objects, every particle of them, each World element are built on the cumulative consciousness of all living people. And thus, if even one segment of consciousness will be changed, the process of the world transformation will begin. That is why, by the way, it is necessary to transform without destruction, but by creation on the ground of creative knowledge. So, when looking at the surrounding World, we, in fact, do not look at something really stable, persistent, but at the place, which we have as a result of averaging and which is most suitable for all living people and creatures, including all the objects in it, to be more exact, we perceive the collective reality within space-time. And that is why our Earth, for example, or the physical agents are just the result of merging of the consciousness of all people, or to be more precise, of all existing consciousness altogether, of both people and other creature and things.

If we know this principle, then we may say that resurrection is simply a proper technological addition into the structure of the universal connections.

So. I will repeat. Everything that exists around us: the Earth, the Sun, stars, space, the entire World - all these, in fact, have been created based on the structure of consciousness, including the consciousness of the Creator. That is why when we know what the spirit is, what consciousness is, we can resurrect, we can create spaces, we can construct the World, we then can perform any creative actions.

In actual fact it is possible to change the reality, because at one time the reality was created by means of making a decision by the consciousness of every person and by the consciousness of every information object.

Therefore, in order to make resurrection possible, to have immortality, in order for everybody to be guaranteed a happy life, this viewpoint must be shared by each individual; each person must take a decision to follow this path. And the more decisions will be taken on choosing this path, the path of eternal and happy life, the faster the reality will begin turning in that direction.

Thus, if we introduce into the collective consciousness the concept that annihilation is impossible, that everyone must be resurrected and that life must be eternal, then everything will be happening exactly this way. Because, when such a belief will become a norm, that is, a part of the collective consciousness, become one of its parameters, one of its beliefs, then this belief, being a part of the collective consciousness, will become stable and start being perceived as objective reality.

In reality physical, that is, certain objective reality as such, does not exist. What it seems to be objective reality, in actuality has been created by the spirit structure, by the consciousness structure. For, I will remind you, consciousness perceives as reality just what exists in consciousness. And that is why, I repeat, our Earth, for example, is just a projection of the collective consciousness on one of its parameters.

On the basis of the collective consciousness the Earth's size can be, let's say, increased, it can be organized so, that additional Earths, additional spaces should emerge. I won`t go into detail on the issue; it has been addressed in my books on the World organization, now I will just state the following principle, pertaining to it.

SPACE DEPENDS ON WHERE DIFFERENT TIME INTERVALS INTERSECT. AS A RESULT OF THAT THE EARTH CAN BE INCREASED IN SIZE (1.15).

A happy infinite life, that is, what people have always dreamed about, what the religions believed in, what is called a paradise, - such a life, finally, may become a reality. I propose the religion which provides the answers to all the questions, which shows how to organize a life which you have a full control of, which is absolutely safe, where one enjoys a complete freedom of action, provided there is a natural creative development of each and all simultaneously. All this is possible to achieve on the basis of consciousness, and I provide specific technologies on how, knowing the consciousness structure to use consciousness in order to obtain solutions and control the reality. Moreover, to control any reality, not necessarily only the Earth or some specific processes. We must understand that everything we see around us, all the processes taking place around us, all these have been formed based on the collective consciousness. And why it is exactly this kind of changes in the soil composition takes place, and why it is exactly this type of photosynthesis process occurs in plants, and why it is that the clouds move exactly this particular way, and why man's present material shape is exactly as it is, and why the Sun is exactly where it presently is – the answer to all these questions is: all these are the phenomena formed based on the collective consciousness. But for each person it happens implicitly and thus not everybody realizes that. By changing the collective consciousness we can change the surrounding reality.

There is an important point to be made here. The fact is that not only people but all one-type objects have the collective consciousness. If, for example, we produce a very large number of computers, then their reality, their collective consciousness might reproduce a control computer. And if their specific concentration per volume unit of information is great, it could lead to a certain life form change. So, what has been written on the subject by the science-fiction writers is not fiction, deep down. Basically it may become a reality. All this must be considered and that is exactly why it is so important to learn the methods of reality control.

By the way, at one time certain animal species, for example, lions, as well as certain types of birds went through the phase of a managerial level, so it is not coincidence that they possess a well-developed instinct. People's instinct proved to be developed for social life. Wild animals, for example, lions, naturally, have the collective consciousness too, which influences our planet as well, but, of course, not to the extent the human collective consciousness does. The priority here is given to man, for though all creatures are God's creation, but man, furthermore, has been created in the Creator's own image and likeness.

The following principle goes with all mentioned above:

THE STRUCTURE OF THE WORLD SHOULD INTENSIVELY DEVELOP WITHIN THE DEVELOPMENT OF OUR OWN CONSCIOUSNESS. (1.4).

Let's sum it up. When we develop our own consciousness, we change the World structure. For by changing our consciousness we gradually change the collective consciousness, and as a result we have the World we need, because it is this World that will be manifested in reality. That is the mechanism of the World transformation.

We shall now formulate a few more principles:

THE TRUE STATUS OF THE WORLD IS IN ETERNAL LIFE. ETERNAL LIFE ENSURES TRUE WORLD STABILITY. THE DESIRE FOR A STABLE WORLD CREATES ETERNAL LIFE.

HE WHO HAS NOT EXPERIENCED DEATH IS THE BASE, WHICH REPRODUCES EVERYTHING ELSE. GOD IS SUCH A BASE. GOD IS ETERNAL, HE HAS NEVER EXPERIENCED DEATH. EVERYTHING ELSE FOLLOWS FROM THIS FACT (1.1)

ETERNAL LIFE IS THE PRINCIPLE OF DEVELOPMENT OF DIVINE REALITY (1.2)

RESURRECTION IS COMPREHESION OF TRUE CONSCIOUSNESS (1.5).

ETERNAL LIFE CONDITIONS THE NECESSITY OF THE DEVELOPMENT OF SOUL (1.6).

To understand any material knowing the key terms, used in the text is always essential. For that reason I will say a few words about the terms being used.

The soul

The soul is the substance that was created by the Creator in accordance with the eternity of the World and is a World element. The soul is firm, stable, unshakable, immovable, inviolable; it basically exists as the World organizing structure and thus it starts the reproduction of such concepts as, for example, spirit, which includes the notion of an act as well. So we may say that in one of the interpretations the acts of the soul are the spirit. Thus perfecting the spiritual base towards the World's creative development, the soul structure may be changed.

The principle (1.6) says that infinite life postulates the necessity of the soul evolution. Indeed, in infinite life as man and the society evolve, more and more new challenges will emerge and therefore, in order for man to adequately face new demands the soul evolution is necessary.

Consciousness

Consciousness is the structure which allows the soul to control the body. The soul, the material part of which is the body, interacts with the reality through the consciousness structure.

But there is also an interaction between the body and the body cells. This interaction is carried out by consciousness too, but this time this is cellular consciousness.

In the wide sense consciousness is a structure that combines spiritual and physical matter.

By changing consciousness it is possible to transform the spirit and therefore to perform acts, that is, events. For the soul is a part of the World, that is, it is present in any event.

True consciousness

The true consciousness is the consciousness, which reflects the World reality in the infinite time and space; it is the consciousness which allows to live eternally and to evolve eternally.

Three characteristics, three features of the true consciousness may be noted.

First. The true consciousness adequately reflects the system of the World development, because it develops concurrently with the development of the World in all its manifestations.

Second. The true consciousness, provided it has been preserved in the primary source, can be readdressed, or delegated, or passed to other beings, together with its all acquired knowledge.

Third. The true consciousness possesses the property of reflecting the entire reality on its each segment, that is, each segment of the true consciousness concurrently contains the entire reality.

We have something similar in holography. When illuminating a holographic plate a three-dimensional object appears in the air, a samovar, for example. And the sense of the samovar real presence is amazing. If we break the plate and have one of its broken pieces, then if we illuminate it the same samovar will appear again, though with limited image definition. If the pieces used are very small, we then have the image blur, the image quality noticeably worsens.

As for the true consciousness, even its small segment ideally reflects the entire reality concurrently.

The true consciousness is formed in the process of the spiritual evolution, that is, the true consciousness first is developed by the soul, then by the spiritual structure and by the body. When I say here "and by the body" I, of course, do not mean, the direct body control. I am talking about a harmonious, balanced interaction of all the cells in the body among themselves and with the consciousness due to the universal connections.

I will note that the evolution, on the microlevel, is inherent in even the tiniest cell as well, which may shift to the macrolevel due to the universal connections mentioned above, so that even the tiniest cell is connected with the entire macroworld.

In the previous chapter the term "an expanded consciousness" was used. Now I will say a few words about this concept.

Expanded consciousness

The expanded consciousness is a concept in many ways explained by the very words of the term. It is a state, when the perception expands and begins to embrace the controlling level of consciousness itself. The concept of an expanded consciousness includes three levels.

1. The perception level of the dynamic World, of the dynamic pattern of the Universe.

If a person looks at the World in his ordinary state, in the state, let's say, of registering consciousness, he then registers static forms. For example, an armchair for him is an armchair, a table is a table, a tree is a tree and that is it. He simply registers these objects as certain static forms.

But if a person is in the state of an expanded consciousness, he now starts perceiving the objects as dynamic forms, that is, for example, as in this case, an armchair or a tree exist in dynamics, in the process of the universal interrelations.

Thus, in the state of an expanded consciousness a person does not perceive objects as static, changeless any more, he begins to perceive the World as a dynamic, changeable form, he begins to see the World as a changeable, transformable structure, and therefore he comes to realize that one may be bettering the World for ever.

We may note that when meeting the resurrected one during the first month after the, the person who met him may find himself in the state of an expanded consciousness and while in this state he experiences the absence of time and the presence of a different state of reality.

2. At the second level consciousness does not limit itself to just a perception of an object, it becomes active, it itself becomes a creative element. For example, during the resurrection, it is the consciousness of the one performing the resurrection that forms the structure of the one being resurrected and this consciousness is an element of the structure of the one being resurrected, the structure that is being created.

3. The third level is a level of one's own state of consciousness. The consciousness of this level is aware of what is taking place and controls the entire situation.

When in the state of the expanded consciousness, a person is able to simultaneously perceive many different processes. And he is able to perceive simultaneously both distant events and events brought closer.

During the resurrection, irrespectively of the fact, whether the resurrection is performed by someone or that person is just being an observer of the resurrection process, being in a state of the expanded consciousness he can see directly the process of the body creation, that is, the creation of the physical matter around the soul of the one being resurrected.

But if it is a question of object materialization, then one may observe the creation of matter around the existing body of information. And at the same time consciousness is present in the object as well (the expanded consciousness!), and consciousness is not just present in the object but plays the role of an active creative element.

As we can see here, in materialization, consciousness carries out the control of the physical matter. However, consciousness may control the spiritual information planes as well, where the term "physical matter" is no more used.

It should be noted that the expanded consciousness is a part of the true consciousness, however in many ways it is an independent element, acting as true consciousness. About space and time we will talk in the next part.

The next principle, the principle of Divinity, relates very closely to the previous principles.

THE PRINCIPLE OF DIVINITY: ASPIRATION FOR IMPERISHABILITY OF BODY, FOR ETERNAL LIFE, AND FOR DEVELOPMENT OF TRUE CONSCIOUSNESS IS THE PRACTICE OF THE UPPERMOST FLOURISHING OF HUMAN EXISTANCE (1.7).

Let's examine this principle in detail.

There are a lot of questions associated with the resurrection. For example, what is the difference between the resurrection that took place shortly after the biological death and the resurrection, which occurred a while after the biological death? And if there are any time fences which, as landmarks, mark the change in the situation.

It turns out that an important role here play the 9th and the 40th days after the biological death. It is not without a reason that there is a tradition to observe these days. Let's consider this question.

## THE 9<sup>TH</sup> AND THE 40<sup>TH</sup> DAYS AFTER THE BIOLOGICAL DEATH AS THE DIVISION ;LANDMARKS SEPARATING ONE FROM ANOTHER DIFFERENT APPROACHES IN RESURRECTION.

The tradition to observe the 9th and the 40th days reflects the principle of information distribution around the physical body.

During the first eight days there is an accumulation, collection of all available information and on the ninth day all the events: spiritual, emotional, physical, that happened in life, are projected into the physical body of the gone one. Further, during 31 days a preparation for the 40th day takes place, when the entire accumulated information as an infinite ray goes out into the informational field into a certain spheroidal segment pertaining to a given person and related to the soul.

If we consider a question of the speed of resurrection, we must say that up to the ninth day the resurrection process moves along faster than it does from the ninth to the fortieth day. And, besides, during the resurrection up to the ninth day the weaker impulses, the impulses carrying the base, core structure of the person, may be sent.

During the period of resurrection up to the ninth day sometimes it is enough to introduce just the information of so called biofields, that is, of what usually surrounds the human body.

During the resurrection from the ninth to the fortieth day the information of the events lived by the person must be introduced, only then can he be resurrected.

During the resurrection after the fortieth day the information that must be introduced, basically, characterizes a person at the level of his/ her creation by God, that is, at the level of the creation of a person's soul.

As we can see from the above, the three different approaches in resurrection are separated from one another precisely by the ninth and the fortieth days.

I will point out an important aspect. The speed of resurrection increases significantly, if till the fortieth day we speak about the gone one as if he were alive. It is desirable not to mention unnecessarily the fact of the departure in the future as well. I will add that the acts performed in the fundamental creative religions after the departure facilitate resurrection.

But if we consider the problem of resurrection at the proper time, that is, when, for example, during an act of rescue the situation demands that a person should be resurrected instantaneously, at that very moment, then in this case a very high access level into control information is necessary, and thus in this case a very high spiritual level is required from the person, performing the resurrection.

The question of the perception of the gone ones is important as well.

ON THE PERCEPTION OF THE GONE ONES

A few more words may be said about how the perception of the reality by the gone ones changes in the course of time. For the gone ones, naturally, a different reality comes into existence. Depending on the degree of decomposition of the physical body the perception pattern of the soul of the gone one changes.

After the occurrence of the biological death the disintegration of different structures, the cellular structure disintegration, begins, however, for approximately the first three days the gone one, nevertheless, continues to perceive the physical reality of the living in about the same way as he did before. Further up to the fortieth day the reality of the living is beginning as if to fade for him, this is a specific transitional process, which I will not go into now.

After the fortieth day the gone perceives the physical reality of the living as a certain ephemeral plane, and he doesn't regard the processes taking place there, as really significant or problematic, because he is now faced with new challenges.

The first challenge he is facing is the synchronization of the physical bodies he used to have in his former reincarnations (of course, if there are any, that is, if he in his time developed them to the point of using the same matter in two or more reincarnations). The organizing center in synchronizing his earlier as well as later incarnations is his soul.

Having accomplished this task the gone one moves to the second level. This level has to do with the enlightenment. The light emerges here, but not the light, usually implied when describing the transition from the state of life to the state of death and a concomitant formation of the corridor system. The light that emerges here is different, it is the light of knowledge, and the knowledge appears before him as an open entity, as an open entity in the sense that the gone one understands that he can gain this knowledge, just as if he himself were indistinguishable from it. It can be compared with what was said about the rose, about knowing what it is, in the Introduction. In a higher state of consciousness it is possible to become one with it, to become indistinguishable from it, and then the truth - its true inwardness - will open up.

Upon reaching the second level, the level of enlightenment, the gone ones begin to perceive the information, coming from the plane of the living. The present situation is that the gone ones as a result of the information they have been receiving begin to show interest in coming back. The matter is that due to the creation of nuclear weapons and their accumulation the mankind has closely come up to the threat of self-annihilation. In case of the nuclear disaster the plane of the gone ones will be affected as well. Due to this at present there is a serious danger for the gone ones, for their history may disappear and even the entire substance of this plane may vanish. This may happen in accordance with the following law of the information development: TOTAL ANNIHILATION OF ONE OF THE MAIN INFORMATION DEVELOPMENT ELEMENTS MAY RESULT IN ANNIHILATION OF THIS ENTIRE INFORMATION AREA AND THUS RADICALLY CHANGE THE FUTURE REALITY. And since the threat of annihilation as a problem has arisen among the living, the gone ones begin to seek resurrection in order to come back and prove that the physical matter of the living is of paramount importance as well as to help prevent the disaster, for it is the living whom the solution of this problem depends upon.

There is another reason, why the gone ones are currently seeking to come back. The matter is that the biological death and following it giving up the physical body as well as the transition to the subtle planes of being have been used before as a way to acquire new knowledge (we've just talked about the second level of the state of being of the gone ones - the level of enlightenment). The body decomposition, that is, in fact the elimination of the physical body, nowadays does not have the same logical expediency it used to before. The biological disintegration of the body as a mechanism, as an act of cognition has already virtually exhausted itself. And this is fully confirmed by the resurrected, who say that when transitioning to the subtle plane as a result of the biological death they didn`t acquire anything there, what they could not acquire when being in an ordinary physical body.

So, it doesn't make sense to abandon the body in order to acquire new knowledge and new experience. One may remain in his body, but raise, for example, his ESP (extra sensory perception) level and gain everything one needs; or develop the level of information control.

Life moves on and, naturally, with change of the situation, there comes a new understanding of the development process.

A NEW STAGE IN THE EVOLUTION OF MAN AND SOCIETY

The question at issue is so serious that it makes sense to discuss it in more detail. Utilizing scientific terms we could start a talk on the paradigm shift, that is, in this case, on the fundamental shift in the behavioral model. But I will remain within the confines of a simple analysis and visual comparisons.

Let's reflect upon how much effort and time it used to take people in old times to get, let's say, from Europe to America. A sailing vessel was used to go overseas. It used to take a very long time. Of course, when you look at the picture of a ship with a lot of sails it is a magnificent sight. But it took so long to sail! And how many dangers awaited a small vessel during a storm. And what about now?

Today it is quite different. Today ships are totally different. They cross the ocean quite quickly. And if you need to reach America very fast, you may take the plane and be there within several hours.  And notice the following: Nowadays it is not only much faster to reach, let's say, America from Europe by sea, but safer as well. And besides, in much luxurious conditions, for the ocean liners have everything necessary: restaurants, dancing grounds, pools and so forth - everything you need.

Or consider the communication problem. How long did it use to take a person from Europe to exchange letters with a friend of his in America? And not that long ago, but, let's say, just in the 19th century? To send a letter and receive an answer? And what is the situation today?

Today teleconferences between different cities have become a common phenomenon, during these teleconferences you converse with people, who are at the other end of the globe, as if they were just in front of you. Or take the final match broadcasting of the football World Championship. A great number of people in all parts of the world stay glued to the television screen and watch the match live through the satellite communication!

The life has changed tremendously. The life conditions have changed. The life rhythm has become entirely different.

And that is why the old slow mechanism of cognition of the highest truths as well as the spiritual evolution by giving up the physical body, a temporal stay in a different form in subtle planes of being, gradual accumulation of the necessary information there and then returning back again into the physical body - this unhurried way of growth does not match the rhythm of the modern life any longer. Thus there is no need to give up the physical body any more or to waste time on all these transformations, but instead remaining in this very body and utilizing special methods to learn entering higher states of consciousness and thereby ensuring one's own spiritual growth.

And those, who have already gone, must be returned back with the help of the resurrection procedure.

I will note that there have always been and are now people, who can live as long as they deem proper. They belong to the category of people, who understand and know from their own experience, what the true consciousness is. And so they particularly understand that life is the simplest, the most available and the most natural reality. And this reality is achieved through the evolution of consciousness.

And what from the conventional perspective is considered to be life, from the perspective of the higher state of consciousness is not yet a true life, because a true life is eternal life. In this sense orthodox biology as well, though the meaning of the word "biology" is "life science", but even biology, in spite of all its advancement hasn't yet come to the true understanding of what life is. And this first of all is due to the lack of understanding, that life has a spiritual base, as well as due to the lack of clarity in what consciousness is and the role it plays.

Consciousness is one of the key concepts. When from the perspective of the World cognition it is not necessary any more to develop the consciousness phase, corresponding to the splitting of the physical matter, death disappears, death becomes unnecessary. Moreover, it becomes a hindrance, for it artificially slows down the pace of the spiritual evolution.

So, the pattern of the spiritual development, used before, that is, the pattern of abandoning, giving up the physical body, does not meet the modern pace of the society development, of the advancement of science and technology. And for this particular reason a person begins to feel at a loss before ever increasing technological complexity as well as before arising general problems, such as the threat of the nuclear annihilation or the global ecological disaster.

A person feels he is unable to cope with growing problems of the external world. And the reason is that the evolution of his internal world is much slower than it is necessary today. To accelerate this evolution and to finally begin to utilize one's own entire potential - that is today's task. Our destiny, the destiny of the entire world depends on the accomplishment of the task.

Talking of potential. Science says that today man utilizes no more than 5% of his brain potential. Bur, it also must be noted that science does not know much yet about the purpose of certain organs, for example, such a part of the brain as the hypophysis. So it is too early to speak about 5% of the brain potential being utilized. Man virtually hasn't even started yet utilizing his potential. By the well-known comparison, man is described as someone who is cramped in the anteroom of a big high-rise building, his own building, but only he doesn't know about it, and is not even aware of the existence of other rooms and floors. Development of all these territories, which can and must belong to him by right is through the evolution of consciousness.

So, we must start using a new pattern of development, a new way, the way through non-dying and resurrection. And then man will be able, at last, to ensure a real harmony of internal and external development. And this will ensure moving towards the full value, joyous and happy life.

The next principle:

IT IS SUFFICIENT TO HAVE ONE PERSON WHO CAN RESURRECT AND RESTORE THE WORLD TO ENSURE THAT IT IS NOT POSSIBLE TO DESTROY THE WORLD. (1.8).

There is a principle in the information area: something once done exists for ever within the time when it was done.

So, if something was ever done, then based on that moment in the past, this act can be reproduced at any other moment in time as well. And therefore if there is, for example, at least a single fact of object materialization, it means that materialization can be performed at any other time as well as be extended to any other object. The same is true for resurrection. Generally, if something was done once, it becomes indestructible.

For a person it means that the idea of the eternity of the World will always result in the realization of the eternal in all realities. And if a person is able to resurrect and restore the World, then the World cannot be destroyed under any circumstances.

RESURRECTION AND ASCERTAINMENT OF THE FACT OF RESURRECTION IS A SIMULTANEOUS FOR THE ENTIRE WORLD PROCESS (1.9).

The fact, that establishment of the resurrection fact happens simultaneously for the entire World means that this event involves all the World structures instantaneously, without transferring the information sequentially from place to place, that is, after the resurrection the information about the resurrection is instantly everywhere. We talked about this phenomenon in Chapter I, when we discussed the lion's abilities.

CORRECT UNDERSTANDING OF THE CORRELATION BETWEEN THE CONSCIOUSNESS OF MAN AND HIS ORGANS PROVIDES RESURRECTION. RESURRECTION IS AN ACT OF CREATION. (1.10).

The resurrection is often seen as consisting of two stages. At the first stage, still during the resurrection process, the one being resurrected does not yet fully match an ordinary living person. At the second stage, when the process of the resurrection is virtually over the resurrected is and looks like an ordinary person made of flesh and blood. However we must note that such a theoretical division of the resurrection process into two stages is a reflection of the hypophysis function at the level of the information of the living one and at the level of the information of the resurrected one. That is, this conditional division of the resurrection into two stages is done by the hypophysis itself. That is why it suffices to only adapt the hypophysis function the proper way, and the resurrection may occur just as a consequence of that. Therefore, this principle says that in order for the resurrection to occur we must just direct the right information to some of our organs, for example, to the hypophysis.

Thus man's awareness of how to access his own consciousness in view of his organs is an important element in the resurrection.

DEVELOPMENT OF MAN SHOULD BE CONSIDERED AS A COMPLEX DEVELOPMENT OF THE ENTIRE EXISTING WORLD (1.11).

This principle resembles principle 1.4, but there I was referring to the evolution of consciousness, and here - to the evolution of the entire person.

When man is evolving, the entire existing World is evolving. Man can develop the World and create Worlds by means of his own intellect, consciousness, spirit, simply put, by means of a new level of his development. When a person can resurrect other people and thus can demonstrate that there is no elimination and that it is possible to never die at all, then, it means that the World has stabilized. The World stability, its eternal essence is an indication of its complexity.

The next principle supports the two previous ones.

THE PRINCIPLE OF THE RESURRECTION CORRELATES WITH THE PRINCIPLE OF MAN'S ORGANIZATION, WHICH TAKES INTO ACCOUNT ALL-TIME DEVELOPMENT OF THE ENTIRE EXTERNAL WORLD (1.12).

The following principle is very important for everyday life: GRIEF, DESPONDENCY AND NOSTALGIA ARE NOT THE WAY TO PERCEIVE THE WORLD. ONLY JOY, LIGHT AND LOVE ARE THE WAY TO COMPREHEND THE WORLD (1.13).

Where all is eternal, where there is no destruction, where man is free, where he can evolve, where all is beauty and joy, love and light reign. There is no room for grief, sadness and other negative emotions; there is just no room for them left, because everything is filled with love and light!

And since there won't be any negative emotions in the future, one must realize that the presence of the negative emotions now hinders a person's evolution, hampers his spiritual growth.

Grief, despondency, envy, hatred and other negative emotions are the World elements, which dissipate. They start to disappear/ vanish with the beginning of the development of spirituality.

Let's recollect the lines given in the Introduction: "… So that you being rooted and established in love, may have the power together with all the saints to grasp what the width, and the length, and the depth, and the height are." We can see that from times immemorial it was known that love plays an enormous part in attaining higher states of consciousness. And not only love but other positive emotions as well. In their turn the higher states of consciousness help positive emotions to become deeper, help all the cells of an organism to be filled with these emotions, which in turn leads to even greater spiritual growth and so on. This process is infinite. And, as already mentioned, transitioning to even higher and higher states of consciousness – that is the way to God.

PERSONALITY REMAINS INTACT AFTER BIOLOGICAL DEATH, INCLUDING CREMATION CASES. IS THIS LAST CASE EACH PARTICLE OF THE ASH, RECEIVED AFTER CREMATION, IS CONNECTED TO THE STRUCTURE OF PERSONALITY OF THAT ONE WHO WAS CREMATED (1.14).

It says here, that the changes the physical body is undergoing are not crucial. It does not matter in which manner the body was changed, in which manner it was disintegrated and translated into the totality of its particles and even microelements. All this is secondary, for on the soul basis the same body may be always fully regenerated. Therefore, this principle tells about the ability of the physical matter to fully regenerate on basis of the spirit, on the basis of the soul.

In connection with what was said, a well-known legend comes to mind about the bird phoenix that used to rise renewed from the ashes. We can see now that the rebirth from the ashes is not just a poetic image, it is a reality.

## 2

We now proceed to the principles of the second level.

The first principle is virtually obvious.

MAN IS AN ETERNAL SUBSTANCE BY THE PRINCIPLE OF HIS CREATION. THAT IS WHY RESURRECTION IS BASED ON REVEALING THE ETERNAL IN MAN (2.1).

The next principle substantiates the importance of the development of the spirit:

THERE IS INTERDEPENDENCE BETWEEN THE SPIRITUAL AND PHYSICAL STRUCTURES. BY CHANGING THE INFORMATION ON THE PHYSICAL STRUCTURE IN THE SPHERE OF THE SPIRIT, WE CAN CHANGE THE SPIRIT TO THE LEVEL, WHEN IT WILL BE ABLE TO CHANGE ANY PHYSICAL STRUCTURE, AS WELL AS TO CREATE A PHYSICAL BODY (2.2).

By raising the spirit to the level, when it will be able not to just change the physical structure, but also to create it, and to create, among other things, a physical body as well, as consequence we have that man can always stay alive. And if man is able to sustain life of his own body for ever, if he is able to always stay alive, he, therefore, can resurrect others.

The next principle:

TIME AND SPACE DO NOT LIMIT THE DURATION OF LIFE. THE CONCEPT OF DURATION OF LIFE IS FORMED BY THE RELATION OF THE SPIRIT TO SPACE AND TIME (2.3).

In the previous segment we clarified what the soul, the spirit and consciousness are. Now we will continue the discussion of the terms used, and I will say few words about space and time.

Space.

Space, like time, is a consciousness construct. Space is a structure for the realization of the acts of the soul as well as of the spirit, of consciousness, of the body. There is soul space, there is spirit space, there is space of consciousness and there is space of the body. The space of the body is the space, within which the body moves, that is, it is a normal physical space.

The space of the soul is a structure of the World organization. And the concept of the physical space is inapplicable there. The space of the soul has a priority over other spaces.

I will note that the soul space is secondary towards the soul itself, the soul is the base.

The soul exists in a certain absolutized space, where God created it. But the spirit exists in the space of action, and here space is associated with the concept of consciousness.

When a person thinks of something, it happens in the space of thinking.

Space can be both individual and collectivized. Every person has his individual space of thinking, but when several people, let's say, in a movie-theater, watch a movie together, the space of thinking becomes collectivized.

Of significant importance is how consciousness reacts to what is going on, for consciousness can transform space, including the physical space. It suffices consciousness to send an action impulse - and space changes.

For those, who are being resurrected, space, in a sense, as if is growing. For the ones being resurrected space is growing on the inside of each cell, of every microelement, of every informational tie, and growing, building up, it fills up the informational structure of the one being resurrected. Thus, in this case, space is also an element of action.

I have developed and to a certain extent implemented technological devices meant for the regeneration of the lost organs and the resurrection of people. Inside them space is compressed to such a degree that the macro level becomes the micro level, that is, consciousness detects both micro and macro processes simultaneously. These technological devices allow to completely restore the entire body, to resurrect a person, and I mean precisely the resurrection, because the spiritual structure of the person is fully identical, is the same. The primary advanced, future-oriented function of such devices is the realization of the algorithm, which allows by analogy to evolve consciousness of a person up to the point when the matter can be fully restored. As we can see, in this case space can be regarded as a working tool for the creation of technological cycles on the resurrection.

People often talk about parallel worlds, about parallel spaces. In actual fact there is nothing parallel in particular, it is just that one and the same spatial region, even one and the same point, may contain everything. To be more exact, everything that can be the manifestation of the collective consciousness in that point.

One of the well-known guests, visiting our space, is yeti, the snow man. He represents a version of man; they are those, who acquired a modified form on account of the transmutation elements, that is, on account of trance states they acquired a mutational parameter and as a result transitioned to a different space. So, they have separated from man and their evolution is followed a different path. There they have a flat infinite Earth and it is quite cold there. Sometimes they fall out into our space and then one may meet them, but in principle, they are beings from another world.

Other well-known visitors of the Earth are the UFO (unidentified flying objects) crews. The UFOs are mainly artificially created objects, which are either alien or have to do with the problem of other spaces, that is, such observable objects do not necessarily come from other planets, it can be just the result of the visualization of other spaces.

People, piloting UFOs, or it is better to say, beings, are representatives of other civilizations and have an appearance of man-like looking objects, biological or of a higher level.

The UFOs themselves are mostly perceived as spheroidal discs, though, generally, they may be of arbitrary shape – it is just through the structure of our space that they are perceived in precisely this way.

An interesting question is the question of dimension of different spaces. In order to better understand it, let's consider a specific example – an organization of a human body.

It is known that within human consciousness many bodies are manifested: physical, ethereal, astral, mental, and others. A well-known matreshka, inside which there are smaller and smaller matreshkas, is in reality a symbol of how man is organized. His bodies, specified above, are each in its space.

The physical space, which we observe with our normal physical sight, in its simplified version is three-dimensional. That is precisely how it is seen by a person having an ordinary state of consciousness. But for a person possessing a higher state of consciousness the physical space can be four-dimensional as well (remember Apostle

Paul's statement, given in the Introduction).

Ethereal space can be seven-dimensional, astral space – nine-dimensional; and the structure of the mental space is twofold - it exists both as six-dimensional and as four-dimensional versions.

But I would like to caution you regarding the following. By no means consider the dimensions I spoke about above, to be fixed once and for all. These dimensions are as such today, but they may change tomorrow. The true life moves on, it consists in continuous evolution of the spirit - I would like to emphasize that in particular. Spiritual growth, spiritual evolution makes it possible to see the dynamics of this process, which in its turn facilitates the development of the spiritual structure. As for the dimensions, the following needs to be considered. Since the spiritual structure includes all known phenomena, it can translate one dimension into another. So the concept of dimension of different spaces is not that important, the main thing is that the spiritual structure is changeable, it can evolve, and it is the spiritual structure that determines all the rest.

Time.

There is more than one way to answer the question, what time is, depending on the perspective taken to consider this question. There is also an approach according to which time, in its ordinary understanding, simply does not exist. But, however, it will be an approach from the perspective of higher states of consciousness, in such states of consciousness the World perception is entirely different, I have talked about it in the Introduction. In this book I will confine myself just to the initial steps in covering the issue of time.

There are several different approaches to consider.

One approach was already mentioned when principle (1.15) was discussed. Namely, time may be considered as a certain space transformer. In this case time may be seen as certain spatial lines of force, along which transformation and movement take place. If we understand this time structure, then the immergence of the required space, as well as the fulfillment of the desirable event, in the right time and the right place, can be achieved.

So, the change of time results in space transformation. But a reverse version is possible as well: by changing space time can be changed. It could be expected, for both of these structures – space and time - are the constructs of consciousness.

We may consider the question of time perception by the gone ones or by the ones being resurrected. Here different aspects may be emphasized too. In the next part, for example, it will be noted that at first for the one being resurrected time is discrete, while for the living one it is continuous.

But the most important in this matter is that for the gone ones as well as for the ones being resurrected time always moves towards live people, towards the living, and thus they all have only one path to follow, which is always only towards life. We may say that the gone ones perceive time as the flow of certain information, as a flow of a river, that pushes them towards life. At present there is very little room left for them, they are involuntarily being drawn closer to one another, they are getting increasingly squeezed. And for the new gone ones there is virtually not enough room.

When the resurrection of a person takes place, a sort of pushing out towards the living is manifested quite unequivocally too: the ones being resurrected have a feeling that the structure of the entire reality constantly moves under them, it moves only in one direction, with greater or lesser speed, and it always moves towards life. That is, in principle, the state of the gone ones, according to their subjective perception, is very unstable. And there is a good reason for it.

Before, during the pre-nuclear epoch, many of the gone ones used to choose a path of reincarnation, the reincarnational system of their development.

That is why they would somewhat distance themselves from this flow of time, they would form the events for their return and only after that would enter the body which had been formed in advance: a born foetus.

Now, during the nuclear epoch, due to the threat of a possible universal nuclear annihilation the gone ones as a result of such a state of affairs experience considerable instability and thus more and more of them begin to orient themselves towards the resurrection. So now they do not distance themselves much from this flow of time. And that is why we may say that time virtually is the structure of existence of some of the gone ones and some of the ones being resurrected, we may even say, of many of them, but not all. Not all of them, since the most enlightened ones can control the situation and find their way out on their own. Those, who do not know the structure, find themselves within very strong flows of time. I will remind you that these flows always move towards life.

I would like to single out another very important aspect. After the resurrection occurred, the information of the resurrected one allows many other absolutely unrelated people in totally different locations to begin to live, as a result of which space increases, the number of people increases, leading in its turn to new resurrections, that is, the process develops like a snowball. Even one single resurrected can reproduce in space, on account of information exchange, many new people, and not based on information creation, but just based on information communication.

The soul of the resurrected one, knowing that it is possible to resurrect the gone ones, gives other people this chance, the chance to come back to life. Here is how it is done. The soul of a resurrected one creates a shape in space, or it is better to say, a human contour, and in many ways, it is the contour of the resurrected one himself. A week after the resurrection a single soul is able to create two such contours, in a month - many times more. Within this contour there is an available path, indispensable life conditions, all necessary events. So that when the gone one finds himself inside this shape, his resurrection takes place. And, as a rule, the fact that the gone one finds himself in this contour is not accidental. He scans space and when he detects such available contour or, in other words, an available space-time cell, he enters it and then his resurrection takes place.

I will note that such a contour from the start pertains to the status of the one, who performed the resurrection. For example, I resurrected a person; further the resurrection begins to develop space. Deep down, it is my status, my information, but it started developing, because the resurrected one sent a new impulse to the World, and the impulse creates new space, new people. As I repeatedly was saying, the resurrection is always very beneficial for all: for the ones being resurrected as well as for the living, who receive additional space and additional positive events.

And it should be added that there is a very important law consisting in that IN PRESENCE OF A PROVEN RESURRECTION TECHNOLOGY, LIFETIME

LENGTHENS OF ITSELF TO THE INFINITY. So, with the resurrection space begins to increase and lifetime becomes infinite.

I can tell you, how the contours actually get occupied. Let's say, I have resurrected a person. And now, I am walking along a street and suddenly see a contour, the contour that looks very much like this resurrected, and somebody, for example, a gone one, often before my very eyes, gets inside this contour, and the resurrection takes place. But the one who gets into the counter does not have necessarily to be a gone one, it can be a living one too, who experienced a discontinuation of his events. He gets into this contour, into this area, into this cell of time-space - and resumes living on. We will come back to this issue, when we discuss Principle (4.3).

We will now continue.

THE PRINCIPLE OF IMMORTALITY AND, THEREFORE, THE PRINCIPLE OF RESTORATION, REGENERATION AFTER A POSSIBLE BIOLOGICAL DEATH IS EMBODIED IN THE PRIMORDIAL CAUSE, IN THE PRIMORDIAL NATURE OF IMPULSES OF MAN'S NATURAL DEVELOPMENT (2.4).

Man's natural development is in principle in harmony with the entire World, and the World is eternal, the very fact of the existence of the World is an element of Eternity. That is why immortality is intrinsically embodied in the primordial nature of impulses of man's natural development.

AN IMPULSE AIMED TOWARDS THE RESURRECTION IS ALWAYS AIMED TOWARDS THE INFINITE DEVELOPMENT OF THE ONE BEING RESURRECTED (2.5).

The resurrection methodology is based on the interconnections of consciousness of the one, performing the resurrection, not only with the one being resurrected, but also with all the events, related to him. What is meant, therefore, is as follows. When the resurrection takes place, the impulse of consciousness of the one, performing the resurrection, must be directed not only towards the realization of the resurrection act, that is, towards the creation, for example, of the physical tissue, but it must be applied to the entire course of events for the one, being resurrected, must specify the entire course of these events. Generally speaking, any impulse is usually aimed to encompass events, but with respect to the resurrection this impulse is of a specific nature: it is always towards the infinite evolution of the one being resurrected.

If the realization of certain events unrelated to the resurrection is needed, then the impulse sent first leads to shaping a certain event, as a result of which other events are shaped based on the existing connections.

It is different when performing the resurrection. The impulse aimed towards the resurrection, is of a generalized character: it is always directed towards the infinite development of the one being resurrected in each event.

THE ONE BEING RESURRECTED ALWAYS SEES AND IS AWARE OF THE RESURRECTION PROCESS, AND HE ALWAYS ACTIVELY PARTICIPATES IN THE RESURRECTION AS AN INITIATIVE PERSON. (2.6).

The resurrection is a process which is always agreeable and right, for it is directed towards life and provides an optimal path of development.

The one being resurrected is always fully aware and in control of this process. And besides, I will note, there is not a single case, not a single fact of the gone one to refuse the resurrection when offered. Quite the opposite, I can say that the gone ones always gratefully accept the offer to be resurrected. The matter is many of them do not have the knowledge with the help of which their consciousness could restore the physical tissue. That is why when they receive an offer from someone else to be resurrected, they gratefully accept it, and I must say, the offer is always accepted by them immediately.

I am telling about it so that it should be clear that ethically one may always resurrect with a clear conscience, and, moreover, any number of people, the main thing is that simultaneously with the resurrection optimal supportive environment for normal living should be insured for these people.

THE ONE BEING RESURRECTED ALWAYS KNOWS FOR A FACT THAT AFTER THE RESURRECTION HE WILL LIVE AS A NORMAL PERSON (2.7).

THE ONE BEING RESURRECTED ALWAYS THINKS THAT THE

LIVING ONE WILL TREAT HIM AS EQUAL, HE DOES NOT FEEL SEPARATED FROM THE LIVING IN ANY WAY, AND HE FEELS LIKE A NORMAL PERSON, NO DIFFERENT FROM THE LIVING (2.8).

It may be specified that the one being resurrected always knows that after the resurrection he will live as a normal person in his normal biological body.

I will note, that during the resurrection the main focus for the one being resurrected is focal aspects of the resurrection process itself, he does not follow the technical details of the resurrection. The reason the one being resurrected does so is to understand the procedure in terms of control and thus later to be able to resurrect other people on his own. I've already mentioned that sometimes for the sake of salvation an instant resurrection is necessary, in which case there is no time to attend to the technical details, and, in general, understanding general principles should always be a priority.

I must say, that at the informational level the one who experienced death will differ for some time from the one, who did not experienced it. The difference is that the one who did not experience death has an entirely transparent informational matrix, which has a free access to all forms of consciousness and matter, while the matrix of the resurrected one has structures associated with an element of matter destruction. This element is more viscous, more ballast, and as a result the consciousness of the resurrected one has a certain delay, for example, in the processing speed of information; but in any case the resurrection is much better than reincarnation, considerably better. Because after the resurrection a person masters the instrument of continuous life and does not die any more, while in reincarnation, though with some exceptions, but for the majority we talk about a totally different person, often with different physical parameters.

And in general, as I have stated earlier, at present reincarnation is becoming inexpedient. At the current stage of development it is the resurrection that is becoming a natural process.

The one, who did not experience death, will always master the processes of control and the resurrection much faster than the resurrected one. For the process of the body disintegration represents a certain disintegration of the intellectual form, which leads, as I have just said, to change in the informational personality matrix, in addition the body disintegration also means loss of time, as the living one during this time has an opportunity to continuously enhance his potential and increase the concentration of his consciousness.

Progress slowdown due to the body disintegration may be compared with the effects of a common illness on school studies. If a student suddenly had to be hospitalized on account of a serious illness, he is clearly at a disadvantage compared to those, who are able to continue their studies.

However, and I would like to particularly emphasize that, after some time, though it may take quite a while, the resurrected on account of a generalized status becomes a complete match to the one who did not experience death. Since life is imperishable, since it is eternal, after some time this is only but a detail for a person if his body has ever gone through disintegration or not; in general this is not an issue for anybody any more, the only exception being the structure of the World stability, which needs the ones who did not experience death. That is exactly why at present the problem of immortality becomes so important. Immortality comes into existence when the resurrection technology becomes known.

AFTER THE RESURRECTION IT IS NECESSARY TO PROVIDE SOME GUIDANCE TO THE RESURRECTED ONE, EXPLAINING HIS NEW STATE, ATTRIBUTABLE TO THE FACT THAT NOW HE HAS A PHYSICAL BODY (2.9).

As it's been already said the gone ones consciously perceive the state they find themselves in after their body disintegration or after its cremation. They take this stage of their life as a phase of the events pertaining to their body. And when the process of the resurrection is over and they acquire a physical body, they clearly realize man's indestructibility. This knowledge of indestructibility of people, of immortality is always in the soul of every person, but, which, may be, not everyone would recognize. After the resurrection the resurrected ones come to realize this knowledge of indestructibility, but only as a one-time act, while the one who did not experience death has this knowledge as a result of continuous flow of life. It is the knowledge of man's indestructibility which is a means of reproduction of life of his physical body. The resurrected one must perceive the knowledge of indestructibility the same way the one who did not experienced death does.

After regaining his physical body the resurrected one has to adapt himself to the conditions of life. Thereby it is necessary to provide guidance for the resurrected to help them adapt themselves to social norms.

Generally they understand it all, because they are normal sensible people, and they may, naturally, say that they will manage on their own, but nevertheless, whatever is necessary for them to know must be verbalized. Yes, logically they understand it all, but the word of the living one contributes immensely to the adaptation of their consciousness to the environment. "First there was a word" – the living one, the one, who did not experience death, must verbalize everything.

With the proper guidance, provided to the resurrected one, his transition from the state of the gone ones to the state of the living significantly accelerates. The adaptation time could take up to a month, sometimes longer, however, sometimes it is an instant transition. Much is determined by the level of the reasoning ability of the resurrected one.

The level of the reasoning ability of the resurrected one depends on how much was done in his environment as well as within his body.

Of course, the resurrected one has his own reasoning ability, however, during the resurrection in a certain sense as if the shaping of his reasoning ability takes place, a certain technology is communicated to him by the one performing the resurrection. So the reasoning ability of the resurrected one depends on the work done on his resurrection. I will note that as a result of this work the reasoning ability of the resurrected one may virtually stay the same, but it depends to a great degree on the quality and the amount of work done, and this work determines his ability to quickly adapt himself to his life in the society.

In my system I introduced the following concept: a level of reasonableness of an emerging object. Because a resurrected one is in many ways an emerging object. The introduction of this concept, that is, the level of reasonableness, allows the possibility for classification. Depending on his level of reasonableness the resurrected one may be attributed to one or another category of people. As a rule, it is the same category, he was attributed to before. Thus the level of reasonableness determines the initial level the resurrected one starts his life with - now in a physical body.

If immediately after the resurrection the level of reasonableness of the resurrected one is quite high, his chances for a fast adaptation are higher, and it may occur, let's say, within a second, an hour or a day. But if his initial level is not very high, the adaptation can take on an average a month, but no longer than three months.

From the above follows a very important fact, - and I would like to emphasize it: the one, who works on the resurrection, paves the way for the one being resurrected.

A RESURRECTED PERSON FULLY RETAINS HIS PROFESSIONAL AND OTHER SKILLS, ACQUIRED EARLIER IN LIFE (2.10).

The content of the statement above is a well-established fact.

THE CONCEPT OF SPIRIT PROVIDES THE TRUTH OF THE STRUCTURE OF COGNITION (2.11).

The spiritual aspect always, in the resurrection too, allows for control of matter and cognition. The cognition structure becomes true, when we are aware of the spiritual aspect instead of accentuating solely the resurrection in the physical body. And it is of fundamental importance that the creation of the physical body, matching the same soul takes place. Virtually, during the resurrection of a person a communication of spiritual knowledge to that person occurs, based on which the soul restores, regenerates its physical part. Thus the cognition structure becomes true, when spiritual and physical structures are combined together.

ONE OF THE ASPECTS OF RESURRECTION IS RESTORATION OF CREATIVE CONSCIOUSNESS OF LIVING PEOPLE. (2.12)

Creative consciousness is in principle inherent in man from the very start of his life. When the body grows, for some time it always creates, until it gets into the system of artificial ideological postulates, farfetched thought-forms, wrong mental sets, which block the development of the body's ties, etc. All this artificially distorts the normal natural development and results in clouding man's creative consciousness. That is why the task of reclaiming the creative consciousness of living people is of prime importance. One of the methods to achieve this goal is meditation, which has been already talked about in the Introduction. The universal method is the practice of the resurrection, which realizes immortality.

After man's creative consciousness has been reclaimed, restored he begins to understand, how he himself is organized, and as a result he is able to resurrect other people by communicating this impulse to them.

THE RESURRECTION PROCESS SHOULD BE REGARDED AT THE SAME TIME AS A PROCESS OF REPRODUCTION OF A FOETUS AS WELL (2.13).

This principle has been formulated in terms of life arrangement and management for the resurrected one. When, according to a biological law, a foetus comes into existence from a man and a woman, a living space for its growth and development is reserved, it is expected from the start that later it will have a legal document, etc. The process of the resurrection should be regarded in much the same way, that is, different organizational aspects should be thought of carefully in advance. Though, as it was specified in Chapter I, the key aspects in the resurrection are controlled by the World structures named in that chapter.

THE SPIRITUAL DEVELOPMENT OF THE GONE ONES DOES NOT STOP. PERSONAL SPIRITUAL DEVELOPMENT ALWAYS CONTINUES AT ALL TIMES. THEREFORE AT SPIRITUAL LEVEL THE RESURRECTION IS UNDERSTOOD AS THE MANIFESTATION OF THE UNIVERSAL WORLD HARMONY. AND THAT IS PRECISELY WHY ON THE SPIRITUAL LEVELALL PEOPLE KNOW THAT THE UNIVERSAL RESURRECTION OF THE GONE ONES IS TO COME. (2.14).

The World is designed so, that man primordially possesses the soul, the God's creation, and man's body is a physical part of the soul. Before the physical body was not regarded as a universally necessary element and thus a biological death meant only a certain status of the soul, when the soul evolution continued in the absence of the physical body.

And in the meantime we know that the spiritual and physical structures are interdependent. See Principle (2.2). The presence of the physical body enhances a faster evolution of the soul. And now, when the world is faced with the threat of global destruction this problem, the problem of a faster evolution of man becomes very urgent.

At present when there is a conflict among people or countries, sometimes they resort to force to resolve the problem. Often a biological death of an enemy is used just to avoid the necessity of attending to the substance of the matter. In actuality it means avoidance of the problem resolution, refusal to fundamentally address the problem.

Now the priority must be given to the physical body, which must become indestructible. As a result development of means of destruction will become illogical and just meaningless.

Because as envisioned by God man is eternal and thus the task now is to reveal again the knowledge about the Creator on a wider scale and to give back to people the consciousness of the true level of Eternity. In this regard the resurrection is seen as return to the understanding of eternity of the World. The resurrection is perceived as the manifestation of the universal harmony of the World.

At heart all people know that the universal resurrection of the gone ones is to come, for the soul is the reflection of the entire World, it interrelates with the entire World. Creating the eternal soul, God created an eternal effect of this soul, that is, we may say, that He created an eternal body as an eternal part of the soul.

## 3

Now we proceed to examine the principles of the third level. It should be noted, that from the standpoint of hierarchy these principles are less important in a way, but sometimes they may become more important than the principles of the second level.

The reader may ask, why this is so, why the principles overlap, and why there are so many of them considered they are called the main principles. This is a serious question, so we will discuss it in detail. Let's imagine a building, for example, the main building of Moscow University on the Vorobievi Gori. To have a complete understanding of what it is you need to walk around it, because only then it can be viewed from all sides. You need to see the inside of it, have a look at the auditorium, classrooms, cafeterias, rooms of the dormitory, teachers' apartments. But if a person possesses a higher state of consciousness, then, as it was said in the Introduction, he can at once simultaneously see the entire building, both inside and outside. The entire building, all the rooms at once. And the number of rooms does not matter. But the one who has not yet acquired the perception of the fourth dimension of space will have to do a lot of walking in order to examine the entire building.

You may be taking pictures while walking around the building. If you look at the building from one side and then, walking around it some more look at it from another side, naturally, you can still see the corner of the building you've just past, though from a different angle. The same will be reflected on the photos. Overlapping is inevitable.

The same is with the principles. In reality there is only one **Principle**, but by ordinary wakeful consciousness it is perceived as sort of multidimensional and thus, as in the example with the building it has to be considered from different perspectives. As a result of that we have many principles. Similarly, in order to become familiar with a building from the photos, one has to go over a lot of photographs. So everything depends on the state of consciousness.

Here is another example. A while ago yoga, mainly hatha yoga, was very popular in our country. In the beginning many people were very enthusiastic about it, however, with time they became less enthusiastic, because they failed to achieve the results they anticipated. But such an outcome is quite natural, and here the situation is quite similar to the one from the previous example. The matter is that there is only one Yoga, and it was created by the people possessing a higher state of consciousness. For an ordinary wakeful consciousness yoga is multidimensional and thus it can only be perceived in parts, only as separate aspects, and these Yoga's separate aspects, Yoga with a capital letter, are hatha yoga, raja yoga, bhakti yoga, karma yoga, jnana yoga. There are other yogas too, but these, to a first approximation, may be considered the main ones.

The purpose of Yoga is raising the level of consciousness and, therefore, moving towards God. The word "yoga" means joining, union, uniting. So the word "yoga" clearly indicates the goal: being in touch with the Creator.

If only one aspect of Yoga, for example, physical (hatha yoga), is taken into account, but other elements - at least the key elements  - of other yoga aspects are disregarded, namely, the proper spiritual aspiration (bhakti yoga), the proper knowledge (nana yoga), the principles of development of consciousness (raja yoga) and understanding of what a proper action is and how it is performed (karma yoga), if these elements are missing, then the hatha yoga practice turns into plain physical exercises, into ordinary gymnastics.

A similar situation is virtually in all the spheres of human activity. Let's consider one of the most important questions –comprehension of the World. Again we have a multidimensional object. And therefore again only its isolated aspects are taken out, and again we have, as we've just seen in yoga, separate approaches, separate paths: the path of religion in its present form, the path of science, the path of art. There are other approaches too, but these are the main ones in the modern society.

Let's take a closer look at these separate approaches, for example, at the path of science. And let's take physics, one of the fundamental sciences, as an example. The advancement of this science, its progress is indubitable. However, due to the impression of the progress science made science has gradually become idealized, its assertions have acquired the status of being a hundred percent true, a word of scientists has become the ultimate truth. For that matter it becomes necessary to see how in general science is created.

The matter is that people, whose profession is other than science, often think that physics, for example, is an exact science, that in physics everything is based on proof, and therefore the assertions scientists make can be relied upon. However, in reality the situation is much more complicated.

The main danger is in initial postulates, based on which the entire building of science is constructed. These postulates do not get proved, they just cannot be proved. If any postulate can be proved, it means it is not original. The very fact that it is possible to prove a certain provision indicates that this provision is not basic, is not fundamental. Fundamental provisions in every science are the provisions that serve as a foundation on which the entire building of this science is constructed upon, these are the provisions, or the laws, from which the rest can be deduced. But they themselves cannot be deduced. They are just declared, and that's it.

As an example we may examine Newton's second law, which we were told about in school. It is one of the laws underlying classical mechanics. It represents an equation, which links three quantities together: mass of a body, force acting on it and acceleration acquired by the body as a result of the force acting on it.

Let us consider briefly all three of these concepts.

We will begin with mass. The problem of mass is one of unresolved problems of modern physics. And it is impossible to completely solve this problem without considering the fact, that anybody, the mass of which is discussed, is a product of the collective consciousness. We already know that. All bodies have been created based on the collective consciousness. As well as the laws, which, therefore, can be changed.

Now concerning force. Force characterizes an interaction of bodies. Four kinds of fundamental interactions are known to the modern orthodox physics: gravitational, electromagnetic, and two other kinds of interactions, pertaining to the nuclear forces. This is what modern science knows. But in reality there are other kinds of interactions as well.

As an example let's consider a case from the recent history. When the Aswan dam was being built after the overflowing of the Nile in Egypt some monuments of ancient architecture, specifically the statues of the pharaohs would have had to go under the water. They were colossal statues made of solid rock. Well, it turned out that current technology is unable to relocate these statues whole and they had to be sawn into separate pieces. The question arises: how is it that the people, who made them, would succeed in the task? The priests of the time knew how to accomplish such a task. They would gather enough people and would properly direct the collective consciousness of these people. As a result the monolith would move to the designated location.

In the Newton's equation the acceleration has not been covered yet. Everybody is well familiar with this concept. It tells you how fast a starting car can gain the necessary speed. Both acceleration and speed are associated with distance and time measurement. And distance is measured between two points in space. It means that in the end the concepts of acceleration and speed come to the concepts of space and time.

We already know that space and time are the constructs of the collective consciousness. And therefore everything that happens can be changed by consciousness.

And also I must tell you what the problem here is: in order to understand what space and time are, one has to possess a higher state of consciousness.

So the original equation of classical mechanics turns out to be very unclear. The similar situation is in other branches of physics as well. And so, all the conclusions from the basic equations should not be expected to be true. And one should be especially cautious in regard to the statements of scientists pertaining to the Universe.

As I've already said before, physical, that is, certain objective reality as such, in actuality does not exist. What people think is objective reality is in fact the manifestation of the collective consciousness. The position of scientists with their belief in the existence of objective physical reality can be illustrated by the following example.

Let's imagine a person in the auditorium of a theater watching a performance. He is taken up by the act. He may also start taking to heart what's happening to one of the characters, start worrying, even his breathing may become affected. He may become so involved that he forgets about everything else and starts accepting what is happening on the stage as a reality. But the reality is quite different. The actors may leave the stage, change their costumes and begin performing a completely different play.

Since their childhood scientists have been watching a long play on the stage of existence. And many of them grow so accustomed to it that virtually automatically accept the surrounding world as objective reality. And it is particularly due to that, by the way, people experience so many problems in their lives – they fail to understand that if needed all they have to do is to change the course of the play or to change the play at all. In reality each person has the keys to his/ her own happiness. We only need to have a good understanding of the situation and properly say: "Open, Sesame!"

Very often what we think is a fairy tale, that is, something made up, in actuality is a picturesque story of the truths hidden behind the outward cover of reality.

So that when I quote as an example "Open, Sesame!" I only mean that this phrase communicates the knowledge of the reality control. And it is this practice, the practice of the reality control, the practice of control of events that is on the current agenda, and that becomes urgent for all of us.

Going back to science, I would like to say the following. The problem is that for a scientist, even an outstanding one, but having an ordinary state of consciousness, the reality looks totally different compared to what opens to someone in higher states of consciousness. I will remind you, that an ordinary wakeful consciousness views the world through the prism of three-dimensional space and time, and it is precisely such model that is used by the orthodox science. From what I've said earlier we can see how limited and problematic such an approach is. The weapons of mass destruction have been made based on exactly this approach.

And thus it is no wonder that the orthodox science, specifically physics, is currently in the state of crisis. And science looks for a way out from this crisis in the wrong direction.

To elucidate the situation I will use a known comparison. Imagine a big branchy tree with a lot of leaves before you. If there happened to be a drought season, the leaves on the tree begin to yellow, wither, and shrivel. If you would like to see the leaves green and full of life again, it would be useless and make no sense to start smoothing them out or doing something else to them trying to help them. To solve the problem you need to go somewhere else, you need to do something different: you need to water the roots of the tree, and then all the leaves will become green and full of life again.

The same is with science. We need to turn to the roots. The roots of the body need to be watered, the state of the body needs to be changed, and the state of consciousness needs to be changed. Your own consciousness must control the reality, and this is the basis which any science must be built upon. Science based on the controlling consciousness of a person allows to neutralize destructive technologies and become man's true protection.

I will repeat again: a person's perception of the World depends on the level of the state of his consciousness. Having attained a higher state of consciousness gives a different World perception, a different understanding, a different kind of knowledge. A well-known utterance refers to this problem too: little knowledge moves one away from God, but big knowledge brings one back to Him again.

I would like to bring your attention to a very significant point pertaining to

Principle (1.3). I will remind you this principle: OUR CONSCIOUSNESS PERCEIVES WHAT EXISTS IN OUR CONSCIOUSNESS AS REALITY. We already know that anything that a person sees around him, all that surrounds him, is constructed based on the collective consciousness. In this connection the following question arises: if the level of the state of consciousness of a certain person is significantly higher than the level of the collective consciousness, then how would, for example, a nuclear explosion affect this person? To answer this question the following comparison can be made. Imagine that you are in the country walking across an open field. And suddenly a thunderstorm breaks out. Storm clouds cover the sky and brilliant flashes of lightning start striking the ground. And being struck by lightning, as we know, does not bode anybody any good. The situation, hence, becomes serious.

However, if during the storm, instead of being in a field you are on board a plane, which is flying high above the clouds, so that the raging thunderstorm is somewhere below, then you may watch with curiosity through the cabin window what is happening below.

And it is all the more better to watch the raging storm from a satellite cabin. From a satellite cabin many other phenomena can be seen as well, for example, a storm rushing through the land, sweeping everything away on its way.

So, just as the hurricane sweeping everything away from its path, can be quietly watched from the height of the satellite, so one can similarly observe what takes place in the sphere of the collective consciousness from the height of a much higher level of the state of consciousness.

And thus the same nuclear explosion won't be able to destroy someone, who has reached a high level of the state of consciousness, for such a person is now beyond reach of ordinary storms – he has already entered the flow of Eternity. There are people like this, and I can say that after some time they will significantly increase in number.

What I've just said can be put in a different manner. As it has been already mentioned, there are scientists, who believe that the surrounding world is governed by certain objective laws.

From this perspective gradually raising the level of a person's state of consciousness means that as this person grows, that is, as he exceeds the level of the collective consciousness more and more, he becomes submitted to less and less number of these 'objective' laws, the less and .less these 'objective' laws are able to affect him.

One of the relatively simple examples is levitation that is, overcoming gravity by consciousness and the flight of the body as a result. I will note that many people just never think of such a phenomenon. And it is because under the influence of the orthodox science there is a preconceived idea in the modern society about the laws as something fixed, as something that represents a certain unchangeable given.

However every person within a comparatively short period of time may learn to change the law of gravity for himself and thereby learn from his own experience what levitation is.

But if the collective consciousness is changed in this respect, it will cause the law itself to change.

In my practice of salvation it is very important not to merely observe and register certain laws, certain situations, but to be able based on control by consciousness to change laws, situations, events in the direction desirable for man.

I think that the significant shortcoming of the orthodox science mentioned above needs more attention, namely, the fact that the orthodox science is engaged in mere phenomena observation and registration of the laws that have been discovered. Such an approach of science, is, of course, explained by the existing belief in the objective nature of phenomena of the surrounding world, in their existence regardless of man, and therefore, the purpose of science is seen as to discover the existing regularities and to describe them.

Let's consider a specific example. Traditionally at the end of December of each year the publishers of "Science", one of the leading scientific journals, select ten most outstanding achievements in science of the passing year. Let's see what is number one among the most significant achievements of the past 1998 year.

The most important scientific discovery of 1998 was recognized the conclusion that our Universe will be expanding forever and at an ever increasing speed.

Here we can see an example of how scientists based on thoroughly conducted experiments merely state the fact they have discovered. And that is all. And this is considered to be a great scientific achievement; when a scientific approach must be fundamentally different.

In this particular example it is not that important what exactly was discovered by the scientists, whether the Universe is expanding or contracting is not the point. The matter is that the true science, that is, the science that I propose, has absolutely different goals and is of an entirely different kind. And especially at this time, when the humanity and the entire world are faced with the real threat of annihilation, science must determine its path based on salvation of the world from the global disaster.

That is why I create my science on principles of achieving concrete results by a number of successive creative actions, and with a complete control of each of them. My science, being also the science of salvation, aims to ultimately attain salvation and at the same time to change the existing reality in the right way.

True science works the following way. Knowing the situation, first it changes the reality in such a way as to achieve the result of salvation. After the salvation has been attained, insuring safety and security is the next priority. And finally, when security and safety are ensured, further development of all the events in the direction proper for the person is set. The same scheme is used to obtain any beneficial result.

As we see, in true science just a plain statement of facts is out of the question. If any existing systems or propositions do not foster obtaining the necessary result, it means that these systems need to be changed, including the system of laws.

The principle criterion in my science is to obtain the necessary result in a creative manner. Verity of the fact that this is the science is in that initially, first of all, the positive result is obtained, for example, a person gets saved or resurrected, or the society gets saved, and only after that, based on this positive result science is created, showing, how to do it.

In order to better understand this important idea, let's refer to something that we all know well. In music we see a somewhat similar situation.

As we know, there is music theory. However, masterpieces of musical art were not created based on music theory, quite the opposite, the music theory is created based on the analysis of musical masterpieces, composed by geniuses. The starting point, therefore, is practice. Theory, which can help beginners make their first steps, is created based on the best pieces of practice.

So, the underlying aspect of my science is practice that is, obtaining a necessary result. And since the most important characteristic of this life is its continuous development, I do not build any systems which are strictly static, like the system of fixed, unchangeable laws, but I build a flexible dynamic system, the based on the necessary result.

If we take the aforementioned example of the discovery of the ever accelerating expansion of the Universe, then a simple question arises: what specifically must be done with regard to this discovery? Because if we just accept the ever accelerating expansion of the Universe as fact, as scientists do, that is, utilize a mechanistic approach , then it becomes obvious  that the control of each stage of this process will be gradually getting weaker and weaker .

So I would put the question in a different way: how to explain this situation, how to show it in such a way that the act of salvation would be possible to attain? How can  we transform consciousness, that is, how can we make the mechanism of perception, the mechanism of development, such, that each act of the external world would be under control?

To answer these questions it is important to define an initial form, through which all the processes may be controlled. We may take, for example, my principle, which states that: ANY ELEMENT OF THE WORLD CAN BE CONTROLLED THROUGH ANY CHOSEN ELEMENT OF THE WORLD, BESIDES, THIS CHOSEN ELEMENT CAN BE SPECIFICALLY CREATED FOR THIS PURPOSE BY YOUR CONSCIOUSNESS. On the basis of this principle the processes of the entire Universe can be always controlled, and from this perspective instead of perceiving the Universe as expanding or contracting, to perceive it just as a system, which is at one and the same stage, but which changes, let's say, its shape as well as changes the implications. And if necessary, certain laws have to be changed too, no matter what they are, or how they have been established.

So, even if the essence of the discovery stays the same, this discovery can be interpreted in an entirely different manner/way, it can be regarded differently. All related elements of the Universe represent information objects. Of course, we may, as it is done by science, find a specific connection between them. However, in order to control this World it is not necessary to observe it from the inside, it suffices to enter macrostructure from one's own consciousness and then control this information, which, most importantly, has to be in the area of control, and this is always possible to ensure.

So, my science provides knowledge on how to resolve this kind of problems, not the problems of registering some processes, but the problems of **control** of any World processes.

The concrete facts of the resurrection of people, given in Chapter I, are convincing examples of such an approach. In Chapter IV we will examine the cases of recovery from various serious diseases. All these examples eloquently illustrate the true science in action: this science does not limit itself to mere stating the fact that a person, for example, has already left this World or that due to the advanced stage of cancer or AIDS he has approached the end of his life. The true science on the basis of the true knowledge of the World as well as with the help of the principles of control first of all obtains the necessary result, in this case a person's salvation: if he has already gone, it brings him back into our world, or, if he is sick, it changes in principle the course of illness, it reverses the processes in his body, so that the person becomes healthy again.

I will give another example from my practice of applying my science .I'm talking about forecasting earthquakes and minimizing their magnitude. In order to forecast earthquakes and other disasters as well as to minimize their affects I applied the formula of the universal reality and the wave synthesis theory, which I have created based on my clairvoyance. Based on these general theoretical provisions I designed and made a special device. I would like to emphasize it. The matter is that I personally can forecast earthquakes and minimize their magnitude without the help of any devices, I personally do not need them. But since we speak about science, it is necessary to create technical devices that everybody could use.

That is why I am now talking about testing the device I have created, which could go into series production. The essence of the device operation as well as of the conducted experiments is as follows.

First of all the device allows to forecast earthquakes. It determines geographical location of the future earthquake and estimates its magnitude. After that the device starts minimizing the magnitude of the future earthquake and continues minimizing it until its technical resources needed for that become exhausted. And only after they have been exhausted, only then the magnitude of the future earthquake is fixed at the level up to which it has been minimized. Naturally, the application of the device with greater resource allows for a greater effect.

This method was developed based on information use of the past and future events. In the aggregate the information of a thousand earthquakes registered in the past was utilized, and the information of the predictive phase was confirmed.

Here is the most of the letter written by Mr. Shakhramanian M.A., Head of the Agency for Monitoring and Forecasting of Emergency Situations MES of Russia, to Academician Kuznetsov O.L., President of RANS (the Russian Academy of Natural Sciences).

"RANS Academician Grabovoi Grigori Petrovich, applying his formula of the universal reality as well as his wave synthesis theory for the purpose of preventive earthquake and disaster forecast, translated the crystal module of the forecast into a digital form. As evidence that proves that the above-stated module allows the realization of a preventive earthquake forecast, earthquake statistics were used, provided by the Central experimental-methodical expedition of the Russian Academy of Sciences geophysical service. Testing of the digital model of the device was conducted on past and future earthquakes. On the earthquakes of the past – by changing the model's initial parameters to the parameters prior to the beginning of earthquakes. On the earthquakes of the future – by software processing of both an electronic terrain map and extrapolation data of the Earth surface monitoring from satellites… In the capacity of the earthquakes that actually happened in the past the data of 1000 registered earthquakes were used for the period from January 7, 1901 through July 4, 1918. In the capacity of the earthquakes of the future in July of 1999 the forecast was confirmed for all the areas where software processing of an electronic terrain map was conducted. … In all the cases the predictive phase was fully confirmed. Presently in order to translate the crystal module parameters in a digital form into the form of a microprocessor which is able to work for a long interval of time without additional calculations the laser radiation characteristics from a physical source have to be translated into a digital form."

Still it is not quite clear how one can make sure that the proposed device really minimizes the earthquake magnitude and that without it the earthquake would be more destructive. Because we just register an earthquake magnitude which we observe, and that's all. And what if the magnitude would be the same without the device?

The answer to this question was obtained earlier when carrying out a series of underground nuclear tests. Several tests may be carried out, exploding a nuclear explosive of one and the same explosive force in the same conditions. During these tests the device is turned off, and the magnitude of emerging destruction is registered. Then the device is turned on and another series of similar explosions, maintaining the same conditions, is carried out. With the help of measurements it is determined what specific changes occur and how they occur when the device is turned on. Measurements were taken at a distance of approximately 20 km away from the epicenter of the explosion. The result of these experiments is truly amazing: even having only one device turned on, the magnitude of the destruction would become virtually half the size. A more perfect and more powerful device may minimize many times the magnitude of the destruction, and the presence of several devices allows to entirely eliminate any destruction.

So, the device has passed a very serious testing and completely proved to be exceptionally effective.

I will add that, when I would join in the work myself, then virtually no destruction would take place.

During the underground nuclear tests the device was adjusted depending on the shape and size of the crystal being used. The graphs obtained served then as a calculation base in the experiments with earthquakes.

Now with respect to the device application during real earthquakes. It is known that from the epicenter of an earthquake there is a propagation of waves, traveling in all directions due to the earth crust deformation. At some distance away from the epicenter the size of these future deformations can be observed. Of course, the size of the deformations depends on the distance and the earthquake magnitude in the epicenter. The beginning of an earthquake can be registered with ordinary devices too. If an earthquake happened to be somewhere, the approximate size of the deformations in the observation location can be determined. However, if after the beginning of an earthquake the device was turned on in the observation location, the size of the earth crust deformations registered in that place would be several times less, not several percents less, but times less.

So given real earthquakes my device has demonstrated an exceptional effectiveness as well. But what else is important is that this device was created based on new science, and for this precise reason it proved to be so effective.

Several words need to be said about what forecasting is based upon. My science solves the problem set before it, I mean obtaining the necessary result, but at the same time it doesn't fixate any particular form of intermediate process. For example, if we take the wave synthesis theory that I've created, in this theory any event is regarded as a result of the interaction of stationary areas with the dynamic ones. It is precisely out of the interaction of the stationary and the dynamic phases of reality that an event comes into existence.

The theory of the wave synthesis is a consequence of my discovery of the creating area of information. This discovery was registered by the International Registration Chamber in 1997. The core of this discovery consists in that IN ANY INFORMATION OBJECT THE AREA OF CREATION OF THIS OBJECT CAN ALWAYS BE SINGLED OUT, WHICH IS THE VERY STATIC PHASE OF REALITY. BUT WHEN YOU PERCEIVE THE OBJECT, THE DYNAMIC PHASE OF REALITY EMERGES, WHICH IS EXACTLY THE ONE THAT CREATES INFORMATION. Hence it follows that all that exists in the World has been created by the collective consciousness, including the consciousness of the Creator. And that is why, through cognition of the laws of consciousness, received from the Creator, it is possible to create any Worlds and ensure eternal life. The application of this discovery gives (ensures) a concrete criterion of the future. That is what forecasting is based on. Further. My formula of universal reality takes into consideration that every person is connected with all information objects. When on the basis of this formula a person realizes that there is a possibility of an earthquake and at the same time he is attuned to minimizing the possible effects of the natural calamity, then the magnitude of the earthquake diminishes. This same task can be accomplished by the properly constructed devices, which are based on the laws of universal interconnections and the functioning of the human consciousness. Under no circumstances do such devices destroy.

Therefore in my science every object is connected with any other object, and all the connections in the World on the basis of consciousness can be very accurately described in precise symbols. And each element - be it, for example, a human being, a bio-system, a general system or even just a formula - works for one general goal – building a creative safe, secure future. And that is why in true science a formal mechanism, which carries out this goal into effect, is at the same time a working tool, which affects the final state of the problem to be resolved.

And all this relates to the application of my science to any phenomena, not necessarily associated only with natural disasters.

The essence of my science is, therefore, that every element of it, including the formal apparatus as well, must change the World in a manner, that the World should be controlled and cause no problems.

So, if the discovery has been made in which the ever accelerating expansion of the Universe is stated, then in my opinion, there should also be, by all means, the recommendations on how to make it possible for man to be able to control the phenomenon and how it could be used for the benefit of all.

For this purpose I would suggest the control through a static unchanging reality of the World. It would seem that it is only the information plane, but the aforementioned letter proves that all information planes can be manifested into reality.

So, I will repeat, comparison of my science with the orthodox science helps better understand that instead of the orientation towards stating any discovered fact, the criterion of scientific thinking must be the orientation towards obtaining the results of an entirely different level, the results that would ensure creative development of the society with full control of all the stages of this development.

If the true science existed at the time, when radioactivity was discovered, the discovery of radioactivity would have never resulted in the creation of nuclear weapon. Unfortunately many orthodox science discoveries can be likened to a jinnee out of the bottle: the control over it becomes problematic.

And this is not surprising. The initial cause of such a situation can be seen from the above example of the second Newton law. The mass of a body, its acceleration and acting force are introduced, and then these three quantities are linked into one equation, but what it is for, whether it is for destruction or for creation, is not clear at all, what's more, this question has not even been raised. Here we clearly see a sign of a complete uncertainty of a primary characteristic, what is typical for orthodox science on the whole.

Any science is associated with the concepts of research and implementation of the research results. The true science at the stage of research should not destroy anything (let's remember the example with the flower given in the Introduction), and at the stage of implementation it must ensure the improvement for all the aspects of the World.

And thus the essence of the true science may be stated as follows: the essence of science is the ability to study, the ability to control and the ability to implement without interfering in the state of an object of study and sometimes even without any contact with it.

It is clear that these two sciences, orthodox science and true science, being so fundamentally different, must utilize a completely different mathematical apparatus. And this is really so. And we can tell right away what this fundamental difference of the apparatus of my science is.

Any discovery, basically, creates an event; therefore, the situation changes. The formulas must reflect this change of the situation. That is why the formulas have to be changing.

My mathematics changes simultaneously with the change of reality and at the same time it itself changes the reality. And it is for this precise reason that it can ensure control of the result at any stage.

Ordinary mathematics for its application presupposes knowledge of the boundary and initial conditions and, in general, the presence of at least some available data concerning the object of research. My mathematics can operate and lead to a desired result even in the conditions, when nothing is known about the object. It allows to always be saved, including those conditions, when the properties of an aggressive environment are not known.

The reason my mathematics is so effective is that it utilizes an operational principle of action, like the one being utilized by the soul. We know that it is the soul that prevents, the soul that saves, it is the soul that regulates the World. Similar is the principle of operation of the true mathematics.

This is completely different mathematics. It's been created in accordance with the structure of the World, it is a part of the World, and hence its main element is a concept of action. And the action, that doesn't destroy, but the action, that creates.

The striking difference between the science that I have presented and the former orthodox science has an explanation. And, perhaps, you have already guessed, what it is. The key is in the difference of the levels of the state of consciousness, that's what it is.

The kind of science a scientist creates is in principle determined by the level of his state of consciousness. And therefore in actuality the word "science" of itself does not say much. For of fundamental importance is the level of the state of consciousness of the one making this science. Thus, there is science consistent with an ordinary level of the state of consciousness, - it is the orthodox science; there is science – which is totally different – consistent with a higher level of the state of consciousness; there is science, consistent with an even higher state of consciousness and so on.

Taking all this into account we may say that the current orthodox science cannot be anything else, but what it is. It is precisely that which is consistent with an ordinary state of consciousness. And that is why I stated above that the way out of the current crisis of science and the key to its qualitative change lies in changing the state of consciousness of the people making it.

What I've just said concerning science, namely, regarding its gradations, its levels, is true for any other human activity. And the words "art" or "religion" also require more precise definition depending on which level of the state of consciousness this or other practice of art or religion corresponds to.

Now we proceed to the principles of the resurrection. And the analysis of science I have just made, will help us as well understand a number of important aspects, pertaining to these principles. For the principles of the resurrection are the example of science, true science. First of all I would like to say the following. Usually principles imply something fixed, something unchangeable. And this is not accidental. We all have an example of familiar to all orthodox science, which deals with fixed, unchanging laws, the analysis of these laws and obtaining consequences of them are conducted by means of the mathematical apparatus that never changes, with fixed formulas. Such fixing of the key positions is inculcated since childhood, just based on the perception of the World, typical for an ordinary wakeful consciousness.

However, we have already seen that real science does not limit itself to plain statement of reality. For reality, as we know from the first paragraph of this chapter, in actuality is very changeable. I can, for example, materialize and dematerialize objects. And therefore, the true science, the real science, utilizes a flexible, changeable mathematical apparatus. Basic laws may change as well.

Similarly each of the resurrection principle may be modified with the course of time. This is consistent with the main characteristic of real life, which is its continuous development.

Other attributes of real science that we have discovered, are present here as well. Here too the existing principles are aimed towards obtaining the necessary result, but provided the absence of any destruction and provided the full control of every intermediate stage.

I would like to draw your attention to the fact, that the division of the principles into four levels and their arrangement into four respective sections should not be perceived statically. The overall approach must be dynamic, flexible. The implementation of these principles by people may be, for example, in such a way, that, a principle from section four can be more effective than a principle from section one. It would seem that, if the principle refers to the first level, it deems to be more effective. However in actuality it can be otherwise, the situation may turn out to be more complex.

It may happen, for example, that a person read the principles of section four but he did not read the principles of section one. But they all are in the information field, and he can perceive them implicitly and thus in fact know them.

And though formally the principles of section one are indeed generally more important, nevertheless, since their effect on a person depends on specific conditions, a specific situation, their general collective effect on a person is more significant. We must bear in mind that all together, in aggregate, these principles represent a living organism. And you, being a living organism too, may have situations, when, let's say, a hand at some point is more important for you than your head. But at the same time nobody is going to deny the importance of the head.

So, the most important here is the general arrangement of the principles and their collective interaction with a person. These principles are, in fact, a system of actions, aimed at the concrete solution of the issues of our life.

The first principle in this section states:

ASPIRATION OF GOD AND MAN FOR UNITY WITHIN RECREATION AND REUNION RESULTS IN MATERILIZATION AND RESURRECTION. (3.1).

As I've already said in the beginning of this chapter, today a new stage in the evolution of man has come. The former path of development, when one has to give up his/her physical body, has completely exhausted itself. It does not meet the demands of the present day. Man is taking a new path, a path of non-dying, a path of immortality. And on this path his spiritual core, his spiritual base begins to show itself much more clearly, and a deeper realization of the verity that man has been created in God's own image and likeness begins to take place.

The resurrection, that is, the regeneration, the restoration of those, who are gone, and their desire, just as the desire of the living, for unity with the Creator reflect the true nature of man.

The resurrection of people, like nothing else, proves that life has a spiritual base.

CONCENTRAION BY MAN OF HIS OWN CONSCIOUSNESS MIGHT RESULT IN A RADICAL CHANGE OF THE WORLD STRUCTURE (3.2).

This principle is closely linked to the principle (1.4). Please notice that the word "concentration" has simultaneously two meanings here.

One meaning of the word is well known, especially to those, who has practiced, let's say, such a discipline as yoga. Some spiritual disciplines explain how by means of concentration of consciousness, for example, on a certain organ of the body the state of this organ can be changed, restored to health.

The other meaning of the word 'concentration' which is implied here as well is the following. As I've already said in part one of this chapter, consciousness is the structure, which allows the soul to control the body, and in a wide sense of the word consciousness is the structure which unites spiritual and physical matter. In this context concentration of consciousness means its real accumulation.

We may draw, but very roughly, an analogy with computers, just to emphasize the idea. Let's remember, what was used to perform calculations at the dawn of the computer era. The first electronic computers occupied several rooms, but a modern computer fits on a palm and is much more powerful.

It is clear that if a certain device initially occupied several rooms and now fits on a palm, then we may say that all those structures that make this device a computer are concentrated in a small volume of this device.

The same applies to consciousness, which, as we know, also represents a certain structure. As a person works on self-perfection, as he develops, as he evolves spiritually the greater and greater concentration of his consciousness is achieved. That is the second meaning of the word "concentration" used in the formulation of this principle.

This second meaning of the word "concentration" is of particular importance. The concentration of consciousness means here, in actuality, an increase of the information compactness, an increase of the mass data in a volume unit. Such consciousness concentration may have far-reaching consequences. When in the process of a person's evolution his consciousness concentration in a certain volume reaches a certain value, this volume begins to submit to the person, begins to submit to his consciousness. In a situation like this the World structure changes and now it is not the World that will determine a person's structure but the person himself will set the tone.

As soon as the concentration of consciousness becomes greater than the substance concentration, for example, of the aforementioned computer, man will become inaccessible, he will be then indestructible. Man's thoughts, words, actions will become a primary element, and machines, buildings, planets, all these and other material objects will be a secondary element. And it will be then the next level of existence. And it is exactly to this purpose that I communicate knowledge, the new knowledge, so that people, having mastered this new system of knowledge should be able to start controlling worlds.

It will be a completely different level of existence. There will be no place for decay, completely different processes will be taking place there. These processes will be the ones of recommencement of Worlds, that is, the processes, when the eternal gives birth to the eternal, when the status of Eternity is translated into the status of next Eternity.

In this case we have an overconcentration of consciousness, which immensely increases the rate of information exchange, so that as a result completely different structures appear, the structures of the highest consciousness, the structures of the highest life. At this level, for example, a thought is now an action and an action is a thought. For this level, for this World structure, for these Worlds an object and an action, physical and spiritual, are the same.

This is the radical change in the World structure that this principle talks about. And a person can achieve it through the concentration of his own consciousness.

PHYSICAL BODY IS ALWAYS A PART OF THE SOUL (3.3).

BOTH THEORETICALLY AND PRACTICALLY MAN CAN BE REGARDED AS A STRUCTURE OF CONSCIOUSNESS THAT HAS A BODY SHELL (3.4).

The wording of the last principle as it is given here, was used in the first section of the previous chapter, where the case of Rusanov's resurrection was examined.

Thanks to the stories of those, who personally visited the other side and then came back into our world again, it is possible to have first-hand detailed information concerning their feelings and sensations at the moment of their biological death and after, and how they perceived our world from there.

Thus, that sealed book, that mystery that has always existed in respect of biological death, now due to the resurrection, finally, ceases to be a great enigma, and the veracity, astounding in its simplicity, uncloses before us. And the core of this truth, the core of this discovery is that now, when the cover has been pulled off from this great mystery, suddenly it became clear that death, as it turns out, is not needed at all. More than that, as we have ascertained a little earlier, it has become an obstacle to a person's further development, and that is why immortality is now on the agenda.

As for Ruslanov's particular experience, he gave a detailed description of the stages his consciousness went through following his departure. During the first month his consciousness was as if contracting, Ruslanov felt that his consciousness was entering a certain single point somewhere around his head, he distinctly felt his consciousness being in that point.

During the first two-three weeks Ruslanov made attempts to restore his body to the level of ordinary life, however then his consciousness shifted to trying to understand, trying to grasp this new stage in his state, the state when his body was undergoing decomposition. And at the same time his consciousness was fully aware that his soul was moving towards God's light. There consciousness and the soul become one.

It should be noted that the stages consciousness goes through after the biological death are quite different for different people. This process is exclusively individual. But I will not go into further details, for we already know that this path, the path of spiritual development through giving up a physical body will soon become a thing of the past, will soon become history. Times have changed. Nowadays nobody would want to use a cart when a car or an airliner is available.

In relation to these two considered principles a few words may be said as to an interesting practice of ancient magicians. The information about it can still be found up to this day, though it is extant mostly in fairytales.

The principles in question mean that it is possible to build a physical body around the soul. But it is not necessarily must be a human body that can be built, but a body of an animal as well. This is the very practice I have in mind, and which ancient magicians were the masters of. They could create a body of an animal, enter it and then come back. We read about it in our childhood. I will emphasize, however, that in order to be able to transfer oneself into animals in such a manner, a fairly fast information processing ability in the structure of the spirit is necessary.

AT THE LEVEL OF CREATION OF INFORMATION CONNECTIONS NO OBJECT OVERLAPS WITH ANY OTHER EXTERNAL OBJECT INCLUDING ITSELF. THE PRINCIPLE OF RESURRECTION OF MAN, OR THE PRINCIPLE OF RESTORATION OF ANY OBJECT, IS IN THE OVERLAPING OF INITIAL INFORMATION ABOUT THE OBJECT WITH THE DEVELOPING INFORMATION ABOUT ITSELF IN THE AREA OF THE EFFECT RELATIONS, WHICH APPEAR IN THE COURSE OF CREATION OF INFORMATION (3.5).

For gaining a true insight into this principle, different aspects of the World at the informational level ought to be understood. The informational approach, I think, will be considered in one of the books of this series, but now I will confine myself just to certain explanations.

This principle virtually states that in the state of ordinary wakeful consciousness a person can resurrect based on overlapping of his initial state of consciousness with the next state of his consciousness, present at the moment of the resurrection. For a person in an ordinary state of consciousness at the informational level of the initial state no object in principle can overlap with any external object or itself. The shift to a higher state of consciousness is necessary in order to make the overlapping of the initial information about an object with the developing information about this object possible, which gives the resurrection of a person or the restoration, the regeneration of any object in general.

Recall the example with a flower, given in the Introduction. In an ordinary state of consciousness a person is not able in principle to comprehend the essence of a flower, as well as of any other creation. He may observe the flower as much as desired but he won't be able to penetrate its mystery, the mystery of its existence. However, in a higher state of consciousness a person is able to become one with a flower, on the language of this principle a sort of 'overlapping' with the flower may take place, and when the person becomes one with the flower, becomes indistinguishable from it, then the comprehension of the essence of the flower comes, the mystery opens up.

The true path towards comprehension of the World is precisely in raising the level of the state of consciousness; it is the higher states of consciousness that pose the golden key, that opens the gates of the World.

The higher states of consciousness will lead to elimination of any destruction. The matter is that in a certain state of consciousness each World element is eternal. Therefore, when the majority of the collective consciousness has achieved such a level, any destruction will be impossible.

THE SYSTEM OF SPIRITUAL VIEWS OF THAT ONE WHO PRACTISES RESURRECTION IS EXACTLY THE PRINCIPLE OF SOCIETY ORGANIZATION AT THE SUBSEQUENT STAGES OF ITS DEVELOPMENT (3.6).

Principle (2.1), which we discussed earlier, states that the resurrection is based on revealing the eternal in man. Thus the one, practicing the resurrection, deals with Eternity. In this connection at the subsequent stages of its evolution the society will be built on the principles of Eternity, which is in line with the designs and ideas of the Creator. These designs and ideas of the Creator are implemented in practice by the one, who practices the resurrection.

DISTANT OBJECTS OF REALITY ARE WHAT IS APPROACHED FOR THE RESURRECTED AND REMOVED FOR THE LIVING (3.7).

First I will explain what this principle is about, and then restate it for it for better understanding.

In this principle one and the same objects, one and the same facts are viewed from two perspectives: from the viewpoint of the living one and from the viewpoint of the resurrected one. If an object is being moved farther and farther away from the living one, thus increasing the distance between them, then for him it will be becoming a farther and farther moved away distant object. However, of all the concepts associated with remoteness, a person's being on the other side is the most remote, for, for example, when the distance increases, one can still speak of certain gradations, but when a person departs, with respect to the living one there are no gradations whatsoever..

However, this remoteness, perceived as such by the living one, for the resurrected one turns to be brought closer. That's what is stated in the formulation of the principle.

By the way, the fact that what is perceived as distant by the living one, turns to be brought closer for the resurrected one, can be discovered during the first month after the resurrection, for example, by examining the cell structure. Cytologic analysis, that is, cell analysis, allows finding out that the cell structure during this period may be somewhat different, for example, in terms of the position of the cell's elements in relation to the nucleus. The cell microelements of the resurrected one may be positioned at a greater distance from the nucleus, and the orientation of their structures is still different compared to all these cell characteristics of the living.

In connection with the aforesaid the principle at issue may be restated as follows. The resurrected one as a control element has a structure, which he has gone through, which he has acquired, for example, through his departure, however, this control element in reality does not prove to be effective, quite the opposite, in order to live a normal life among the living much work has to be done by the resurrected one as to re-acquire the characteristics of the living and to become one of them in all respects.

This principle may be looked at from a somewhat different angle. In terms of action and development the resurrected one perceives reality, especially in the beginning, so, that Eternity appears to him to be a flexible structure, while for the living one Eternity is an absolute structure.

It is the transition through the departure and return structure that leads to the perception of Eternity by the resurrected one as a dynamic and flexible structure. And due to this a problem of adaptation to the world of the living arises, the necessity to properly attune various perception elements, so that Eternity changes and becomes static and absolute.

What I've just said is, in fact, one more formulation of this principle. Due to its importance I will repeat it again, more laconically.

In the beginning after the resurrection the resurrected perceives Eternity as a dynamic structure. In order to become adapted to the living he has to regain their perception, the perception, which reflects the absolute reality, namely, the static structure of Eternity.

The circumstance that in this regard the resurrected has a distorted picture of reality comes from the fact that during the resurrection out of the overall picture he singles out only one element: the resurrection phase - and as a result, he sees only one of the aspects of Eternity statics, the statics, which for those, who did not experience death, is an absolute reality and which for them reflects an absolute character of Eternity.

This principle, pointing out the significant difference in the beginning between the resurrected and the living, virtually speaks of the necessity to assist them in their adaptation process. And I do not mean only social adaptation. The resurrected experience cell rearrangement as well, their structure somewhat changes, certain atoms move to the proper place into the proper structure. As a result of these processes the elements of the separation from the living I was speaking about, gradually fade and become insignificant for the further evolution of the resurrected one. That is why special concentration methods should be given to the resurrected one to facilitate the said processes in the body.

Now here is one more formulation of the principle at issue. The resurrected has a structure of consciousness, which was formed, among other things, also due to the departure, and for that reason this new structure needs to be adapted to the structure of the consciousness of the living, of those, who did not experience death, so that after some time their structures of consciousness should not in fact differ from each other.

THE RESURRECTED ABSOLUTIZES SPACE AND DETAILS TIME. DURING THE INITIAL PERIOD TIME IS DISCRETE FOR HIM, WHILE FOR THE LIVING ONE TIME IS CONTINUOUS (3.8).

In what sense does the resurrected absolutize space? He absolutizes space as a structure based on which anything is possible, for example, both the body's decomposition, and its being assembled back again.

Absolutization of space by the resurrected one is also due, as we have discussed earlier, to the tie to a certain place.

The living one doesn't absolutize space due to the fact that he has never been tied to a certain place. And since he has never been tied to any particular place, since he has never had such a tie, he could not apply it to the eternal structure.

It is different for the resurrected one. For some time he was tied to the space in a certain point, in a certain area. That specific segment was a structure of Eternity for him. That is why that stage of his, during which he was a gone one, absolutizes space for him as a structure of Eternity; though in actuality the situation is quite different. Videlicet, we know that space can be controlled, let's say, by means of a thought impulse, or it may even be changed at all, as I have explained, through the collective consciousness.

As a matter of fact, the resurrected understands that space is changeable, transformable; it is even natural for him, it is just obvious for him, because he himself has just been transformed in the same way. Nevertheless, both the gone one and at first the resurrected one absolutize space, make it absolute, that is, impart uniform characteristics to space for the perception process. As a practical consequence it follows that man can be resurrected in any place in space, wherever you wish, regardless of time.

One may notice that such space perception, generally speaking, persists in the consciousness of the resurrected one, however, gradually he stops noticing it regarding it as unessential.

Now concerning time. In what sense does the resurrected one disaggregate time in the initial period? In the initial period the resurrected disaggregates time in the sense that each element of the World is in different time for him. It can be understood if we look at the process of assembling the body. During the resurrection when the body was being assembled at the cellular level, each cell was being restored at a different time. The difference in time could only be small fractions of a second, and yet, different cells were being restored at a different time.

Here a principle difference may be seen from the case, when a person is born normally. In normal birth, the body is also formed, but it is formed monolithically, synchronously, there is no asynchronism which is observed in the resurrection. As I have said, during the resurrection some cells are formed faster, some - slower, and a person feels it. He perceives it, as if the flow of time is different for different objects. If, for example, he sees a plant before him, he may think that time flows, let's say, faster than for any other object.

So, time disaggregation by the resurrected one is due to the fact that for him time in the beginning flows differently in different objects, in different processes. It leads to the time being as if discontinuous for the resurrected, one kind of time is here, another kind of time is there, which results in time being at first discrete for him. The discreteness, the discontinuity of time is, therefore, one of its disaggregation aspects.

This time discreteness or its disaggregation in general, pertains to the problem of perception. Logically it is clear that the World can be perceived in quite different ways. The consciousness of the resurrected one has gone through the phase, where any views are present, where time is both continuous and discontinuous. Thus, when in the beginning the resurrected observes that time is different in different phenomena, he, in fact, just observes a discrete picture of the World.

Special courses may help the resurrected one restore his time perception, make it similar to the one of the living, within quite a short time, two weeks at the most.

Particularly the discreteness and the aggregation of time are seen when a human body is assembled from the ash. In this case a human body is disintegrated into small particles, the ash particles, and the ash may happen to be widely scattered, and some particles may happen to be in totally different surroundings.

The ash particles are further broken down into microelements. And for the scattered particles the collective consciousness of a sort emerges, which controls each element of the ashes. And each element has its own flow of time, its own rate at which time passes for it.

A person in this case is as if scattered, since all his particles are scattered. However, even in such a state he clearly understands that he is the same soul, the same consciousness, the same person, that his present state will be followed by the resurrection, because the soul just must resurrect the body in order to have additional opportunities for a faster growth.

Compare: if a person is sick, he is out of shape, he is not feeling very well, because a sickness is a departure from the norm. And the gone one perfectly understands that he, being in a scattered state, is far from the normal state, thus he tries to bring the norm, which is his natural status, back.

Compared to the gone one, the living one is in incommensurably more advantageous position: he doesn't have to assemble anything, he can devote all his efforts and time to whatever needs to be done. And since he has a physical body, he has additional capabilities, for example, he may pick up a receiver and dial a number, when the gone one is devoid of such a capability. One must clearly understand altogether that it is no joy to be on the other side, and furthermore, in the future one will have to assemble his/her body anyway. So, there is no need to waste time.

As I have said, the reincarnation path for the gone is becoming a thing of the past, now the resurrection is becoming the primary path.

And all the gone ones will resurrect regardless, at present in this respect they have a narrow choice. There is also another variant of development of events: when the number of the resurrected will reach a certain specific quantity, we may say nominal mass, then all the rest will resurrect all at once. This process of the resurrection is already under way.

1 think, it is worth mentioning, that space and time perception depends on the level of the state of consciousness, on the level of the spirit. If a person is not enlightened, he perceives space and time at the current moment. But if a person possesses a higher level of the state of consciousness, he can perceive the World by means of clairvoyance. In that case he is able to see diverse spaces and diverse time and a different kind of spaces and a different kind of time at all, specifically, for example, absence of time. So, the concepts of space and time are individual for each person, and everything is determined by the level of the state of consciousness.

THE PRINCIPLE OF AUTONOMY OF INFORMATION FUNCTIONING WITHIN DIFFERENT TIMES (3.9).

First of all I must say that autonomy here means independence. This principle says that the information of the past, the present and the future, or just the past, the present and the future as separate elements are independent from one another, independent relative to the instantaneous impulse of the consciousness of the one, performing the resurrection, or from the standpoint of the one, being resurrected.

© Г.П. Грабовой, 2001

Let's examine the essence of this principle at greater length. When somebody wishes to resurrect a person and gives an impulse of consciousness for his resurrection, this impulse must by all means contain certain information elements respectively towards the past, the present and the future. The past must be taken into account, the future must be formed and the present must be directed at the technological aspect: how to perform the resurrection, what has to be done now, in this particular situation.

Information contents of the past, of the present and of the future exist independently; they have different structures and different focus. In fact, these information contents are, naturally, interconnected, however at the same time they exist independently in different times. And when all three independent systems come together, a certain principle of trinity is realized, and in this case we have a system of interrelations of the resurrected one and the external and the internal world. This is one of the viewpoints of this principle, the principle of autonomy of information functioning in different times.

Another aspect, another angle of this principle means that during the resurrection each information element can exist independently. Here is what it means. For example, a certain person exists in the past till the moment of his departure. The departure phase represents an autonomous area, that is, an area independent of other areas. For this reason the departure phase may be easily eliminated. We have already seen the application of this principle, through the example of V.'s resurrection in Chapter I, though a somewhat different wording was used to describe this event and this principle, there we talked about the breaking up of the event. But the meaning, of course, is the same.

Thus, the principle of autonomy of information functioning within different times is based on the fact that each information element, in accordance with the organization of the World functions independently, alternately stated, functions by its own laws for each time. That is, an element of time is an element of the information structure. In this case, time, therefore, is viewed as a structural information form.

As a matter of fact, by utilizing a more in-depth approach, it is possible to show that the resurrected is basically as alive in the past as he is in the future. And it is possible to show what specifically must be done for the practical realization of this proposition.

The eternity of life results from the combining of the entire time in the present moment. And vice versa, all the past and the future, and, therefore, eternal life, may be obtained from the present moment.

So, from the perspective of applying this principle to the resurrection, the resurrection can be achieved by just taking out the point of departure. This is first. And second, by imparting autonomous characteristics to the impulse of consciousness, that is, by imparting finished forms for the past, the present and the future to the impulse of consciousness. As I have already said, for the past - it is taking into account the specific circumstances that took place for a particular person; for the present - it is the methodology, which is applied in the resurrection, it is what the one performing the resurrection does and the way the one being resurrected responds to it, and, finally, for the future — it is the formation of the future in the proper direction, depending on the specific situation.

TRUE RELIGION IS AIMED AT PROMOTING THE CREATIVE DEVELOPMENT OF SOUL, BODY, AND SOCIETY (3.10).

So, now that we have earlier discussed the problems of science, we now proceed to the issue of religion.

At the very beginning of this section I have already said that for a person who has an ordinary state of consciousness comprehending the World is rather difficult. The reason for the difficulties is that for ordinary wakeful consciousness this task is multidimensional and thus such consciousness is not able in principle to embrace it in its entirety. And if so, isolated aspects of the matter have to be taken out, as in the example with the main MSU (Moscow State University) building or with yoga. And these isolated aspects, these isolated approaches, these isolated paths do represent, for example, the path of religion, the path of science, the path of art.

It is clear that this division into isolated paths is artificial, this is a compulsory measure, and it has to be this way, since a higher state of consciousness has not been reached yet by all people simultaneously. In a higher state of consciousness this division just does not exist, there is only a single whole there, and, hence, it is clear, that the higher state of consciousness a person attains, the fewer the differences between science and religion.

At the present time attempts are being made to build up a greater understanding between science and religion, for example, conferences are held attended by the church and scientists representatives, the conferences proceedings are published; but the basis for the disagreements actually lies in the state of consciousness. One has only to start working on raising the levels of the state of consciousness this problem, the problem of mutual misunderstanding will begin to dissolve by itself, for, if I may say so, science will tend to become more religious and religion - more scientific. On the very top there are no differences at all.

However, now when I am talking about religion and science, I will be considering only the nearest higher levels of the state of consciousness, and thus certain difference between these two approaches will still remain, but it won't be so big any more.

The word "religion" has ancient roots; it derives from the word, which for consciousness correlates with the word "reality". Thus, religion is a science about reality. As you can see, the word 'religion' is already accompanied by the word 'science' And we may notice, how they have drawn closer together. Indeed, very briefly the essence of science may be characterized as control of reality. Of course, I am talking about the true religion and the true science which I propose.

So, religion is a science about reality. And that is why first of all I would like to address those reality distortions, those misconceptions about reality which pertain to religion.

My religion does not accept a passive attitude towards life with an erroneous idea that in the course of earthly life one should only be preparing for some true life. This is absolutely a misconception, it has already done a lot of harm and continues to deprive life of its best attributes and take away from life its true significance.

Such ideas have nothing to do with what Christ spoke of, with what He taught. Christ spoke in parables, and not everybody proved able to understand the true meaning of his words. He called to reject not this life, not the life here, but the life in the state of ordinary consciousness, for life in such a state of consciousness cannot yet be called life in its true divine meaning. Christ urged to awake from that state, which he compared to sleep, and enter into the Kingdom of God, the Kingdom of Heaven, into Eternity. It is quite obvious that by his resurrection Jesus Christ called to eternal life in a physical body.

By the Kingdom of God Christ meant higher states of consciousness ("The Kingdom of God is within us"). By calling to give up everything for the sake of attaining the Kingdom of God, Christ thereby was calling for attaining higher states of consciousness by man. He was calling, therefore, for man's evolution, for the realization of his divine nature, which would make it possible for man to finally begin to really live, to live in this world in this physical body, to live here and now. And in conformity with the true purpose of life a call to live here and now means a conscious control of events of any time.

Enormous harm of the orientation towards the preparation for a better life is also that a person erroneously thinking that real life will begin someday in the future and the present life is only a preparation for it, enormous harm of this false mental set is that a person, having such an outlook on life in this world does not appreciate the present moment, does not appreciate the moment in which he finds himself now, does not appreciate the very moment the only real life he has. To live here and now! - is great wisdom. Only by actually living through each moment mindfully one may feel the taste of life, only then one may feel the verity of life, only then man is able to open up to real life, true life.

One of the most important features of my religion is its practical orientation, its orientation towards obtaining a specific result, namely, towards ensuring a creative evolution of the soul, the body and the society. And thus a supporter of my religion is at the same time an empiric too, who makes his life and helps others make their lives based on a creative principle, the principle that reflects the real laws of the World. And thus, with his work he most fully reflects and most fully embodies the purpose of the Creator.

And the cooperation of individual people and groups is important for a constant technology exchange on creative development.

Usually in every society there are people, who by their combined effort are capable of directing the development of the society, they can shape the society's creative development as well as improve the technologies needed for that. The union of such people may be called a leadership group, or a group of leaders, or the center.

Close interaction of separate individuals with the leadership group is a significant aspect of my religion. If, for example, a useful technology appears, it must be passed on to the center right away so that it belongs to everybody, thus contributing and promoting a more successful development of the entire society as well as the collective progress.

So, the true religion emphasizes the common, the common for all, the common for individual people, for the leadership group and the society on the whole. Any action in the World is simultaneously reflected in each individual as well as in what is common for all. Besides, the action simultaneously reflects the technology of creation as well.

I have already said that my religion is practice oriented. Religion, as science about reality, must adequately reflect the existing World. And it must address vitally important problems and above all, of course, urgent problems. The most serious problem is the existing threat of global annihilation.

Therefore, in the present situation the primary objective of religion is to develop technologies, intended to prevent the global disaster.

It is such behavior that will be the reflection of reality, for all God created creatures, that were created for life, for development, and  more so people, created in God's image and likeness - they all have the right to life and free development. And hence, at the threat of global annihilation, the first impulse of every creature, naturally, must be towards the Creator, and the impulse must be always towards an actual implementation of God's given right to life, which in fact means the need for every possible action towards the universal salvation.

My religion, therefore, gives both, practice, action, and a direct belief, and the concept of belief includes the oration to the Creator through specific technological principles, through specific external actions towards the support and the development of life. And at the same time simultaneously an action directed inward is present, directed into the depths where the entire accumulated experience is stored and where a direct guidance from the Lord can be received on how to act properly in every particular situation.

As can be seen from the above in true religion unification of an inward action and an outward action takes place, and due to this an infinite creative development is assured. For, as we know, the outside world is built based on consciousness, and consciousness represents a structure, which unifies spiritual and physical, and that is why, when an action comes from within, from the very center, from the source within the very soul, then such an act, basically, becomes now a Divine act.

The same may be expressed in different words. Namely, an outward action must take place with a person's concurrent awareness of himself, awareness of his action, of the entire situation.

I now have been speaking about one and the same, but from somewhat different angles. As far back as in the Introduction it was noted that man's progress, his evolution are first and foremost associated with the evolution of his consciousness. True religion asks for raising the level of the state of man's consciousness, but it does assist him in this process. True religion says that the practice of self-awareness and of being aware of one's actions is quite effective for the development of consciousness.

I would like to explain what I mean when I speak of self-awareness and of being aware of one's actions.

Imagine that someone was at home writing something, when suddenly someone called and asked him to come to a certain place immediately due to an incident. When coming back home and wishing to resume his work, which was interrupted, he finds out that his pen is missing: it's neither by the armchair, where he had been sitting before the phone rang, nor on the table by the phone, and now he does not know where it is, he just can't remember where he in his haste put it. This exactly means that he put the pen somewhere mindlessly; he was not aware of himself or his actions at that moment.

We are all familiar with such a situation, this is a frequent occurrence. And the analysis of such cases indicates that by becoming more and more aware of ourselves and our actions we may be raising the level of our consciousness more and more, and moving towards higher and higher states of consciousness, as we know, is precisely the way to God.

The world is in reality organized as a structure of manifested consciousness, the consciousness of the supreme being, that is, of God.

God has created the World in His own likeness. And since God himself is eternal, He created the World so that each World element is eternal. This way God implements His idea, that His own life in Eternity acquires Eternity in beings of His creation. And therefore, a supporter of my religion must seek eternal life in the physical body, for then he will reflect in himself the essence of God as well.

However, you shouldn't think that man must only work on himself. People's evolution must be passed on to all other creatures as well, for example, to aforementioned lions so that they too could simultaneously, synchronously develop into Eternity. So, the objective of every believer, of every supporter of my religion is to ensure the infinite development for any creative element. And when I say 'to any element', I do not mean only animals, birds, insects, sea inhabitants, but also trees, flowers, grass, all plant life and all the objects of the World in general, that is, I am speaking of ensuring infinite development and immortality truly to all elements of the World. It will be recalled that they all contribute to the entire collective consciousness.

Since the Creator has underlain eternal life and the eternal development as the very foundation of the World, it becomes obvious that all that promotes destruction is not God's true purpose. That is, the evolution should take a radically different path., there should be no place in the society for things like nuclear weapons. And thus life must be transformed on the spiritual basis, and true religion, being the science about reality, just shows people the way.

For any person his first priority is raising his level of the state of consciousness. The desire to be aware of oneself and one's actions contributes to it to a great extent and it is advisable to have some time set aside for this practice every day. As important are the exercises for everyday of the month given in Appendix G.

The core of my religion is the proper understanding of all that exists in accordance with the plan of the Creator himself. Such proper understanding allows any, even a seemingly dangerous; process to be transformed into a worth-while and creative one.

In connection with what I have said in my religion an important place is given to technology, the technology of one's own immortality, the technology of knowledge transfer to others, the technology of transforming any processes into creative ones and, finally, the technology of entirely different type of thinking, of thinking towards supporting and maintaining eternal life of all elements of the World and their eternal evolution.

And importantly my religion is technologically substantiated in practice by the existing level of development; it is largely substantiated even by that. In Chapter IV I will tell you, for example, about technical devices, developed to implement my technologies for the resurrection of people or for the regeneration of their lost organs. So my religion indeed has been already validated to a large extent even technologically.

RESURRECTION IS THE MOST REAL, THE MOST PRAGMATIC, THE MOST RATIONAL AND THE MOST CONVINCING BASIS FOR THE CONSEQUENT DEVELOPMENT, FOR DEVELOPMENT OF THE THINKING OF THE GENERATIONS TO COME (3.11).

It is perfectly obvious that the resurrection is the most real, the most pragmatic, the most expedient and the most probative base for further development. So, I will say just a few words on the role of the resurrection for the development of thinking of posterity. However, prior to that I will explain the meaning of certain terms. I am talking about what intellect, mind, knowledge, a thought and a feeling are.

Intellect.

Intellect is a structure, which consolidates the reactions of consciousness, of the body, of the spirit and of the soul. This is the system of their intertwining at the perception level, informational or actual intertwining.

The word 'intertwining', used here, gives an idea, how the reactions mentioned would be seen as a whole when taking an outside perspective. And it should be noted that consciousness, the body, the spirit and the soul exist in perception at the level of their effect, the effect on perception as well as on the perceiver.

In which case is the intellect harmonious? The intellect is harmonious when the soul, the spirit, the body and consciousness, and, besides, we need to add here the phenomena of reality too, so, when all these elements, when all these objects are in harmony with one another, then the intellect is harmonious. In this case, in the case of harmony, one may speak of the true intellect. It may be also called the intellect of development, the intellect of a person. To define intellect more laconically we may say that intellect is the structure of a person, who is aware of the relations within the phenomenon under consideration and at the same time aware of the connection of this phenomenon with all other World phenomena by having control of them.

Mind.

The mind is a way to react to information, to the external influence. Since any object may react to information, to the external influence, the concept of the mind may be applied to any object. But we will be speaking of the human mind. And the examination of the characteristics of the mind as it develops is of particular interest to me.

During the resurrection, in the process of the resurrection, the mind's organization starts from the cellular level. The mind formation occurs, of course, on the basis of the soul. The information on the creation of each cell element, even of each microelement, of each atom, of each nucleus and of the elements of still deeper levels is embedded in the mind.

The mind may serve as a certain characteristic of an object. For example, if you try to prick a cell with a needle and it tries to resist it, this cell may be called clever compared with the cells, which offer less or no resistance at all.

The mind may be regarded as a notion unifying the soul, the spirit, consciousness and the body. Identification and unification of entities according to the mode of their reaction and response takes place in the mind.

It should be noted that the problem of the resurrection is as well to a significant degree a problem of the mind. If the mind of a person is evolved enough, the resurrection does not appear to him as something extraordinary, he regards this phenomenon as natural. The same goes for immortality. If a person recognizes immortality as a normal state, it means that this person's mind is highly evolved; in this case we may even say that his mind is the reflection of Eternity and of the Creator.

Above I virtually defined the mind as a structure that unifies different elements according to the technology of their reaction, their response. Now I will add to this the following: the mind is also an organizing structure for reaching goals, for achieving anything at all. That is, the mind can be viewed as a mechanism for accomplishing, a system for achieving, for example, the resurrection or immortality, or something else.

Knowledge.

Knowledge is both moving from consciousness into the soul and then back from the soul into consciousness and the result of this moving. In simple terms it can be explained as follows. There is a certain element in consciousness, which from time to time calls on the soul reservoir, draws information there and comes back, let's say, more enlightened. As a result consciousness accumulates knowledge, that is, basically, the consciousness structure becomes transformed due to its contact with the soul. So, knowledge is what we have as a result of such a contact. That is, in actual fact, knowledge is a contact of consciousness with the soul. Knowledge may be acquired, for example, through reading, however, it should be kept in mind, that according to the law of universal connections, whatever has been read in fact primordially exists in the soul. The same is true as for any other ways of acquiring knowledge as well. I will note that clairvoyance is based on the direct perception of knowledge held in the soul. The soul controls knowledge. The control status belongs to the soul.

After acquiring knowledge the problem of its implementation arises. The mind is responsible for knowledge implementation.

The above said may be illustrated as follows. Let's think of a big reservoir. We may identify this reservoir with the mind. The reservoir, that is, the mind, holds knowledge. The mind regulates the outflow of knowledge from the reservoir.

We also need to mention a specific role of knowledge for the resurrected. During the resurrection the one being resurrected goes through knowledge formation, and knowledge forms in the process of registering everything that takes place, knowledge comes as a result of a sort of processing of the events taking place. As a result during the initial period it is knowledge, that is, what the World represents in perception that becomes the criterion of the World evolution for the resurrected one. This is one of the differences between the resurrected one and the living.

The living one is connected with the entire reality right from the moment of his birth. But the resurrected one was for some time in a different state; he lived without a formed physical body. That is why when his body is assembled and as a result of registering the undergoing processes his knowledge of the World is formed, this knowledge is an intermediate connection element between his formation and the external reality, and therefore, during the initial stage it is knowledge that for him is the criterion of the entire developing World.

Hence we can see that in the process of the resurrection knowledge also serves as a certain mechanism. This circumstance is utilized in the technological devices I have developed for the resurrection of people and the regeneration of lost organs and tissues. Here is the idea. From the direction of the device comes the needed information, perceived from the other side by the one being resurrected as real. Interconnectivity of these two sides is provided by the intermediate mechanism, the mechanism of knowledge, this is its precise purpose of use in this case.

With the use of clairvoyance the speed of the resurrection increases manifold and the resurrection may even be instantaneous.

The purpose of creating technical devices for the resurrection of people is to create the collective consciousness, which will allow every person to perform the resurrection based on his own spiritual core.

Of course, there is still a number of specific technical factors, for example, the fact that the information preferably be communicated to the one being resurrected by portions, discretely, especially during the first hours so that he could be restoring, regenerating as if walking up the steps. It is important to give the information by certain portions, because that particular knowledge is the reality criterion for the resurrected one, and through that particular criterion he interacts with the reality.

The transition to the reality criteria, used by the living, usually takes about a month to occur, in rare cases a month and a half – two months. When this transition period is over for the resurrected one, then not the knowledge, but the reality itself becomes for him the criterion of the World.

Thought.

The thought is the information, which is a connecting link between consciousness, the spirit and the body. At that the thought is organized by the soul.

The correlations among the concepts involved may be better seen through the example of the following analogy. Let's picture to ourselves a waterfall. Water cascades down under gravity. Gravity may be compared with the spirit, water - with consciousness. A riverbed, along which water runs, corresponds to the body; a riverbed carries water. And the soul corresponds to what has created all this: the Earth, gravity and water.

Basically the soul participates in the creation both directly and through the thought. We may say that the thought is unified with the entire World structure and means a specific action of a person in this general structure.

Feeling.

A feeling is the soul's manifestation in the dynamic of the spirit and in the part, where the spirit is connected with consciousness and the body. When the soul organizes the body, the feeling is that structure, on which the body is built. The feeling presents, therefore, the base, the ground, upon which the body is built. And that is why it is thought that a feeling comes out from the body.

When interacting with reality, the feeling perceives information faster than the thought does.

Now I have already proceeded to the discussion of <u>what the distinction between a thought and a feeling is</u>. The feeling reacts faster. That is why a person often may say or do something first and only then realize that he shouldn't have done it.

Another distinction is as follows. When a person thinks then the feeling is in the control phase. And when a person feels then the thought is in the control phase. I am talking now about control of reality. We see that a thought and a feeling can switch places, switch their areas, their roles. When this happens, when, for example, the thought is in the control phase, the feeling can unfold, develop.

The thought and the feeling may share the same space, but herein they for the most part can't be in the control phase simultaneously. The exceptions to this rule are certain special cases, such as these: when a foetus is being conceived and is developing, or when a certain cell is healing, or, in general, in the process of recuperating from a certain illness, or during the process of the resurrection. In these particular instances the thought and the feeling can be unified and thus they can be in one and the same phase simultaneously.

There is one more important distinction between the thought and the feeling. Imagine that a person encounters a certain phenomenon. Naturally, he has both certain thoughts and feelings pertaining to this phenomenon. However they are formed in different ways.

The thought is formed by consciousness based on all information about the external and internal world related to this phenomenon. The feeling towards this phenomenon is also formed by consciousness but differently. In this process consciousness is aware of the body, goes through the body, utilizes the information of the body, and being in full interaction with the body consciousness forms the feeling.

There are even more subtle distinctions, but I will not go into further details in this book.

Now with respect to <u>what the thought and the feeling have in common</u>.

The common ground between them is that both thoughts and feelings determine sequence of actions in the structure of consciousness. We may speak about the existence of order in the processes of consciousness, where there are their own laws of development, so, thoughts and feelings are the ones that control and determine order.

To illustrate this we may take a look, let's say, at the way an architect works. If without going into details, well, as, for example, when in the process of working on a painting an artist doesn't paint with a painstaking detail, but paints with large brush strokes only what is basic, then we may say that an architect's thoughts determine a building layout, and his feelings may assess this layout in relation to harmony as well as may be manifested in the architect's desire to have either lunch or a cup of tea on completing his work.

So, thoughts and feelings may perform the same function, namely, determining sequence of actions in the structure of consciousness.

I may, perhaps, give another interesting example of the area, where the thought and the feeling have a common ground. It is the way an external object, for example, a rock or a plant, reacts to man.

Here I have to elucidate that not only plants but rocks also have certain elements of reaction, of response, corresponding to human thoughts and feelings. Of course, they are totally different, but nevertheless, a rock lives its own life too, and again, you shouldn't forget that all entities make their contribution to the general collective consciousness. Each entity's contribution is different, of course, but it exists, and that's what matters.

What could from man's perspective be called the rock's thought and the rock's feeling? The rock's response to the outside environment may be called the rock's thought. The feeling is also a reaction, a response to the outside environment, but of another type, well, for, example, it can be a deformation. Something fell on a rock, some object, or, let's say, the water began dripping on it causing deformations to occur, even if only very small, the size is not important, the fact is that they exist, and they can be considered as a sensory evidence of a rock, as its feeling, which resulted from the interaction.

So, it comes out to be that if a person looks at a rock, the rock's arising reaction points along a straight line, connecting the rock with the person, and towards the person; and this reaction is often both the rock's thought and the rock's feeling at the same time, that is, both the rock's feeling and its thought here are unified.

When a person looks at a plant, the plant's thought and feeling also become unified, but only unlike the rock's the plant's response is perpendicular to the line connecting it with the person. If you have an indoor plant, comprehension of its thoughts and feelings will allow you to come into contact with it and you will never have a problem with its watering: the plant will tell you whether to water it or it's not yet time for it.

The discourse on the rock's reaction in the form of thoughts and feelings, at first glance may seem abstract to someone. However in actuality that is not true at all. If we consider a case, when the rock's thoughts and feelings are unified and if we understand why it happens, then we can understand altogether how the thought is organized in terms of diffusion of knowledge from one object to another. What is more, since the generalization of the characteristics when transmitting them to other structures gives the law of connection, then based on this we can comprehend the entire reality altogether and transmit the technologies of eternal development to any entities of the World.

Imagine that you transmit your thoughts and feelings, for example, to a stone or to a plant. Now, the stone and the plant, based on one of the attributes, are in the same world as man. And, in that event, it is possible to learn everything about them, to be precise, all their functions.

Here we can draw an analogy with my mathematics, I have already told about it in the beginning of this section. Through the use of my mathematics I can acquire information on an unknown entity as well, I can determine all its functions. This is new mathematics. Its operators reflect the World organization. And hence it is not necessary to know all the entity attributes, including destructive ones. Putting this circumstance to use is particularly important in preventing disasters by structuring one's consciousness in the area of controlling clairvoyance. The objective of clairvoyance in this area is not to externalize negative information, but to form positive events to maximum effect.

It is worth-while to employ controlling clairvoyance also when the data on the start of a disaster have been already fixed. I have already prevented several global disasters by this means.

I would like to add the following. When there is generality between structures, then one structure can always be translated into the other. And, hence, with proper, though possibly longtime, practice one may learn to translate a thought into a feeling and a feeling into a thought. Or, else, one may learn to translate one reality into another.

Basically, everyone knows from his own experience that a thought attracts a certain feeling and vice versa, a feeing may attract a thought. A person who has an ordinary state of consciousness often confuses a thought with a feeling, he may take one for the other. For example, one may *think*, and quite sincerely, that he loves somebody, and still in actuality he may just not know yet, not yet have experienced and not even suspect, what true love is. Such confusion of thoughts with feelings in life continually leads to misunderstandings and sometimes even to serious complications.

You can see that the discourse on thoughts and feelings opens new layers to speculate upon. For that matter we may remember the motto 'Know thyself'. One of its aspects is just the issue of feelings and thoughts. If one understands the problem, then one may start working on creating one's own cognition construct.

Now we may go back to the discussion of the principle under consideration. I have been talking about the importance of the resurrection for further development and particularly, for the development of thinking of future generations.

The resurrection, as we already know, is always beneficial. The resurrection on a broad scale will bring about a change in the collective consciousness. For example, children's intellect, mind, knowledge will be of a different kind. Their thoughts and feelings as well as their body altogether will be noted for greater harmony. They will be able to acquire information with much greater ease (remember what I said in the Introduction on different ways of acquiring information). As a result a child will be able, for example, to create prose, poetry, to compose music or to know advanced mathematics from beginning to end. And in so doing it won't require of him any Herculean efforts or overwork. It's just that his intellect, mind and all the rest will be new. He himself will be different. And I will also add that the resurrection on a broad scale will bring about a global change in knowledge altogether. And not only knowledge.

Future generations will have to receive information and material objects from their own thinking, from their own spirit. Thus the problem of the scantiness of our planet's resources will no longer exist. I, for example, in order to spread the technologies carry out materialization of objects, thus demonstrating the real possibility of doing that.

Thus, the resurrection brings about the establishment of greater harmony between man and the Universe.

THE LIVING ONE, WHO HAS NOT EXPERIENCED DEATH, CAN ALWAYS REGENERATE, RESTORE THE GONE ONE WITHIN A SHORTER, MORE OPTIMAL TIME AND AS A MORE DESIRED OPTION THAN THE RESURRECTED ONE CAN (3.12).

First of all about the fact that the one who has not experienced death can always regenerate, restore the gone one within a shorter, more optimal time. When discussing principles (2.7) and (2.8) we already saw that on the informational plane the one who has not experienced death has significant advantages as compared to the resurrected one.

If we refer to the fundamentals of the World structure, to the level, from which everything originates, we may speak of the matrix organization of the World. On the informational level each person has his own informational matrix. And since the true life status is nonexistence of death, that is, eternal life and continual development, then in accordance with the true status of life the one who has not experienced death has a totally transparent matrix, fully which has access to all forms of consciousness and matter. That is why the one who has not experienced death has a higher speed of information processing and, therefore, is able to regenerate, restore the gone one within a shorter, a more optimal time.

Now as to the second part of the principle, about the fact, that the one who has not experienced death can restore, regenerate the gone one in a more desired variant. First of all, what does it mean: to restore, regenerate the gone one in a more desired variant? There seems to be just one variant, isn't it?

Of course, there is just one variant for the resurrected one, because the resurrected one is the very same person who he/she was before. It is clear. When I say 'in a more desired variant', I mean in a more desired variant in terms of the creative organizational plan, that is, the one who has not experienced death restores, regenerates the gone one in such a way that the priority of life comes first and, therefore, this is the most desired variant for all.

I may, perhaps, remind that with time the resurrected one can remediate his deficiencies related to his previous biological death, he can compensate for them with his further proper development and in accordance with his status, become in no way different from the ones who has not experienced death.

THE PRACTICE OF RESURRECTION, THE PRACTICE OF RESTORATION, REGENERATION IS NOT CONTRARY TO ANY RELIGION, TO ANY LAW, NOR TO ANY CREATIVE TREND (3.13).

This proposition is perfectly obvious, since, as I have repeatedly said, the resurrection is always an event beneficial for all, and presently is altogether a fundamental principle of the universal salvation.

THE RESURRECTION OF PEOPLE MAKES IT POSSIBLE TO RESURRECT AND RESTORE ANY OBJECTS (3.14).

Let's go back to the beginning of Principle (1.1):

The true status of the World is in eternal life. Eternal life ensures a true World stability. The desire for a stable World creates eternal life.

Since the World is truly eternal, any object exists for ever. This fact is utilized in a technical apparatus, which I have developed to regenerate lost organs. The idea of the approach is as follows.

Time may also be considered as a system of parallel screens. Then, naturally, the object exists behind one of the screens. Hence, in terms of technology to restore, to regenerate an object means just to go behind the right screen and that's all.

A real apparatus has up to, let's say, a hundred parallel screens. They can be very thin. A light pulse carrying the information of the organ of concern is passed through these screens. The pulse, as it passes through one of the screens, specifically the screen sought after, passes through the structures, where the organ of concern still existed, where it was intact. As a result the pulse simply transfers the information of this healthy organ to the right place in the person's body. And the organ regenerates.

If we look at the World in this connection, nothing vanishes in it, and therefore, it is always possible to take something from one place and move it into another, that is, to perform a simple rearrangement.

That is why it is for a reason that instead of space-time I take displacement as a basis. If as a basis we take space-time, then we have to calculate coordinates, which is needless, unnecessary work, whilst if we draw on displacement, we then do not need to calculate anything, we don't need to figure out, where the object in question appears, since the displacement immediately shows its location.

Thus, one can always enter the time wanted, take the object sought after and transfer it here, into our time. I researched into these matters, when I was about twelve. Aside from that I've discovered, that when I in my physical body go into the past, I exist there too. Of course, it is possible to enter any time and any space point through the spiritual structure, but now I am talking about entering specifically in the physical body. There are mechanisms to travel in the physical body anywhere, so, you may at will instantaneously find yourself in any point of the Universe.

I would like to pinpoint an important circumstance. Principle (2.2) speaks about the interdependence of the spiritual and the physical structures. That is why the popular quotation 'A sound spirit in a sound body' may be read vice versa: 'A sound body in a sound spirit'. We can see that the second utterance is somewhat like a reflection of the first one. In actuality we have here an example of reading the text by reflection. The ancient Greeks, for example, read many texts through reflection, however to modern people this technique is unknown.

The utterance 'A sound body in a sound spirit' means that a body is in the spirit, and, therefore, in the soul, that is, a body is a part of the soul.

Above I presented an idea, based on which the apparatus for organ regeneration operates. But technical devices are just a temporary helper, worth-while before an adequate level of the spiritual development has been achieved. But when this level has been achieved no auxiliaries are needed any more, the strength of spirit is now enough for to resurrect. And then it becomes apparent that the resurrection means that the soul, the spirit, consciousness – generally all, that pertains to a person, reflects the existing World to the fullest extent, in the most harmonious way; and a total reflection is, in fact, the creation of the World. The resurrection embodies this verity. And therefore, the resurrection of people really makes it possible to resurrect and to regenerate, to restore any objects. Always entities which existed in the past, even if they turned out to be destroyed in the present, can be fully restored, regenerated, always. In fact true understanding of these principles allows to restore, to regenerate any entity. And this regeneration, restoration can be instantaneous.

To illustrate this here is an example from my practice. For example, once on the plane an instrument board failed, and the plane started to fall down as a result. I brought the card back to normal in real time in the falling plane, and the situation straightened out, the plane continued its normal flight. This fact was evidenced by the data, obtained as a result of the flight data recorder tape interpretation.

## 4

We shall now proceed to the final section of the core principles of resurrection.

## RESURRECTION IS CONTROL OF THE ENTIRE EXTERNAL SPACE (4.1).

During the resurrection we deal with the following interesting fact: the entire external space (which includes the entire outside environment and the entire outer space) plays sort of the role of pressure. This situation may be compared with the one, in which each one of us indwells on the surface of the Earth. I am talking of the air pressure. Air represents a fairly rare medium, its density is scant compared to the density of solid substances. However the depth of the atmospheric layer is huge and due to this it presses down on each square centimeter of the Earth surface with the force of one kilogram. So that every square centimeter of our body experiences a force action equal to one kilogram.

So, during the resurrection the operation of the following physical and at the same time biological principle may be observed: each element being restored experiences pressure of information, of informational systems, of biological systems, of physical systems. That pressure occurring during the resurrection, acts on each and every cell, on every molecule, on every element being restored, regenerated.

It should be noted here that, when the restoration, the regeneration of a certain element is taking place, in order for it to be materialized, space has to be actually moved apart, as well as time, but predominantly space, external space, since the resurrection is brought about by an impulse, coming from within, it is an inner impulse, it is an impulse of the soul.

It follows that the proper way to send a spiritual impulse, created, as they say, at the inner level, that is, at soul level, is in fact the mechanism of the resurrection. We can see therefore, that given proper soul pulsations, so to speak, the body is eternal. Or, in other words, when control of the entire external space is proper, man becomes immortal.

If we consider the re-creation of the elements of an object being restored, regenerated sequentially, there is a point to be made. For example, a cell was re-created as a result of an impulse of consciousness. Now the entire external space has to be controlled so, that this cell would not disappear, that it would survive and that one more cell would be created. Now we have two cells and the external space. We continue adding cells. And now we have an organ and the external space, then a number of organs and, finally, the whole person and the entire external space. Certain properties of the event must be added here as well, for instance, where precisely the resurrection is to occur.

It took us some time to sequentially analyze the resurrection process element-by-element, however in reality this process can happen very fast, and in fact even instantaneously.

Another way of formulating the essence of the principle is this. External space may be perceived as a precision system, in which case, provided there is a specific response to this system during the process of the resurrection the resurrected one or a restored, regenerated object appears. And this is in fact one of the resurrection technologies, when space is utilized to restore, to regenerate an object.

It is also worth noting that during the resurrection two approaches may be utilized: within and without. In the first approach the one performing the resurrection looks at the external space from within, through the one being resurrected and as if presses the right space point. In the second approach the one, performing the resurrection, vice versa, looks from without, from the external space. The final result, of course, is the same.

So, during the resurrection process t, all World connections are involved, they all start changing, and thereunder the entire external space must be controlled in such a way that the resurrection act should take place.

MAN IS THE ENTIRE EXTERNAL AND INTERNAL WORLD SIMULTANEOUSLY (4.2).

Man holds an entirely special place in the World. I have already said that. And it is because man has been created in God's own image and likeness.

Previously I have told about the eagle, about its amazing abilities, about its command of teleportation, about its ability to create antigravity and so on. So, when we consider the internal and external worlds of the eagle, it turns out that its internal world is represented to a lesser degree than the external world. In other words, eagle's information of the internal and external worlds is different, whilst for man it is one and the same. And we may even say that, if a certain object's information of the

The Resurrection of People and Eternal Life From Now On Is Our Reality! 141

internal and external worlds is one and the same simultaneously, it means, this object is man. And we may add: as the analysis of the World evolution shows, all information objects are evolving towards man. In general the entire World tends to man, to his shape, to his mode of response, reaction and evolution.

The manifestation of this can be seen everywhere. Let's turn, for example, to the work of astronomers. Scientists armed with telescopes study stars, constellations, globular clusters, galaxies, in short, everything that is laid out before their eyes. Let's take a look at the scientists' actions from the outside. We can make the following comparison.

Imagine that all of a sudden you find yourself inside a human body, say, within the interior of the lungs, and having looked about, started entering in the log everything you were observing from your position. You too, could register different objects and all sorts of clusters and assemblies, for example, of same cells. That is what you would see from the interior. So, the scientists do not realize that through optical telescopes they observe a huge organism from within. If they could look at this organism from without, from outside, they would see the informational representation of man.

And then as a revelation comes a new understanding of the saying mentioned before: 'Man has been made in the image and likeness of God.' This saying, like any great truth has many facets, it has many aspects.

If the objects of the Universe, observed by the astronomers, are approached from the perspective just given, then it is possible even to forecast how these objects and the Universe itself will be evolving further on. To do this one just needs to know the development of man here. Knowing the development of man here, we can speak of further evolution of the Universe. We can say, for example, what the dynamics of Eternity will be. I can say that static images will pass into dynamic. There won't be a notion of space there anymore. Space over there will be pulled into the soul structure, into the structure of the spiritual impulse. And, therefore it turns out, that there the soul, the spirit are in the truest sense the base, and it, the spirit, forms everything.

By analogy with man, by applying the similarity principle, we can say, that the mutual shaping of perception and the World is taking place now at the level of atoms, molecules, cells. From now forward the concentration of matter will be increasing, organs will become apparent, though their formation is already under way, the brain will become apparent, and the interaction between the separate parts of this giant organism will take shape.

And when I say that the salvation of the World in one place is at the same time the salvation of everything, then this too, will be easily understood on the basis of the similarity principle. If a person has a certain serious disease, for example, a heart ailment or a kidney disease, his life may be threatened as a result of that. But if the functioning of these specific organs is improved, if they become restored, become healthy again, then the person too, in whole will become healthy. The same applies to the World. And another thing to be kept in mind is that all has been created based on the principles of interaction, intersection, and mutual conditionality.

So, now make up of the Universe is mainly at the level of atoms, molecules, cells, however the processes of both their concentration and therefore, make up of organs-like formations as well can already be observed, for example, the heart, and further on there will be the transition to the pulsation levels such as beatings of the heart. Thus, what scientists call the expansion of the Universe, is actually only a taken out phase in one of the beatings of the emerging 'heart' as well as 'lungs' expansion associated with it.

Knowing all this, it is possible to create such telescope systems, which will allow to see space from the other side, and thus it will be possible to observe stars, globular clusters, galaxies from either direction, both from within and without. And what is more, knowing, how the Universe evolves, it is possible to make such optical systems, which will be able to see a future structure of an object, that is, what this object will look like in the future. We may recall that in ancient times crystals were used for such purposes: the images appearing inside them would give the information sought-for. Though, of course, the easiest way to obtain such information is through clairvoyance.

In connection with the above said I would like to mention space travels too. Everything, as I have already said, rests upon the image of man, on his shape, on functioning and interaction of his organs. If we know how blood travels throughout the human body, how human heart functions, how the entire human body works altogether, then we can build ships, which will travel by utilizing the natural level of space motion. Perhaps, I'll say a little bit more about this.

I will say it again: we are now at the level of development, characterized by the fact that we predominantly perceive the molecular structure of the Universe. That is precisely how the observational results of the astronomers can be interpreted. However, if we adopt such a viewpoint, then we immediately can say how a spaceflight must be organized.

If we take a particle of blood, a tiny one, which is now, let's say, in the region of the leg, then after a while due to the blood circulation through the vessels, through the body channels, this particle will find itself in the region of the heart. Mind you, without any efforts on our part. Its travel is attributable just to the fact of being inside within a living body. Our Universe is also a living organism, just very large. The analogy that we've already used, allows the possibility to understand that no engines for a space-ship are in fact necessary. The only thing to do to make a space travel possible is to spot the ship within the proper channel and that's all. And then in a while the ship on its own will find itself in the location that we need. More than that, if we go deeper into these issues, it will become clear that our ship is able to even instantaneously find itself, for example, in another Galaxy altogether. Virtually, having attained a certain level of spiritual development, any person without any ships is able to find himself at will in any point of the Universe.

Here is another important example of my science application, relevant to this subject.

Presently I have developed a spacecraft creation technology navigated through an optical system. This system is crystal- based. It suffices to send a mental signal to the crystal for it to begin to set in motion the entire mechanism, and it suffices to specify only the destination coordinates in the initial impulse; the crystal will do the rest. On its own it will single out the proper channel, and on its own will position the ship into the desired point. The principle of similarity, similarity between the Universe and the human body underlies this fundamentally new principle of space flights.

As I have said earlier, based on this similarity one may make forecasts regarding further development of the Universe. However, to be deep, thorough, these forecasts must be based upon the knowledge of laws, the laws of development. Thus, if we would like to understand the course of further evolution of the Universe by applying similarity principle, not only must we have a good understanding of the human body organization, but as well study both man's psychology and modes of his interaction with other people, and gain insight into how in general communication in the human society is carried out. Having found the answers to these questions it will become possible to control much larger areas of the World. So, the approach is quite simple here.

The similarity principle that is being considered now can be applied to the development of new technologies, to creation of fundamentally new technical devices, like those space-ships I have just spoken about. And what is very important, this principle will ensure the harmonicity of development.

I will give a few more examples from my practice of similarity principle application. When transforming one object into another, an object must be transformed according to the principles of the organization of man. When I, for example, transform one substance into another, the human form, the human matrix can serve as a transformation form. When I, let's suppose, started looking at a certain substance and began acquiring information it was giving, then irrespective of what kind of knowledge exists about the substance, be it symbolic or as formulas, irrespective of that, in this substance, in each of its elements, everywhere we can see man.

If we look once again at the aforementioned lion, we will see that it represents the structure of man's thought-forms. If we look at the eagle from that same perspective, it will become clear that it represents the structure of the events man would wish to accomplish. We may continue this sequence into infinity. If we go deeper into all this, we may discover that the entire outside environment, outside in relation to man, is created in the similitudes of his manifestation. That is, to understand, why animals or other entities, or matter in general, have been created the way they have, to understand this we have to look at man and his actions. Everything man is surrounded with is his current actions and the effect of his previous actions. It follows that when man extirpates a certain species he thus virtually affects himself. Genuine ecology is in understanding of this fact.

Based on the knowledge I provide we can say at once what will happen as a result of extirpating a certain animal species by man, what evolutionary species will emerge in the future, that is, what specific form the next animal species will take. We can also say what specific changes will result from the technogenic path of development. Knowing all this, we can balance and create the forms desired.

In the future crossing of species and genera, their synthesis won't constitute a crucial problem any longer, as distinct from what we have today. And if we decide to create a certain mixed species, this will be possible to do. The technology is simple enough here: one has to know the organization of man.

So, a well-known old-time motto 'Know thyself!' as we can see, has many aspects. Comprehension of this principle gives a true understanding of the World organization, and its realization leads to the effective opening of the flower of life.

TIME DILATATION, ITS REMOVAL OR APPROACHING MEANS RESURRECTION FOR SOME ASPECTS OF SPACE (4.3).

It has already been stated in section II of this chapter that time is a construct of consciousness. Time is created with respect to space by people's thoughts. For people who have an ordinary state of consciousness, introducing time, it may be said, is very worth-while, even necessary. Having time is very convenient for them. Take, for instance, a train timetable or a flight schedule. The schedule ensures regulating and safety of traffic. And in general the notion of time is applied to almost all areas of life.

The creation of the concept "time" also means both the creation of information and the creation of space, of such space, in which the concept of time is in existence. This principle is about time dilation, its moving off or drawing near for some aspects of space. This refers to those spaces, in which time exists. And, besides, to the fact, that not only time is connected with space but also has its properties, for example, such as, dilation, moving off or drawing near.

For the resurrected one the space, in which a concept of time is in existence, means life. And time in relation to space, as I've just said, is created by people's thoughts. That is why we can mentally dilate time, move it off, draw it near. And since for people with an ordinary state of consciousness many events are associated with time, as, for example, the notion of departure, they come to understand that by dilating time, by moving it off or drawing near it is really possible to carry out the resurrection. The issue under discussion now can be looked at from a somewhat different angle. In relation to the notions of life and the resurrection, time dilation, its moving off or drawing near mean in fact an introduction of a thought form of the resurrection. And the introduction of the thought form results in structural change of reality.

I will now clarify the term "a thought form".

The thought form.

A thought form - is a structure, perceptible through the man's consciousness, relating to the information content called thought. That is, a thought form is in fact a specific geometric shape, which contains a thought of a person.

If we take the space of thought (one may either visualize it or enter it directly), then, for example, a table represents one information configuration, a chair does another, a person represents still another. That is, a thought form is expressly a shape, which, according to the thought it carries, corresponds to a certain information object.

Summing up, we can put it quite simply: a thought form is a shape of a thought, containing some specific information.

As I have said, a thought form is perceived through man's consciousness. When in life you encounter a certain entity, you can look at it from different perspectives. If it is, for example, a plane, you can have a look, let's say, at the cockpit, or at the airplane's wings, or its tail. The same is with a thought form. Since it is indeed a real object, a real shape, then when perceiving it consciousness can touch it from different angles. And just as in case with a plane when you can see its different elements, so in this case when consciousness touches different aspects of a thought form reception of sort of different thoughts occurs.

Consider a specific example. Let's say, someone went to the store to buy a bottle of mineral water. The corresponding thought form carries the person's idea to buy a bottle of mineral water, but not only that. It also contains a sense of occasion: he knows where he will go, which way, and, the notion that he probably will have to get dressed, if it is wintertime. All this as well as many other things are contained in this single thought form.

Using scientific language we may say that a single thought form carries many conceptual parameters. Scanning rate of a thought form to identify these parameters, that is, processing rate of the information contained in the thought form, may differ depending on the level of a person's development, and the difference can be very substantial. A person with an ordinary state of consciousness, as a rule, in general perceives only a portion of a thought form. But if the level of a person's spiritual development is high enough, all aspects of a thought form are taken in simultaneously, that is, in full and instantaneously.

The consideration of the thought form notion proves to be important also from another practical point of view. I'm referring to control of technical systems. Let's examine this issue.

There is such a fact: thought forms without fail interconnect geometrically with one of the soul's aspects. Such is life. That's the way things are. The thought is hierarchically connected with the soul either directly, which, to tell you the truth, rarely happens, or indirectly, through the structure of gathered experience. That is why the thought form is controlled directly from the soul. And since the soul responds to the reality of fundamental nature, therefore, the thought form exchange process with the external world turns out to be decelerated or for some period there is none at all.

So, the thought form is controlled directly from the soul, and thus an impulse from the external world can't reach it, can't change it and, therefore, control through the thought represents the most immune control system.

At first glance it would seem that technical means must be the most resistant to control technical devices, technical equipment, that they allegedly must be more resistant than the thought. However, in reality it is not so. In actual fact the thought is the most resistant system and thus, the control of technical devices, technical equipment by the thought or the thought form is the most reliable kind of control.

A specific example will help to understand it. Let's say, a plane is flying by an autopilot. The contact of a technical device, in this case the autopilot, with the external environment is permanent, which represents a substantial potential danger. The autopilot may, for example, get hit by a missile or it may get disabled in any other manner. But if we have the thought as a controlling system, it, virtually, may have no contact with the outside environment at all. And though, of course, basically, contacts are present between all elements, but in this case I am referring to the duration of the contact, to the fact that a thought contact can be instantaneous, while an autopilot contact both with a plane and with the external space is permanent. And if the contact of a controlling thought with a plane is instantaneous, then the external environment is unable to alter this thought. And thus the plane can fly the planned route without any problem and it will make it through, no matter what.

I would like to note in particular here that the safety component of any object as well can be put into the thought. The capability to do so is based on the thought immunity to the outside environment.

I have received an invention patent for information transmission and control by thought device.

We now turn back to the question of the use of thought forms for the resurrection. Having formed the desirable thought form, it is now possible to restore, to regenerate the body anywhere, even where, suppose, there is no suitable for life environment, where, let's say, there is no air, but vacuum. However, if the thought form has been formed properly, then in this environment oxygen and everything else needed will appear, instead of vacuum and everything will be all right.

Once I was asked to regenerate, to restore an indoor plant perished a long time before. I created a proper thought form and the plant came alive and grew green again, though due to the lack of water the soil in the pot had long since dried out. A proper thought form transforms the outside environment in the desired way.

How can such phenomena be explained? The following fundamental principle underlies such phenomena:

THE WORLD CONSISTS OF INTERACTING STRUCTURES. THUS CHANGE OF ONE STRUCTURE RESULTS IN CHANGE OF ALL OTHER STRUCTURES. PERCEPTION AND CONSCIOUSNESS ARE ONE OF THE WORLD STRUCTURES. THEREFORE, BY CHANGING PERCEPTION AND CONSCIOUSNES THE WORLD CAN BE CHANGED.

That is why the reality reacts to a thought form, responds to it, and our objective is that the reality's response to a thought form of the resurrection would lead to the resurrection itself. In fact, it is similar to the training of the reality. Yes, the reality is organized in such a way that one can train it, one can teach it. You may, for example, quietly sit down and start practicing. The purpose of this practice is as follows: the reality must be trained so that it yields and produces the resurrection as a result. That is, the reality in this case is viewed as a controllable and trainable environment.

We can look at these procedures still yet from another angle. Though in substance, of course, all along we've been speaking about one and the same, just the wording is different. For someone who has an ordinary state of consciousness, in the space, in which the notion of time is in existence, there is a notion such as "life". We enter the word "resurrection" and begin sort of moving it: moving it away, drawing it near, putting it in different positions relative to life. If we get at once into the region of space-time, where the notion of life is consistent with the element of its eternity, then the resurrection happens instantaneously.

In section 2 of this chapter I talked about how the resurrection of a person occurs when he enters a specific space-time cell. I also spoke there of the fact, that there is a possibility of a person, who had experienced an interruption of events entering such a cell. He enters this cell – and resumes living. Now I will give an example of one of the possibilities of interruption of events.

There are many cases, when a person would suddenly disappear, often in public. He was here a moment ago, was talking to someone, - and suddenly disappeared, vanished into thin air. Sometimes after a while he would reappear, looking absolutely the same: the same clothes, the same age, and for him this disappearance would go unnoticed, to him it lasted only an instant, though a hundred or two hundred years could have passed. This person sort of fell through a certain space-time crack, and now he is here again. If much time has gone since his disappearance, his clothing, the way he talks, the words and expressions he uses immediately suggest a different epoch to people around him.

The essence of this phenomenon is that in such cases a person falls out into the space, where the notion of time is not in existence. When in discussing Principle (2.3) I was spoke of a temporary interruption of events for a certain person, I meant such cases as well.

WHAT MAN THINKS, WHAT HE SAYS AND WHAT HE DOES IS OF ETERNAL NATURE (4.4).

I have already said, when discussing Principle (1.8) that in the information area there is such a principle: something once done exists forever within the time when it was done.

The thought ranges among actions as well. That is why if a person thought of something, that thought is registered in the database. Moreover, it stays there forever, for there is nothing there similar to computer viruses, which exist in ordinary computer networks and can erase the information stored there. In the Cosmic Net database information is preserved forever.

Saying words, that is, speaking also ranges among actions. As a matter of fact, this principle ensues directly from the fact that man has been created in God's image and likeness, God is eternal and his every act is eternal; that is why anything man does has an eternal character. It is quite easy to understand this principle.

THE PRINCIPLE OF ETERNITY. IT GIVES THE GONE ONES AN INSIGHT INTO THE FACT THAT THEY WILL BE RESTORED, REGENERATED (4.5).

The principle of Eternity states that in the eternal system of connections the existing connections have been put into place in such a way that the gone ones will be alive again. However, the spiritual aspect is more important here, it is, in essence, a spiritual principle.

We already know that life is eternal in principle; this has been enshrined into the World structure. And since the notion of Eternity has been primordially embodied into the notion of spirit, the living one knows, always knows, at least at the soul level, that he will not die, that he will live forever and that provided he has a good command of the proper technology, he can resurrect others. And thus the consciousness of the gone ones and their soul understand perfectly well, both on their own and due to coming in touch with the consciousness of the living, that they will be restored, regenerated.

And therefore, this principle, the principle of Eternity, acts as a bearer of light, as the light that can guide a person and evolve him.

It should be noted that, when a person's departure occurs, from the very first moment after the departure, this principle the gone ones come to understand this principle, and they perceive it not only at soul level, but also quite consciously. Many of those, who have experienced clinical death, tell about an unusual calm, serenity, peace that would pervade them in that state, and about the light that would emerge. The serenity, the peace and the light come from the contact with Eternity. This is the Creator who gives the one, trying to depart, such an angle of understanding of Eternity. Through the emerging light God imparts the knowledge of eternal life. Those, who have expanded their structure of consciousness to the level of perception of this knowledge, come back straightaway.

I remind that while staying in a normal physical body, it is possible to quickly achieve the capability of experiencing the described states and understanding this and other principles. To do so one has to raise the level of the state of consciousness. In higher states of consciousness all these principles are just manifest truths.

THE MOVEMENT OF THE GONE ONES AROUND THEIR COUNTRY OF LIFE, MAGIC FOR OUR UNDERSTANDING, ACTUALLY IS REALIZED TROUGH THE STRUCTURE OF OUR CONSCIOUSNESS (4.6).

What does this statement - the movement of the gone ones around their country is actually realized through the structure of our consciousness - mean? This statement contains several aspects. We have already discussed one of them in relation to the previous principle (4.5). Namely, even if the living one is not well familiar with the resurrection technology or doesn't know anything about it at all, nevertheless the knowledge of the fact that the gone ones will be restored, regenerated has already been enshrined into the structure of his consciousness. It already exists in the structure of consciousness of the living. And thus, as I have said, the gone ones have this knowledge both at soul level and as a result of the contact with the consciousness of the living.

There is yet another aspect of the statement under consideration. The movement of the gone ones is done through the structure of our consciousness, because in our consciousness the notion of the departure and of the gone ones still exists. It is our belief that the departure is a normal, natural occurrence that enables it to happen. It is only because our consciousness allows the existence of the gone ones that they exist. When with better general understanding of the fact, that life in actuality is eternal, that death is unnecessary, that it, contrarily, only slows down man's spiritual development, when with man's growing realization of these veritable realia of life the notions of the departure and the gone ones have disappeared from the structures of his consciousness and this new understanding has become a collective consciousness constituent, then everybody will live forever, there will be no departure and no gone ones any more. So, it suffices to understand the World correctly and there will be no gone ones, everybody will live forever.

In the formulation of the principle the word 'movement' is very important. But what is at issue here is not about the dynamics which exists while in the state of clinical death and about which tell those, who have come back from that state into our world. The corridors they describe, becoming calm, serene, at peace, the emergence of light — all these are true indeed and are the result of the contact with Eternity. However, I'm now speaking about the entirely different movement, about the dynamics which is radically different.

I am talking about the assemblage of the microelement and event base. In the state in which the gone ones are in reality the notion of stoppage or cessation of processes does not exist. Immediately after the occurrence of the biological death the assemblage begins, the assemblage in accordance with the structure of Eternity. The motion of, for example, information starts, basic laws of being start being embodied, certain microprocesses get underway and so on. These processes are directed inward a person, as it should logically be when assembling his microelement and event base.

Thus, as soon as the moment of the departure comes and the biodegradation of cells begins that is, as soon as the body decomposition gets started, immediately at the same time the processes, necessary for the resurrection begin as well, an inward-directed assemblage begins.

All this, essentially, proves a sheer nonexistence of the idea of death. There is only life and its eternal evolution.

What has just been said in relation to the microelement and event base assemblage after the departure allows seeing yet another aspect of how the movement of the gone ones through the structure of our consciousness occurs. Here is what I mean. When the living commemorate the ninth and the fortieth days or participate in some ceremonies or celebrations, such as, for example, Christmas, they thus lend a substantial support to the gone ones. For our consciousness, as we already know, is organized so, that it contains the principle of restoration, regeneration, that is, the resurrection, and since during the mentioned celebrations the interaction of the structures of consciousness of the living and the gone ones is particularly strong, the consciousness of the living, even if unaware of the fact, nevertheless, their consciousness helps the gone ones to be actively regenerating. That is the primary purpose of appropriate celebrations and ceremonies. They help the resurrection of the gone ones, facilitate their transition into the inner structure, and cause the assemblage process to accelerate.

Knowing the principles of organization of man, his assemblage can be achieved instantaneously. Likewise coming of a biological death can also be instantaneously stopped. In modern medicine a high-voltage impulse is used in order to bring a person back out of the state of clinical death. It is a shock of a sort. However since this is a mechanical method, it by no means always works.

In ancient China they could regenerate a person even from a much decomposed state. For these purposes the acupuncture was used. Naturally, different degrees of decomposition require different approaches. If, for example, no longer than three days would have passed after the coming of a biological death, then the extremities acupuncture points would be used. Inserting needles into proper points would result in the resurrection. However this approach is mechanical too, it is based on utilizing mechanical principles. And for that reason I won't dwell on these methods. Because in the first place I'm giving spiritual principles.

Though, perhaps, maybe it is worth mentioning another interesting phenomenon of the past. In ancient times in certain localities they knew the secret of "preservation" of people, provided they gave their consent. It was primarily applied in relation to warriors. When it was necessary to transport the warriors at long distance they got archived, that is, were merely stacked in a certain place, well, the same way the papers which may be needed in the future, are archived. The warriors would shrivel and in such a state, being just a mass of matter, they could be indefinitely preserved. But when the need in them appeared, a needle would be inserted in the right place of every warrior, or a specific mixture would be poured upon them, or a proper impulse of consciousness would be given - and the warriors would come back to life. Similarly, provided the specific conditions are met, certain mummies too, can come to life.

We now turn back to Principle (4.6.) It refers to the movement of the gone ones about their realm of life, which from our perspective is a fairyland. Of course, we could say that the movement is not about the land but about the realm of life. I, however, purposely use here the word 'land', and more than that, the expression 'fairyland'. For the word 'fairy' in this case conveys a deeper meaning.

The matter is there is an interaction between the world of the gone ones and the world of the living. Not only we, the living, speak, but they, the gone ones, speak too. They speak from there. And a fairy tale is an intermedium. A fairy tale, a legend, a sage, an epic include not only what was said by us, but also what was said by them. And when they speak, for the living their words come out in fairy images. Using scientific language we may say that a fairytale is a transformation system, an information transformation system from there to here, and this information comes to us in the language we understand.

Many fairytale elements are child friendly. Exposure to even two or three good fairytales significantly facilitates the process of further development of the child. He thereafter develops dynamically.

Of course, besides the tales, a very specific technology can be given to children and then, they will be able to become eternal almost at once, from the very beginning. And they will begin to develop as they should. Though, the external world may orient them differently, nevertheless, children may be given such a program due to which the transformation of the society will take place and within a short time.

So, two –three fairytales may be enough for a child to acquire a dynamic form of development. And if in addition children have been given an appropriate technology, then from the beginning they will be able to evolve according to the principles of self-regeneration and eternal life. Then everyone becomes introduced to the status of Eternity from the start.

CHANGES OF GEOGRAPHICAL LANDSCAPE, RESULTING FROM EARTHQUAKES, OR FROM SPLIT OFF OF BIG ROCKS DURING AVALANCHES, LEAD TO GENETIC AND STRUCTURAL CHANGES IN MAN, BECAUSE MAN REACTS TO THE ENTIRE SPACE (4.7).

First of all let's go over what Principle (4.2) states: Man is the entire external and internal world simultaneously. Therefore, geosystem, common earthquakes and the entire surrounding world in general - all this in fact is the manifestation of man's status.

But why is it specifically the changes in geosystem resulting from earthquakes and rock shearing during avalanches that have been pinpointed in the wording of the principle? Because it is these changes above all others that lead to genetic and structural changes in man, since the landscape and rocks have a longer formation period and thus they are more connected with man's overall genetic structure.

The important role played by existence time can be seen also using the example of buildings. A building starts effecting genetics, if it was built, let's say, more than a thousand years ago. In this case one may, in a sense, speak of eternity. Of course, this number, a thousand y years, is, frankly speaking, relative, but nevertheless it reflects the existing situation: such buildings do have effect on human genetics. And they have a particular influence on human perception. This is due to the fact that the longer a building exists, the more it is adapted to the collective consciousness. Such a building creates a certain status. We know the expression: the attraction of a building. Such buildings, such structures or their remains still exist and the fact, that they attract streams of tourists is not coincidental.

The same is true for works of art. With the course of time they increase in value. Auctions are a good evidence of that.

In addition to what I said I will note that the evolution of Eternity largely consists is in raising not only the status pertaining to time, but also to space as well. It means the more new land is inhabited, the more areas are developed, the more stable the structure becomes. That is where man's desire for exploration comes from.

Let's go over Principle (4.2) one more time: Man is the entire external and internal world simultaneously. This principle gives us an indication as to how to act properly in our external activity. If we, for example, construct buildings, they need to be built so, that they tend to man's image and likeness. If we take, let's say, London and notice how it is situated, it will become clear that it represents man's head. Moscow tends to the heart representation.

There are two approaches in construction in man's image: based on external areas and internal areas. They are different approaches. The external areas are the areas of a greater manifestation of the collective consciousness. They are out of the physical body of man. And the internal areas are the areas of greater manifestation of the individual consciousness of a person. They are inside man's body.

Why, for example, were there for a long time religious prohibitions against an autopsy of man, a taboo to see what's inside the human body? The reason for that is that the formation of informational interconnections between man's external and internal areas in the image and likeness of God was still under way, as was the formation of man's consciousness.

If you carefully read the exercises, given in the Appendix, you will see that the concentration I present is predominantly on external objects. This is because man's internal system frequently changes and changes radically, whereas the external objects possess stability in terms of their permanent existence in perception.

We need still yet to clarify the following point. When I say that buildings must be built in man's image and likeness, on no consideration one needs take it literary, that is, that buildings have to be in the shape of little men. This question calls for a deeper analysis. I am referring to connections and interactions of shapes. One needs, for example, to understand, the interconnection between the plane and man's shape, or the interconnection between the sphere and man's shape. With this knowledge, we can build absolutely stable eternal structures, including the ones based on antigravity. Buildings, and generally all kinds of structures, built in this way, will harmonize with man and thus with the Creator.

As to the problem of shape, interconnection between shape and information as well as other related questions, all of them will be inquired into in one of the books of this series.

## SUMMARY OF CORE PRINCIPLES OF RESURRECTION

### 1

1.1. HE WHO HAS NOT EXPERIENCED DEATH IS THE BASE, WHICH REPRODUCES EVERYTHING ELSE. GOD IS SUCH A BASE. GOD IS ETERNAL, HE HAS NEVER EXPERIENCED DEATH. EVERYTHING ELSE FOLLOWS FROM THIS FACT.

1.2. ETERNAL LIFE IS THE PRINCIPLE OF DEVELOPMENT OF DIVINE REALITY.

1.3. OUR CONSCIOUSNESS PERCEIVES WHAT EXISTS IN OUR CONSCIOUSNESS AS REALITY.

1.4. THE STRUCTURE OF THE WORLD SHOULD INTENSIVELY DEVELOP WITHIN THE DEVELOPMENT OF OUR OWN CONSCIOUSNESS.

1.5. RESURRECTION IS CONPREHENSION OF TRUE CONSCIOUSNESS.

1.6. ETERNAL LIFE CONDITIONS THE NECESSITY OF THE DEVELOPMENT OF SOUL.

1.7. THE PRINCIPLE OF DIVINITY: ASPIRATION FOR IMPERISHABILITY OF BODY, FOR ETERNAL LIFE, AND FOR DEVELOPMENT OF TRUE CONSCIOUSNESS IS THE PRACTICE OF THE UPPERMOST FLOURISHING OF HUMAN EXISTANCE.

1.8. IT IS SUFFICIENT TO HAVE ONE PERSON WHO CAN RESURRECT AND RESTORE THE WORLD TO ENSURE THAT IT IS NOT POSSIBLE TO DESTROY THE WORLD.

1.9. RESURRECTION AND ASCERTAINMENT OF THE FACT OF RESURRECTION IS A SIMULTANEOUS FOR THE ENTIRE WORLD PROCESS.

1.10. CORRECT UNDERSTANDING OF THE CORRELATION BETWEEN

THE CONSCIOUSNESS OF MAN AND HIS ORGANS PROVIDES RESURRECTION. RESURRECTION IS AN ACT OF CREATION.

1.11. DEVELOPMENT OF MAN SHOULD BE CONSIDERED AS A COMPLEX DEVELOPMENT OF THE ENTIRE EXISTING WORLD.

1.12. THE PRINCIPLE OF THE RESURRECTION CORRELATES WITH THE PRINCIPLE OF MAN'S ORGANIZATION, WHICH TAKES INTO ACCOUNT ALL-TIME DEVELOPMENT OF THE ENTIRE EXTERNAL WORLD.

1.13. GRIEF, DESPONDENCY AND NOSTALGIA ARE NOT THE WAY TO PERCEIVE THE WORLD. ONLY JOY, LIGHT AND LOVE ARE THE WAY TO COMPREHEND THE WORLD.

1.14. PERSONALITY REMAINS INTACT AFTER BIOLOGICAL DEATH, INCLUDING CREMATION CASES. IS THIS LAST CASE EACH PARTICLE OF THE ASH, RECEIVED AFTER CREMATION, IS CONNECTED TO THE STRUCTURE OF PERSONALITY OF THAT ONE WHO WAS CREMATED.

1.15. SPACE DEPENDS ON WHERE DIFFERENT TIME INTERVALS INTERSECT. AS A RESULT OF THAT THE EARTH CAN BE INCREASED IN SIZE.

## 2

2.1. MAN IS AN ETERNAL SUBSTANCE BY THE PRINCIPLE OF HIS CREATION. THAT IS WHY RESURRECTION IS BASED ON REVEALING THE ETERNAL IN MAN.

2.2. THERE IS INTERDEPENDENCE BETWEEN THE SPIRITUAL AND PHYSICAL STRUCTURES. BY CHANGING THE INFORMATION ON THE PHYSICAL STRUCTURE IN THE SPHERE OF THE SPIRIT, WE CAN CHANGE THE SPIRIT TO THE LEVEL, WHEN IT WILL BE ABLE TO CHANGE ANY PHYSICAL STRUCTURE, AS WELL AS TO CREATE A PHYSICAL BODY.

2.3. TIME AND SPACE DO NOT LIMIT THE DURATION OF LIFE. THE CONCEPT OF DURATION OF LIFE IS FORMED BY THE RELATION OF THE SPIRIT TO SPACE AND TIME.

2.4. THE PRINCIPLE OF IMMORTALITY AND, THEREFORE, THE PRINCIPLE OF RESTORATION, REGENERATION AFTER A POSSIBLE BIOLOGICAL DEATH IS EMBODIED IN THE PRIMORDIAL CAUSE, IN THE PRIMORDIAL NATURE OF IMPULSES OF MAN'S NATURAL DEVELOPMENT.

2.5. AN IMPULSE AIMED TOWARDS THE RESURRECTION IS ALWAYS AIMED TOWARDS THE INFINITE EVOLUTION OF THE ONE BEING RESURRECTED.

2.6. THE ONE BEING RESURRECTED ALWAYS SEES AND IS AWARE OF THE RESURRECTION PROCESS, AND HE ALWAYS ACTIVELY PARTICIPATES IN IT AS AN INITIATIVE PERSON.

2.7. THE ONE BEING RESURRECTED ALWAYS KNOWS FOR A FACT THAT AFTER THE RESURRECTION HE WILL LIVE AS A NORMAL PERSON.

2.8. THE ONE BEING RESURRECTED ALWAYS THINKS THAT THE LIVING ONE WILL TREAT HIM AS EQUAL, HE DOES NOT FEEL SEPARATED FROM THE LIVING IN ANY WAY, AND HE FEELS LIKE A NORMAL PERSON, NO DIFFERENT FROM THE LIVING.

2.9. AFTER THE RESURRECTION IT IS NECESSARY TO PROVIDE SOME GUIDANCE TO THE RESURRECTED ONE, EXPLAINING HIS NEW STATE, ATTRIBUTABLE TO THE FACT THAT NOW HE HAS A PHYSICAL BODY.

2.10. A RESURRECTED PERSON FULLY RETAINS HIS PROFESSIONAL AND OTHER SKILLS, ACQUIRED EARLIER IN LIFE.

2.11. THE CONCEPT OF SPIRIT PROVIDES THE TRUTH OF THE STRUCTURE OF COGNITION.

2.12. ONE OF THE ASPECTS OF RESURRECTION IS RESTORATION OF CREATIVE CONSCIOUSNESS OF LIVING PEOPLE.

2.13. THE RESURRECTION PROCESS SHOULD BE REGARDED AT THE SAME TIME AS A PROCESS OF REPRODUCTION OF A FOETUS AS WELL.

2.14. THE SPIRITUAL DEVELOPMENT OF THE GONE ONES DOES NOT STOP. PERSONAL SPIRITUAL DEVELOPMENT ALWAYS

CONTINUES AT ALL TIMES. THEREFORE AT SPIRITUAL LEVEL THE RESURRECTION IS UNDERSTOOD AS THE MANIFESTATION OF THE UNIVERSAL WORLD HARMONY. AND THAT IS PRECISELY WHY ON THE SPIRITUAL LEVELALL PEOPLE KNOW THAT THE UNIVERSAL RESURRECTION OF THE GONE ONES IS TO COME.

# 3

3.1. ASPIRATION OF GOD AND MAN FOR UNITY WITHIN RECREATION AND REUNION RESULTS IN MATERILIZATION AND RESURRECTION.

3.2. CONCENTRAION BY MAN OF HIS OWN CONSCIOUSNESS MIGHT RESULT IN A RADICAL CHANGE OF THE WORLD STRUCTURE.

3.3. PHYSICAL BODY IS ALWAYS A PART OF THE SOUL.

3.4. BOTH THEORETICALLY AND PRACTICALLY MAN CAN BE REGARDED AS A STRUCTURE OF CONSCIOUSNESS THAT HAS A BODY SHELL.

3.5. AT THE LEVEL OF CREATION OF INFORMATION CONNECTIONS NO OBJECT OVERLAPS WITH ANY OTHER EXTERNAL OBJECT INCLUDING ITSELF. THE PRINCIPLE OF RESURRECTION OF MAN, OR THE PRINCIPLE OF RESTORATION OF ANY OBJECT, IS IN THE OVERLAPING OF INITIAL INFORMATION ABOUT THE OBJECT WITH THE DEVELOPING INFORMATION ABOUT ITSELF IN THE AREA OF THE EFFECT RELATIONS, WHICH APPEAR IN THE COURSE OF CREATION OF INFORMATION.

3.6. THE SYSTEM OF SPIRITUAL VIEWS OF THAT ONE WHO PRACTISES RESURRECTION IS EXACTLY THE PRINCIPLE OF SOCIETY ORGANIZATION AT THE SUBSEQUENT STAGES OF ITS DEVELOPMENT.

3.7. DISTANT OBJECTS OF REALITY ARE WHAT IS APPROACHED FOR THE RESURRECTED AND REMOVED FOR THE LIVING.

3.8. THE RESURRECTED ABSOLUTIZES SPACE AND DETAILS TIME. DURING THE INITIAL PERIOD TIME IS DISCRETE FOR HIM, WHILE FOR

THE LIVING ONE TIME IS CONTINUOUS.

3.9. THE PRINCIPLE OF AUTONOMY OF INFORMATION FUNCTIONING WITHIN DIFFERENT TIMES.

3.10. TRUE RELIGION IS AIMED AT PROMOTING THE CREATIVE DEVELOPMENT OF SOUL, BODY, AND SOCIETY.

3.11. RESURRECTION IS THE MOST REAL, THE MOST PRAGMATIC, THE MOST RATIONAL AND THE MOST CONVINCING BASIS FOR THE CONSEQUENT DEVELOPMENT, FOR DEVELOPMENT OF THINKING OF THE GENERATIONS TO COME.

3.12. THE LIVING ONE, WHO HAS NOT EXPERIENCED DEATH, CAN ALWAYS REGENERATE, RESTORE THE GONE ONE WITHIN A SHORTER, MORE OPTIMAL TIME AND AS A MORE DESIRED OPTION THAN THE RESURRECTED ONE CAN.

3.13. THE PRACTICE OF RESURRECTION, THE PRACTICE OF RESTORATION, REGENERATION IS NOT CONTRARY TO ANY RELIGION, TO ANY LAW, NOR TO ANY CREATIVE TREND.

3.14. THE RESURRECTION OF PEOPLE MAKES IT POSSIBLE TO RESURRECT AND RESTORE ANY OBJECTS.

## 4

4.1. RESURRECTION IS CONTROL OF THE ENTIRE EXTERNAL SPACE

4.2. MAN IS THE ENTIRE EXTERNAL AND INTERNAL WORLD SIMULTANEOUSLY.

4.3. TIME DILATATION, ITS REMOVAL OR APPROACHING MEANS RESURRECTION FOR SOME ASPECTS OF SPACE.

4.4. WHAT MAN THINKS, WHAT HE SAYS AND WHAT HE DOES IS OF ETERNAL NATURE.

4.5. THE PRINCIPLE OF ETERNITY. IT GIVES THE GONE ONES AN INSIGHT INTO THE FACT THAT THEY WILL BE RESTORED, REGENERATED.

4.6. MOVEMENT OF THE GONE ONES AROUND THEIR COUNTRY OF LIFE, MAGIC FOR OUR UNDERSTANDING, ACTUALLY IS REALIZED

TROUGH THE STRUCTURE OF OUR CONSCIOUSNESS.

4.7. CHANGES OF GEOGRAPHICAL LANDSCAPE, RESULTING FROM EARTHQUAKES, OR FROM SPLIT OFF OF BIG ROCKS DURING AVALANCHES, LEAD TO GENETIC AND STRUCTURAL CHANGES IN MAN, BECAUSE MAN REACTS TO THE ENTIRE SPACE.

# CHAPTER III
# THE METHODS OF THE RESURRECTION OF PEOPLE

The methods of the resurrection of people are based on the fundamental laws of the World. They reflect the understanding of the role of consciousness in our life and of how consciousness can be used for resurrection. Knowing that life is eternal is also essential.

The methods of the resurrection of people are based also on a thorough understanding of the fact that the information of resurrection can be communicated to the soul of the one being resurrected. And there are countless ways to do it. Of all the variety of practicable methods I selected fifty. This number, as a matter of fact, equals the number of the core principles of resurrection, given in the previous chapter. If you count them, it will be exactly fifty.

When we communicate the information of resurrection to the soul of the one being resurrected, we rely heavily on the fact that his soul understands the principles and the methods of resurrection. At soul level everyone possesses this knowledge. This knowledge has been embedded into the structure of consciousness of every person. It is another matter that as yet not everybody has woken up to this knowledge. But this is a problem of a personal spiritual growth. As man evolves spiritually, as the level of his state of consciousness raises, all these truths will be easier and easier to understand.

Since different people are at different levels of development, when practicing the suggested methods of resurrection, the following should be kept in mind. First of all, one should realize that resurrection occurs through proper perception, proper understanding of the text of the book. The awareness should be focused on each person's individuality.

Some people may succeed right away. However, many will realize their unpreparedness. It's O.K. For this only means that you have to continue working with the book.

Carefully reread Chapter II "The Core Principles of Resurrection". These principles should be thought through. You must start having the feeling that you understand them. Also reread Chapter I "Concrete Facts of The Resurrection of

People". These are living illustrations. The analysis of the cases described will help you understand the aspects, characteristic for resurrection. The given facts already contain all the necessary knowledge of resurrection.

You should reread Chapter IV "The Principles of Resurrection and Everyday Life" as well. The questions discussed there will add to your understanding of everything related to resurrection.

And, finally, you need to read one more time very carefully the commentary to Principle (3.10), where practical recommendations on self-cultivation are given. It is very important to follow those directions as consciously as possible.

And then, with time you are bound to succeed. It is precisely with this in mind this book has been written: to aid you to achieve success. This is your innate ability, internal ability. Everyone has it from birth. One only needs to achieve its practical realization. When you communicate the information of resurrection to the soul of the one being resurrected and embark on work, he himself too becomes an active participant of this work. This was discussed in Chapter II. Remember about it. And always consider particular circumstances, in which the resurrection takes place.

Why did I come up with so many resurrection methods, fifty? The matter is we all are very different. And this is natural. Each one of us has his own inclinations, his own views, his own preferences. A large number of the methods allow each person to decide on the one which appeals to him most, which he likes best, and, most likely, this particular method will be most effective for him. This may be the case at the initial stage. With time you will be able to use most of these methods with equal success.

Another reason for my coming up with so many resurrection methods is as follows. At first sight these methods appear to be very different. However, when reading them, when thinking them over, you will gradually begin to feel, that though they may differ in form, in actuality underneath they all have one and the same thing in common. Underneath them all is what unifies them, what virtually makes them the methods of resurrection. The variety of forms of these methods will help you better feel and understand their one whole fundamental nature underneath them.

Understanding the material set forth is an important factor. Doing the exercises given in the Appendix also leads to resurrections and eternal life, helps you achieve a greater harmony with the surrounding world. When better understanding and greater harmony have been achieved, the resurrections will begin to occur much faster.

The first few methods are given in considerable detail. Closer to the end only the main idea of the method discussed is presented.

The name of each method is listed next to its number. The material has been presented by me in such a way that after becoming familiar with a method, transfer of knowledge to the soul of the one being resurrected will be ensured by simply focusing on the name of the method. It is of course better, though, to follow through all the recommendations given there.

Now we are coming directly to the methods of resurrection.

1. RESURRECTION ON THE BASIS OF OPERATION OF DISTANT SITES OF CONSCIOUSNESS.

First we have to understand what the distant sites of consciousness are. Imagine that you are deliberating on a question, trying to understand it. The degree of understanding may vary. The understanding may be clear or not very clear, or not clear at all. And since understanding lies within the space of consciousness, then the degree of understanding can be associated with normal distance in physical space. We may say that what you understand well is in the nearest segments of consciousness, and what you don't understand that well is in its distant sites.

So, the segments of your consciousness, associated with questions you did not understand, or did not go into, thinking that you would concern yourself with them at a later date, or questions you just do not attach any importance to, these segments within the frame of this method are called distant sites of consciousness. Now, it turns out, that resurrection may occur on account of the operation of such distant sites of consciousness. This process is very capacious. It may be used when you are not able to simultaneously embrace all the processes that are taking place.

During resurrection micro- and macrostructures undergo changes, the regenerative processes in the cells are under way, and organs are being formed. These different processes are a great many, for a human physical body is being created. If you are not able to embrace all these processes, then, you may not understand them. However, it is this lack of understanding that is used in this method. The lack of understanding in this case turns out to be a positive factor. Because then distant sites of consciousness may be used. When you use distant sites of consciousness, you do not need to know and take into account all the connections simultaneously, no need to keep them in mind, no need to focus on them, etc.

And now let us move to how distant sites of consciousness can be used for resurrection in practice.

I suggest two options of this method:

i. In the first option a mental geometric object – a sphere – is used.

Imagine distant sites of consciousness in the shape of a sphere. Place this sphere straight before you at a distance of 25 cm away from the surface of your body. The radius of the sphere must be 5 cm. Now focus your attention in the center of the sphere. Concentrate on the image of the person you intend to resurrect as well as on the idea of his resurrection. Thus you are in fact creating a transmission channel. This is a method of communicating the information to the soul of the person you intend to resurrect.

ii. In the second option the law is used, which states:

WHEN A PERSON REACTS TO INFORMATION, DEPENDING ON THE DEGREE OF HIS REACTION THE INFORMATION IS PLACED EITHER WITHIN NEARER OR WITHIN MORE DISTANT SITES OF HIS CONSCIOUSNESS.

If a person's reaction is weak, the corresponding information is placed in more distant sites of his consciousness. Therefore, in the distant sites of a person's consciousness there is information, which he either did not understand properly, or did not understand at all, or did not understand because he did not give it due attention. It is these distant sites of consciousness that are used in this method. The advantage of their use, as it's been already said, is that you do not need to have a clear picture of all the connections and of all the processes, taking place during resurrection.

In order to use this method affectively it needs to be thoroughly understood. Besides, the core principles of resurrection have to be thoroughly studied. Then you will be able to resurrect others as well as restore any objects.

The direct work on resurrection based on this approach is performed in the following way.

Focus your attention on the image of the person you would like to resurrect. Consider this image as part of your consciousness. For the image is really in one of its segments. You are now in the space of consciousness. The image of the one being resurrected is in one of its segments. And now create the reflection of this image in another segment of your consciousness, and in another segment create one more reflection. Continue to create more and more new reflections of the image of the one being resurrected in different parts of your consciousness.

Some amusement parks have an attraction like this: in a room lots of mirrors are arranged in a special way, so that when a person enters the room, he sees countless reflections of himself.

You have to do something similar when applying this method of resurrection. You must have more and more new reflections in different parts of your consciousness. And when your consciousness holds a great many reflections of the image of the one being resurrected, the image will pass into reality – the resurrection will occur.

The information is communicated to the soul of the one being resurrected through the segment of consciousness, where the image of the one being resurrected has been formed as well as through those segments, where reflections of the image have been formed. By creating the reflections of the image in different areas of your consciousness and by gradually increasing and increasing their number, more and more areas of your consciousness thus become included in communication of the information.

This process has an analogy in radio engineering. We will be talking about antennas. Due to prevalence of television almost everybody knows about antennas. And many people know that if suddenly something goes wrong with a television picture, one of the reasons for this can be problems with the antenna. Antenna is an important element in transmitting and receiving information.

So, for transmitting and receiving signals special devices, called antennas, are used. A single antenna represents a single radiating element. Its work is characterized by certain defined parameters. If however we have many such radiating elements, then an aerial array may be created. And the aerial array now possesses the properties, which single radiating elements are lacking.

So is in our case. An element of consciousness, which contains an image reflection and transmits information, may be regarded as a single radiating element. By increasing the number of reflections of the image, you thus increase the number of radiating elements. Given a very large number of the elements, a qualitative change in the way information is transmitted and received happens. The accumulation of information elements in distant sites of consciousness sufficient for resurrection to occur takes place.

We have already discussed these questions in the Introduction. Remember what was said there about the brain function and laser radiation. The analogy given there is valid here as well.

In the context of the questions of transmitting and receiving information the famous "Bhagavad Gita" comes to mind. Let's recall how the book begins. A ruler, seated in his chamber, asks a clairvoyant, who is there with him, to tell him what is happening on the battlefield while both of them are in the palace. And the entire "Bhagavad Gita" is the clairvoyant's account of the events, taking place on the battlefield. In this case the clairvoyant shifts the area of his consciousness, corresponding to the distant events, to the area of consciousness, which is brought closer enough for precise perception of these events.

2. CONTROL OF RESURRECTION THROUGH THE ELEMENTS OF FLORA.

In this method a plant is used to communicate the necessary information to the soul of the one being resurrected. You may use either a tree, or a bush, or grass, in short - anything you like. Instead of the whole plant you may concentrate just on a single leaf.

You consider this leaf as the structure of the World, as an element of the World. And since everything in the World is connected, this leaflet is connected to all the elements of the World, including the soul of the person you intend to resurrect. It is clear that these connections look a certain way.

So, the kind of connections a plant leaf has may be seen by closely examining the leaf contour. You may either visualize a leaf or look closely at a tangible physical leaf.

Your task is to detect the connections, serving as the channels in the plant, through which the information is transmitted to the soul of the one being resurrected

In order to succeed in transmitting the information the following technical moment has to be considered. I am referring to a plant orientation. It is you who sets a spatial orientation by your body position. For, it is you who are the active participant. That is why a plant's position must be mentally tied to the position of your body.

Here is an example: suppose, you work, for instance, with a tree. The tree axis, that is, a line from its roots towards the top, should always coincide with your axis, that is, with the direction from your feet towards the head. For example, if you, using this method, work in the standing position, then, since a tree grows vertically upward too, in this case it is all right. But if you are, let us say, in a horizontal position, you must visualize the tree in a horizontal position too, so that in your mental picture it should be, so to say, parallel to your body.

In such a case the tree is used as a transmission channel. You mentally focus your attention on the way the tree is growing, on the way its sap is circulating from the roots towards the top, towards the tips of the branches, towards the edges of the leaves. Into this movement from the roots towards the crown you put in the information for the soul of the one being resurrected, you invite him to be resurrected. We already know how the gone ones act in such cases. Having received the information, that they are to be assisted, they immediately become active participants of the resurrection process.

Actually the elements of the plant life are not the only elements which can be used in this method of resurrection. By the method described it is possible to communicate the information, for example, through the structure of a rock, of a crystal, through the structure of mountains. You may use, let's say, a mountain, which is directly before you, or mountains, visible in the distance. The distance does not matter. You concentrate on the tops of the mountains and using them transmit the information you would like to communicate to the one being resurrected.

3. THE METHOD OF THE SOUL EVOLUTION OF THE ONE BEING RESURRECTED, WHICH FORMS COGNITION ABOUT RESURRECTION IN

## THE WORLD OF THE LIVING.

As the name of the method suggests, its purpose is to communicate the information to the soul of the one being resurrected to be used by his soul to regenerate his physical body in the world of the living.

For our purpose the practical application of this method can be divided into four stages.

i. Focus your attention on the soul of the one being resurrected so, that it becomes illuminated, that is, that it acquires a clear light of knowledge.

ii. You tell mentally to the soul of the one being resurrected about the fact, that in the present-day situation, when the world is faced with the threat of nuclear elimination and ecological disaster, for the sake of universal salvation it is necessary to be able to regenerate the physical body. This regeneration of the physical body, its formation occurs based on the knowledge you are already familiar with. You must give the one being resurrected a sufficiently detailed and accurate account regarding all these things. And in your conversation with him his individual characteristics should be considered. Remember that he is still a personality. So, the conversation with him must be very concrete.

iii. In order for the one being resurrected to better apprehend your information you must be in the state of serenity, calm. And it will be very beneficial, if at the same time you are aware that your state of serenity and calm is the source of knowledge for the one being resurrected. We may say that your state of serenity and calm is sort of a beacon of light for him, which lights his way and helps him orient himself in the ocean of information.

iv. You are to determine the location of where exactly the resurrection is to take place. This place should be mentally shown to the one being resurrected so that he knows where he is to resurrect. Of course, the one being resurrected, being his own master, may have his own opinion about this. He may make his own suggestion. This is not important. In that case you just have to specify the meeting place to him, where he is to come after the resurrection, that is, in his physical body.

When you mentally show the one being resurrected the meeting place, you have to visualize very clearly and accurately the area, for example, the street, or the room, or some other place, where your meeting is to happen. You must visualize the one being resurrected approaching this place. And where he is coming to it from. You must clearly visualize the scene at the very least within the radius of about one hundred meters relative to the place of meeting. I will repeat: you must visualize very clearly, in every detail, how he will walk these one hundred metres, you must visualize, see him walking and follow very closely his every step all the way through this section up to the place of meeting.

Now a short addition. In the first part of this method and previously in the book I used the term "enlightenment". Now I will tell you, what it means.

<u>An enlightened person.</u> <u>Enlightenment.</u>

An enlightened person is he, in whom the light of the soul is seen. It means that the soul of such a person has the light of knowledge, the light of the future, the light of creation. When emphasis is on the light and therefore on enlightenment, creative aspects of the soul are meant, its focus on light.

Thus, an enlightened person is that one, who brings the knowledge of creation, the knowledge of development, the knowledge of harmony.

And enlightenment as a process is a spiritual growth, a spiritual evolution of the person, who becomes enlightened.

4. ACQUIRING THE KNOWLEDGE OF RESURRECTION TECHNOLOGY BY FIXING ATTENTION ON THE BOUNDLESS SURFACE OF WATER.

Imagine that there is an ocean before you. Boundless expanse of water extending in all directions. Boundless, infinite. This ocean is as infinite as your knowledge of the World that your soul possesses.

You would like to resurrect a certain person, wouldn't you? Wonderful. Your soul already possesses the knowledge of how to do it.

A question arises though, how in that ocean of knowledge that you have to find precisely what is needed for the resurrection of that particular person at the given moment. Surely you wouldn't be going over this infinite amount of data piece by piece, this could take a very long time.

In fact, I have to tell you, that the time it takes to examine even an infinite system is always finite. There is such a law. That is, even having an infinite system of knowledge, the time it takes you to go over it is always finite. Though, of course, it will require some time, and the time it will take depends greatly on the level of a person's development. Based on the level of a person's development it may take a few seconds or several hours, days, etc.

The important feature of the method being considered is that it allows one to perform a resurrection instantaneously. That is why it is useful especially in those life situations, when it is necessary to resurrect instantly.

Imagine, that the pilots piloting an airliner, suddenly passed away, let's say, from poisoning,, and now the plane is left without control. Such a situation requires an instantaneous resurrection. Saving the pilots in this situation means saving lives of many people.

Or take, let's say, a person responsible for control of a nuclear station. Suffice it to recall the Chernobyl disaster and its consequences in order to understand the importance of the work of each operator. But what if suddenly something went wrong at the station and at that very time the operator suddenly experienced a biological death, what then? In such a situation he must be resurrected immediately, so that he could restore the normal operation of the station.

Another example can be, let's say, the nuclear cargo transportation. In life similar situations can be plentiful. Therefore, it is necessary to master the method of the instant resurrection of people.

We now go back to the description of the method. You need to concentrate on the ocean of knowledge and find the point in it, where the resurrection of a given person occurs instantly and in the right place.

However a question arises: how is it at all possible to instantly find exactly what is needed for the resurrection of a particular person in the boundless ocean of knowledge? The question is how to find the knowledge instantaneously, for we are talking about an instant resurrection.

Let's suppose for a minute that you already possess this knowledge. Then, the problem has been immediately solved. Because the World is organized in such a way that the knowledge necessary for resurrection, this knowledge in itself is the fact of resurrection. Provided, all the necessary requirements are met for this particular situation.

All, therefore, comes to acquiring the knowledge of the resurrection technology. And since we are talking now about an instant resurrection, it is clear that you can't be looking for this knowledge, you just do not have the time.

However, it turns out you don't need to look for it. You have to do something else. You are to attain such a spiritual status when the entire reality should begin to change in the right direction for you.

The matter is that the center of the ocean of knowledge is you yourself, your spirit, your soul, and, naturally, your mind, your intellect, consciousness and all the rest. And since you are the center of the ocean of knowledge, then all this knowledge is yours. Based on this knowledge you must form the information in such a way that the reality, in response to the information, would manifest itself as the resurrection.

We need, therefore, to understand, how to form such a response of reality. The method for this is as follows. You regard yourself as one of the World elements, the very element, which organizes the fulfillment of the goal you established, in this case a person's resurrection. By impersonating yourself with this element of the World you can see, how exactly and to what extent your spirit has to be developed in order for the desired event to occur.

The state of the spirit is reflected in a corresponding inner state. As your spirit evolves the intensity of your inner luminosity, the brightness of its light increase. I mean, that you, as sort of burst, should be able to instantly achieve the level of luminosity, the level of the state of spirit, which ensures an instantaneous realization of the desired event.

And at the same time you do not need to look for anything. Though, of course, that point in the ocean, that knowledge, needed for this particular resurrection, this knowledge, of course, is necessary. This is so. But you don't have to look for it.

It is known that moths fly to the flame. It takes only to turn on the light in the darkness – and here they are, swarming around it. They are drawn to light.

The same is in our case. You are the light in this World. Realize it. But your realization should not be formal, intellectual. Your entire being has to realize it. If you realize it, you will suddenly discover that you do not need to look for anything. Everything will come to you by itself.

Do you need to resurrect this particular person? Excellent. By impulse shift to a higher state of spirit, to a higher state of consciousness, and you will see that the resurrection has already taken place. So even if this higher state of spirit hasn't become your natural state yet, it's all right; even if you were in this higher state for only an instant, but for that instant you became the light, the bright light – and the necessary knowledge of resurrection came to you on its own from the boundless ocean, and the reality immediately responded to this flash of light with the resurrection.

So, the idea of this method is to come to yourself through fixation of attention on the boundless surface of water from the infinite ocean of knowledge by raising your spirit, and you need to raise it to the extent when the necessary event would form around you on its own.

## 5. CONTROL OF THOUGHT FOR THE RESURRECTION OF PEOPLE.

In this method for the resurrection of people you control thought, that is why it is important to understand that the thought must be very concrete. That is, you must perspicuously formulate the thought about the resurrection of a particular person, if it is a single person, or of particular people, if there are several of them. This is the first.

Further this thought needs, so to say, to be objectified, that is, to be transferred to an object and associated with it. The right little finger is the best choice for this purpose, any flat object may be used as the second choice, followed by three-dimensional objects as the next choice.

In order to objectify a thought you need to concentrate on the selected object, for example, on the little finger of your right hand, and visualize the thought. You must visualize this thought of the resurrection as a specific information element. "To visualize the thought" in this case means, that you have to clearly see those people you would like to resurrect, their images must be distinct, vivid, in color. You must scrutinize them.

If you are not very successful at that, then you may just concentrate on this thought while looking at your little finger, either a physical one or in your mind, and in this case the concentration should last no less than five seconds. As a result of this procedure you associate your thought of the resurrection with the specific object, that is, you objectify it. In this case your right little finger became that object.

Further the question of control of an objectified thought arises. For that purpose you must use your consciousness. Your consciousness acts here as a controlling system. And it is important to ensure that your consciousness, a certain element of your consciousness to be exact, its certain area, should completely envelop this thought, so that the thought should become a part of your consciousness and that it should become a part of your consciousness in a particular place, for example, in the area of the object you concentrate upon.

This situation can be elucidated using an analogy with a hen's egg. We will associate an objectified thought with the yolk and the area of consciousness, surrounding it, with the egg white. The yolk is inside the egg white altogether. In much the same way an objectified thought is completely inside a certain area of your consciousness.

The thought and the area of consciousness, surrounding it, can't be seen with physical eyes.

The same as the yolk or the egg white cannot. And only an exterior covering of an egg - an eggshell - can be seen. In our analogy during the resurrection a physical body of the resurrected one corresponds to the eggshell, this exterior covering of an egg. It too, like an eggshell, can be seen with physical eyes.

If we have a whole egg, its internal structure can be seen with the help of specific devices. Similarly, man's internal structure, his thoughts can be seen by means of clairvoyance. By means of clairvoyance even the entire process of the resurrection can be seen.

We now go back to the question of control of the objectified thought. The above analogy helps understand, that the entire process of resurrection can be divided into the internal part, which includes what can't be seen with physical eyes, and the external part, which includes what can be seen with physical eyes. So, the control of an objectified thought must be done in such a way, that in the first place the thought should be transferred to the area that can be seen with physical eyes.

I would like to draw your attention to the fact that here, as everywhere else certain specific laws work. And control of the thought during the resurrection should be consistent with them. And these laws state that you must bring your thought of the resurrection to a specific physical location, and it is to stay in that specific physical location.

This situation here is similar to this. For you can, for example, take a book from your desk, bring it to the next room and put it on a bookshelf in the bookcase. And it will stay there. The same is with the thought. You need to remember that a thought is a real object.

Thus, if the resurrection is intended to happen at a certain specified location, then it is this very location that the thought of the resurrection of this particular person should be placed into. If the one being resurrected would like to resurrect elsewhere, then you place the thought of his resurrection at the location of the scheduled meeting.

How in fact do we place a thought into the designated location? This problem is solved through thought objectifying. And there are two different ways to do it.

i. You objectify the thought of the resurrection on an unrelated object, for example, on a sheet of paper. On a sheet of paper you visualize the image of the one being resurrected. You focus your attention on this person keeping in mind the thought of his resurrection. After that in your mind you transfer this sheet of paper to the place, where the resurrection is to occur or where your meeting is to take place.

ii. But if in order to objectify a thought instead of an unrelated object you use one of the elements of your body, let's say, your right little finger, then the image of the body element is not transferred. What gets transferred is the image of any object within the immediate proximity from you. Here, however, I do not mean that the selected object has to be within the utmost proximity to you. Any object near you will do. You decide. Trust your inner feeling. The way you tune in to these actions is your personal approach to communicating the data. When you think individually, when you communicate the information your own unique way, the resurrection occurs faster.

6. THE METHOD OF CONTROL OF CONSCIOUSNESS AT WHICH CONSCIOUSNESS FORMS THE THOUGHT OF RESURRECTION.

What is this method based upon? We know that everything in the World is related to everything else. We live in the World of different relations. When, for example, walking along the street or when thinking of something, you may have various thoughts which reflect certain connections. When walking along the street, you notice certain things, certain buildings, or cars, or what is happening around. You perceive this information, you may as well analyze what you see. When you perceive something, it is accounted for the work of your consciousness. But when you act, in this case we speak of a different consciousness level, of the level of consciousness development.

So, when you observe the surrounding reality, it provokes certain thoughts in your mind. Now, the essence of this method of resurrection is to reverse the cause of actions. Namely, using your consciousness you need to form a thought, which will cause the necessary event, the resurrection in this case, to occur. By means of your consciousness you need to form a thought of the resurrection and this thought must be of the proper shape and of the right content.

How is it done in practice in this method? See how the objects closest to you are positioned, arranged. If you do it, you will be able to have a simple principle. Here is what I mean.

When you look at your surroundings, wherever you are at the moment, you may always observe certain connections, for example, in terms of the position of the objects. One object is closer to you, another is further away. Therefore, there is such a notion as distance. Distance, of course, can be measured in meters, but it also can be perceived as a sensation or as a certain image. Thus, you may regard such a simple notion as distance as a connection. And now translate the distance into the image and you will have a resurrected person. Such is the principle.

You must identify those places, where you can create the one being resurrected basically as an image, and as soon as it has been created in a certain place, you transfer the image closer to you, that is, transfer it to that level of your consciousness, which is more propitious for you, where, you feel, the one being resurrected or the one who has already resurrected, will feel comfortable, and then it is this particular consciousness level forms the thought for you.

After you have formed such consciousness, the shape of the thought can be determined later, in a little while, for instance, several seconds later, but sometimes, may be even a few days later. It is important to note here that, when we speak about thought formation through consciousness, it needs to be understood that we are speaking about the fact that consciousness itself must be evolving towards the thought formation of such a status. Unlike, let's say, the thought concentration on the basis of consciousness, here consciousness itself forms a thought and it is consciousness itself that must bring the thought into the desired structure. And when your consciousness functions this way, you can, watch this entire process as if from the outside.

7. CONSCIOUSNESS EVOLUTION TO THE LEVEL OF SELF-COMPREHENSION WITHIN THE AREA OF THIS SAME CONSCIOUSNESS.

This method uses the fact that your consciousness is evolving. And consciousness is evolving as if of its own accord, you need only to set the desired characteristics to it. With infinite evolution of consciousness you become able to process information extremely fast, and as a result any act becomes possible, including the resurrection. Moreover, resurrection becomes possible within the timeframe you determine yourself. And, therefore, it will be possible to control the time interval of the resurrection as well.

So, you regard consciousness as a self-developing system. And it is important that consciousness be evolving in harmony with your personality. That is, while staying in the same social setting, communicating with people as before, exhibiting the same behavior, your consciousness must expand to the extent of becoming infinite in relation to the body of the information to be processed for the resurrection.

The concept of infinity is relative here. Infinitude of one volume of information with respect to the other means that the first volume is incomparably larger than the other one. And this second information volume, that is, in this case full information necessary for the resurrection, this volume of information can be very large, even infinite. However, you already know that your consciousness can process even an infinite information volume within a finite time. And in no way such notions as volume of information, finite or infinite arrays of information can affect the information processing rate.

The most important for you is to clarify for yourself what is control for you. When I say that consciousness evolves infinitely, first of all, it means that your spiritual base knows it, your spiritual core is able to do it, your soul controls it all and your soul agrees with it. Basically your objective here is to attain inner harmony, to attain inner concord, to attain concord with yourself, because then your consciousness will be evolving infinitely fast.

So, attaining such concord is based on a very simple principle. You must realize that in order to develop normally it is necessary to have the eternal future, it is necessary to have the systemic future, it is necessary to have the future, safe and secure for development. And when you have set such a goal, you must clearly formulate exact objectives. Specifically, in order for the world not to be destroyed, for people not to be eliminated, resurrection has to be mastered, we must show that the body can be fully restored, regenerated based on the knowledge of the soul, and at any point of space-time. All that will provide the framework for the eternal development of your consciousness.

And since any process for your consciousness, including the infinite process of evolution of consciousness itself, can be controlled, in fact, the control of this process may sometimes take only seconds, even milliseconds and even less, this process, in terms of form, has a finite size. That is, in actual fact in terms of consciousness infinite evolution may have a finite size.

It becomes clear that the shift of your consciousness to the state of infinite development is achieved through your understanding and through your acceptance of this postulate, of this method. And when you set your mind on that, your knowledge will begin to develop infinitely. And in order to be able to resurrect taking the time component into account, that is, so that the process of the resurrection includes the time of the resurrection as well, all you need to do is to include the time of the resurrection as a thought in the infinite evolution of your consciousness, and then the consciousness will evolve in such a way that you have the resurrection mechanism, which includes control of the duration of resurrection. Though, of course, this is not obligatory. However, it will give you one more control parameter. You will be able to control the duration of the resurrection as well. And you will be able to change it at your own discretion, depending on the circumstances.

8. DIVISION OF CONSCIOUSNESS INTO EXTERNAL AND INTERNAL

AREAS, AND RESURRECTION AT THE BOUNDARY BETWEEN THEM.

This method is as follows. You apply the principle, which enables you to distribute your consciousness in a certain way. Namely, you imagine your consciousness divided into two parts, inner and outer.

You consider the surrounding environment as the inner part of your consciousness. That is, it is what you see with your eyes or perceive through the sensations of your physical organs. Generally, all what happens within the physical reality, for example, shopping, visiting a cafe, various relations among physical objects – all these belong to the inner part of your consciousness. And all the objects and the processes outside physical reality, such as, let's say, a thought - all these you should consider as the outer part of your consciousness.

I will say at once that this division of consciousness into outer and inner structures is relative. You could easily swap them. This is not important. The division is important.

And now, when you have this division, you are to determine the connection between the inner and outer parts of consciousness. And this relations finding between the inner and outer parts of consciousness enables you to resurrect people at the boundary between them.

In its essence this method is based on the following principle. When you view the outer part of consciousness, that is, what from your point of view is outside the physical reality phenomena, you enter the fundamental structure of the World. The fundamental structure of the World is based on the collective consciousness, on the consciousness of all, on the consciousness of the Creator. And your objective is to act in accordance with the way the consciousness of the Creator evolved. In this case your consciousness will have the proper characteristics. That is why you must always be in the right place, either in the inner or outer part of your consciousness, but always where the consciousness has the proper characteristics.

The boundary region between physical processes and the processes outside physical reality is the area, where it is possible to create. When I, for example, materialize an object, I often simultaneously create matter in different places within the boundary area and at the same time bring all matter together in one contour or in one place. It results in object materialization, or in organ regeneration, or in the resurrection of a person. You may act in a similar way.

So, in this method you must divide the structure of your consciousness into the outer and inner parts. And when you have done it and have found the links between them, you will discover that you have resurrected a person in the boundary region.

## 9. BODY CONTROL IN RESURRECTION.

This method is based on the fact, that through the control of your body you may in fact create the space around it, where a person will be able to resurrect. And your body must serve as a certain standard for him. That is why, the one being resurrected, being some distance away from you, has to see your body, its dimensions. He must see, for example, how you quietly move around, work comfortably, undisturbed, solve all your problems level-headedly, and this is a canon, an example, a model for him. Remember that you are one of the representatives of the living for him.

As to the body of the one being resurrected or the resurrected one, its function must be in coherence with the function of a reference body, taken as model. And since in this case it is you, who performs the resurrection, then, naturally, it is your body that serves as a model. This method is about your realization of this fact. For that matter you should seek to ensure the highest health level for your body, because it is your level of health which will be perceived by the one being resurrected. The information communication of the methods of forming a healthy body is achieved through tuning in to the harmony with the surrounding world. The general rule is as follows: the more you practice resurrection, the healthier you are to become, up to reaching perfect health. The circumstances of your life and of those close to you are bound to be improving too.

So, the control of the body in resurrection to a considerable degree is in its development, in obtaining its highest health level, and thus the body restoration, the body regeneration of the one being resurrected will be occurring significantly faster.

## 10. RESURRECTION BY IMPARTING SPECIAL FUNCTIONS TO CERTAIN PARTS OF ONE'S OWN BODY.

In this method resurrection takes place by means of imparting, on the information level, special functions to certain parts of one's own body. Specifically, the little fingers of both hands are used.

You consider both little fingers as elements of the World. The right little finger can be viewed as a World element of the infinite level, and the left little finger as the finite point of the entire information. If you mentally join the little fingers of both hands together, then at the place where they touch you will be able to have the resurrection of a person. For this purpose you need only to do this mental joining close to your physical body and then to transfer the thought to the planned location of the resurrection.

## 11. APPLICATION OF NUMBER CONCENTRATION.

When using this method, you need to concentrate on a number sequence or on each separate number of this sequence in consecutive order. At the same time you must think of the resurrection of a particular person. And, besides, you may by means of a number focus this thought for example, on a plant. The use of a plant is one of the options, I will tell you about other options as well.

Thus when reading a number you must always transfer this number onto a plant, along with the thought of the resurrection. That is, you visualize that the thought of the resurrection is on a number while the number itself is on the plant.

And here are specific numbers, needed for this concentration.

Numbers 1, 2, 3, 4, 8, 1, 4 – this is a numerical concentration on plants.

Numbers 8, 2, 7, 5, 4, 3, 2 - concentration on rocks and crystals.

Numbers 2, 1, 4, 5, 4, 3, 2- concentration on the image of the one being resurrected.

If for resurrection you use the number concentration on a plant, then while reading the corresponding numbers in consecutive order you may just be looking at the plant.

Instead of reading the numbers consecutively, you may also do the following. First you concentrate simultaneously on the first and the last numbers of the numerical row, then on the second and the one next to last, then, on the third from the beginning and on the third one from the end, and, finally, on the central number. Each of the rows above consists of seven digits. Through this practice you can achieve resurrection.

The numerical concentration on rocks and crystals is performed in similar fashion.

Now regarding the concentration on the image of the one being resurrected. Visualize the image of the one being resurrected some distance away from you. The numerical row you are using must be somewhere between you and the image. You may just write these numbers on a sheet of paper and place it between you and the image. During the concentration your contact with the image must be in the straight line through the numbers. It is very important to remember that when you concentrate on the numbers, the thought of the resurrection of a particular person must be always present.

As in previous instances you may either go through the entire numerical row digit by digit consecutively or start with the extremes and gradually reach the central digit.

## 12. VISUALIZATION OF THE SENSATIONS OF THE ONE BEING RESURRECTED.

In this method you need to perceive the sensations of the one being resurrected and to create his image based on these sensations. In order to translate the sensations into the image in the general case the following needs to be done.

The sensations must be visualized as information, namely, as an image, which must be infinitely distant from you. And when you are able to visualize this image, which is infinitely far away from you, it will mean that this image is indeed a sensation.

So, if you are able to perform the visualization of the sensations of the one being resurrected, his resurrection will take place.

## 13 APPLICATION OF ALTERNATIVE WAYS OF PERCEIVING.

This method is based on the fact, that you consider reality as a system of alternative, conditionally opposite, knowledge. If, for example, the process of the resurrection is occurring in one location, you immediately transfer this resurrection to another location, which conditionally may be called an opposite location. For example, if, let's say, the location of the resurrection is close to you, you transfer it somewhere far away. If, vice versa, it is far away, you bring it nearer to you. Or if the resurrection is to take place, for example, in the daytime, you shift it to the night time, and if it is to occur during the night, you perform it during the day time. Thus you must mentally be reversing your perception, which accelerates the resurrection.

This method is primarily used to shorten the time required for the resurrection.

## 14. VISUALIZATION OF JOINED ELEMENTS OF PHYSICAL REALITY.

In the surrounding physical reality we may often see instances when one element is joined with another. Let's take, for example, a tree. We may see a branch growing from another branch, that is, they are joined together at a certain point. And that's exactly what is used in this method.

With your physical eyes you see a branch growing from another branch. And here we can draw an analogy with resurrection. For resurrection, indeed, is growing too, a physical object growing from the existing world. A branch growing from another branch -- you translate this element of physical reality to resurrection, and you regard resurrection as the one being resurrected growing from this world. That is, you consider one branch to be the world of the living and the other, the one, which grows from it, to be the one being resurrected.

You need to concentrate on the point, where one branch grows from another. By concentrating in this manner you can achieve resurrection.

## 15. TRANSLATION OF AN EVENT OF REALITY INTO AN EVENT OF INFORMATION.

Let's examine an event. Imagine that you, for example, are walking over a bridge. You have air above you, and below, under the bridge, there is, let's say, a road or a river. If we translate this event, that is, the fact that you are walking over the bridge, into information, then to do so at least three elements of physical reality may be used. In this case, if we look along the vertical, it will be, for example, the air above, secondly, you and the bridge you are walking over, and, finally, also what is under the bridge. Generally any event can be translated into information using three elements of that same event, as we have just done.

Another example. You are passing a tree. Or standing near it. The first element is the tree, the second element – you again and your position in space, and the third element is the outside environment.

When you translate an event into information, it is very important to make this translation the simplest possible way. Well, for example, a physical act may be translated into a thought. And here is how this translation is done in practice.

You concentrate on your right little finger, then - on your right thumb, from the thumb you pass the information to your left little finger, and further to your left thumb. When you pass the information from finger to finger, you must vividly visualize this information transfer. The given procedure translates physical reality into informational reality.

This procedure, as a matter of fact, represents training of your consciousness and your perception. It is, in fact, training in reality control.

In our life we deal with information perception at every step. When we gaze at a splendid landscape or watch TV, we perceive what we see. However, we have to learn not only to perceive the information, but to optimize and communicate, transmit it as well. What you perceive you must be able to communicate, to transmit.

The described training on communicating, transmitting information will result in your acquiring this ability, and then, you will be able to focus, to manifest your wish into physical reality. Here is what is important. When you are assembling the information, you must clearly understand your objective, the resurrection in this case. Having assembled the information you transform it so that its transfer would result in the desired event manifested in the physical world.

So, having set the task of resurrection, you collect information from the events of physical reality, then transform it in such a way that after communicating it to the one being resurrected it should manifest as his resurrection in the physical world.

16. ESTABLISHING THE CONNECTION AMONG DIFFERENT ELEMENTS OF THE WORLD.

In this method you examine relations among different elements of the World. Your understanding of the World is the basis for establishing these relations.

Let's consider an example. Imagine that you walked into a store and are buying a certain item there. This item is linked to many things. First of all, it is important to know where it was made, who manufactured it. For a customer it always matters. Secondly, this item carries a price. And, finally, now this item is connected with you, you have purchased it. As in the previous method I have limited myself to three elements.

Pay attention that in the example above I listed the connections in the chronological order, that is, as consistent with their successive appearance in time.

Indeed, first this item was manufactured somewhere, then it was delivered to the store and was priced and, finally, you saw it and bought it.

We can see how the connections appear successively in time. So, your objective is to establish the connections among the elements of the World irrespective of time. That is, your perception must carry no time element, only the connections must be present. When you are able to orient your consciousness in this manner, you will have resurrections, and under entirely different conditions.

## 17. SHAPING THE IMAGE OF THE ONE BEING RESURRECTED FROM YOUR CONSCIOUSNESS PERSPECTIVE.

Your consciousness contains the image of the person you would like to resurrect. The form (shape) of the image may vary. You may see, for example, the person in full-size or only part of him

To elucidate the idea, let's take a photograph. It may be, let's say, a full-length photograph. If for the resurrection you take this photograph as a basis, then it makes sense to have this particular photo as a form (shape). If the photograph contains just a face, then, if desired, a face may serve as a form (shape), implying here the entire body. In general you choose the form at your discretion.

So, you form in your mind the image of the one being resurrected. And the form also includes such details as, for example, the clothes you would like to see him wearing, when resurrected. Here is why forming (shaping) the one being resurrected with due regard to such details is important. For then the one being resurrected does not have to think of the form, in which he is to appear before you. You relieve him from additional concentration.

In order to communicate the information regarding the form to the one being resurrected, you, of course, must establish a rapport with him. The contact is achieved by focusing your consciousness on his image in the form (shape) of your choice.

## 18. USING EXTERNAL ENVIRONMENT AS THE ANALYZER OF EVENTS OF REALITY.

Usually when we look around, we view the environment from our own perspective. This method consists in reorienting your consciousness, in looking at yourself and the surrounding world from another object's perspective. You may take, for example, a tree, or a rock, or air (let's say, one cubic meter of it) and see, what you or the surrounding world are from their viewpoint.

You may take any of your actions, for example, your movements. From a tree's perspective they have an infinite structure in a bounded form. From a rock's point of view your movements are very abrupt, jerky. From the air's perspective you have infinite connections, you are in the center, surrounded with an infinite environment. The way a tree, a rock, air or other objects perceive the surrounding world may be learned using clairvoyance.

We can see how different world perception by different objects is. And since everything is based on the collective consciousness, then, having such a variety of perceptions, it is not that difficult to compose them so as to have the perception of the one being resurrected and thus to ensure the resurrection to occur within a shorter timeframe. All one needs to do is to establish a telepathic communication with the one being resurrected and invite him here.

## 19. TRANSFORMATION OF THE ESSENCE OF NUMBER FOR RESURRECTION.

In our life we constantly have to deal with numbers, starting with the date of birth. You live in a building which has a number. Your passport has a number. Your phone has a number. Every car is provided with a number. Each day of a month is numbered. Numbers are used everywhere.

What happens in our consciousness, when we see a certain number? In accordance with the essence of number, the number determines the location of one of the elements of our consciousness at the moment of perception. For every number there is a specified element of our consciousness corresponding to this number. Thus numbers determine our perception. We see them – and their location emerges, or comes out, in our consciousness. In other words, when we perceive a number, we perceive it with that element of our consciousness, which is the location of that number.

So, the idea of this method of resurrection is that the essence of number principle be used backwards: not from the perception towards the corresponding element of consciousness, but from the element of consciousness towards the perception. That is, let your consciousness come up with the date and place of the resurrection, for example, with a building number or an apartment number, and the resurrection will take place on the day and at the designated location.

Such use of numbers is called transformation of the essence of number.

20. APPLYING THE CONNECTIONS AMONG SURROUNDING OBJECTS FOR THE RESURRECTION.

In our life we are always surrounded by a lot of different objects. And each one of them may be viewed from several perspectives. The variety of possible perspectives is explained by the fact that every object has many connections, I have already spoken about it before.

This method is that when looking at various objects from different perspectives you would find semantic connections among them, always remembering that resurrection is the manifestation of development of all connections. Acting this way will enable you to have the methodology for resurrection as well as self-resurrection.

21. ESTABLISHING THE CONNECTION AMONG DIFFERENT INFORMATION OBJECTS AND RESURRECTION BY MEANS OF TRANSFORMATION OF THESE OBJECTS INTO THE ELEMENTS OF ONE'S OWN CONSCIOUSNESS.

When we look at an element of reality, for example, at a tree, at a house, at stars or consider a certain process, we have all these objects in our consciousness. However, your task is to have them in your consciousness not in terms of perception, but in terms of their control. You must learn to control any process. The idea, therefore, is that you could have an access at the level of consciousness to any information object.

To obtain such an access and, accordingly, the possibility of control, you must do the following.

You must carry yourself mentally, but virtually with your consciousness, with your spirit or, if we look at it all from even more fundamental positions, then with your soul, to carry yourself over to the place, to the environment where you intend to perform the control. As you know, a soul is an infinite structure. That is why your soul is both in the place where your physical body is and simultaneously where the object you are interested in is or where the process you are interested in is proceeding, combining which one can speak of the environment you are interested in. Your soul superimposes this environment on your consciousness in the place where you perform the control of this environment.

It is a good idea to start practicing using simple concrete things. Take, for example, an apple or a pear, or a tomato. Start with fruits. Project an apple on your consciousness from outside. Projecting an object, in this case an apple, on one's own consciousness means transforming this object into an element of one's own consciousness. When you have projected an apple on your consciousness, eat it and watch the way the surrounding world responds to it.

Observing the reaction of the surrounding world will allow you to find the necessary level of control and you will realize that to control the resurrection process is quite simple, because this process in fact is a projection too, but only now it is the projection of your consciousness on the physical reality.

22. APPLYING DISCRETE VALUES OF THE NUMBER AND DISCRETE ELEMENTS OF THE WORLD TO CREATE CONTINUOUS DEVELOPMENT.

Suppose, we have a set of positive integers: 1, 2, 3, 4, 5, 6, 7 and so on to infinity. If we limit ourselves to only positive integers, then the sequence above includes all such numbers and that is why we observe a continuous transition from one number to another.

But if we take only three elements of this sequence, for example, numbers 1, 10, 20, these numbers represent a discrete set of numbers. There is no continuity here, because there are eight omissions between the numbers 1 and 10, and nine omissions between the numbers 10 and 20, and any subsequent numbers are missing at all. However, by using these three elements many times, we can, by adding one element to another, get all the numbers between 1 and 10, then between 10 and 20 and so on. For example, 1 + 1 = 2, 2 + 1 = 3, 10 + 1 = 11. As we can see, due to addition we already have the numbers 2, 3 and 11. As a result of such addition of separate elements we can have a continuous series of all positive integers out of a discrete set of numbers.

Another example is a bridge construction. Single piles (discreteness!) are driven into the bottom of a river as support to later have a continuous construction– a bridge

– as a result.

The given examples show that connecting discrete elements of the World is the way of construction, is the creation of a continuous development. And when discrete values of the number or discrete elements of the World begin to connect – we have the resurrection.

For the resurrection you always have at least three discrete elements. The first element is the salvation system, the second one is, as always, you yourself, and the third element is the surrounding environment.

In the example with the numbers we saw that by connecting discrete elements the entire continuous series of positive integers can be obtained. Something like that happens during the resurrection as well. In order to do it you only need to connect all the elements together in your consciousness.

## 23. THE TECHNOLOGY OF THINKING FOR THE ONE BEING RESURRECTED IN ORDER TO RESURRECT HIM.

The one being resurrected at the deep, profound level, at soul level, has full knowledge about the physical body. At this level he has, specifically, the thoughts, related to the physical body. You need to direct the one being resurrected towards the awareness of this connection, serving as a standard. Since you are a live person who has a physical body, you have a connection between the thought and the body. This connection can serve as a model for the one being resurrected. He too must have a similar connection. Therefore, your objective is to communicate your thought to the one being resurrected and thus he will have the connection between the thought and the body similar to yours. It will immediately shape the resurrection and it will happen significantly faster.

So, the resurrection occurs through your communication of your thoughts about the physical body to the one being resurrected. At the Worldview level these thoughts, in fact, coincide with his thoughts, and for you they are your own.

## 24. REGISTERING THE THOUGHT OF THE ONE BEING RESURRECTED IN A DISTANT AREA OF THE WORLD.

The method is as follows. You examine the thoughts of the one being resurrected, transfer them to the infinitely distant part of the World, into the past or into the infinite future, and watch these thoughts creating an image of the one being resurrected, both physical and spiritual, watch them ensuring the infinite development of this person.

With proper orientation towards infinite remoteness, this method provides a fast resurrection.

## 25. THE TRANSFORMATION OF THE WORLDVIEW ON THE BASIS OF SYMMETRY.

The idea of this method is as follows. Viewing the entire World, place it, for example, onto a plane or onto a sphere. The Worldview may be as well created as certain notions. The point here is to assign symmetry, not necessarily mathematically. What will be symmetry for you in this case is not that important. You decide. You may assign symmetry, let's say, relative to a point or a line, or a plane, or even relative to a thought. Having chosen the element, relative to which you assign symmetry, your objective is as follows. While transferring your Worldview through the chosen element, which defines symmetry, you must communicate your knowledge to the one being resurrected at the very moment of crossing this element.

To clarify what was said I will give you a specific example. Let's take a sheet of paper, lying on the table. Having viewed even only a part of the World, for example, the side of the sheet, facing you, you turn the sheet over and fractions of a second before its other side touches the table, that is, at the very moment of its being turned over, you must instantaneously communicate your view, your concept of the World to the one being resurrected.

So, on the basis of any chosen conditional symmetry you transform the Worldview and at the moment of this transformation you almost instantaneously transmit your knowledge to the soul of the one being resurrected. And in this case the resurrection will be the result of your World transformation. And this is a mechanism and a method of the resurrection.

## 26. THE CONTROL OF THE WORLD IN THE AREA OF ITS SELF-ORGANIZATION.

The World is created by God. In his own image and likeness.

When the question arises of how the Creator was organized, the answer to it is as follows. He organized himself. And the answer to the question of what was there before God's self-creation is this: it should be taken into account that it is only our ordinary consciousness perceives the World through the prism of time. In higher states of consciousness the situation is entirely different. Let's recall once more the words given in Introduction, which distinguish one of the characteristics of higher states of consciousness: "And swore… there would be no time". In Divine reality there is no notion of time.

In the process of self-organization the Creator was creating all the elements of the World including man. To every animal, plant, to every microstructure and macrouniverse and, generally, to every World element, corresponds precise information of its interconnection with man. Mentally communicating this knowledge to the one being resurrected, you, in fact, communicate the method of self-organization to him, the same that was used by the Creator himself.

## 27. THE WORLD TRANSFORMATION INTO THE AREA OF ITS EVOLUTION.

You view the World. There is a multitude of connections in it. You know some of them, suspect some others, and there are connections, you will know about in the future. So, your aim is to transform the World into the area of the future, into the area of its evolution. And it is the resurrection that must be this evolution of the World, it is the eternal life that must be the evolution of the World, and it is this image that you must disseminate into the future.

In practice it means that by means of your inner spiritual impulse you must wish it, you must demand it from the World, and you must try to evolve it at once to an infinite level. And as soon as you have done it, it will become significantly easier for you to resurrect and understand all the processes, related to the resurrection methodology.

## 28. TRANSFORMING THE SURROUNDING ENVIRONMENT INTO THE AREA OF YOUR THINKING.

From the information point of view the transformation of the surrounding environment into the area of thinking is done by means of two or three impulses, directed towards mastering this environment. That is, as you master the environment, you simultaneously transform it into the area of thinking.

In practice it looks as follows. When doing some professional job, or doing some work around the house, or, doing anything at all, you must see all this, the entire process, in the area of your thinking. Because one may perform acts automatically, without being aware. So, your aim is to do everything mindfully; in the area of thinking you must see what exactly is happening, you must see the entire picture, including yourself, as if from the side. And when you are able to act in this manner and transform the surrounding environment into the area of your thinking against the background of the thought of the resurrection, you will be able to resurrect.

29. PHYSICAL REALITY CONTROL, DIRECTED TOWARDS OBTAINING MATTER, NECESSARY FOR THE RESURRECTION.

This kind of control of the physical reality is that you take the physical matter, needed for the one being resurrected, out of space, out of air, out of water and out of food.

In practice this control is done as follows. You examine the area of the whereabouts of the one being resurrected irrespectively of the existence there of air, water, food, etc. You create all this by yourself as if anew, that is, re-create by control, mentally. As a result the one being resurrected comes to the area created by you. Next, the adaptation to the collective consciousness area, that is, to the entire World, takes place, as a result of which from the very start the resurrected will not be separated from the living. That is, using this method the resurrected won't be separated from the living right from the first moment after the resurrection.

30. THE TRANSFORMATION OF THE SYSTEM OF KNOWLEDGE OF THE ONE BEING RESURRECTED INTO THE SYSTEM OF KNOWLEDGE HE WILL NEED FOR THE RESURRECTION AS WELL AS AFTER THE RESURRECTION.

The one being resurrected, of course, has his own system of knowledge. However, for the resurrection he has to possess the very knowledge, necessary for the resurrection. He can, of course, mentally refer to certain information either in advance, before the resurrection or directly at the moment of the resurrection.

As I have said, for the resurrection he must have transformed knowledge. I am speaking of the system of knowledge, which will allow him to always be in the state of life, to never die, to have his own methods for achieving it and so on.

You've got to help him make such a transformation of knowledge. Here is how it is done in practice. You focus your attention above his image, above his head, and communicate your knowledge of life, of the resurrection, of the infinite development to him. And it will lead to the resurrection.

It is worth noting that this same method can be applied for health restoration. You may apply the described procedure to any person. And besides health restoration it also gives a person an understanding of the resurrection and the development of the immortality ideology, that is, of eternal life.

31. CONTROL OF LIVE REALITY APPLIED TO ALL OF ITS ELEMENTS.

You apply everything, related from your perspective to the notion of life, to all elements of reality, and as a result the resurrection occurs in one of these elements. Application of the notion of life to all elements of reality is done in the following way. You are aware that life germinates and grows everywhere, in all systems, in all places. In this case it comes out that you are a life bearer, you are a bearer of its evolution, and that is exactly why the resurrection takes place in one of the elements of reality.

Methodologically it may look like this. We may examine the life of a person or of a butterfly or of a plant. We observe these particular phenomena around us. A plant, for example, interacts with the soil. The soil provides it with nutrients, and owing to it a plant grows. This is a common situation. But what if we raise a question about the possibility of a plant growing, for example, inside a rock? Considering such a situation requires a mental effort. So, you must visualize how a plant could develop and grow inside a rock. And when you develop these images to the level of actual control, that is, when real plants can grow out of rocks, then the resurrection can be achieved.

32. CONTROL OF THE PHYSICAL REALITY, DIRECTED TOWARDS THE RELATIONS HARMONIZATION BETWEEN YOU AND THE ONE BEING RESURRECTED, AND AFTER THE RESURRECTION BETWEEN YOU AND ALREADY THE RESURRECTED.

What is the harmonization, mentioned in the name of the method? The matter is that the one being resurrected regards you as someone, who initiates him and helps him, but the resurrected considers you and himself to be at the same levels of development. So, the harmonization of relations is that during the period of the resurrection the one being resurrected must be at the same level with you, even though he himself might think that he depends on you to a certain extent. And when you guide him into the structure of full control, that is, of complete freedom and independence, then the one being resurrected, being, of course, in contact with you, will be very stable and independent as a result of the knowledge you have provided him with. And besides, this method of the resurrection will enable him to communicate more knowledge to others.

33. THOUGHT CONTROL, DIRECTED TOWARDS THE EXISTENCE OF THOUGHTS IN

ALL THE ELEMENTS OF REALITY, IN THE ENTIRE WORLD, IN ALL THE SEGMENTS OF THE WORLD.

When you develop your thought so that it starts to exist in the whole World, you then have the resurrection of a person in the right point of space-time. Indeed, when a thought is in the entire World, in all of the World elements, then it is, naturally, also where this resurrection has already occurred, in the right point, at the right time. This approach provides also the methodology of the thinking that controls reality.

34. THE RESURRECTION OF A PERSON BY MEANS OF TRANSFERRING HIS IMAGE FROM THE FUTURE INTO THE PRESENT.

The suggested method is based on the following. Not only what takes place at present, but also what may happen in the future needs to be regarded as the elements of reality. The future already has this particular person, who you intend to resurrect, resurrected. This is an element of reality of the future. And when you transfer this element of reality of the future, which contains the resurrected, as an image here into the present, then you thus perform the resurrection.

35. ADVANCING THE IMAGE OF MAN INTO ALL THE INFORMATION ELEMENTS, INTO ALL THE WORLD ELEMENTS.

This method of the resurrection consists in your attempting to bring into life the reality, similar to human life, everywhere. And you realize the necessity of human development in God's own image and likeness. Visualizing the image of man in all the sections of the World and thus, in fact, as if advancing the image infinitely further away from you, you, naturally, at the same time advance infinitely away the image of the person, you intend to resurrect. Acting in this manner, you advance his image to the point of space-time, where the information will work towards the resurrection.

36. GAINING HEALTH UNDER THE CONDITIONS OF THE DEVELOPMENT OF THE SURROUNDING WORLD AND GAINING HEALTH FOR THE INFINITE DEVELOPMENT OF THE ONE BEING RESURRECTED, FOR THE INFINITE DEVELOPMENT OF THE LIVING ONES, AND FOR THE INFINITE DEVELOPMENT OF THE WORLD.

Gaining health is based on the soul – body connection. You must be gaining health by means of your observation of the body functioning on the basis of the knowledge of the soul. This knowledge can be enhanced, using consciousness. That is, in this way, virtually, one can evolve infinitely.

37. RECEIVING INFORMATION THROUGH THE DIRECT VISION CHANNEL.

You must look with your physical eyes and receive the information on the resurrection along the line of your physical sight. Further you act according to the information received.

38. GAINING THE CONNECTION AMONG DISTANT AND CLOSE ELEMENTS OF AN EVENT.

You must be able to gain the connections between distant and close elements of an event. In this way you will be able to control the resurrection.

39. GAINING THE CONNECTION LINES AMONG EVENTS.

You must concentrate on the events until you gain the connection lines. The resurrection may occur within these lines. And you will be shown the way and the method.

40. INFORMATION TRANSFORMATION TOWARDS THE RESURRECTION.

If there is information regarding a person's departure, you must transform this information, and in such a way that the departure information with all the departure concomitant circumstances after its transformation should work towards the resurrection, that is, that by means of this transformation you should perform the resurrection.

## 41. REALIZING THE PLANS OF THE ONE BEING RESURRECTED WITH REGARD TO ETERNAL LIFE.

Under present-day conditions each one being resurrected strives for eternal life. You must review his plans after the resurrection and help their realization. You need to start working on that right away. You may learn about the plans of the one being resurrected by means of clairvoyance. If you start helping the one being resurrected in realization of his plans right away, his resurrection will occur faster.

## 42. ACQUIRING THE RESURRECTION SKILLS FOR THE INFINITE DEVELOPMENT.

Seeking to master the practice of the resurrection, from the very start you must assume the principle of infinite development as a basis. Then the first resurrection will happen sooner.

By practicing the resurrection, you, naturally, as with any practice, acquire the appropriate skills. So, these skills must become such that you should be able to resurrect always, everywhere and in any circumstances.

## 43. RECOGNIZING THE SIGNS OF THE ONE BEING RESURRECTED IN THE ELEMENTS OF REALITY.

In various elements of reality you must detect the sensations, which were or could be near a live person. Based on the perception of these sensations you must see, feel whether the resurrection is in progress or it has already occurred and you only need to achieve a meeting with the resurrected. In short, wherever you are, your reality perception must be such that you should be able to detect these nuances.

## 44. ACQUIRING SUCH A THINKING STATUS WHEN THE THOUGHT OF THE RESURRECTION BECOMES AN EVER PRESENT THOUGHT.

The gist of this method is as follows. Your thinking needs to be such that you should always, in any circumstances, along with any other thoughts, have in mind the thought of the resurrection. That is, the constant presence of the thought of the resurrection must become a characteristic feature of your thinking.

## 45. RECOGNIZING THE ONE BEING RESURRECTED IN IMAGES.

If you look, for example, at a tree or at any other element of reality, then among the variety of the perceptions being received, you must recognize the image of the one being resurrected. You may see, let's say, his entire, full size figure, but it may be only his face.

In our childhood many of us used to scrutinize picture puzzles. The drawing may look, for example, like a tree with some bushes nearby, and you are to find a hare. You are looking at the drawing but are not seeing any hare. It seems it's just not there. You start turning the picture in different directions. Nothing. No hare. However, continuing your scrutiny of the picture, you, at some point, suddenly distinctly see the hare. It is, for example, under a bush with its ears close to its head. And now you are surprised at how you could have failed to see it right away.

You must do something similar in respect of the image of the one being resurrected when perceiving the elements of reality. And the image must be such that it should lead to the resurrection or to the specific location of the resurrected, if the resurrection has already taken place.

## 46. INVOLVING THE ENTIRE EXTERNAL INFORMATION FOR THE RESURRECTION.

You need to search for and involve any external information in the process of the resurrection. Though it is always better to use your own thoughts and your own knowledge based, first of all, on the principles of the resurrection.

## 47. INVOLVING THE SUPERMIND LEVEL, GOD'S LEVEL, FOR THE RESURRECTION.

The gist of this method is to turn to God for the resurrection.

## 48. TURNING TO GRIGORI GRABOVOI FOR RECEIVING THE INFORMATION ON THE

## RESURRECTION AND FOR RECEIVING DIRECT ASSISTANCE.

You may refer to me as the one practicing the resurrection and the one, who created its theory. You may ask me mentally for establishing a telepathic communication and for receiving the information on the resurrection necessary for you. You may turn to other people as well, to those, who practice the resurrection.

## 49. GAINING THE SIGNS OF THE RESURRECTION THROUGH EXTENDING CONSCIOUSNESS TO YOUR ENTIRE FUTURE.

It is necessary to extend your consciousness to your entire future in a way as to become aware of your eternal future in the eternal evolution of the World. Such awareness allows for the instantaneous resurrection.

## 50. GAINING THE SIGNS OF THE RESURRECTION BY MEANS OF EXTENDING YOUR CONSCIOUSNESS TO THE ENTIRE INFORMATION OF THE PAST, THE PRESENT AND THE FUTURE ALTOGETHER.

You must extend your consciousness to the entire information of the past, the present and the future, so that your consciousness should perceive this entire information in real time and that you should know for sure that this consciousness is extendible absolutely everywhere, as in time so in space. In this case the resurrection will occur exactly as you wish.

Having read all these methods from beginning to end, having linked all this with the main principles of the resurrection, with the entire book content and having practiced them, you will have the concrete instrument for the resurrection of people. It may also be used for health restoration, for restoration of any information object, for control of events. But its primary purpose is the salvation of people from the threat of global destruction. And that is why you must always have this concrete thought in mind that all your actions are aimed towards the salvation of people from the threat of global destruction.

# CHAPTER IV
# THE PRINCIPLES OF RESURRECTION AND EVERYDAY LIFE

In this chapter we'll consider the connection of the principles of resurrection with everyday life. We've already known that the principles of resurrection are the laws of everlasting development of life. And so the using of these principles in our everyday life leads to its favorable transformation. With the mastering of these principles and bringing them in the everyday practice, our life acquires the firm base for the creative development.

First of all I'll tell about new medicine, i.e. the medicine of future millenniums. But I want to underline that this medicine has already started to work. Its era has already begun. This new medicine sets its main task, which is eternal life of living people that is immortality. Immortality is already becoming reality of the present.

An important task of the new medicine is also resurrection of "gone" persons.

The theory and the practice of resurrection underlies the new medicine. These are exactly the theory and practice of resurrection that define the principles of the new medicine and, first of all, the principle of full regeneration of matter.

The World can be considered as the totality of cause-connected phenomena. The Creator created the World the same way He had created Himself. Therefore, in this chapter we will consider any development as that one, which happens on the basis of those laws, which were realized by the Creator for His self-creation. Based on this, it's possible to say that the expression "in God's image" means first of all, how each creative element of the World can be self-created.

IT IS CLEAR THAT THE CREATOR IS TRULY MAN BECAUSE HE CREATED HIM. THUS MAXIMUM AND SALUTARY DISPLAY OF CREATOR IS HIS INCARNATION AS MAN AND HIS WAY AS MAN. AND THEN THE CREATOR CAN PASS KNOWLEDGE TO EVERYBODY AS A MAN TO A MAN.

When we use the expression "in God's image", it's said not about the outer likeness but about some profound ties and interaction of forms.

When we speak about the principle of likeness, we also mean that the Creator, having taken the image of man and having formed him, reproduced the whole surrounding World. Reproduction of the World is carried out in such way that the image of man leads to the creation of each element of the World. And the principle of self-creation has been laid down in each element of the World. Therefore, on the basis of the form of the physical body of man and his thought forms it's always possible to get any necessary information about any event in the World. At present there are devices, which register thought-forms.

Any event can be transformed into a favorable one, when you learn to change a thought form purposefully. The structured consciousness can purposefully change thought forms. This approach of consciousness structuring for control of thought forms makes the foundation of my Teachings "About Salvation and Harmonious Development". This Study has been officially approved in the Charter documents of UNESCO. My long-term practice fully confirmed all provisions of my Teachings. The received results are included in the three-volume edition "The Practice of Control. The Way of Salvation." The main provisions of my Teachings are such that any person can master them easily irrespective of his age. So, my disciples begin their practical work immediately and quickly achieve results in saving and harmonious development.

When the question of what the real salvation is of all people is asked, the answer is the following. The real salvation of all people and for all times is passing of real knowledge from the Creator. And each man, who received this knowledge, must spread them as extensively as possible. This is exactly the way my Teachings "About Salvation and Harmonious Development" is constructed. The Teachings provides technologies of cognition, practical application of the knowledge and their spreading. When everybody will be developing in such a way, then the systematic safety of the development of the World will be guaranteed. All mentioned above makes it possible to see that the World has absolutely exact shapes, absolutely clear system, and each action in the World has its corresponding link, a definite structure and absolutely precise coordinates. All events in the World, past and future, have absolutely precise coordinates, if we consider the World as developing one from the form of the Creator.

Using the picture of the World, which I've just described, that is, in fact, using this principle of the form, image and likeness, which the Creator has spread to all phenomena of the World, applying this principle to the practice of your life, you can see that those principles of resurrection and those methods of resurrection, which I've stated, are applicable for restoration of any object of information.

In fact, the principles and methods of resurrection are the principles and methods of control of reality. If you consider all principles and methods of resurrection from this point of view, you'll see that their application to any process of reality for its full recreation means also complete control of a corresponding element of reality. Based on this and on the picture of the World, which I've just introduced and which shows that the world is recreated in the image of God, based on this, you can see a concrete technology showing, how the principles and methods of resurrection of people are applied to restoration of health, to control of events. And, of course, control of events is a significantly wider notion: recovery of health is included in control of events as its natural and harmonic link.

The principles of resurrection of people are fundamental laws of the World. The same way as you can use every day the force of gravity for various purposes you can use fundamental laws of the World for solving concrete tasks.

Further I'll show how main principles of resurrection are applied for cognition of the World, for control of events and for treatment. Of course, these are only some kinds of their application. Like any fundamental laws, they can be applied everywhere. Application of principles of resurrection in everyday practical activity proves that resurrection is a usual process in people's life.

## PARAGRAPH 1. THE NEW MEDICINE AS ONE OF THE CONCEQUENCES OF THE PRINCIPLES OF RESURRECTION.

In this paragraph I'd like to show that understanding of the principles of resurrection results in understanding of the essence of the new medicine. For this purpose I'll again consider one by one the main principles of resurrection, but this time I'll do it in short.

1.1. THE TRUE STATUS OF THE WORLD IS IN ETERNAL LIFE. ETERNAL LIFE ENSURES TRUE WORLD STABILITY. THE DESIRE FOR A STABLE WORLD CREATES ETERNAL LIFE. HE WHO HAS NOT EXPERIENCED DEATH IS THE BASE, WHICH REPRODUCES

EVERYTHING ELSE. GOD IS SUCH A BASE. GOD IS ETERNAL, HE HAS NEVER EXPERIENCED DEATH. EVERYTHING ELSE FOLLOWS FROM THIS FACT (1.1).

The first part of the principle is about mutual movements: aspiration for the stable World creates the eternal life, and the eternal life provides the true stability of the World. Here the principle of mutual aspiration and interdependent development is stated. It follows from this principle that any element of the World in the dynamic of its development exists as a structure, consisting at least of two components. The second part of this principle is about God who is the basis, which reproduces all the rest.

You can apply this principle to consideration of any phenomenon. And you must also take into account that that has been said in the beginning of this chapter. For example, there is a need to regenerate a plant. Regeneration of the plant at the level of thought results in regeneration of this plant in the physical reality.

Or let's consider, for example, regeneration of some organs of a body. Regeneration of any organ at the level of thought results in regeneration of this organ in physical reality. The reality is controllable. We discussed this issue when we considered principle (4.3) of the second chapter.

1.2. ETERNAL LIFE IS THE PRINCIPLE OF DEVELOPMENT OF DIVINE REALITY.

The whole World is developing According to this principle. Each element of the World is created is such a way that a moment is its eternal status of development. Based on this, it is possible to restore any object.

It is also possible to control any events. For this you should proceed from the principle of eternity of this event in one point. This chapter first of all is about health. Thus, first of all I mean that the required event is health recovery. This principle, first of all, regenerates blood circulatory and cardio-vascular systems, and then, as a result, the organism as a whole. Regeneration of the organism occurs through the notion of eternity of each element of development.

It is important here to consider exactly the status of t Divine reality, because the real Divine reality is always developing in the direction of the eternal.

### 1.3. OUR CONSCIOUSNESS PERCEIVES WHAT EXISTS IN OUR CONSCIOUSNESS AS REALITY.

It follows from this principle that any element of reality can be reproduced by our consciousness. Understanding of this provides control of any reality including your own health and health of other people. This principle first of all regenerates cellular system and metabolic processes in an organism.

### 1.4. THE STRUCTURE OF THE WORLD SHOULD INTENSIVELY DEVELOP WITHIN THE DEVELOPMENT OF OUR OWN CONSCIOUSNESS.

If you consider this principle in terms of health and control of events, you can see that the whole World is reflected in the consciousness, and intensive development of the World generates your own organism and generates an event.

When you realize a new origination of each element of the World as the fact of the following life, it becomes clear to you that the medicine of the future will consider each element in the past or future as a moment of new birth of an organism. By connecting these discrete elements of birth, which originate from your soul, you achieve that your own consciousness can already control an element of development.

### 1.5. RESURRECTION IS COMPREHENSION OF TRUE CONSCIOUSNESS.

On the one hand, restoration of an object helps it to become eternal and an eternal object always possesses maximum possible information value, and it has maximum possible number of metabolic processes and connections. On the other hand, the real truth is characterized by the maximum comprehension of an object. Thus, when we say that resurrection is comprehension of true consciousness, it means that the ability to restore any object characterizes the truth of consciousness.

Hence it is clear that the ability of control arises as a spiritual characteristic.

### 1.6. ETERNAL LIFE CONDITIONS THE NECESSITY OF THE DEVELOPMENT OF SOUL.

On the one hand, eternal life conditions the necessity of development of soul. On the other hand, the status of soul should be considered as an initial one, it is exactly it that forms eternal life. We again see here the principle of mutual aspiration and interdependent development. The principle enables anyone to control endless number of events.

1.7. THE PRINCIPLE OF DIVINITY: ASPIRATION FOR IMPERISHABILITY OF BODY, FOR ETERNAL LIFE, AND FOR DEVELOPMENT OF TRUE CONSCIOUSNESS IS THE PRACTICE OF THE UPPERMOST FLOURISHING OF HUMAN EXISTANCE.

To apply this principle to control of events, you must consider the status of imperishability of body as the true status of any event.

By building an event around the eternal body you'll get control of the event and full health correspondingly.

1.8. IT IS SUFFICIENT TO HAVE ONE PERSON WHO CAN RESURRECT AND RESTORE THE WORLD TO ENSURE THAT IT IS NOT POSSIBLE TO DESTROY THE WORLD.

According to this principle proceeding from a single perception, which is from the perception of a single person, it is possible to have the eternal World. This can be explained in the following way: though the perception of a single person is described, the soul of man is an infinite ion its volume, it is a part of the World and it is available in any event, moreover, the soul of man is an organizing structure of the World.

Awareness of this makes it possible to transfer of control events to the level with control of time. It means that you can use this principle to control events on the required time.

1.9. RESURRECTION AND ASCERTAINMENT OF THE FACT OF RESURRECTION IS A SIMULTANEOUS FOR THE ENTIRE WORLD PROCESS.

When you apply this principle for control of some personal events you should consider yourself as a bearer of the status of the World that means that the World is also a manifestation of your soul in common perception. Besides, you must take into account the simultaneousness of ascertainment of the fact of resurrection for the whole World mentioned in the wording of the principle. Proceeding from this, you see that any element of the world is as displayable as you are, and thus it is controllable. You begin to understand the mechanisms of the manifestation of the World and get control of the universal reality.

## 1.10. CORRECT UNDERSTANDING OF THE CORRELATION BETWEEN THE CONSCIOUSNESS OF MAN AND HIS ORGANS PROVIDES RESURRECTION. RESURRECTION IS AN ACT OF CREATION.

In order to understand fully measure the action of this principle, you should take into account one more important principle, which says: A man is the base of the world. The form of a man creates elements of the world and defines events MAN IS THE BASIS OF THE WORLD. THE FORM OF MAN CREATES ELEMENTS OF THE WORLD AND DETERMINES EVENTS.

As an example I can say that even a simple doll, having the form of man and put in vacuum, in some time can create oxygen near itself. And it will happen only because that doll has the form of man.

The stated above principle is closely interrelated with principle "MAN IN THE WHOLE EXTERNAL AND INTERNAN WORLD SIMULTANEOUSLY". When you consider some organs of a person who is being resurrected, it means that their construction depends on the consciousness of man, that comprehension of the form of man creates organs the person who is being resurrected. Preceding from this, with the help of concentration on your different forms and with the help of control you can receive full regeneration of an organism.

Thus this principle says that a form forms events. When you see some event in front, then the cognition of the form of the participants of this event or even of a form of some nearby object provides you with control of the event.

## 1.11. DEVELOPMENT OF MAN SHOULD BE CONSIDERED AS A COMPLEX DEVELOPMENT OF THE ENTIRE EXISTING WORLD.

Complexity in development is, first of all, the involvement of all parts in the process, of all elements of the structure. And the important role here plays the notion of simultaneousness. Only simultaneous coverage and accounting of all elements of the World can provide its stability in the process of its uninterrupted development.

When you consider application of this principle to control of events, you see that control is carried out through the complexness reflected in the development of man.

## 1.12 THE PRINCIPLE OF THE RESURRECTION CORRELATES WITH THE PRINCIPLE OF MAN'S ORGANIZATION, WHICH TAKES INTO

ACCOUNT ALL-TIME DEVELOPMENT OF THE ENTIRE EXTERNAL WORLD.

When we speak about organization of man, we mean not only his physical form but also organization of his thinking and actions. If you take into account the whole all-time development of the entire external World, you see correspondingly organization a man and hence you see each of his events. This is a fundamental principle, which enables you to control on the basis of understanding.

1.13 GRIEF, DEPRESSION, AND NOSTALGIA ARE NOT THE WAY OF UNDERSTADING THE WORLD. ONLY JOY, LIGHT, AND LOVE ARE THE WAY OF UNDERSTANDING OF THE WORLD.

Any creative event is an event, which is built in a creative way. And creative building of an event takes place faster on the basis of the positive emotions. That's why exactly a creative event always contains joy, light, and love as the elements of building of the structure of such events. And that's why exactly joy, light, and love are the way of understanding the World.

1.14 PERSONALITY REMAINS INTACT AFTER BIOLOGICAL DEATH, INCLUDING CREMATION CASES. IS THIS LAST CASE EACH PARTICLE OF THE ASH, RECEIVED AFTER CREMATION, IS CONNECTED TO THE STRUCTURE OF PERSONALITY OF THAT ONE WHO WAS CREMATED.

This principle makes it possible to understand that there is everything in each partial element of the event contains everything related to the entire event. That's why any event can be reconstructed just on the basis of some characteristics of the participants, or based on the name, or even without any name just with the help of clairvoyance.

For control of events this principle means the following fundamental law: "IT IS ALWAYS POSSIBLE TO CARRY OUT A CREATIVE CONTROL BECAUSE EVERYTHING IS RESTORABLE." And as a consequence of this there is another fundamental law: "IN ANY COMBINATIONS OF EVENTS IT IS ALWAYS POSSIBLE TO RESCUE THE WORLD". Proceeding from this, any creative control always results in the desirable result.

1.15. SPACE DEPENDS ON WHERE DIFFERENT TIME INTERVALS

INTERSECT. AS A RESULT OF THAT THE EARTH CAN BE INCREASED IN SIZE.

Time can be considered as an element, which in the process of its development coexists with space. This means that each time interval can be considered as an element, correlated either with the space itself or with some object in the space, if we have a relocation of an object, we can introduce a time coordinate. The same, of course, can be done if we have several moving objects. If there are no relocations, we can introduce a time coordinate proceeding from our perception, that is to say based on our certain feeling, a certain reaction we experience. And then time is clearly displayed as construction, the connection of which with space is turned to be formed on the basis of dependence on our consciousness. Time can be indicated in your consciousness, though you can avoid doing this, that is to say, time can be excluded from the sphere of perception.

So, if an object is moving, then, quite naturally, you have to describe somehow its movement, and then you have to introduce time. If the objects are immovable, you just appoint time in your consciousness. However in reality these situations can occur in the consciousness simultaneously and moreover there might be several objects.

Taking into account connection between consciousness and space-time, you can see that appearing crossings of time intervals can result in change of space. Increase of a volume turns to be connected with the increase of the amount of information. Generally, it is always possible to control any event, increasing the amount of information.

We may have a bit different approach to understanding of this. Suppose there is a movement of some object. If you just look at it, then, nevertheless, you can get an impulse in your consciousness, based on which another object can start moving. That is to say movement of one object on the basis of principle of transfer of information can cause movement of another object. So, this movement can happen due to your will and then, your spiritual level will pride a possibility to increase space. I'll remember you that space and time are constructions of consciousness.

For explanation of the considered principle I gave here concrete examples of movement, but it's possible to manage without them. If to consider the essence of the stated above, it is clear that you always can increase any information as much as you need to realize the desirable event.

2.1. MAN IS AN ETERNAL SUBSTANCE BY THE PRINCIPLE OF HIS CREATION. THAT IS WHY RESURRECTION IS BASED ON REVEALING THE ETERNAL IN MAN.

Detection of the eternal in any object of information results in your ability to always see the structure of the given object in all of its manifestations. And in this case the object becomes absolutely controllable.

2.2. THERE IS INTERDEPENDENCE BETWEEN THE SPIRITUAL AND PHYSICAL STRUCTURES. BY CHANGING THE INFORMATION ON THE PHYSICAL STRUCTURE IN THE SPHERE OF THE SPIRIT, WE CAN CHANGE THE SPIRIT TO THE LEVEL, WHEN IT WILL BE ABLE TO CHANGE ANY PHYSICAL STRUCTURE, AS WELL AS TO CREATE A PHYSICAL BODY.

This principle makes it possible to understand the following important approach to control of events. Let's suppose that some object participates in an event we are interested in. Then, by changing information in the sphere of this event we can change it so that it can influence on the event itself. That is to say it is possible to control an event by changed of the informational structure just in one object of information. However the change of the informational structure of the object makes it different. That is why the control is carried out in fact through another object, through the object, in which you've changed the informational structure in the way you need.

2.3. TIME AND SPACE DO NOT LIMIT THE DURATION OF LIFE. THE CONCEPT OF DURATION OF LIFE IS FORMED BY THE RELATION OF THE SPIRIT TO SPACE AND TIME.

This principle says that in reality any object is always eternal. When you look at some object it always exists. Transferring this spiritual state on the element of the required event, you receive that the event itself gets fully under your control.

In the particular case you receive absolute health because your mood in the relation to health in this status of the Eternity allows you to make your health eternal.

2.4 THE PRINCIPLE OF IMMORTALITY AND, THEREFORE, THE

PRINCIPLE OF RESTORATION, REGENERATION AFTER A POSSIBLE BIOLOGICAL DEATH IS EMBODIED IN THE PRIMORDIAL CAUSE, IN THE PRIMORDIAL NATURE OF IMPULSES OF MAN'S NATURAL DEVELOPMENT.

Referring to control of reality this principle says that the principle of restoration of any object after its destruction has been laid in the very base of any object. Control of any object can be called an event. You bring into it many various elements of events, for instance, the direction that the World will not be destructed. This introduction in of the elements of events is carried out in the following way. You introduce the method of development into the principle of restoration by your will or spiritual effort, and then not a single element of the event can be destroyed. An appearing harmonic structure provides you with such a control of the event that you don't have to make any efforts, and the event, is developing as if independently in a more favorable for you way.

2.5.   AN IMPULSE AIMED TOWARDS THE RESURRECTION IS ALWAYS AIMED TOWARDS THE INFINITE EVOLUTION OF THE ONE BEING RESURRECTED.

Any impulse, directed to resurrection, is always directed to the infinite development of the person who is being resurrected. Such directivity of this impulse is explained by the fact that full restoration of man underlies this principle. And as a result based on the law on the universal connections for all elements of information you get absolutely full restoration at all levels.

2.6. THE ONE BEING RESURRECTED ALWAYS SEES AND IS AWARE OF THE PROCESS OF RESURRECTION AND ALWAYS PARTICIPATES IN THE RESURRECTION AS AN INITIATIVE PERSON.

This principle makes it possible to understand that any object of the information always reacts to changes, which take place in your consciousness. When you control an event or, as in the concrete case we've considered, restore an object of information, on the creative level this object of information always aspires for facilitation of harmonious development of the events. It means that each element of information during its restoration always facilitates movement to the maximum harmony. This happens on the basis of the principle, which was provided in the beginning of the chapter and which says about the development in the image and likeness of God. And the likeness of God is at the same time God's creation. And as the harmony has been put in each element of reality, it is quite naturally that each element of reality interacts with you harmonically. And thus when you control an event you can use any number of elements.

2.7. THE ONE BEING RESURRECTED ALWAYS KNOWS FOR A FACT THAT AFTER THE RESURRECTION HE WILL LIVE AS A NORMAL PERSON.

This principle allows to understand that any event, which you control, any your organ, any element of information, all of them are actually constructed in such way that absolutely precise information on what they must be, was initially put in them.

Therefore, when you perform some action, for instance, you regenerate an organ of a person, standard sample has been already put in this process, in regeneration of the organ, because this organ contains information on what it must be, and thus, after its regeneration it will always be as it has initially always been.

If you carry out spiritual materialization of some absolutely new object, which has never had any analogues before, anyway it will always be harmonic and maximum developed in the image and likeness of God, in other words, as a matter of fact, in line with the God's will.

The mentioned above relates to creation of new systems and new technologies as well. The given examples help to understand that each element of the World was initially created by God. This is exactly what the considered principle means.

When you control an event, and simultaneously control the level of an element, which was initially created by God, your control will always be harmonic.

2.8. THE ONE BEING RESURRECTED ALWAYS THINKS THAT THE LIVING ONE WILL TREAT HIM AS EQUAL, HE DOES NOT FEEL SEPARATED FROM THE LIVING IN ANY WAY, AND HE FEELS LIKE A NORMAL PERSON, NO DIFFERENT FROM THE LIVING.

There is a principle of equality of all objects of information. In line with it ANY OBJECT OF INFORMATION EQUALLY COEXISTS WITH ANY OTHER

OBJECT OF INFORMATION. This is a law of the World. Being aware of this law, you can control any event by forming the status of freedom for it. In other words control is often ensured by that that you add the status of freedom to an event or an object, which they previously hadn't got or just hadn't been aware of.

So, you can regenerate your own organism or organisms of other people, you can control reality by adding the status of freedom to events and objects. All mentioned above helps to understand that the principle of full freedom of each person is a natural spiritual principle of development.

2.9. AFTER THE RESURRECTION IT IS NECESSARY TO PROVIDE SOME GUIDANCE TO THE RESURRECTED ONE, EXPLAINING HIS NEW STATE, ATTRIBUTABLE TO THE FACT THAT NOW HE HAS A PHYSICAL BODY.

This principle enables anyone to control events based on their consequences. This is another method of control of reality

A bit earlier we discussed another mechanism. In that approach we changed at once in the situation as required and further on the events had been developing in the favorable for us direction.

The approach, we are discussing now, is quite different. We do not change the initial situation; we begin from its effects. To be more exact, with the help of clairvoyance or by some other way we can follow up development of the event, see its further way. Possessing these data, we can choose a moment from the future we have watched, or, it would be better to say, from the seen by us further development of events, which were going to take place. Changing this chosen moment in the area of controlling information, that is to say, by change of one of the effects of the initial situation, we through this change of the effect implement change of the initial situation. And the new initial situation results, of course, in some new further development of events, by the way, exactly to that one, which we need.

Apply this approach to your health, and you get absolute health. Like with any other correct approach.

2.10 A RESURRECTED PERSON FULLY RETAINS HIS PROFESSIONAL AND OTHER SKILLS, ACQUIRED EARLIER IN LIFE.

There is a principle: EACH ELEMENT OF REALITY ALWAYS PRESERVES

ALL INFORMATION ABOUT EVERYTHING. On the base of this principle each recreated object always preserves information, related, in particular, to it. Thus, resurrected person fully retains all skills he had acquired earlier in his life.

The knowledge of this principle makes it possible to control any object of information from any point and anytime. And it doesn't matter, for instance, that by the beginning of control the selected object had already moved to another place and functioned in quite different conditions.

2.11. THE CONCEPT OF SPIRIT PROVIDES THE TRUTH OF THE STRUCTURE OF COGNITION.

We know that spirit is the action of the soul. And the truth of the structure of cognition for any object of information and, first of all for man, is his characteristic embedded in his status. I have already mentioned this issue in the Introduction, when we discussed the receiving of information from the universal Cosmic Net.

On the base of this principle a control can be fast and simple, if your spiritual state is such, that it provides the following: the reaction of an object or a situation must be such that in the given moment it would give the biggest harmony of the World for your consciousness and at the same time on all levels. Thus, the control here is the awareness of that that it is necessary to introduce your own spiritual element into any event and as such to provide more harmony. In other words, you should have the necessary spiritual state that will exactly implement control.

Thus, the principle under consideration enables you to receive control through cognition, through the state of spirit at the maximum possible highest level.

2.12. ONE OF THE ASPECTS OF RESURRECTION IS RESTORATION OF CREATIVE CONSCIOUSNESS OF LIVING PEOPLE.

Reconstruction of creative consciousness of living people is one of the most important tasks. For its solution you can act in the following way.

When you look at any object, then by some kind of will effort you can pass creation to it. Thereby you can control an event by reconstructing the element of the creative development in it. If you want, for instance, to recover health, or you wish to control some event, related to your private affairs, or, let's say with business, then, first of all, you can reconstruct creative consciousness of those people, who participate in the event, including, of course, yourself. Or you can provide further development of creative consciousness of a person, if he's already had it. Or you can do something useful, for example, through your consciousness, through spirit make some ecological clearing of environment and as a result to get the control accordingly.

Thus, on the basis of the considered principle you get the control either by reconstructing and development of creative consciousness or just by a creative action.

2.13. To the process of resurrection we ought to approach (come up) at one and the same time as to the process of the reproduction of a fruit THE RESURRECTION PROCESS SHOULD BE REGARDED AT THE SAME TIME AS A PROCESS OF REPRODUCTION OF A FOETUS AS WELL.

Any process should be considered subject to its further development. This is what the discussed principle about. It says that you should control any event in such a way that you ensure that any of your actions would provide the necessary further development of this event.

2.14. THE SPIRITUAL DEVELOPMENT OF THE GONE ONES DOES NOT STOP. PERSONAL SPIRITUAL DEVELOPMENT ALWAYS CONTINUES AT ALL TIMES. THEREFORE AT SPIRITUAL LEVEL THE RESURRECTION IS UNDERSTOOD AS THE MANIFESTATION OF THE UNIVERSAL WORLD HARMONY. AND THAT IS PRECISELY WHY ON THE SPIRITUAL LEVELALL PEOPLE KNOW THAT THE UNIVERSAL RESURRECTION OF THE GONE ONES IS TO COME.

Each element of reality always possesses information about the possibility of full restoration of any other element. In relation to organism it means that reserve capacities of any organ are available in any other organ. This means that the structure of each cell is such that it contains a powerful reserve for a restoration of each element of another organism. In other words, any cell actually contains all elements of organism, and therefore we can restore the whole organism with the help of just a single impulse directed at restoration of one cell. The same is related to any event. According to the principle of universal connections each element of an event contains all other its elements. Therefore, we can reconstruct any event or control it from any point and with the help of any of its element.

### 3.1. ASPIRATION OF GOD AND MAN FOR UNITY WITHIN RECREATION AND REUNION RESULTS IN MATERILIZATION AND RESURRECTION.

We can also speak about God's aspiring for and generally of any object of information for personification of the idea of the Creator exactly within recreation.

The wording of the principle is about the aspiration of God and man for unity within recreation and reunion results in resurrection and materialization. This means not only materialization of an object but of an event as well. Based on this principle you can actually control any event, including a future one, which at present moment hasn't been displayed yet in the physical reality.

### 3.2. CONCENTRAION BY MAN OF HIS OWN CONSCIOUSNESS MIGHT RESULT IN A RADICAL CHANGE OF THE WORLD STRUCTURE.

This principle for the purpose of health improvement contains the following control. Consider your consciousness as an element of the World. Place it in the necessary for you area of the World, for instance, into some of the inner organs. As a result this inner organ will changed in line with what you put in your consciousness. Put perfect health in your consciousness and you will be able to fully recover both your health and the health of any other man.

### 3.3. PHISICAL BODY IS ALWAYS A PART OF THE SOUL

For recovery of one's health on the basis of this principle you should always consider body as a part of the soul, as manifestation of the soul. Using this approach you can rather easily restore your own organism or the organism of another person. Herewith it is important to understand that body is just a part of the soul.

Through the inner organs, through the organs of thinking, through any part of your organism you can get skills and any information from your own soul. It's possible to receive all this directly from the Creator. Because the soul of man is created by the Creator, this is His own creation. The soul is the light of the Creator.

When you can get knowledge straight from your own soul, it means that you have already been approached to God. But it's possible to get knowledge straight from the Lord. In this case you have direct knowledge. And in this case the unity with the Creator takes place just at the level of physical body. And as the soul, like direct knowledge, also descends directly from the Lord, then it turns out that you can have the status of the soul there, where the unity with the Creator takes place at the level of physical body. This means that physical body is a part of the soul.

And hereof it follows that each organ of physical body is structured based on the same principle of multifaceted functioning. So you can always reconstruct any of your organs or of any other man. This thereafter can be done with the help of concentration on your organs or on organs of any other person.

You can act in a different way. You can mentally pass this knowledge to another person and then he himself will be able to do for his health anything that is needed.

3.4. Either theoretically or practically a person can be considered as a structure of consciousness, having a body shell. BOTH THEORETICALLY AND PRACTICALLY MAN CAN BE REGARDED AS A STRUCTURE OF CONSCIOUSNESS THAT HAS A BODY SHELL.

Let's s consider, how we can use this principle for control of events. Each element of reality can be considered as a structure, which can bring to some actions in physical or in any other areas of reality. What can we say in the case, when we consider consciousness of a man in the relation to some object? The answer is this: the area of man's consciousness connected with the object is the area of reactions of this object or the area of its creation.

Appealing directly to the Creator one can see how the event is being created. Any event we can consider as manifestation of the will of the Creator. Understanding of the laws of development of the World, comprehension of that how God controls the World makes it possible to control any events.

3.5. AT THE LEVEL OF CREATION OF INFORMATION CONNECTIONS NO OBJECT OVERLAPS WITH ANY OTHER EXTERNAL OBJECT INCLUDING ITSELF. THE PRINCIPLE OF RESURRECTION OF MAN, OR THE PRINCIPLE OF RESTORATION OF ANY OBJECT, IS IN THE OVERLAPING OF INITIAL INFORMATION ABOUT THE OBJECT WITH THE DEVELOPING INFORMATION ABOUT ITSELF IN THE AREA OF THE EFFECT RELATIONS, WHICH APPEAR IN THE COURSE OF CREATION OF INFORMATION.

First of all, this principle makes it possible to understand what the autonomy is, that is independence of each element of the World. When some element of the World is being created, there is autonomy in every action within the process of its creation. And independence, selfness in every action is actually the freedom of will of the object of information.

When you consider some event from this point of view, on the basis of the principle of freedom of will, then, the situation for you looks absolutely transparent. You understand all ties of this event, and moreover you can see them far ahead. That is to say, you clearly see all ties: not only those, which exist at present, but those ones, which existed in the past, and those, which will appear in the future. That circumstance that you can see appearance of the future connections defines the exact technology of control of an event. To be more exact, the principle under consideration makes it possible to control any event on the basis of understanding of its further development.

Referring to health this principle means the following. In order to be completely healthy be harmonious connection of the organism with all elements of external reality is necessary. Understanding the role of these elements and taking into account their availability in your events, you can get remarkable health.

3.6. THE SYSTEM OF SPIRITUAL VIEWS OF THAT ONE WHO PRACTISES RESURRECTION IS EXACTLY THE PRINCIPLE OF SOCIETY ORGANIZATION AT THE SUBSEQUENT STAGES OF ITS DEVELOPMENT.

When you consider society as created on the basis of principle of self-creation and existing on the basis of full self-organization, that is, when you accept the way of development the Creator passed through, you, thus, accept the following principle of the Creator, the principle of the universal and eternal creation of Him exactly in all elements of the World and at all stages of development. And then each moment of creation and self-creation provides exactly this essence of development.

Therefore, when your development takes the way that realizes your movement in the likeness of God, you come to the World, which exists in harmony with you and in which each element possesses universal reserve ability. This universal reserve ability means that any object can create any other object.

This knowledge makes it possible to understand many mechanisms of development of events, for instance, why sometimes events develop in such a way that some little object can restrain realization of events, or some small problem can for a long time and in a determinative way influence all events, and why it is often enough just to get to know this problem, just knowledge, in order to completely solve the issue, for instance, of self-restoration or restoration of other people.

For recovery of health you should first of all determine the cause of its worsening, the initial cause. You can also completely restore the whole organism by eliminating the cause and restoration of normal state.

This is one way. But there is another one possible. The principle which is being discussed now being applied to control of event means that any element of the World can be with the help of any other World element. Thus, a person of high spiritual level can just at once change everything in such a way that the organism will be completely restored.

## 3.7. DISTANT OBJECTS OF REALITY ARE WHAT IS APPROACHED FOR THE RESURRECTED AND REMOVED FOR THE LIVING.

We know that the resurrected is a person who had different structures of consciousness due to his passing away and subsequent return. In a similar way any restored object also had different states. Any changes in the state of the object which is being restored can be compared with those changes, which take place when you form the required event. Understanding of this makes it possible to control events in the following way.

The event which is being formed can be considered as consisting both of distant and approached areas in relation to the elements of this event.

We can say that that one, who controls, who creates, always works with distant elements because for him they are external realities. And that that has already been created, can serve as an approached element because it happens to participate in the creation of the next, adjacent to it element. Imagine, for example, that you glue a broken vase. You collect it from separate pieces. Then, that piece, which you have just adhered to the available ones, can be considered as the element approached to the vase in comparison to that one, which you will add to it.

Being aware of everything stated above you can restore your health based on principle of an approached image. For this you look through your own organ, if it is healthy, or through the organ of another person, or imagine this organ, and this image of the healthy organ you approach or even just overlay it on the sick organ, which you have to heal. This is the essence of the principle of the approached image, which makes it possible to restore sound health quickly.

3.8. THE RESURRECTED ABSOLUTIZES SPACE AND DETAILS TIME. DURING THE INITIAL PERIOD TIME IS DISCRETE FOR HIM, WHILE FOR THE LIVING ONE TIME IS CONTINUOUS.

This principle makes it possible to implement control of events on the basis of the following fact: when some event starts being organized, time during the initial period is highly detailed, it means that time seems to be discreet. Later on when the event has already been formed time for the elements of this event appears to be continuous.

The above mentioned makes it possible to understand the following. When we want to control a starting event, we should proceed from that that each of its elements can be perceived as an isolated one, i.e., separately from others. Therefore, different elements of a starting event don't always depend on one another essentially in many senses. However in due course, as far as the event develops further, their dependence on one another increases.

And now about the exact application of this principle to restoration of health. If the disease hasn't become a chronic one yet, it means that it is in the initial stage, in the process of formation. Therefore it is possible to restore the organism through healing of separate sick organs, of course, taking into account the forming connections. The organism at that might be conditionally considered as a discreet structure.

If the disease has already become a chronic one, I mean that the state of the disease has already been formed, it is necessary to consider all steady connection for health restoration. In this case the organism should be considered as a comprehensive whole.

3.9. THE PRINCIPLE OF AUTONOMY OF INFORMATION FUNCTIONING WITHIN DIFFERENT TIMES.

Based on the analysis of the principle, stated in Chapter 2, we know that time is of autonomous, to be more exact of independently functioning structure. It means that within different time that is within the past, present and future control can proceed from different time, different in term of duration of controlling impulse. And as far as different processes in the organism have different specific you can restore health by choice of the required duration of impulse. Moreover the recovery of people who are around results in restoration of that person, who treats. This demonstrates the mechanism of self-restoration when a healed person heals consequently people around him. .

## 3.10. TRUE RELIGION IS AIMED AT PROMOTING THE CREATIVE DEVELOPMENT OF SOUL, BODY, AND SOCIETY.

This principle makes it possible to understand a very important intention of the Creator: any object of information should favor creative development of any other one. Moreover, it should promote permanent increase of the level of this creative development. The Creator laid down such principle in every element of the World.

The way by means of which any object of information promotes increase of the level of creative development of other objects, determines its own ability to create, its level, and its specific status. Each object of information, each element of an event there contains specific inner status. Anyone who has understood this specific status will be able to control any event.

I would like to emphasize once again an important moment, which is fundamental for ensuring sound health. I mean the existence of the unbreakable connection of man's body and his soul. If a man's physical body loses contact with his spiritual essence the man has the firm ground slipping away from under his feet. Hence body is a part of soul. Understanding of this is a decisive factor to ensure healthy physical body.

True religion helps to ensure harmonic interaction of the soul of man with his body as well as of every person with the entire society. And this favors creative development of all.

## 3.11. RESURRECTION IS THE MOST REAL, THE MOST PRAGMATIC, THE MOST RATIONAL AND THE MOST CONVINCING BASIS FOR THE

CONSEQUENT DEVELOPMENT, FOR DEVELOPMENT OF THINKING OF THE GENERATIONS TO COME.

From the viewpoint of control this principle means the following. Resurrection or in general case restoration of makes it possible to contact the true essence of the World. Such its aspect as Eternity makes it possible to always have any specific object, to be always in contact with it, and, therefore, to be always able to control it. Actually means the possibility of eternal control, possibility of the eternal creative harmonious development.

Full harmony is the everlasting interconnection; it is a multifold interaction between all elements that ensures creative development. Such harmony organizes absolute health. The control on the basis of the principle, which is being discussed, plays a significant part in the new medicine. It demonstrates that full restoration is the consequence of the principle of the adequate regeneration and infinite development of organism.

3.12. THE LIVING ONE, WHO HAS NOT EXPERIENCED DEATH, CAN ALWAYS REGENERATE, RESTORE THE GONE ONE WITHIN A SHORTER, MORE OPTIMAL TIME AND AS A MORE DESIRED OPTION THAN THE RESURRECTED ONE CAN.

Control of the process of restoration is realized through the awareness of the harmony of the World, which is reproduced in the consciousness of the person, who is resurrecting, Mastering this control had been initially laid down into spiritual structure of each of us.

However there are some differences in the speed of this process, in its quick action. To be more exact, the person, who has never died, has always higher speed of control than that one who has lived through passing away and consequent return. Since it is clear that one can faster control through the object of information that is more harmonic than through the object, which bears some traces of previously available destructions, and which, in particular, is a subject to more intensive harmonization. In relation to health, all said above means the following. The restoration of your organism or of the organism of another person can be easily implemented through a healthy organ. If you concentrate your attention on a healthy organ and then extend your consciousness to the entire organism you will be able get good health of the entire organism.

3.13. THE PRACTICE OF RESURRECTION, THE PRACTICE OF RESTORATION, REGENERATION IS NOT CONTRARY TO ANY RELIGION, TO ANY LAW, NOR TO ANY CREATIVE TREND.

This principle makes it possible to understand that when any object is being restored the elements of creative development are embedded in it. Let's assume, for example, that there is some object which had previously been problematic for people around it. Then the restoration of this object on the basis of the impulse of creation enables it to be developed in such a way that it turns to be in harmony with the environment. I'd like to emphasize here that any process of full restoration is sure to result in harmonization of the object with the environment.

Referring to such objects as destructive systems harmonization in this case means that the control results in full neutralization of all destructive functions of this object.

Elimination of destructive functions and development of creative ones means real control of the event.

Based on this principle you can receive important consequences for improvement of health. Let's consider, for instance, a smoker, who wishes to give up smoking. Taking into consideration the following approach could be recommend. First, one should isolate the cigarette in the consciousness and only then give up smoking.

It makes sense to give a general clarification here. Any disease actually always develops first of all at the level of information. And only when it has developed and formed to enough degree, it will display itself at the physical level, that means that it will be discovered in the physical body.

Based on this it is clear that treatment just of the physical body is the treatment of the effects. Once the treatment is started, the causes should be always taken into consideration. The causes have their roots at the ethereal levels of existence. Therefore, effective healing can be quite easily ensured due to the active usage of one's consciousness.

Consider once again attentively those approaches to healing, which I offered to you when we discussed the previous principles. I, for instance, said, "Form in your consciousness the image of the healthy organ and just overlay it on that organ, which you want to heal".

This is the universal approach and this is an exact example of the practice of control.

3.14. THE RESURRECTION OF PEOPLE MAKES IT POSSIBLE TO RESURRECT AND RESTORE ANY OBJECTS.

Restoration of any objects makes it possible to create any structures of reality and as such actually to control any events. In particular one can control health.

4.1. RESURRECTION IS CONTROL OF THE ENTIRE EXTERNAL SPACE.

This principle makes it possible to control events in the following way: - you transfer the whole external space exactly into the event and based on this you get the control.

How the above can be used for restoration of health? You should consider all harmony of the external world within yourself, you reflect it within yourself, you display it within yourself;-so it begins to sound within you, and your harmonized organism, is already radiating wonderful health.

4.2. MAN IS THE ENTIRE EXTERNAL AND INTERNAL WORLD SIMULTANEOUSLY.

Referring to health this principle means the following. Health is the state determined by many factors. The fusion of all factors means health of each organ, of each cell.

4.3. TIME DILATATION, ITS REMOVAL OR APPROACHING MEANS RESURRECTION FOR SOME ASPECTS OF SPACE.

From the point of view of health this principle provides understanding of one important point. Each organ can be considered as an object existing in time. Some processes take place in it. It lives its own life; it has its normal course of time. And it's not obligatory that its course of time should coincide with the course of time of processes in the adjacent organ. So, when you see that the processes, going on in different organs, differ, let it be insignificantly, by the course of time, this means that you have complete health.

4.4 WHAT MAN THINKS, WHAT HE SAYS AND WHAT HE DOES IS OF

ETERNAL NATURE.

Based on this principle one can understand that each organ was created in such a way that it can function eternally. If man understands it, but not just formally, not just by his mind, if man realizes it as a whole person, then he will never have any health problems.

4.5. THE PRINCIPLE OF ETERNITY. IT GIVES THE GONE ONES AN INSIGHT INTO THE FACT THAT THEY WILL BE RESTORED, REGENERATED.

Reality and every its element are built in such a way that principles of complete restoration exist as a result. Thus every living one always has knowledge about the everlasting life. In a similar way any object of information always has knowledge about its complete form.

If to mention some objects with destructive properties, for instance, bombs, then, it is necessary to note that these structures are deprived of harmony, these are structures of that sphere of consciousness, where the creative element hasn't become dominating one yet, hasn't yet become determinative. Thus in this case your consciousness should isolate the bomb, it should prevent it exploding. And the isolation of the bomb in your consciousness should result in change, well, of political situation, and the bomb issue would fall away and negotiations would become the basis disputable issues.

Thus, the principle of Eternity doesn't destroy the bomb, but it changes, for instance, the organization of the society or the structure of the event so that as a result over time the bomb loses those functions, which were initially embedded in it. Here I mean that after being stored for some time, due to decomposition of its components or other similar processes, it will not be dangerous, actually it will stop being a bomb. This principle is embedded into form of objects. When there is an element, which can damage something, it works in line with the form of self-destruction. Thus, when we speak about eternity of an object, we mean about that these elements connected with destruction are moves out into the structure, where they are not able to destroy themselves or other elements of reality.

So, correct control results in the fact that all elements, which can destroy, over time are self-transformed. And herewith, I would like to emphasize, we do not interfere with their initial structure.

Thus, based on the principle of eternity the restoration of harmony is ensured.

4.6. MOVEMENT OF THE GONE ONES AROUND THEIR COUNTRY OF LIFE, MAGIC FOR OUR UNDERSTANDING, ACTUALLY IS REALIZED TROUGH THE STRUCTURE OF OUR CONSCIOUSNESS.

Referring to health this principle makes it possible to understand the following.

We will consider the elements of reality through the structure of our consciousness, that is to say we will set ourselves the aim to change the reality by change of our consciousness. We'll see that there are many connections, which depend on the structure of our consciousness, on that how we perceive the reality. If you understand this, if you see these connections, you can understand the disease; you can understand its cause and heal both yourself and others.

4.7. CHANGE OF GEOGRAPHICAL LANDSCAPE, RESULTING FROM EARTHQUAKES, OR FROM SPLIT OFF OF BIG ROCKS DURING AVALANCHES, LEAD TO GENETIC AND STRUCTURAL CHANGES IN MAN, BECAUSE MAN REACTS TO THE ENTIRE SPACE.

Any change in the World, on the basis of the law of universal connections, results in other changes. This principle makes it possible to understand that any movement of an organism, any thought, any change in consciousness result in response of all elements of organism. This knowledge makes it possible to heal any disease.

So, we have considered once again the principles of resurrection, given in the Chapter 2. This time we used them for control of events and, in particular, to restoration of health.

For the same purpose the methods of resurrection of people stated in Chapter 3 I might have been considered in a similar way. However I will not do this, at least in this book, however I strongly recommend you to think over these issues independently and try, at least based on several methods of resurrection, to see, what recommendations you can get from then for control of events and for the restoration of. This will be a good practice for the comprehension of the material provided in Chapters 2 and 3.

I would also like to draw your attention to the following. The principles of resurrection from the point of view of control of events are the reflections of the laws of the World, and the methods of resurrection are the laws of the World in the dynamic manifestation. Any fundamental structure, which is the expression of the World's laws, is always and by itself initially the law of the World from the point of view of its application.

Thereafter you can make the next step in the understanding of the construction of the World, though we spoke about it in Chapter 2. The next stage could refer to formation of the structure of the World based on the principles through their application. That is to say, to create such laws of the World, that will bring to creation. You can create these creative laws. Because the principles that reflect the laws of the World after being comprehended by everyone, become fundamental laws of the World on their own.

**PARAGRAPH 2. THE MAIN PRINCIPLES OF THE NEW MEDICINE, WHICH IS THE MEDICINE OF THE FUTURE, AND THE PRESENT.**

Now I am going to discuss the main principles of the new medicine. These principles are arranged in such way that they form two parts.

The first part includes nine principles. These nine principles, in their turn, are divided into three groups with three principles within each group.

These three groups correspond to three different levels of the principles. However this level based division of the principles is conditional exactly the same as I described in Chapter 2 when the main principles of resurrection were discussed.

The second part includes eleven principles. All of them are approximately of one level and thus are given consequently one after another without any further division.

Part 1.

1

1. IT IS NECESSARY TO ENSURE THE DEVELOPMENT OF THE SPIRIT UP TO SUCH LEVEL THAT WILL ENABLE MAN TO REPRODUCE HIS PHYSICAL BODY ON SPIRITUAL BASIS.

The new medicine should not just ensure the processes of life of physical body, but should also ensure the development of the spirit of man up to the level that will enable man to reproduce on spiritual basis his physical body and events in any world, in any space, in any space-time.

2. THE NEW MEDICINE HAS TO ENSURE CREATION OF SPECIAL SPACE-TIME AREAS WHERE REPRODUCTION OF MATTER WILL BE REALIZED.

The reproduction of human body should take place in conditions, say, of bioorganic inner and outer environment, on the basis of which the body will function depending on the spirit, the soul and all information. So, the new medicine has got a task that is not related directly to human body. This task is the creation of special space-time areas, such areas, where in fact the reproduction of matter will be carried out, and thus physical body will be able to function freely there.

3. THE PHYSICAL BODY, WHICH WAS REPRODUCED BY THE SPIRIT, WILL BE ABLE TO REPRODUCE OTHER BODIES; WILL BE ABLE TO RESTORE THEM IN INTERACTION WITH THE SOUL AND THE SPIRIT.

This will be exactly the healing in its true meaning.

If to speak about more developed persons, about more developed souls, they will be able to reproduce the body of another man, and moreover they will be able to structure separate segments of his soul in the direction of eternal creative development.

The thing is that the World is constantly developing, circumstances change, and therefore quick reaction to some new changed situation should exist. I mean here the following. If somebody was the first to notice that the reaction should be sharply changed, that some changes should be introduced for the world harmony to develop further, then, he should be able straight away to structure the necessary element of the soul of another man and to do it without any thought, without any words, without any intermediate action, for another man to have it right away. This technology will be a special part of the new medicine.

Currently the formation of the body and the formation of the soul are referred only to the action of the Creator. So, the subject, the new medicine will deal with, will be not just the formation of body, it will deal with the practice of structuring of some segments of soul as well. Moreover, it can be done instantly.

2

1.    THE NEW MEDICINE WILL CONSIDER THE INTERACTION OF THE PHYSICAL BODY WITH THE SPIRIT AND OTHER BODIES AS THE INTERACTION BETWEEN VARIOUS OBJECTS, WHICH ARE ALL EQUIVALRNT AT THE INFORMATION PLAN.

Physical body lives in some space. The interaction of the body with the spirit and other bodies produce some changes both in itself and in the outside space. This interaction one can consider as an interaction between different objects of information. The universal creative development forms the equivalence of these objects at the information plan.

I'd like to draw your attention to the fact that I introduce more general meaning than just treatment into the concept of medicine. I think that medicine should ensure man's health in any space-time continuum, in any space-time area. Therefore the new medicine should have a special part, which will be engaged in the results of interaction of different objects of information: bodies, spaces, space-time objects and so on.

2.    AS A RESULT OF MAN'S DEVELOPMENT EACH CELL OF HIS PHYSICAL BODY WILL BECOME AS INTELLIGENT AS HE IS.

Currently there is a well-known notion Homo Sapience, that is, an intelligent person, translated literary, or in other words, man as an intelligent creature. So, the hallmark of the new medicine will be the existence of the notion of clever cell in addition to the notion of intelligent man. The cell will be as intelligent as man is. It is quite a new phenomenon, hitherto not known.

The mechanism of influence on the external circumstances will changed due to the cells that will become intelligent. The influence upon the external circumstances will be exerted both through the inner and outer cellular systems. These are the positions of intercellular and supracellular medicine correspondingly.

Based on the above, related to the cells, the body will have a more complicated system of hierarchy, because additional possibility of control from each cell appears.

3. THE DEVELOPMENT OF HUMAN BODY, INCLUDING THE DEVELOPMENT THROUGH THE CONSCIOUSNESS OF ITS CELLS, WILL RESULT IN ABILITY OF THE BODY TO ACT AS AN ACTIVE ELEMENT OF

CONSTRUCTION OF THE WORLD.

Anything created by God can change synchronically together with the development of the World; moreover, the change will be controllable. The development of human body will also occur through the consciousness of its cellular structure, through the consciousness of cells. Human body will become an active element of construction of the World. Better to say, due to the development, the body will not be just a consumer; it will also become the creator of itself.

This is quite a new branch of medicine. It'll be connected with reconstruction of both spiritual and material processes, for instance, intracellular, supracellular ones. The development of the spirit will occur based on a complicated principle. We could say that the spirit, brain, and body will be the same things as the soul, brain and body. In Chapter 2 I described the difference between the spirit and the soul. However, based on the above it follows, that in the course of human development this difference will be effaced. Altogether, the new medicine will have unification of some elements because the act of creation will become the act of instantaneous manifestation of all of its consequences.

Man will act as the creator of the Worlds. He will be able to create completely new elements, that is to say, such elements which are not available on the Earth. During the demonstration of materialization I have already created the elements of matter unknown before, and this fact was documented officially. I will tell of it in detail in my other works. This process is many-sided. Any subject, a nail, for instance, can be made with the help of a machine, and it can be received with the help of materialization by one's consciousness.

3

1. PHYSICAL BODY, THOUGH IT WILL REMAIN INDIVIDUALIZED, AT THE LEVEL OF THE SPIRIT AND SOUL WILL BE ABLE TO BE PRESENT EVERYWHERE.

Physical body will have to remain individualized, and at the same time, that is to say, it should be really spread to many objects of information. Should be spread means that body exactly as soul will be able actually to implement all procedures on control of the external reality.

It means that not only the soul, but even physical body at the level of the spirit, and the soul will be able to be present everywhere. At the same time it will be necessary to solve the tasks of individualization of each body and determination of real spheres of habitation of soul, spirit, body and intellect. These listed items have endless number of degrees of freedom. Each of these degrees of freedom is displayed in a definite perspective, that is to say, in the definite systems of access, in the definite elements of understanding, etc. however all this exists only for those, who understand this.

The task of the new medicine will be identification of the individual features of persons. This is a special task, it is important for the reproduction of the following generations. The principle of individualization is the basis for the reproduction of the following generations of people, animals, birds, plants and all creatures in general.

You see that this principle could be referred to the first level as well. I placed it here in the third group because it is easier to perceive and easier to understand the construction we are receiving from every quarter.

2. THE EVERLASTING LIFE OF MAN WILL BE ENSURED BY THAT FACT, THAT IT WILL NOT BE POSSIBLE TO CHANGE THE CREATIVE WAY OF DEVELOPMENT.

This principle is intended to connect the concept of development with the concept of access to any space-time structure. Provided that the access to space-time structure is available, one will always be able to make any required changes in it. These changes are made with the help of the impulse of consciousness, the impulse of soul. The track of the influence of this impulse will be kept both for the past and for the future, but, first of all, for the past in order to exclude such situation, when a single person could change the accumulated bulk of information, could change the created constructive scheme of development. This is a kind of a safety measure.

The knowledge I provide is safe. It develops man only for the better. And it ensures the observance of the principle of safety. Because it is organized in such a way that the access to any space-time structure will be granted only to that one, who knows and who knows how. The matter concerns the creative knowledge and the creative skills. That one, who doesn't know, and doesn't know how to do will not be able to get access to space-time structures, and thus will not be able to change anything. This is the special technology the principle of safety is based on.

3. THE REPRODUCTION OF LIFE WILL BE REALIZED IDEPENDENTLY OF NUTRITION.

Due to the access to information it will be possible to realize the formation of structures of organs development, and it will be possible to realize the formation and development of organs independently of nutrition. That is to say, the reproduction of life might be realized independently of nutrition. This part of medicine will join technologies ensuring eternal life, because food will not be required for satisfaction of the needs of man. Any needs, excluding, of course, destructive ones, any needs will be satisfied in a creative way through infinite development.

I speak about all of this this because it is one of the steps; one of the elements of movement to the new medicine, where everything is transformed in the creative direction based on the will of soul. And as a result any person will depend neither on external nor internal world circumstances. The ideal state of personality, which will be characterized by full control and realization on its part, will be achieved.


Part 2

1. THE STRUCTURE OF MATTER IS SUCH THAT CONSCIOUSNES IS ABLE TO RECREATE MATTER IN ANY POINT.

This principle makes it possible to understand that in the new medicine the synthesis of consciousness and matter will be a well-known process that will provide known in advance result for each point. In reality the possibility of synthesis of consciousness and matter are already well known now for those, who practice the structuring of consciousness based on my system of salvation.

So, the work of consciousness will be shown on the level of those processes, which in fact are connected with the process of reproduction of the World.

A concrete example. When you plant a tree, your consciousness functions together with your body in this process of reproduction of life. And the tree in its turn supports the life of the body by producing oxygen.

This principle will be used in all devices, in all settings of the new medicine, as well as in all of its analytical approaches. As a result the analysis will be made not only from the view point of what is going on in the organism, but from the view point of how the organism interacts with reality. This is an entirely new approach. It will provide doctor with new possibilities for the health recovery.

2. WHEN YOU CONSIDER REALITY AS A STRUCTURE FORMING YOUR CONSCIOUSNESS, YOUR CONSCIOUSNESS IS ABLE TO FORM YOUR BODY WITHIN THIS REALITY, AND THE BODY, IN ITS TURN, FORMS THE FOLLOWING NEW REALITY FOR ITSELF.

This principle could be worded differently. Namely your consciousness is able to form reality in such a way that each next step in its formation brings to the creation of reality that is the most favorable for you. It means that every person with every new stage of development becomes more and more harmonic.

As a result, such concepts as old age, diseases, loss of workability disappear. The flourishing of person takes place in every respect. And each new stage of development results in the increase of the level of this development. When each person develops in such a way, the task for the new medicine will be actually creation of conditions for such development.

3. THE DEVELOPMENT OF ECONOMIC, POLITICAL, SOCIAL AND ECOLOGICAL FOUNDATION FOR RECREATION OF MAN WILL RESULT IN ETERNAL DEVELOPMENT THAT WILL FORM ETERNAL CONSTRUCTIONS OF THE WORLD, WHICH WILL BE SECURED BOTH BY LEAGL AND SOCIAL SPHERES.

On the basis of that foundation, which is mentioned in the wording of the principle, the development of person will be so harmonious, that universal love will develop in each element of the development. This will contribute to the birth of the new Worlds. Then man as their creator will organize the next stage of development on the basis of universal love.

Actually this principle could be formulated as follows. Man, acting as a creator, relies on love and at the same time develops it. This is exactly the approach God originally based development on. That is to say love is the basis for the construction of the Worlds. And just as the unlimited love of the Creator, being invisibly available is constantly directed towards each of us, exactly the same way each of your actions should always be permeated with love, and then, creating, you will act the same way as God does. And then the construction of organism and healing of yourself and other people will reveal itself as manifestation of universal love.

4. ANY PROCESS OF REALITY WILL BE CONSIDERED AS INTERRELATED WITH MAN

This principle is clear and can be easily realized in healing of man, in his actions and in his development provided that the concrete connections of man with every object of information are visible. This principle makes it possible to see the interaction of various current events that take place in man's life, and the future events as well. As a result a man will be able to receive specific recommendations in relation to what he should do in the future, how he should behave to ensure normal development of his life and good health.

5. ANY EVENT HAPPENING WITH ANY OBJECT OF INFORMATION, INCLUDING ANY EVENT IN THE LIFE OF MAN, WIIL BE CONSIDERED AS CONTRIBUTING TO RESTORATION OF HARMONY IN THE MAN WHO NEEDS ANY ASISTANCE.

The treatment in the new medicine will not be restricted to medications or some special technologies created by consciousness for this very person. In the new medicine the treatment will be realized due to development of consciousness of this man into the area of interaction with other people. As a result the healing will be realized due to the perception of harmony with any other man. The technicality of this principle will look as follows. The devices will improve health of all people and simultaneously restore all objects of information; as a result the health of this very person will improve as well.

6. ANY TECHNOLOGIES AND ANY TECHNOLOGICAL DEVICES OF THE NEW MEDICINE UNDER NO CIRCUMSTANCES WILL LIMIT THE LIBERTY OF ACTION AND WILL OF ANY PERSON.

In reality the new medicine will be based on the liberty of action and will of every person. So, the devices for the analysis of the state of health will be created so that in no way they would limit the freedom of thinking and the freedom action of any person, but, on the contrary, would contribute to the development of this freedom. Hence, first of all, complete freedom of thinking is an indefeasible condition of creative development of person.

How will these ideas be realized practically? I will just explain the structuring of consciousness, I have told about already.

This new technology is aimed for the treatment that will mainly take place on the basis of man's consciousness. The structuring of consciousness will result in the ability of the consciousness to reproduce any medication structure, that is, to materialize the required medicines. And these will be quite different medicines. Not those, which are made artificially on the basis of chemistry. The medicines created by consciousness are completely harmless, without any side effects and do only good. With their help it's possible, for instance, to restore the health of any organ. But, of course, one will be able, on the basis of consciousness, just to restore straight away the required organs within himself. Or organs of another person. If you carry out the structuring of your consciousness for the control of reality, then unlimited possibilities are opened before you.

7. TECHNOLOGIES AND TECHNICAL DEVICES OF THE MEDICINE OF THE FUTURE WILL WORK WITH HUMAN ORGANISM WITHOUT ANY TIME RESTRICTIONS.

In the future man will show more striving for full freedom of action and, in particular, to real travel to different space-time areas. It means that the medicine of the future will have to ensure complete health of man in any point of all these space-time areas. That is why this principle says that technologies and technical devices, which will be created, will have to be directed not only towards the present, but towards the whole past of this organism and towards its future state, its future structure. That is to say, the new technologies will work with each organism without any time restrictions.

8. THE ANALYSIS OF MAN'S MOVEMENT IN SPACE AND TIME, AND THE PARALLEL ANALYSIS OF THINKING MAKES IT POSSIBLE TO ACHIEVE CONCRETE STRUCTURING OF CONSCIOUSNESS THAT ENSURES PERFECT HEALTH.

We are able to observe and analyze the movement of man in space and time. On the other hand, we are able to observe and analyze simultaneously the movement, which takes place at the level of thinking. Connection of the elements of these two movements makes it possible to get the concrete form of consciousness that results in arising of understanding how thought should be expanded in order to have perfect health.

9. THE NEW MEDICINE WILL NOT JUST ELIMINATE ANY AGE RESTRICTIONS FOR MAN'S BIRTH IN THE NATURAL BIOLOGICAL WAY BUT WILL ALSO RPOVIDE A POSSIBILITY FOR CREATION OF MAN TROUGH CONSCIOUSNESS STRUCTURING.

Permanent improvement of health and improvement of organism functions will make it possible to eliminate any age limitations for natural biological birth of man and to eliminate any time frame limitation for childbearing. At the same time the natural level of man at time of his birth will permanently increase as a result of continuous progressive development.

In parallel with the possibility of childbirth in the usual way, complete creation of man through consciousness structuring will become possible. It will be the same way of creation of man as God used to create him. Creation of man through structuring of consciousness will mean full freedom of action. The birth of person in that way will ensure him perfect health. He will also possess the ability of instantaneous perception and transfer of any information. Thus the task of the new medicine will be the transfer of information to new man actually instantly as far as possible.

10. THE MAIN TASK OF THE NEW MEDICINE IS ENSURING IMMORTALITY.

The movement of the society towards immortality, to the realization of eternal life and endless development should take place simultaneously for all of its members, that is to say, each man should move along this way and each man should become immortal. Therefore, the task of the new medicine is distribution of correspondent knowledge and technologies among all members of the society for every person to be able to freely develop in this direction.

There is another possibility that can be used, that is to ensure instantaneous transfer of all the data when the foetus has just begun to develop.

## 11. WITH THE DEVELOPMENT OF CONSCIOUSNESS OF MAN EACH ELEMENT OF REALITY WILL BECOME MORE CONTROLLABLE AND MORE COMPLIANT WITH THE MAN'S WISHES.

With the development of man's consciousness each element of reality will be changing towards more compliance with man's requirements. In this connection the character of control of reality elements will be changing gradually. The control will be no more based on force approach, without help of pure conation. Due to establishment of more harmony in the World the control of the elements of reality to a greater extent will take place on the basis of coordination with them of supposed actions. For this they will preliminary receive all the required information. As a result the reality will developed in a coordinated way. Ensuring such development is one of the tasks of the new medicine.

So, this principle is about that thing, that with the development of man's consciousness each element of reality will become more and more controllable, more and more coordinated with the demands of man, more and more complying with man's wishes. Ideally each element of reality should become such as man wishes it to be.

The both parts include equivalent principles. However these parts are built differently. The first part includes block like construction of the principles, while the second one includes consecutive construction. As a result when you master them you receive different structuring of your consciousness.

According to this, due to the inner comparison, you comprehend block-consecutive or, in other words, discrete-continuous structure of consciousness that enables you to control based on the same laws the World has been built.

The first paragraph of this chapter includes the principles of resurrection that were given in the application to the events control by means of explanation of the methods of their use. And the current paragraph provides mastering of the principles of control of events due to the unification of discrete and continuous ways of perception. This is exactly the same way all elements of the World are formed. Since any event is formed from the cause-effect and discrete-continuous elements. In our case the cause are the principles of resurrection, and the effect is the application of these principles to the events control. As for discontinuity, it is the block structure of the first part, and the continuity is the consecutive arrangement of the principles in the second part. The control of events based on the above takes into consideration the variety of all connections of the World, which provide harmonious creative control.

## PARAGRAPH 3. CONCRETE FACTS OF CURING DISEASES, WHICH ARE CONSIDERED TO BE INCURABLE.

Currently traditional medicine looks for the methods of curing diseases, which it is not able to cope with. These diseases include cancer and the fourth stage of AIDS.

With the spiritual approach there are no incurable diseases in principle. Moreover, if you understand the principles given in this book and follow them then no illnesses will ever emerge. Since you will always be in harmony with the World. And any disease can be considered as an effect of violation of this harmony. So, the recipe for any disease curing is very simple: you should restore harmony with the World.

I have already healed people from many diseases, which at present are considered to be incurable. All these cases are documented. A part of them is included in the three-volume edition of Grigori Grabovoi "The Practice of Control. The Way of Salvation." All the three volumes were published in Moscow in 1998 by the publishing house "Soprichastnost'"". In this paragraph I am going to refer to materials included in the third volume.

I chose four cases from the great number of particular facts: three cases of healing from cancer and one case from AIDS, all diseases were in the fourth stage. In one case the patient applied personally to me, in another based on recommendation of relatives, in another one the patient didn't know that his relatives applied to me and he didn't know anything about his diagnosis. The cases are very different.

1

Antipova Galina Stepanovna. Diagnosis: intraductal breast carcinoma. The source of the material cited is v.3, pp. 713-716 "The Practice of Control. The Way of Salvation." (In this book – APPENDIX B, pp.327-332

Galina Stepanovna applied to me after her visit to the oncologic dispensary where on the basis of analysis the diagnosis of intraductal breast carcinoma was established for her. Intraductal breast carcinoma is actually incurable form of cancer. According to the data of the World Health Organization the patient with this form of cancer has only several months to live.

I conducted remote treatment of Galina Stepanovna, that is to say, staying at a distance. When in several months, she again had oncological examination at the same dispensary and by the same doctor, it was established that she had no cancer at all.

For healing I use the principles and methods, which are presented in this book. I will outline briefly the approach I used.

At first I build all the required following events. Then I connect them with the real cells. I tune all the cells to self-reproduction. Then I tune all the events to that very reproduction in order to have coordination of the healthy cells and of the whole organism with the favorable way of further events, and the cancer is healed. Like any other illness.

Let's think over the following thing. What did the recovery of man from the disease, due to which he had to die in several months, mean? In the essence it means resurrection, just removed in time. Now let's distract from the cases of such sharply pronounced diseases. Many people at present die from the old age. However, the old age, in the final analysis is also a disease. And, therefore, the recovery from the disease, called "old age" is also resurrection. And hence, in general, we can say that in essence eternal life is a continuous self-recreation. We came to the wording of one more important principle:

ETERNAL LIFE IS A CONTINOUS SELF-RECREATION.

This principle makes it possible to see the connection between the new medicine and the principles of resurrection.

Actually the main task of the new medicine is the guarantee of eternal life, and eternal life is based on self-recreation. And therefore, the new medicine actually appears to be one of the consequences of the principles of resurrection and self-recreation.

Furthermore, the formulated principle establishes the deep connection between two most important concepts, resurrection and eternal life. The influence of these words by itself is exceptionally beneficial. If to make an audio record of words "resurrection" and "eternal life" their repeated reproduction destroys cancerous cells.

This is an experimentally established fact. This is the force of action of these words. These words are the key ones in this book. The title of the book begins from them. After her recovery Galina Stepanovna decided to tell people her story. Those who heard all this received an impulse of restoration. They restored themselves and restored those surrounding, thus they restored the entire World, and as a result its light became brighter. In other words, beneficial effect of this recovery extended to all phenomena of the World. In turn, all these positive events contributed so that the life of Galina Stepanovna became valuable and there were no any diseases in it.

2

Belyakov Mikhail Gavrilovich. Diagnosis: the fourth stage cancer of ascending section of colon with metastases into the kidneys and liver. The source of the material cited is v.3, "The Practice of Control. The Way of Salvation." pp. 738-742. (In this book – APPENDIX B, pp 339-340

This case is interesting because the patient knew nothing about the dangerous diagnosis and that his daughter of Serbina Nadezhda Mikhaylovna and granddaughter Serbina Diana Yanovna asked me to cure him.

They applied to me on September 25, 1996 after the fourth stage cancer of colon with metastases into the kidneys and liver was diagnosed for Mikhail Gavrilovich. The same day I conducted one session in the absence of Mikhail Gavrilovich.

Ultrasonic examination carried out next day, on September 26, showed the absence of metastases. The next examination with the use of computer laminography carried out on September 30, confirmed the absence metastases in the entire organism. After my session, Diana Yanovna, the granddaughter of Mikhail Gavrilovich, watched how restoration process was going on. Asking her grand-dad correct questions and talking with him she additionally improved the process of recovery and as a result complete recovery was achieved just within several days.

Here, indeed, the following important information should be added to the aforesaid. After applying to me with the request to cure her grand-dad Diana Yanovna studied my technology of structurization of consciousness based on the system of salvation and she tried to master it practically. This circumstance made its contribution to the fast recovery of Mikhail Gavrilovich. This completely reflects the principles of the new medicine. Any person who participates in the process of treatment can pass on the necessary knowledge to the patient and thus help him to restore health.

From the point of view of orthodox medicine a man with such disease as cancer of the fourth stage, has to leave our world within several months. The fact that he survived means that the pulse of resurrection was transmitted directly into his future. Furthermore, this pulse was transmitted to him also in the current time directly by the conversation with him of his granddaughter, moreover, of course, in the form of the indirect words, indirect in the sense that the word "resurrection" or another similar word was, quite  naturally, not mentioned in this conversation. Mikhail Gavrilovich was offered additional aid and support by his daughter Nadezhda Mikhaylovna who also participated in his treatment.

As I've already mentioned, fast recovery was achieved in this case. And the usual state of health was achieved. On the whole it should be mentioned that the transfer of the pulse of resurrection to the future, where tragic outcome should have occurred, corrects this future and always ensures good health exactly at present.

I will tell once again about the importance of propagation of knowledge about resurrection, about the importance of transfer of this information. The following principle is valid here: the more you transfer knowledge about resurrection to people around you, for example, from this book, about the principles and methods contained in it, the more favorable structure of events is being established around you and the closer you approach to absolute health.

The considered case shows that a patient might even not know what his concrete diagnosis is, he might not know that his relatives asked for help, and nevertheless he can also get fast and effective recovery.

3

Buza Vladimir Georgievich. Diagnosis: malignant tumor of the head of pancreas with germination into duodenum. The source of the material cited is v.3, "The Practice of Control. The Way of Salvation." pp. 747-749.  (In this book – APPENDIX B,. p.342-343

Vladimir Georgievich applied to me for help based on the urgent request of his wife Buza Ludmila Ivanovna. What does this detail tell about? It tells that another people can contribute to the recovery of this very person, i.e., other people can contribute to the course of events in direction desirable for the person and even give impetus to exactly this course of events.

In the considered case the pulse of resurrection was formed on the basis of Ludmila Ivanovna's information that finally resulted in the recovery. I developed this pulse and restored Vladimir Georgievich in the future with the help of the pulse of recovery in the present. At the end of his statement Vladimir Georgievich writes: "Actually Grabovoi Grigori Petrovich healed me from inoperable cancer of the head of pancreas with germination into duodenum within one session".

This is really so. One session proved to be enough in order to save the man from the desperate condition.

I'd like to stress here one crucial point. I mentioned above the pulse of resurrection and the pulse of recovery. So, both of these pulses are completely identical. And they are completely identical with the pulse of restoration of any matter altogether. So, actually all these cases are about the formation of one and the same pulse. This is the pulse of consciousness, this is the pulse of necessary knowledge, this is the form of necessary knowledge, and all this together is following the example of actions of God in similar situations.

This is spiritual approach. Additionally to it, in this chapter dedicated to the new medicine, I will present another approach to cancer treatment. I will describe developed by me procedure of treatment of cancer on microelement basis.

However, first I will repeat some general provisions related to the process of recovery. Orthodox science considers that there is objective physical reality. I refer this "objective" reality to the static area of consciousness. Why exactly to the static? Well, let us recall how in general this reality is formed. The reality perceived by us is actually the product of collective consciousness. This reality appears as the result of averaging over the huge amount of ideas of various individual consciousnesses. Each consciousness has its own ideas indeed. The received averaged idea becomes stable already. Let's recall the experience with the tossing of a coin. If the coin is tossed up many times, then the ratio of the number of heads to the number of tails will be equal to one. As a result of the averaging we obtained stability. The target relation became the constant number.

Therefore the averaged idea proves to be steady exactly due to the averaging of ideas on the basis of a very big number of different consciousnesses. And the stability of idea means the constancy of the picture of perceived reality. In particular the constancy of laws, for example, as the law of gravity. Well and any constancy can be considered                              as                              statics.

The aforesaid makes it possible to understand what the field of research of orthodox science is. This is a part of perception related to the statics of consciousness, which is accepted as objective reality by orthodox science.

The practice of achievement of the desired reality (in this case healing from cancer) shows that the desire objectively exists both at the level of the understood reality (presence of disease) and at the level of the realization of the desire (recovery). Realization of the desire I refer to another form of consciousness, i.e. the dynamic one.

The observed phenomena of the physical world that relate to the static area of consciousness are only a part of a more general World of phenomena, which includes the dynamic consciousness as well.

Hence appears an objective law related to the influence of consciousness on the existing reality. The change of thought forms changes reality.

Now it is possible to go on to specific recommendations. In this case I will content myself just with the first case considered in this paragraph, because now I just want to explain the idea of the method developed by me and to show the exact way of its application.

From the point of view of microelement basis my practice of treatment of cancer is that I increase the content of magnesium (Mg) in the brain. I increase magnesium concentration by 0.5%. In this process conversion of thinking energy into healthy cells simultaneously takes place as well.

How can one get this recipe of recovery? When I changed my thought form for the purpose of ensuring the recovery of Antipova Galina Stepanovna, the objective instrument analysis showed that the content of magnesium in her brain increased by 0.5%. This registered fact made it possible to understand that it was possible to treat carcinoma by the increase of the percentage content of magnesium. And this can be easily achieved by physical therapy and remedial measures carried out as out-patient treatment in any health center.

Thus, after examining the change of the content of microelements in the organism of patients at the time of my healing pulses, it is possible to create a procedure of healing by substance. In this case, the procedure of healing from breast cancer can be magnesium increase in the brain by 0.5%.

Let's consider the fourth case. It is about the recovery from AIDS.

## 4

Mgebrishvili Gvantsa Ramazovna. Diagnosis: AIDS of the fourth stage. The source of the material cited is v.3, "The Practice of Control. The Way of Salvation." pp.705-711. (In this book – APPENDIX B, pp. 344-352. Before Gvantsa Ramazovna applied to me, AIDS had been diagnosed for her based on medical examinations more than three years before. The sizes of lymphatic glands were increased and there were spots of different size and color everywhere on the body: black, green, yellow. It was already impossible to save the person on the basis of standard methods of treatment.

I conducted treatment in the absence of the patient, at a distance. I was in Moscow, and Gvantsa Ramazovna was in Georgia. First her increased glands began to resolve, then the Kaposi's sarcoma began to disappear, all the spots on the body gradually disappeared and the skin became completely clean. Medical examinations which were carried out and tests showed the absence of AIDS. So, the person was completely healthy within two months. I would like to draw your attention to one interesting detail. Officially Gvantsa Ramazovna applied to me through my representation in Georgia, in Tbilisi. However, before that when she just made the decision to apply to me, I telepathically perceived this her appeal, her request about help, and therefore I began the treatment immediately, before she submitted her official application.

I tell about this for you to know that it is possible to apply to me in my absence. You can ask me to resurrect someone or to help you to do this yourself. It is possible to apply not only to me, but also to other people, to those, who know how to resurrect, or who originally was able to do it or to those who learned how to do it.

The considered cases of resurrection and recovery show that the distance makes no difference. The pulse of resurrection can be transmitted anywhere; it is attached neither to space nor to time. And this is quite natural. Since the pulse of resurrection is the pulse of consciousness, and space and time are themselves constructions of consciousness.

The pulses of resurrection and recovery, as I mentioned, are of the same nature and of the same structure. And that circumstance that these pulses of consciousness have no attachment either to space or time confirms that we deal with the universal system of control, such system, which actually makes it possible to make the World eternal.

## PARAGRAPH 4. RESCUING PEOPLE DUE TO PREVENTION OF ACCIDENTS AND THE ANTICIPATORY FORECASTING OF POLITICAL, ECONOMIC AND SOCIAL EVENTS. CONCRETE FACTS.

This paragraph will, first of all, include some concrete facts of people rescue due to prevention of accidents. Materials cited here are presented in first and second volumes of my work "The Practice of Control. The Way of Salvation". These examples are about prevention of accidents under various conditions: underground, on the earth, above the earth in the air, and in the outer space.

1

An experiment on possibility of extrasensory determination of locations of accidents in a mine as well as the number of injured people and their location. The source of the material cited is v.3, "The Practice of Control. The Way of Salvation." pp. 284-286. (In this book – APPENDIX C, pp.. 357-359

A commission that included independent experts provided me just with a diagram of the mine ventilation. No maps of the area were given to me. I'd like to mention that the diagram of ventilation was just a sheet of paper with lines without any fix-up to the location.

Furthermore according to the experiment condition the commission members did not prepare the questions for me in advance. They asked me that question, which occurred during our meeting. No one previously knew either what diagrams of ventilation exactly would be given to me.

After the task was received I approximately within one second correctly determined the place of the fire origin, locations of the two injured people in the air gate, and the places of ventilation violation. The experiment showed that it was actually possible by extrasensory means to diagnose instantly a situation in a mine correctly on the basis of its diagram. Thus the carried out experiment confirmed that any object of information (as, for example, the diagram of ventilation) had information about everything. I mentioned this when the principles of resurrection were considered. The considered case of diagnostics of the mine is just one of a number of concrete examples. In the general case diagnostics of any objects makes it possible to anticipate the place and reason of a possible accident and due to this to prevent it. As a result it is possible to avoid loss of people. And this means their resurrection. And this gives an excellent example of control of events, in this case this is an example of the change of the future in a favorable direction. We had a similar situation when we considered the healing from fatal diseases.

The pulse of resurrection based on its spiritual content is applicable to all cases of life, it brings salvation everywhere. Its spiritual status is originally inherent in everyone. This is the status of universal unity. And since this status is originally inherent in all of us, it means that each of us has originally the ability to resurrect and to contribute to the universal salvation. This is exactly what my religion is based on. As well as on the true knowledge, first of all on the knowledge of that how the Creator, creates.

2

Prevention of automobile accidents. The case described by Kuzionov Sergey Petrovich. The source of the material cited is v.3, "The Practice of Control. The Way of Salvation.", p. 354 and the reverse side of the page. (In this book – APPENDIX C, pp. 360-361

Sergey Petrovich was introduced to me on January 3, 1995 in Uzbekistan, in Tashkent. At that time he was greatly interested in the question whether the future was single-valued or could be changed. We have already learned that the change is possible. Moreover, this should be the daily practice of each of us. Every man must be the architect of his own future, happy future. This book, in particular, is written for each person to be able to become happy.

Answering Sergey Petrovich's question, I said that I had already changed his future during our conversation. This was really so. I saw that the car, by which Sergey Petrovich came to the meeting, and which belonged to his father, was in a dangerous condition. This could result in a tragedy. Quite naturally I wanted the car to be repaired. I wanted Sergey Petrovich to understand the necessity of the repair and at the same time I wanted everything to be safe for him.

Therefore, when Sergey Petrovich left the garage the next morning, I dematerialized in the car slits in the place of the articulation of the control shaft and the shaft of the worm reducer and in two planes I dematerialized parts of the bolt in the place of articulation. Sergey Petrovich immediately saw, that he could not leave the garage for the road since when he was turning the control wheel the wheels were not turning. He stopped immediately without leaving for the highway. Then at the station of maintenance the car was completely repaired. At the same time it was found out that the insurance bolt was cut simultaneously in two planes what could never happen, and what was unfulfillable in practice. However, exactly this was really done for the safety of further drives.

I selected this method of answer to Sergey Petrovich's question because he, by that time, had been studying irregular phenomena for 16 years. He studied parapsychology and issues related to poltergeist and UFO. He was a member of commission for research of irregular phenomena of the Geographical Society of the Academy of Sciences of Russia, he worked at the American center in New York on study of anomalous phenomena and treatment of abnormal injuries.

Therefore, he as a specialist was interested to see in one practical answer to his question both a change in the future that was vitally important for him and the practice of control of events at a distance with introduction of substantial changes into his automobile exactly at that moment, when he and all other were guaranteed safety as well as the way he was forced to repair seriously his car, moreover in this case a phenomenon of the annihilation of matter of some parts was used. Later on Sergey Petrovich told about this case in the video recording specifically for the United Nations.

The three-volume edition includes the cases when I corrected energetically different mechanisms and systems of automobiles, changed the state of materials and many other things. The included exact facts are presented both by individuals and by organizations.

3

Prevention of accidents of aircrafts. The source of the material cited is v.3, "The Practice of Control. The Way of Salvation.", pages 43, 44, 45 and the both sides of pages 43 and 44. (In this book – APPENDIX C, pp.362-366. This is about my practical work on prevention of air crashes. This work was documented as experiments, in which the possibility of extrasensory diagnosis aircrafts was checked. The organizers of the experiment were to find out how effectively it was possible predict the occurrence of failures, deviations from the technical conditions of operation, and complete failure of systems. The works in Uzbekistan were carried out on the basis of an agreement with the Uzbek Administration of Civil Aviation.

In this case I carried out diagnostics visually, staying at a distance of 100-200 meters form the aircrafts. The mentioned above pages include a number of forecasts made by me for various aircrafts. I will dwell on the last example: the forecast for the aircraft Il-62, identification number 86704.

I predicted the appearance of malfunction in engine No 3, to be more exact, the material damage in the area of combustion chamber of engine No 3. In ten days in this place they revealed the burnout of the nozzle apparatus and the engine was prematurely withdrawn from service. The flaw was detected in proper time because on the basis of the preliminary forecast this place was under intensive monitoring. Based on the experts' conclusion, hadn't the engine been taken off timely, the chipping of blades would have taken palace in a flight and the board would have been broken in a flight. And this results in a catastrophe due to depressurization. So due to the correct diagnostics it was possible to avoid an accident and to save the lives of people.

The accuracy of the forecast in this case as well as in all others was 100%

All in all, only the first volume of my work "The Practice of Control. The Way of Salvation." includes more than 400 exact facts with 100% confirmation throughout the entire volume of tasks. At first glance, it may seem that the presented material just included some cases, in which actually due to extrasensory diagnostics it was possible to avoid people casualties. However this is a much more profound issue and one should consider the presented facts from a more general point of view.

Diagnostics and prognostication are indeed the elements of control of events. Correct diagnostics with the appropriate actions ensures rescuing of people. The presented examples prove that it is possible to remove from our life tragic casualties that no one wants. Moreover it is possible to do this on the basis of science, on the basis of true science. The principles of resurrection presented in this book are an example of this science. The principles of resurrection make it possible to create a society, which will be able to develop only in a creative way on the basis of true knowledge and with the help of the principles of control.

The following example is from Vol. 1, page 229 and the reverse side of the page. (In this book – APPENDIX C, pp.367-370 This time I was offered to conduct extrasensory diagnostics of two aircrafts AN-12. Based on the conditions of the experiment I had to conduct the diagnostics from the distance of 20-25 meters and no longer than within two or three seconds.

In one aircraft I revealed corrosion in the area of the $62^{nd}$ frame, while in another cracks on the planes of the right and left parts of the wing. In several days these forecasts were confirmed as a result of the instrument inspection since it was not possible to detect these defects by physical sight. Thus, it was proven, in particular, that it was possible to see the internal structure of materials.

As a result of the conducted forecasting technical defects, which could result in a catastrophe in the future, were identified. Due to the elimination of these defects it was possible to save the lives of people. This once again confirmed the possibility of control of events due to the detection of technical malfunctions and their elimination. The first volume also includes practical evidences confirming that it is also possible with the hundred per cent accuracy to carry out the diagnostics of equipment on the basis of diagrams and identification numbers, moreover it can be done at any distance from the technical device.

The third example is from Vol. 1 "The Practice of Control. The Way of Salvation." pages 234-235. (In this book – APPENDIX C, pp..371-374

This case is about the test flights of aircraft Tu-144. The test flights were carried out by the famous all over the world pilot Veremey Boris Ivanovich. His wife Veremey Inna Andreevna leaned from a telecast that I possessed the ability to diagnose the state of aircrafts. Therefore she applied to me with a request to conduct diagnostics of the technical state of the aircraft her husband had to test.

I followed her request. I recorded on tape my data on the diagnostics of the aircraft with the description of possible defects and with the recommendations for the pilots. Inna Andreevna immediately gave the cassette with this record to her husband.

My predictions were fully confirmed. The data related to the work of the pitch angle indicator (this is the instrument, which shows the aircraft tilt angle) proved to be especially important. It was very important to know if the sensor really showed that very aircraft tilt, which really took place. My data made it possible to save the lives of the crew members and to save the aircraft. Since if the pilots hadn't got my data on this device, the aircraft would have struck with the tail assembly upon landing and would have been destroyed. There was also a recommendation to increase the speed against the calculated one.

Here I would like to emphasize again the skill of Veremey Boris Ivanovich. No wonder he is famous all over the world. His great practical experience joined the information, which he received from me, and as a result of this synergy a more powerful and more stable system of contact of man with the machine emerged. Such system possesses a much bigger capacity to save and to improve any tested equipment.

Actually acquired by man, in the process of his work, experience, skill and intuition indicate his approaching to the ability to control events. By this my book I offer to put this process on the scientific basis.

4

Prevention of accidents and diagnostics of controlled space vehicles.

The forecasts presented here were made to order of the Russia Space Flights Control Center. The material that describes all these cases is presented in Vol. 1 "The Practice of Control. The Way of Salvation." Pages 239, 240, 241. (In this book – APPENDIX C, pp. 375-377

In the first case, I had to give a forecast on the outer dock of orbital station "Mir" (Russia) and space shuttle "Atlantis" (USA). The docking was scheduled on 27

September, 1997. The task was given on 26 September in the daytime.

Immediately upon receipt of the task I informed on what was going to happen. I told that the docking would take place, but just before it there would be a deviation from the axis. The forecast was fully confirmed.

Simultaneously with the first task I received the second one. I had to give a forecast about the work of the on-board computer of space orbital station "Mir".

I answered immediately that the on-board computer would have worked for five days. This was what really happened. The on-board computer had worked for five days, and then it was replaced.

In three days, on September 29 in the daytime, I was asked to diagnose the engine of the space shuttle "Atlantis". I gave the answer in several seconds. I informed about the change in the parameters of the lower engine of space shuttle "Atlantis". This was an important characteristic because with the change in the parameters of the engine, acceleration of the space shuttle could fail, and that could result in a change in its trajectory and possible accidental collisions. My diagnostics was confirmed completely. On the whole, any forecast information is especially important for space technology for prevention of accidents.

I received the first two tasks when I was in the Space Flight Control Center, but the third task was given to me when I was walking along Novyi Arbat. I received this request on the cell phone.

Pay attention to the conditions, under which I received this task. Novyi Arbat is always very crowded at day time. So, I received this task walking along the street and being surrounded by many people. And nevertheless, in spite of this situation just within several seconds, i.e., practically instantly, I gave the correct forecast.

I tell about these concrete circumstances in order to emphasize one important point. In actuality the mastery of any matter can be considered complete only if man is capable to solve a stated problem under any conditions. This is completely necessary for the resurrection. You should know how to resurrect under any conditions, wherever you were or whatever you were doing at the moment when this was required.

I should also mention that according to the data of an independent expertise the accuracy of all my forecasts and my diagnostics was 100%. Only this fact confirms that what we have here is an accurate science built on consciousness.

I noted above that the presented facts are not a collection of happy chances. It's exactly the opposite. There are too many facts. And the accuracy of all of the forecasts is 100%. So, all these facts evidence that I used a new science, the science of a higher level. Exactly such science should be used for people rescue in order to guarantee rescue at any circumstances. Let us once again think over what, for example, means my information that there were cracks in the material of the aircraft wing. What the result could be? The defect was eliminated on the basis of the provided information and the new material ensured a favorable course of events. Correct diagnostics changes the course of events. And this is reflected in the materials cited. Look at them from this point of view. You will see internal movement in the presented protocols. The movement in favorable direction.

Therefore we deal here not just with the accurate science; we deal here with the science, which defines development in creative direction.

The final desired event determines those actions, which should bring to it. The diagnostics of equipment, in this case, and prognostication of possible deviations from the norm provides information for control, for control of events in the required direction. Realization of this control brings to the required result, to the desired future. Based on this we can make a conclusion that you can use your consciousness to control any event at any distance between you and the object of control.

The same program of actions is also used in my mathematics. I have spoken about this already. Each symbol in it is a controlling one; each symbol ensures movement to the required result. This is guaranteed by the fact that first the desired future is considered, i.e., that result, which should be obtained. This result joins the operator base. The operator in the form of the necessary symbol already exists in my answer and therefore he always controls the development of the movement exactly to this desired answer. And therefore any deviations to the side are impossible, since this movement to the answer is controlled.

All sciences should be developed according to this principle. And therefore the nature of the existing orthodox science should be converted in this direction. Let's also consider accidents, which are caused, for example, by the entry of a bird into the engine of an aircraft. I should mention that this only from the point of view of the science, which examines the static area of collective consciousness, such incidents are random. The science of the higher level makes it possible to predict such phenomenon on the basis of vision of many different processes.

In this case two approaches are possible. With one of them a usual calculation is performed the same way as in any science. I can do this. With another approach it is possible not to carry out all these calculations, but to look immediately what result they give, i.e., just to see the answer. Usually I do so.

These two approaches are familiar to each of us even from school. Let it be, for example, we should solve some problem in mathematics. Then it is possible to attentively read condition, to consider it, then to begin the search for the way, which leads to the solution, and if you manage to find the correct way you will conduct all necessary calculations and obtain the answer.

But it is possible to use another approach. It is possible to open the assignment book in the necessary place and to see the answer. My Teachings registered in the regulation documents of UNESCO include a section devoted to education. It explains what the structure of preliminary and higher education, or better to say of any education should be, and what principles it should be based on. In the future I will also share my personal experiment in the area of teaching.

Now, discussing the example with the solution of a mathematical problem I show the principal existence of another opportunity. If you are interested in the eventual result it is possible just to open the book in the required place and to see the answer. However, actually I speak, of course, about another book. The Book of the Universe should be always open for you.

Let us return to the diagnostics of technical systems. We understood that diagnostics and prognostication result in rescue of people. In other words, in certain cases actually as if in their resurrection. And the ability for diagnostics and prognostication can be acquired on the basis of correct structurization of consciousness. It means that structurization of consciousness makes it possible to realize resurrections of people even just due to the development of the ability to ensure correct work of technical systems. In this case we have an example of such structurization of consciousness, which for resurrection realizes the skill to prevent man-made catastrophes. This shows the commonality of methods of consciousness structuring based on the system of rescuing. Commonality means here that any mastered method can be used in completely different situations.

Thus, one of the steps is to be able to diagnose engineering equipment. Then you begin to resurrect on this basis. Moving further and after having learned to see deeper the functioning of technical units, you will be able to see how the soul of man should function for man to be resurrected by his own soul.

Now let's proceed to the methodology of anticipating prognostication. The element of rescuing in this prognostication includes both anticipating information, and straight opportunity to undertake concrete preventive actions.

Prognostication in political, economic and social areas is connected with the activity of very many people as well as organizations, societies, and other structures. Therefore this prognostication has a number of special features. For example, mentioning of a concrete surname or an exact date in political prognostication might result in displacement of the forecast information. However, if necessary it is possible to indicate exact dates and circumstances, which make it possible to determine concrete individuals. I can give confirmation of my forecast related to the development of the process of presidential elections in Russia in 2000 as an example (Appendix C, pages 531-549).

In the practice of political, economic and social prognostication it is frequently necessary to convert information in direction favorable for everyone. The information of people about their future placed into the collective consciousness is of special significance in this case.

If there is negative information it is necessary to break it up at the moment of realization of the forecast. For example, there was abundant information about the possible end of the world in August 1999. Therefore, forming in July 1999 information of the forecast about the further course of events, I converted the information about the possible end of the world into the information of the absence of global catastrophe and into the information of favorable harmonious development.

"The end of the world is cancelled," this was the title of the article with this my forecast.

I consider that actually any forecast should be an act of control, which forms the creative course of events.

Examples of such forecasts are included in the published results of my works.

## PARAGRAPH 5.  THE PHENOMENA OF MATERIALIZATION AND ANNIHILATION OF MATTER. CONCRETE FACTS.

I have already given the example of annihilation of matter in the previous paragraph. Now we will systematically examine a whole series of examples of materialization and annihilation of matter and will consider these phenomena in detail. Although actually we discuss exactly these phenomena throughout the book. In fact, what is resurrection? Resurrection indeed is one of the very clear examples of materialization.

From the point of view of physical body, its presence or absence, the gone could be considered as people who went through the process of annihilation of matter. With the help of the reverse process, that is materialization, it is possible to bring them back. Physical human body is materialized by the soul. Materialization of any object takes a similar way. Your soul creates this object.

Let us recall principle (2.1): MAN IS AN ETERNAL SUBSTANCE BY THE PRINCIPLE OF HIS CREATION. THAT IS WHY RESURRECTION IS BASED ON REVEALING THE ETERNAL IN MAN.

This is exactly the information about the eternity of any object that provides the opportunity of its materialization.

Let's turn now to the specific facts of materialization and annihilation of matter. We can start with the statement of Glushko Svetlana Pavlovna, a reviewer of newspaper "Megapolis - Kontinent" (Vol. 2 "The Practice of Control. The Way of Salvation.", p. 426. In this book, Appendix D, page 391).

Svetlana Pavlovna was interested in the phenomenon of materialization. Therefore during our conversation on September 22, 1994 she invited me to materialize some objects in her apartment. She turned to me with this proposal because she wanted to write an article on this topic and give a specific living example.

I had never been at Svetlana Pavlovna's home. She wrote in her article that she didn't tell me her address to ensure the cleanness of the experiment.

I complied with the request of Svetlana Pavlovna. In eight days she found in the anteroom of her apartment two objects, which had never been there before. No strangers entered the house during that period. The fact of materialization was present. Moreover the objects were of such composition that could they not be created with physical methods.

When conducting such experiments it is very important to ensure the following. The person should preliminary know that materialization will take place and who will specifically realize it. It is necessary to ensure the avoidance of the possibility of a stress for the person. I mentioned about this in the first chapter. If a person knows everything in advance the change of his cells will not take place with the perception of the result of materialization. The next case is materialization of a key.

It is presented by Babaeva Tatiana Pavlovna (Vol. 2 "The Practice of Control. The Way of Salvation.", p. 437.). (In this book – APPENDIX D, pp. 395, 396. Tatiana Pavlovna stayed at the same hotel I was staying. And once it happened so that she lost the key to her room. She checked all her pockets and the bag but she did not find the key. Then to be sure Tatiana Pavlovna shook out everything from the bag so that it would be possible to examine everything better. However, the searches were in vain. There was no key. She was upset greatly. The situation was such that she had to enter her room urgently. So she decided to apply to the senior person on duty when I interfered. It happened so that at that time I was sitting in the hotel lobby and therefore was able to observe what was going on.

I decided to help Tatiana Pavlovna and materialized the key in her bag. I advised to her to look once again for the key in her bag. She followed my advice and looked into it once again; to her surprise she unexpectedly found the key in the bag. Tatiana Pavlovna understood well that this was the result of my work.

Loss of keys is a never-ending story. You will hardly find a person who had never had this problem. However, in the following cases materialization and annihilation of matter of keys were carried out as an experiment.

The first two cases are represented in the statements Livado Ekaterina Ivanovna

(Vol. 2 "The Practice of Control. The Way of Salvation." p. 462 and 460). (In this book – APPENDIX D, pp.. 397, 398. The first experiment referred to annihilation of matter of a key, the second one to its materialization. A key weighting 10 g was used. During annihilation of its matter I stayed at a distance of 10 meters from it. I carried out the process of annihilation of matter within 20 minutes.

When the annihilation of matter of the key was registered I began its materialization. During this process I stayed at a distance of 3 m from the appearing key. The materialization lasted for 5 minutes.

This experiment is of important significance. This is not the key or any other concrete object that matters. This experiment is crucial to establish a correct understanding of the World. It is important for understanding of the fundamental picture of the World.

The carried out experiment showed that materialization of the key took less time than annihilation of its matter, approximately four times less. Hence it follows that the process of resurrection can also last four times less than the process of passage from clinical death into the state of biological death. However, you should take into account that now I speak from the point of view of the nearest higher levels of the state of consciousness with respect to the ordinary consciousness. With the use of very high levels of spiritual development a resurrection, of course, can be accomplished instantly.

The description of two more experiments gives Lavrushkna Nadezhda Borisovna in her statement (Vol. 2, pages 464-467 and the reverse sides of pages 466 and 467). (In this book – APPENDIX D, pp.. 398-403

This time I conducted first not complete, but partial annihilation of the key matter. Then its restoration was accomplished. A key weighting 10 g was located at a distance of 50 cm from me. In this case there was no physical contact with the key. The entire experiment lasted for 5 minutes.

Four photographs were made during the experiment. They are represented in the Appendix.

The first photograph showed the key, which was used in the experiment. The second photograph showed the received result.  It was visible that the rod, which connected the knob and the base of the key, was practically not seen (partial annihilation of matter, annihilation of matter of some parts of the object).

Thus, it is seen on the second photograph that the connecting rod was absent. Its matter was annihilated. One part of the key still existed, though another one was absent. It is interesting to know where the information about the entire key and about its form was. It is everywhere: it was in the remained parts of the key, in the space between them, and near the former complete form.

The fourth photograph shows the result of first step toward the complete annihilation of the key matter. The key disappeared but information about it remained as before. The information was just seemingly scattered, however it was always available, it stored the image of the object and that object could always be restored.

The above said about the key can be compared with the annihilation of the matter of a physical human body. A human body can be annihilated and disappear, but information about it always remains in the soul of man. Therefore the physical body can be completely restored any minute. The same refers to any object. Actually no object is dead; there is no object that can be described as lacking any elements of consciousness. Indeed all bodies are created on the basis of collective consciousness. Therefore each object has the elements of consciousness. And therefore it is possible to establish a contact with any object. It is possible as if to agree, for example, about annihilation of its matter. It is possible seemingly to persuade it to go through this process. However, after annihilation of the matter the object, or to be more exact, the substance the object was composed of, keeps information about its past form. The essence of the conducted materialization is actually in reminding the matter about its past form, and the object is materialized.

The statement of Salnikova Svetlana Pavlovna (Vol. 2, p. 458). (In this book – APPENDIX D, pp.404-405

Svetlana Pavlovna prepared a book for publishing. This book was about me. In the process of work she found out that the document about my meeting with Philippines healer Yuko Labo was missing. Nevertheless she handed over to me the prepared material for review. When I took the manuscript I immediately understood that this document was missing. Therefore I materialized it so that it appeared at the desk of Svetlana Pavlovna. Moreover the quality of this materialized document was much better than that of the copy. Because the letters were clearer, the font was better as well as some other details. This practice means that from the point of view of the principle of complete restorability of matter any object can be restored in maximally good form. The resurrected, who passed away due to a disease, return healthy.

The statement of the spouses Babaev Victor Bagirovich and Babaeva Tatiana Pavlovna (Vol. 2, p. 439). (In this book – APPENDIX D. 406, 407. The Babaevs departed together with me for an official trip to India. When we had a passport control in the airport of Tashkent it was found out that my passport lacked the stamp, which permitted departure from the country. The border-guards were really astonished that such thing could happen. However, the spouses Babaev were more astonished, because they had seen that my passport had been stamped and my documents had been in complete order.

This was done by me in order to show that should someone wish to, it is possible in an extrasensory manner to delete a stamp from an official document. And not just a stamp, but generally any sign or any part of the text.

I'd like to draw your attention to the ethical moment related to the considered phenomena. No one's interests by no means should be affected when such phenomena are demonstrated. Exactly this happened, for example, when the stamp in my passport was annihilated. Similar facts indicate that if a resurrected person wishes, the records about his passing away might disappear.

Babaeva Tatiana Pavlovna testifies about one more interesting case, which happened to her in India (Vol. 2, p. 430). (In this book – APPENDIX D, pp., 408, 409

It happened so that she lost her airline ticket. All searches for it were useless. I decided to help her and offered her to look for the ticket in the shopping bag, because just before that I materialized it exactly there.

Quite naturally before that Tatiana Pavlovna searched everything including the bag. But based on my advice she glanced into it once again and on the bottom of the bag really found the airline ticket, jammed and slightly soiled with the juice from the apple which was there.

I deliberately materialized the ticket in this form for Tatiana Pavlovna not to be stressed when she saw it. It happened so. When she saw the ticket on the bottom of the bag rumpled and soiled with juice from the apple, and then she immediately calmed down, because she finally found the ticket and because its state showed that it had been there. Just in a moment, after recalling that she had also searched in the bag, Tatiana Pavlovna understood that the ticket was materialized. But by that time she had already calmed down. So, the proper understanding of the situation took place at the required moment.

In general with the realization of materialization it is necessary to consider always the degree of susceptibility of the man. The main thing is to avoid causing stress when a person encounters a new phenomenon. Materialization in life can be realized when it is necessary in reality as in the cited case with the airline ticket. Similarly it is possible to restore passports for the resurrected, if there is no desire to obtain them anew.

There is one more case with the loss of an airline ticket and its teleportation that is presented in the statement of Balakireva Elena Damirovna (Vol. 2, p. 419). (In this book – APPENDIX D, p. 410. Elena Damirovna who lived in Tashkent lost her annual airline ticket on the way home from Moscow. Due to this she applied to me for help.

I saw where the ticket was and simultaneously revealed that it was mechanically damaged. Therefore first I restored it, i.e., conducted partial materialization, and then teleported it to Elena Damirovna. As a result the ticket was found by its owner in that place, where she hadn't found it earlier.

It is possible to act the same way with the resurrection. If the tissue hadn't decomposed completely it is not necessary to create it anew. It is just possible to finish building it in order to obtain the restored organism. Thus, partial materialization can also take place in resurrection.

The following two statements confirm annihilation of matter of an article carried out by me. Gusarova Galina Alekseyevna (Vol. 2, p. 454.) (APPENDIX D, pp. 411, 412 and Tsvetkova Anna Mikhaylovna (Vol. 2, p. 455) (APPENDIX D, p. 413 both participated in the experiment. The daughter of Anna Mikhaylovna was also present.

The described article was typed on usual ten typewritten sheets and was in the apartment of Anna Mikhaylovna in the desk drawer.

I conducted annihilation of matter of this article and ten sheets of paper disappeared from the drawer without leaving a trace.

I'd like to remind here that if creation of some information occurred it exists everywhere and always. Therefore, if an article was written, the corresponding information exists regardless of the fact that the article was dematerialized or not, and even, generally, regardless of existence of its any material basis. Similarly any book created by someone always exists.

The resurrected person always transfers information about his resurrection. This information becomes accessible always and everywhere. Publication just about one case of recovery from cancer of the fourth stage or about one-only resurrection ensures that this process becomes natural for all times, becomes eternal.

The following statement is about the living sound of one's voice that can be reproduced at any distance.

The statement of Chutkova Tatiana Ivanovna (Vol. 2, p. 471). (APPENDIX D, 414, 415

Tatiana Ivanovna contacted me about the disease of her grandson. I said that I will conduct a session without his presence. Natalia Vadimovna, the daughter of Tatiana Ivanovna came to her child to the hospital by the beginning of the session. I carried out a remote session, at a distance. While waiting Natalia Vadimovna looked at her watch, she was worried. She did not know my name and patronymic. "What's his name?" she asked herself. In order to quiet her I decided to answer her question. As it is written in the statement she clearly heard: "My name is Grigori Petrovich. I work with your son. Don't fear, I will help him." Natalia Vadimovna sincerely thanked me. She heard exactly the physical sound; this was emphasized in the statement of her mother although I was not near her. In reality we see here one more example of materialization, in this case it is materialization of sound vibrations. Moreover the voice of man in such cases does not differ in any way from the voice that could be heard in case the person is nearby. And this case as any phenomenon of materialization is one more example of how it is possible to control the elements of physical reality.

Statement of Shelekhov Vadim Vladimirovich (vol. 2, p. 424). (APPENDIX D, p.. 416 In his statement Vadim Vladimirovich told, that during his meeting with me he was impressed by the fact that I unexpectedly for him happened to be in the car that was closed.

In general there could be anything instead of the car, for example, any other place, any planet, any galaxy, any region of the World. The principle of control of space is used in such cases. On your desire you can appear in any of space-time point. And if you want you can create there conditions for life. So it is possible to move to any area and it is possible to create life under any conditions.

Thus, in reality the current discussion is about an important and serious science that is the true science. First, after moving apart the medium, you can move to any space-time point, and then supply the formed space with oxygen and other necessary vital conditions. On the basis of consciousness you can create worlds and be there really. Foresight of the future can also be referred to the phenomenon of materialization, that is to say, to materialization in the present of the information of the future.

Statements of Olekhnovich Lev Petrovich, Doctor of Chemical Sciences, professor of the Sores Foundation, the chairman of the department of chemistry of natural and high-molecular compounds of the Rostov State University, and Kornilov Valery Ivanovich, Candidate of Chemical Sciences, assistant professor of the Sores Foundation of the same department, the head of the laboratory of chemistry of carbohydrates of Scientific Research Institute of Physical and Organic Chemistry of Rostov State University (vol. 2, p. 383 and 385). (APPENDIX D, pp. 417, 418

The two mentioned above scientists offered me to determine what version of intermediate state was preferable in the chemical process, shown in the Application on the first of the two pages indicated above. This was a serious task. Its solution could be obtained either theoretically on the basis of complex quantum-mechanical calculations, or by means of an experiment with the use of the methods of magnetic nuclear resonance. At the moment when I received the task I was in my office in Moscow. I immediately answered the question and gave a written conclusion in favor of a certain structure. Furthermore, I gave additional information that the realization of the third structure was possible in the magnetic field; the authors did not take into account that fact. They didn't tell me anything about their research of the mentioned process precisely in the magnetic field. I immediately saw both: that the experiment was conducted in the magnetic field, and that this field was capable of influencing the nature of the intermediate state. My forecast was confirmed completely.

The second question, asked by these scientists, related to a chemical process, depicted in Appendix D on page 418. It was required to determine the order of the number of migrations for the acetyl group in this process. And here again I gave the answer practically instantly in writing. I told that there will be 20-30 migrations per second that was completely confirmed in the subsequent experiments.

Statements of Kurbatov Sergey Vasilyevich, Candidate of Chemical Sciences, assistant professor of the Department of Chemistry of Natural and High-Molecular Compounds of Rostov State University, and Kornilov Valery Ivanovich, the Candidate of Chemical Sciences, assistant professor of the Sores Foundation of the same department, the Head of the laboratory of Scientific Research Institute of Physical and Organic Chemistry of Rostov State University (vol. 2, pages 384 and 386). (APPENDIX D, pp. 419, 420

In the first case it was required to determine the number of migrations of the same group, however in another reaction. This reaction is given on page 601 534. My immediate answer was: $10^6$ per second (i.e., one million per second). This forecast was confirmed completely.

Here I'd like to note that it was practically impossible just to guess this number the same as in the similar example in the previous statement. The thing is that the number of migrations in such type of connections can vary within very wide limits from $10^{-6}$ to $10^6$ per second. The mentioned limits are the numbers, one of which is greater than another by a huge number of times, to be more exact, $10^{12}$ times, in other words, the relation of limits is expressed by the number with twelve zeros after number one. It is obvious that it is completely impossible to guess the number within such a wide range of choices. The answer must be known.

The second task was to assess the rate of transformation of one substance into another. The both substances were given in the text of the statement. I answered immediately that under the given conditions there would be five transformations per second. Later this forecast was confirmed completely both with the help of the carried out subsequently calculations and by the experiment. It is important to note that by the moment when I gave my information no experiments or calculations that confirmed it hadn't been carried out yet.

We observe here an ability to immediately see the answer to any question. I have possessed this ability since childhood. I used it widely both in school and university. For example, at the university during the tests I immediately wrote answers in the received tasks to all presented questions without doing any calculations. My University friend Rumyantsev Constantine Alexandrovich testified to this fact in his statement (vol. 2, p. 372, 373). (In this book APPENDIX D, pp. 421-423 In this statement he informed about the concrete facts of clairvoyance that had taken place in academic year 1982 - 1983. That academic year I began to come to the classes at any time, often by the end of the test. In those cases there was not enough time to copy from the board the test tasks. I was just able, through clairvoyance, to put down the answers to the tasks. The University was characterized by democratic attitude to class attendance. The main thing was to know the subject when the student passed a test or an examination. But the phenomenon of the precise answers to the task without solutions began to attract the attention of the instructors strongly. First some of them conversed with me, and then the curator of the group began publicly declare about my abilities in the presence of the entire group.

In the future, to avoid drawing attention, I again like in school, began to write some intermediate actions before the answer. After receiving the Diploma of University, in my practical work based on my specialty, I used to provide precise answers through clairvoyance with the complete right of the degreed specialist. Similarly you can after mastering this book refer to it as to a usual educational course. The Ministry of Education approved my author's program that was based on my technologies and gave the right to grant the state diploma for the second major degree.

When clairvoyance is used the answer to any stated task actually exists. Since this was exactly the intention of God when He created the World. The World was created so that you could always accomplish any of your tasks in the infinite space-time. And this is the ideal of the development of man and society. If you want, let us say, to resurrect a man the answer to the question how to do it, preliminary exists. Having received this answer you can resurrect.

Why is this theme (obtaining answers) placed into this section? Because such obtaining of answers can be considered as a phenomenon of materialization. In fact, if a man is asked a specific question its answer can take a lot of time without the use of clairvoyance. Sometimes several years could be required for the solution of a problem. In other words, in the usual way the answer would be obtained only in the future. Therefore the knowledge of this answer just now, in the present, actually means materialization of the future. I received many of the principles of resurrection presented in this book by means of my clairvoyance from the information about the future. Materialized in the present they make it possible to conduct resurrections at the physical level now.

There is one more additional crucial point, which I would like to note in relation to the considered statements. The presented precise forecasts, related to the migration of acetyl group, evidence that it is possible to foresee processes at the molecular level as well. I should say that I directly see how the chemical reaction occurs, how separate micro-particles interact. So, molecules, atoms, electrons and other objects of micro-level can be seen although of course not by physical sight.

Statements of Yakovleva Olga Nikolaevna (vol. 2, p. 456 and 457). (In this book APPENDIX D, pp. 424-427

The first statement of Olga Nikolaevna is the evidence to the fact of change of the content of audio cassette by extrasensory action. The cassette had a record made during a conversation with me. Extraneous sounds were present there as well. I removed all the extraneous sounds. Moreover, by an extrasensory action I added additional text with my voice to this cassette. Later on the available previously record was compared with the text that appeared on the film due to my action. The comparison showed that the both records had the sound of one and the same voice that was mine.

This evidence confirms that it is possible to materialize sounds on an audio film by extrasensory action. Summarizing it is possible to say that through the structurization of consciousness it is possible in the required place to create necessary sonic forms on concrete physical carriers.

Materialization of sonic forms is useful in the resurrection. For example, creation of a suitable sound of wind contributes to more rapid adaptation of the resurrected person.

In the second statement Olga Nikolaevna told that I in a completely specific way deleted a part of the record from the audiocassette. The film recording consisted of three sequential parts. By extrasensory action I deleted the middle part but in such a way that during the subsequent hearing the third part directly followed the first one. There were no pauses. That is to say, there was no empty place remaining on the film. There was no background noise at the place of the received joint of the first and third parts.

Especially I would like to draw your attention to the circumstance that the physical parameters of the magnetic tape remained the same. Its length did not change. As a result it came out that there appeared to be much less information on the tape with the same length of tape and with the same speed of its winding. The deleted record was indeed rather long, thus the loss of information was significant.

Thus, despite the fact that a part of the record was deleted from the tape and the physical length of the tape remained the same, despite all this the tape had no empty places. This demonstration shows that you can you can dispose any information as you like. At the same time physical conditions and physical parameters will comply with your control. Therefore, if it is necessary it is possible with the help of consciousness to increase the Earth to the extent required for all the resurrected.

Statement of Ladychenko Constantine Vladimirovich (vol. 2, p. 469). (In this book APPENDIX D, p. 428

Constantine Vladimirovich reports in his statement, that he witnessed how I annihilated the matter of a computer diskette. The diskette contained 1.44 megabytes of information. I was not informed about the location of the diskette.

This example shows that if it is required, for example, to exclude some additional information undesirable from a creative point of view it is possible for this purpose to use a phenomenon of annihilation of matter causing harm to no one and nowhere in this case. This phenomenon can be made an element of control system. This approach can be extended to all phenomena of the World. Thus, the principle of annihilation of matter can be at once placed into the creation of completely new machines. This is the new generation technique developed by me. Its distinguishing feature is that it under no conditions will be able to destroy a man. This can be ensured with the fact that with the appearance of a threat to man from the side of the machine it will either annihilate or teleport itself to any vacant places of the nearest parking.

Statement of Valitov Rafik Tafikovich (vol. 2, p. 293, 294). (In this book APPENDIX D, pp. 429-431 Rafik Tafikovich reports that he was a witness of the following demonstration of the abilities of clairvoyance. I was offered to diagnose twenty diskettes for availability of a virus. In this case, of course, no computer technology or specialized software intended for detecting viruses was used. I had to determine the virus on the basis of visual view of the diskettes, just looking at them. I exactly determined all five diskettes infected by a virus.

Then it was required to remove the virus by extrasensory way. Usually if a diskette has a virus when its program file is copied to a fixed disk the virus remains and passes to the fixed disk. However when I copied the file from the diskette saving it on computer I destroyed the virus and therefore it was not transferred to the fixed disc. This was confirmed after scanning by the computer antivirus program.

Furthermore, I did so that the program file was carried to the hard disc in the volume, which was 10 times less than the original. The demonstrated elimination of the virus showed that it was possible to introduce changes into information traffic changing it at one's discretion with the help of extrasensory effects.

When we visualize some object, then at the level of thought we see a certain image. A certain picture appears before our mental look. At the same time each element of reality gives its specific picture. Virus has completely specific color background. It is possible to clean a file by an impact on this background, by change of its color spectrum, by levelling it off.

When we mentally see a man who is to be resurrected he thereby is already resurrected at that level of reality, which corresponds to thinking. We have only to move him into physical reality for him to come back.

With the normal flow of things life should be eternal. There should be no passing away in principle. From the point of view of all stated before it is possible to say that there is a task to clean the reality from virus. Actually, in other words, biological death is the virus, which has to be cleaned off from the reality in order to fix the reality up.

So, in the example above, when the file was copied and saved, the virus was removed. As a result normal software appeared on the fixed disk. In a similar way after cleaning the reality from death, we will obtain exactly that reality, which should be.

Statement of Babaeva Tatiana Pavlovna (vol. 2, p. 434).?

Tatiana Pavlovna reported that she together with her husband used to watch how I without touching the button of the elevator made it move in the required direction and stop on the required floor. I carried out these demonstrations in April 1994 in the hotel, in which we lived during our stay in Delhi (India). In the mentioned cases I closed the electrical circuit by extrasensory action and set the elevator into motion without touching the button.

In line with this example let us consider one more, which also relates to the closing of an electrical circuit.

In the previous paragraph I considered the statement of Kuzionov Sergey Petrovich (vol. 2, p. 354 and the reverse side of the page), a specialist in the field of research of irregular phenomena. Sergey Petrovich also told about the continuation of my extrasensory action after the case when for the prevention of the accident I dematerialized the slots and parts of the bolt in his car. Once he turned out circuit plugs (disconnected the circuit) in his apartment, nevertheless the house had electrical lighting and the fax was on and received messages. I realized that situation in order to provide Sergey Petrovich, who was a serious researcher, with one more opportunity to observe personally manifestations of work of consciousness he was interested in.

The turned out plugs meant a disruption of the electrical circuit. I showed that staying at a distance I was able to close the disconnected circuit. Moreover in this case I did not use the phenomenon of materialization. I used another phenomenon. In reality I just modelled in my consciousness a lacking part of the conductor. How did I do it? I input into the right place information that a closed electrical circuit is required there. And the image created in the consciousness functions as a physical conductor. This example shows that consciousness can fulfill any functions.

This experiment also proves that it is possible to create technologies required for eternal development using no resources just on the basis of consciousness functioning principles. Moreover, such technologies are absolutely safe. For example, when I modelled by consciousness the lacking section of the conductor and the electric current appeared, the fundamental advantage was that there was no danger of electrocution in the place of the lacking section of the conductor. Based on this, on the basis of consciousness or at the technical level by means of optical systems, it is possible to build safe and invisible by physical sight devices just in the air.

In other cases described by me, the cases of materialization, the image created in the consciousness, passes into the physical image. This is the essence of the process of materialization.

We act in a similar way with resurrection. We create in the consciousness the image of the man we want to resurrect. And this image created in our consciousness we transfer into the physical image, which since that moment exists in the usual three-dimensional space. This is a natural process. And it confirms the fact that life is built on spiritual basis.

Therefore, if we understand that man was created for eternal life, that there should be neither passing away nor those who passed away in principle, if each person considers eternal life to be natural, life will be exactly like that, and physical reality will be exactly like that. Since an image in consciousness determines and forms physical image. This is the way physical reality is created. This is the way to create really happy eternal life.

## PARAGRAPH 6. THE USE OF TECHNICAL DEVICES FOR THE RESURRECTION OF PEOPLE AND FOR RESTORATION OF LOST ORGANS.

First of all, I should say that all technical devices are auxiliary means. They are intended for use by those people, who have not yet completely achieved structurization of consciousness in the area of restoration of health and in the area of restoration of organs and resurrection.

Actually these technical devices are called to help people who master technology of structurization of consciousness, technology of development of soul, spirit and creative ideas in the reality of the eternal World. Being auxiliary these devices are called to develop abilities man has to possess.

I have already said that all knowledge on eternal life, on resurrection, on restoration of organs, on recovery from any illnesses is originally laid into man upon his creation. However not everyone has awaken to awareness of this and to communication with his soul.

It is possible to communicate with the soul directly. In this case we have an example of work with the soul directly. The soul is originally created by God and it cannot be supplemented with any technical devices.

Technical devices can be used when we work not with the soul but with the consciousness. In this case these devices seemingly supplement those structures of knowledge of the soul, which haven't been completely transferred into the consciousness.

In other words, these technical devices supplement the structures of consciousness and this way they work together with the consciousness of people who haven't accomplished proper structurization of consciousness yet.

I have already created a number of such devices that really work. They are built on the basis of fundamental discovery made by me. I presented this discovery in my Ph.D. thesis in Physics and Mathematics based on which I received Doctor's degree.

The essence of the discovery is as follows. People become aware of any phenomena of reality through perception. The perception indeed can be achieved by different methods. For example, with the help of physical vision, or sensations, or mentally. When we fix the things that we perceive in our consciousness we can always see some light image. This light image is seen with spiritual sight. It can also immediately appear in consciousness. Using scientific language we can conditionally say that man has a certain system of conversion, which can transfer his perception into light images.

This our system of conversion, the optical system, is used also in resurrection. The image of man who is to be resurrected in this specific process of the World control might be considered as an optical signal. This signal in the spiritual space (the image of the person who is being resurrected) corresponds to the perception of this person in usual physical world. From this point of view resurrection is the process of the transformation of an optical signal from spiritual space into three-dimensional physical space.

Similar optical systems of conversion can be created at technical level. These are exactly the technical devices which are described in this section. These devices supplement the abilities of man in the space of control. In other words, all the auxiliary technical equipment should work according to the principle of complementation.

An example of such an auxiliary means is a developed by me software product that is based on my discovery. I created the model of archive storage of information in any point of space-time (certificate-license "Archive Storage of Information in Any Point of Space-Time") APPENDIX E, p. 437

Reproduction of matter in any point of space-time might be provided on the basis of information that is archived in this point. Moreover this point can be chosen in any substance, in air or vacuum, that is to say, really in any place

The method is as follows.

Space is considered as the structure of time revealed in perception. Time is considered as the function of space. The reproduction of matter is considered as the consequence of the reaction of time to the change of space. In this case it is possible to calculate the points of contact of space with time. These points are the points of archive storage of any information.

Knowledge of the points of archive storage of information makes it possible to create technological systems on the basis of computers, which can archive the required information in any point of space-time. This circumstance makes it possible to create a form of intellect that can be considered as an intellectual machine (machine sapiens i.e., intellectual machine, by analogy with Homo Sapiens).

The archived information of the past is the static construction of this machine. Archive storage of the future provides its dynamic construction. The area of the present ensures control of this intellectual machine. Thus it is possible to create a required form of intellect that completely controls the intellectual machine on the basis of human consciousness.

This form of reason will not destroy the creator or other objects, since in the current time it is always manifested only in the form of functions of creative control. This is an example of an intelligent machine, safe for man, animals and other objects of information.

The distinctive feature of this discovery is that information can backed up not only on floppy disks or other currently known media, but in vacuum as well. And I do it through single pulses of a special set-top box to a computer.

You can also archive information in the air by means of reflected from floppy pulse or in any substance by continuous recording.

Archived in this way information at the physical level can be placed, for example, in an area of a match head size (diameter less than 3 mm).

A completely new type of computer equipment can be created on the basis of this method of information archiving. It can be used to create the desired form of mind in vacuum, air or any substance. Similarly a reader for archived information can be made. As a result in practice we get an intelligent machine that occupies no place and is located where necessary. This machine is a controlled form of reason. On our desire it can be targeted at creation of substance, space or time. There is one more my method (certificate-license "Computer Technology of Remote Control") (APPENDIX E, p.438 that can be used for creation of completely new types of computer technology. I developed a technology of transfer of information of any event into geometric forms. A special computer software first transfers a certain considered event into a corresponding to it geometric form. Further this initial form is converted into another one, namely such, which corresponds to the development of this event in the required direction. This is the way of events control realization. Moreover, control can be exercised at any distance. In the particular case computer can be used for creating the required form of reason at the selected point. This reason at the selected point arises from the action of controlling single pulses from a special set-top box to the computer.

I have built several different installations of this type. They work great. They use interaction between space and time to create substance. This is one more principle that I discovered it is officially registered (Certificate-license "Time is the Form of Space"). (APPENDIX E, p. 439

This document states that I have developed computer technologies that make it possible to transfer time into any substance. Thus completely new possibilities for creating substances are offered. These computer technologies make it possible to ensure control of material, organism tissues regeneration, possibility to instantly obtain the required form of material, construction of buildings, creation of mechanisms and machines, controlling machines, and much more.

Due to these and other created by me technologies you can forget once and for all the energy crises and the problem of energy. Energy can be obtained, for example, from the time of past events. This energy source is unlimited.

I think it makes sense to make one more comment to the above. You may wonder how it is possible to archive information not on the traditional media, such as diskettes, but without any media in vacuum.

Let us recall again that space and time are the constructions of consciousness. And since space and time are the constructions of consciousness, information can be placed into any point of space-time including vacuum. Since vacuum, so to speak, "empty space" is also a construction of consciousness. For this very reason some scientists though on the one hand consider vacuum as a medium, which does not contain material, on the other hand are forced to admit that one can get everything from vacuum. And in order to justify somehow this position they began to call vacuum as physical vacuum. Creation of names is often a way of avoiding problem solution. It will never be possible to make ends meet if we continue to keep to the concept of objective physical reality that does not depend on consciousness. Since, as we know, such reality just does not exist.

In fact the essence of the question is simple. Vacuum, the empty space, is the same construction of consciousness as anything else. And since vacuum is the construction of consciousness, it is indeed possible to get everything from it. Because it is possible to get everything from consciousness. All bodies are created on the basis of consciousness.

And therefore, it is not surprising that at any point including vacuum it is possible to archive any information. And thus it is possible to create a required form of reason at the selected point.

Thus, on the basis of the presented discoveries I created special software products. This is a normal computer software; however, it works according to the principle of extrasensory effect. It properly supplements the information of control and as a result tissue appears, or otherwise, the tissue is created. And as a consequence of this, for example, the destroyed cells are restored.

When recovering organs and physical body altogether, the tissue that is sure to be connected with the soul of man is created. We have to keep in mind that one of the manifestations of the soul is highly concentrated information. Connection of the created tissue with the soul takes place due to the coordination of information.

By the way, since the soul is an infinite by the volume structure and since one of the manifestations of the soul is highly concentrated information, it is obvious that this is archive storage of information at all points of space-time. So the principle of archive storage of information is one of the fundamental principles of the World. Therefore its use, which was discussed above, is completely natural. And therefore possibility to create such form of reason that will constantly restore man at any point of space-time is quite natural. It will not just restore his organs or resurrect him, but generally will ensure the constant level of normal health.

This work will be implemented, as I said, on the basis of the principle of complementation. In other words, technical devices will implement this work when human consciousness is diverted to something else or if structurization of one's consciousness hasn't been completed in this area yet. This is exactly how the devices created by me work based on the principle of complementation.

In resurrection and restoration of lost organs conducted with the aid of technical devices the question related to the identity is especially urgent. Indeed the resurrected person should be exactly the same one, who he was before. He should be exactly the same. The same refers to his organs, to the physical tissue. In the general case the recreated object should manifest itself identically in physical reality. This problem is solved on the basis of my discovery (Certificate - license "Reproducing self-developing systems, which reflect the external and internal areas of the variety of creating spheres" APPENDIX 6, p. 440

The fact of the matter is as follows. I discovered the complete identity of any objects of information with respect to the creating area of information that provides complete identity of the restorable objects with their originals. I made the discovery of creating area of information using the knowledge about the soul. Complete identity achieved in the processes of restoration was demonstrated in practice. The protocols of these results are notarized in the United Nations.

I proposed concrete technologies that make it possible to use the creating area of information without its destruction. Moreover, it is shown how it is possible to ensure its self-development.

There is a detailed technique that enables you to find such creating information areas. The idea of this procedure is as follows. We get the form of a sphere from the past known objects of information. Actually on the inner surface of this sphere we have reflections of objects of the current time on the basis of the principle of common connections. Now let us choose an object, which must be restored. We find its reflection on the inner surface of the sphere since we know the past. This will be the area of creation of this object. As a result the object can be completely restored.

Real technologies that I created work exactly in line with this principle. They restore entire person, either his individual organs or separate cells. These technical devices work on the basis of developed by me special computer software and optical systems.

The above discoveries are presented in my work "Applied Structures of the Creating Area of Information". On the basis of the principles presented there I made one more invention that was registered under invention patent No 2148845 named: "Method for Prevention of Catastrophes and a Device for its Realization". APPENDIX E, p.. 441-449 We have already discussed this device when we spoke about prevention of earthquakes. However earthquake is just one type of catastrophes. There are different types of catastrophes. Cancer or AIDS of the fourth stage are also catastrophes but of human organism. Illnesses, which are not so serious can be considered as smaller-scale catastrophes. Since this device is created on the basis of true science it is of universal action. And therefore it can be successfully applied for prevention and elimination of organism catastrophes, i.e., for recovery. And for resurrection as well.

I'd like to remind that this device works as follows. First it decreases the force of the approaching catastrophe. If it has enough technical capacity it just eliminates the potential danger. But if its capacity is insufficient for complete elimination of the catastrophe, it maximally reduces the impending danger as much as possible in line with its potential and then it reports when and where this catastrophe might occur. Then it is possible to concentrate on crystals with the thought on prevention of the catastrophe or recovery and in this case the capacity of the device will increase many times.

The device intended for resurrection and for health recovery is based on the same operating principle.

This device is an optical system created on the basis of crystals. If something is wrong in a human organism it suffices to place this device near the person or to direct toward him the receiving surface of the device in order to restore normal health.

If to direct this device toward the sick organ or toward its X-ray photograph, restoration of this organ occurs. If to direct this crystalline module toward the photograph of the person who passed away, you can implement his resurrection. By directing the module to the schedule of some event, you can normalize all actions connected with it.

Thus, this technical device is a universal one based on its ability to restore normal state. You may be interested to know how it gets information about the norm the organism should be brought in line with. Or about the norm of some other object? It reads information about the harmonic norm in the space, that is to say, about that norm, which was laid by the Creator for this very development stage. This device adjusts the corresponding system to this norm. And information about the required norm exists at each point of space.

I am going to repeat once again that such devices controlled by the consciousness of man have been working already in practice. The technical devices of the future will be created based on the same principles.

The set out principles can be also used for creation of devices for transmission of information. One of such devices created by me has already passed all tests successfully. For it I received the patent of invention "Information-Carrying System" No 2163419. APPENDIX E, p. 450-458

It works as follows. You should mentally, to yourself, pronounce a phrase. This phrase can be considered as a message you want to transfer. Of course if you have accomplished the structurization of consciousness, you are able to transfer this message telepathically without any devices. But if you haven't mastered such methods yet, special devices can help you.

The transmitting device built on the basis of principles discussed above transfers your thought. And at other end another crystal device converts your thought into words or images based on your desire. Actually this is a new form of communication built without the use of electromagnetic waves. One newspaper publication named my invention telepathothrone. It is possible to use laser emission instead of the operator for the transfer of video or audio information. Then it will be possible to transmit television and radio broadcasts, exchange computer data and so forth. I developed a technology that makes it possible to connect the abilities of the normalizing and transmitting crystalline modules. Based on this technology it is possible to produce a miniature crystalline system, which can be accommodated on the bracelet of a wrist watch, which will restore a man, and moreover it will transfer data about his health to the central crystalline system. If the central system receives information that the state of the organism should be improved, the human health is restored by the central large crystals. Such technologies of restoration can be extended to any objects of information.

The transmission of information is done instantly. The distance doesn't matter. You can transmit your thought to any point of space, to any Galaxy. Moreover there are no such areas where this could be prevented. And furthermore, the sent mental signal will always be individual, since it is sent by a specific person. The individuality of the thought and consequently of the signal always remains in line with the set of the signs. Therefore such communication systems are ideal from the point of view of interference immunity. And moreover they are completely controlled. The same way the devices created for restoring organs and for resurrection are also completely controlled when they work.

## PARAGRAPH 7. RECOVERY FROM ANY ILLNESSES WITH THE HELP OF NUMBER SERIES.

We have already discussed the use of numerical sequences. Let us recall the eleventh method of the resurrection of people from the third chapter. The method included usage of seven number sequences for resurrection. Moreover the sequences were different for the different cases of concentration.

Possibility of resurrection of man with the help of certain number series means that this method can be used to cure people from any illnesses. Since the resurrection of man can be considered as his recovery from a very serious disease. Other illnesses are easier. So this simple method is very effective in reality

Since the simplicity of the method is its big advantage, I used this approach when I wrote the handbook for recovery from any illnesses.

This book has been written already. It is called "Restoration of Human Organism by Concentration on Numbers". It includes more than a hundred pages. There are about a thousand of disease names with corresponding number series of seven, eight or nine numbers for each disease. Being tuned to any particular number series you cure yourselves from the corresponding disease.

The question arises: why such simple procedure as concentration on a specific number series, proves to be so effective for recovery from diseases? What is the matter here?

Here is the thing. Each disease is a deviation from the norm. This is a deviation from the norm in the work of separate cells, organs, or entire organism as a whole. Recovery from any disease means return to the norm. So the number series provided by me just ensure return to the norm. By concentration on a particular sequence of numbers, by being tuned to this number series, you are setting your organism to the state that is the norm. As a result everything is fixed as the recovery from the disease.

For the explanation of the essence of this treatment I would like to give some information about the vibratory structure of numbers.

Our life is pierced with rhythm. Planets periodically rotate around the Sun. For the Earth this means recurrent alternation of winter and summer. The Earth revolves around its axis and the regular change of day and night occurs.

And at the micro-level the picture is the same. Electrons in the atom make regular movements around the nucleus. Each of us after listening can hear regular beating of the heart. Each cell in our organism has its rhythm. And the totality of the cells has its rhythm although a different one. And the big totality that is at the level of an organ has another one. There is a specific rhythm at the level of connection between organs.

Organism in this respect can be compared with an orchestra. Orchestra when performs a work should not play falsely. The same refers to organism. Organism sounding should be harmonious. And if some organ or some connection in its work deviates from the norm, in other words it begins to play falsely; this is an exact indication of the beginning of a disease. And then you as the conductor of your orchestra have to wave your conductor's stick and restore its harmonious sounding.

Rhythm can be also found where it is not available at first glance. Let us consider an example of rainbow, which sometimes appears in the sky after rain. We will see splendid paints, saturated bright colors. But what are these colors from the point of view of science? We perceive this one or another color due to the action of an electromagnetic wave of a specific frequency. The vibratory frequency in the violet part of the visible spectrum is approximately two times higher than the vibratory frequency in the red area. Thus, the difference in the perception of color depends on different vibratory frequency.

When a person perceives numbers it is not obvious for him that they are related to a vibratory structure the same way as color. We have found out that a specific vibratory frequency corresponds to each color. Exactly the same thing takes place in the case with numbers. Each number is correlated with the corresponding to it vibratory structure. The same refers to the sequences of numbers.

By the way, each number series can be considered as a specific combination of numbers. Let's again consider the spectral colors; there is a big experience in the use of their combinations in science and technology. For example, in color television. All those different beautiful colors, which you see on the screen, are in reality received by the mixing of just three colors: red, green and dark-blue. A certain brightness of each of these colors is used on the basis of the required image.

An orchestra sounds differently from any separately used instrument. Each collection of spectral colors gives its specific effect. The same refers to sets of numbers.

A bad set of numbers in the identification number of an aircraft can result in the appearance of undesirable vibrations. And vice versa, a suitable, or we'd better say, correct set of numbers contributes to a favorable course of events, to establishment of harmony. This method of treatment is based exactly on this property of correct combination of numbers.

I have already said that in case of any illness correct sequence of numbers results in recovery, in other words, it adjusts organism to the norm. However, now as we have learned that each number and each sequence of numbers is related to the corresponding vibratory structure, recovery with the use of this method can be described in a different way. A correctly selected sequence of numbers results in adjustment of organism to the norm because the numerical sequence related to a certain vibratory structure is the norm itself. It is the required sounding, correct sounding. And concentration on this sequence of numbers indicates tuning. Exactly the same way musical tools are tuned based on the sounding of a tuning fork.

Now let us return to my handbook. The book consists of 27 chapters. Each chapter includes a collection of specific diseases. The first 25 chapters actually include all known diseases. The 26th chapter provides concentrations for recovery from unknown diseases and conditions.

Following the name of each chapter there is a restoring number series, which applies to all diseases together placed in this chapter. It is always possible to use it and especially when the exact diagnosis is not known, when it is just known that the disease relates to this chapter. If the diagnosis is known the number series that follows just after the name of the concrete illness should be used. It is also possible to use additionally the general number of the chapter, as I've mentioned before.

The content of the book presents the names of diseases each followed by a number series that cures this disease.

As an example here is the beginning of the first chapter.

CHAPTER 1. PRINCIPLES OF TREATMENT FOR CRITICAL CONDITIONS – 1258912.

ACUTE RESPIRATORY FAILURE – 1257814 –pathologic state of the organism when maintenance of the normal gas composition of blood is not provided or is achieved by the effort of compensating mechanisms of external respiration and is characterized by:

- Decrease of $pO_2$ of arterial blood ($paO_2$) below 50 mm Hg when breathing air;

- Increase of $pCO_2$ of arterial blood ($paCO_2$) above 50 mm Hg;

- Disorder of mechanics and rhythm of respiration;

- PH decrease (7.35).

ACUTE CARDIOVASCULAR FAILURE (CONGESTIVE CARDIAC FAILURE)– 1895678 –lost ability of heart to provide adequate blood supply to organs and systems, break of capacities of heart and needs of tissues for oxygen, is characterized by low blood pressure, reduction of blood flow in tissues.

CARDIAC ARREST (clinical death) – 8915678 –transient condition between life and death: this is not death yet, but it is not life already. It begins from the moment of termination of activity of the central nervous system, blood circulation and breathing.

TRAUMATIC SHOCK, SHOCK AND SHOCKLIKE CONDITIONS – 1895132 – grave condition caused by an injury, which is accompanied by the expressed disturbances of functions of vitally important organs, first of all blood circulation and respiration.

Further I will give just the names of the following chapters with the appropriate restoring number series.

CHAPTER 2. TUMOR DISEASES – 8214351.

CHAPTER 3. SEPSIS – 58143212.

CHAPTER 4. SYNDROME OF DISSEMINATED INTRAVASCULAR COAGULATION OF BLOOD – 5148142.

CHAPTER 5. DISEASES OF THE ORGANS OF BLOOD CIRCULATION– 1289435.

CHAPTER 6.  RHEUMATIC DISEASES – 8148888.

CHAPTER 7.  DISEASES OF THE ORGANS OF RESPIRATION – 5823214.

CHAPTER 8.  DISEASES OF THE ORGANS OF DIGESTION – 5321482.

CHAPTER 9.  DISEASES OF KIDNEYS AND URINARY TRACTS – 8941254.

CHAPTER 10.  DISEASES OF BLOOD SYSTEMS – 1843214.

CHAPTER 11.  ENDOCRINE AND METABOLIC DISEASES – 1823451.

CHAPTER 12.  OCCUPATIONAL DISEASES – 4185481.

CHAPTER 13.  ACUTE POISONINGS – 4185412.

CHAPTER 14.  INFECTIOUS DISEASES – 5421427.

CHAPTER 15.  VITAMIN DEFICIENCY DISEASE – 1234895.

CHAPTER 16.  CHILDREN'S DISEASES – 18543218.

CHAPTER 17.  MIDWIFERY, FEMALE DISEASES – 1489145.

CHAPTER 18.  NERVOUS DISEASES – 148543293.

CHAPTER 19.  MENTAL ILLNESSES – 8345444.

CHAPTER 20.  SEXUAL DISORDERS – 1456891.

CHAPTER 21.  SKIN AND VENEREAL DISEASES – 18584321.

CHAPTER 22.  SURGICAL DISEASES – 18574321.

CHAPTER 23.  DISEASES OF EAR, THROAT, NOSE – 1851432.

CHAPTER 24. EYE DISEASES – 1891014.

CHAPTER 25. DENTAL AND ORAL CAVITY DISEASES – 1488514.

CHAPTER 27. NORMAL LABORATORY VALUES – 1489999.

It case of some indisposition it might be difficult to determine diagnosis, or even determine the type of disease, that is to say, indicate the chapter related to this illness. To help to cope with such situation I included an additional chapter into the book, the 26th: "UNKNOWN DISEASES AND CONDITIONS – 1884321".

The essence of the method in this case is as follows.

Human body is considered as consisting of seven parts. I will cite them below; moreover I will place the appropriate restoring number series next to each body part.

1. Head – 1819999.

2. Neck – 18548321.

3. Right hand – 1854322.

4. Left hand – 4851384.

5. Trunk – 5185213.

6. Right foot – 4812531.

7. Left foot – 485148291.

Now I'll explain how to use these data. Let us assume that a man had a headache. In this case he can use the number series intended for head. If a man experiences some painful sensations in two or more body parts simultaneously, it is necessary to concentrate consecutively on the numbers, which correspond to these areas. Several words about numbers with a different number of digits. Let us compare sequences, which consist of 7, 8, and 9 digits. If the sequence consists of 9 numbers, as a rule it ensures recovery from one or two specific diseases. If the number series is of 8 digits, it cures on the average from five diseases. If the number series consists of 7 digits it can cure ten or more different diseases. In other words, a number series of 7 digits possesses a greater capacity; the area of its applications is considerably wider. For this very reason I used mainly these number series in the handbook.

I have already described practical work with number series in Chapter III when I explained the eleventh method of resurrection of people. It is possible to pass through numerical sequence from the beginning to the end. But it is possible to begin from the outermost numbers and gradually come to the center.

When you work with number series it is possible to act differently in another aspect. When you pass from one digit to another you can concentrate for equal time, on each digit. And it is possible to stay on some digits for one period, and for another period on others. It is possible to concentrate on each of seven digits for different time.

In this case we should return for a minute to color television. As I said, only three colors are used for creation of a colored image: red, green, and dark-blue. Combination of these three elements gives a new color. The resulting color can be changed by changing the intensity of these three components.

When the duration of concentration on some number is changed, the effective force of this number is changed. Therefore, when the duration of concentration on separate digits of a certain number sequence is changed, its quite different sounding appears, and thus it acts a bit differently. In your practical work you should rely on your intuition although regenerative effect is achieved at any duration of concentrations.

I would like to draw your attention to the following. When you concentrate on numbers, you should at the same time be aware of yourself, perceive your organism, see it inwardly, and see it to be absolutely healthy. This is important for quick restoration of normal condition.

This method can be used for treatment of other people.

The meaning of the entire handbook is that on the basis of ten numbers: 0, 1, 2, 3, 4, 5, 6, 7, 8, 9 you should be able to know how to cure any illnesses and further maintain the achieved normal state of health.

In order to achieve normal health some restoring moods are frequently used, i.e., specific texts, which consist just of several phrases. Correctly comprised mood texts possess great effectiveness. In form it's kind of a similar method. Since a specific sequence of words is used in the mood text, and in that method, which we discuss, a specific sequence of the numbers is used.

Word is also a symbol. Actually, if we take any object, for example, a table, we can easily find that different peoples have completely different words to name the same object. Nevertheless, although word is a symbol everyone knows well what force it possesses. This can be explained by the corresponding spiritual-energy vibratory structure related to each word.

Let us return to number. If to express the same at the fundamental level, we can say that each number, exactly as each word, is related to spiritual-energy vibratory structure. This ensures their effectiveness.

The most different phenomena of our life could be analyzed on the basis of this approach. For example, music. Each sound is also related to spiritual-energy vibratory structure. That is why music can have such striking effect on the listeners. As you understand, once there are number series for recovery from diseases, it is quite natural that number series for the solution of other vital problems should exist. And this is really so.

In life we have to make decisions at every turn. For example, shall we agree to the proposed work or not; will this work prove to be that activity, which will help your development, or not; is currently existing situation favorable for some enterprise or not; have you chosen the best way to solve the problems you face or not; is the partner who appeared on your horizon suitable or not; does your desire coincide with what you really need or not, and so on to infinity. It is possible to give, for any type of life situation, an optimizing number series, which will help you to solve the problem you face.

At the same time the number series fulfill the task of structuring of consciousness for control of events. This is their usefulness. The number series can help you to cope better with many tasks and generally to be much better oriented in the manifested world.

Appendix G includes two number sequences for each day of month. One is of seven numbers, another is of nine. You may concentrate on them consecutively: on the first one and then on another one. Or separately, at different times.

These number series, exactly as those given by me for recovery from diseases, are connected with control coming from the spiritual sphere. And therefore the work with them contributes to the development of the spirit.

You should also do two other exercises, given in the Appendix. This will help your development and establishment of harmony with the pulse of the Universe.

**PARAGRAPH 8. METHODS OF CREATING ANY MATTER ON THE BASIS OF YOUR CONSCIOUSNESS.**

We know well the topic that is the creation of matter. We consider it throughout the book. Now I will give you the methods of consciousness structuring, these are the methods to construct your consciousness so that you could be able to create any matter from your consciousness. The mastery of these methods gives understanding how the Creator created matter. These methods actually provide that technology of development which was laid by God

These methods give the precise understanding how each element of reality interacts with other elements. They make it possible to really build matter and to really control this process.

Understanding of interaction between elements means very much. Let's consider, for example, resurrection of people. I can say that it suffices just to bring one parameter to the norm, let us say, from the point of view of the microcell of man, and due to this the man could be resurrected. That's what the understanding of the normal connections gives.

The methods set out by me are fundamental. If you construct correctly, for example, one element of micro-level, a single cell, you might be confident that you are capable of resurrecting man. This practice gives real knowledge about the methods of realization of eternal life.

Thus, you should consider the methods set out here exactly as the methods of construction of any matter on the basis of your consciousness.

## 1. CONSTRUCTION OF MICROMATTER.

In order to construct micro-matter you should isolate a distant site in your consciousness. We have already met this concept in the very beginning of the third chapter. You should know exactly what the distant section of consciousness means for you.

You have to tune to your distant section, to isolate it for you personally, and this distant section will be the micro-matter that is connected to all other elements of reality. What this exactly micro-matter might be for you? It depends on you. This might be, for example, a molecule, i.e., the smallest particle of substance. And this can be the element of a deeper level, i.e., any structure, which creates matter. This structure of a deeper level implies the base in it on which the matter is built.

Thus, the first method of construction of matter is as follows: you isolate a distant part of your consciousness and assign it to be micro-matter, a micro-element. You can isolate as many of such areas and respectively micro-elements as you wish, at your discretion.

## 2. CREATION OF MACRO-ELEMETS FROM MICRO-ELEMENTS.

According to the first method you have an entire collection of micro-elements. These are, in fact, the chosen sections of your consciousness. You begin to move them in your consciousness, and during their motion you began to see certain symbols, certain images. These images, in turn, also begin to move, and you see their joining up. The process continues, and as a result you receive a certain object, for example, a connection of molecules.

You can thus create tissue and restore organs, resurrect people, cure illnesses, and materialize any objects. For this, of course, you will have to direct the creative process described above. Based on this method you can build any reality, physical or spiritual, any in general, if you just refer it to the macrocosm. In this method you pass from micro-matter to macro-matter.

I will repeat once again the basic features of the first two methods.

In the first method you isolate several the most distant sites of consciousness. You consider them as micro-elements. You appoint them micro-elements. And if you understand correctly the normal connections you can thus get the entire object.

In the second method you watch the movement of these micro-elements. The movement can be chaotic or system, this is not important. The main thing is to have, as a result of this movement, these micro-elements joined up as if sticking to each other into a single whole and as a result the creation of macro-matter takes place.

You assign in the first method, and you already get the second one.

## 3. CONSTRUCTION OF REALITY WITH THE HELP OF THINKING.

This method can be considered as the consequence of the first two ones. You should take the isolated by you micro-matter and macro-matter constructed in your consciousness and instantly, with a very high mental speed, connect these areas. The area built this way is the isolated part of the thought and serves to be a kind of platform; your thinking rests on this platform and as a result achieves construction of any matter. This case refers to the construction of any matter from the point of view of basics.

However, it is possible to act differently in this method. This is another approach. You do not need to allocate micro-areas in your consciousness and build macro-areas with their help. You can create substance just on the basis of thinking. In other words it is just enough to think. Therefore, with this approach you isolate that thinking component, which is a controlling one, which builds reality.

This way you can construct a table, a computer, a plant, a man, anything.

## 4. CONSTRUCTION OF THE ELEMENTS OF EXTERNAL REALITY DUE

TO THE REFLECTION ON THE INTERNAL ELEMENT OF YOUR CONSCIOUSNESS.

You fix a certain internal element of your consciousness and watch how the image of the external reality approaches you, or to be more exact, this internal element of your consciousness. And here when the border of this element of perception is crossed you fix what you want to get.

Simply put, you introduce your desire into the element of perception. And then it turns out that you build what you need where your perception is located. Perception in this case is located in the area of control.

Thus, in this method, the zone of control is located in the area, which is isolated by you; your perception is located in this area, and the required physical or spiritual reality is achieved there.

5. CONSTRUCTION OF THE INTERNAL CONTENT OF ALL IMAGES OF EXTERNAL REALITY.

You can perceive objects by physical sight. You look, for example, at a computer and you see its exterior view. You can perceive the computer, also, at the level of thinking. It's a different perception. Your task in this method is to use an additional approach. You have to construct mentally the internal contents of an object, let us say, a computer, so that your construction would reflect the way the Creator implements this construction.

The Creator is present in the construction of each element of reality, including the construction of each element of computer. To act like the Creator, means in this case to comprehend the structure of computer, to see internal connections in it, to isolate them into the microsystem and thus to realize, how, for example, the molecules are attached to each other. If you can instantly realize all systems of connections, their interaction, you have already understood from these connections the meaning of this device. And you can create it. Or if it has already been created, in case of breakdown you will always be able to repair it. Moreover, for this you do not necessarily have to understand how its concrete physical elements are built.

You just need to know the connections between the elements of information that are the content of this object, let us say, a computer. You just need the knowledge of the connections between the elements of information and you will always be able to restore the work of the object as a whole.

## 6. DISCRETE CONTROL THROUGH CONTINUOUS THINKING.

In this method you should choose any object and imagine it as if consisting from parts. Man is an exception. Man should always be seen as a whole, his image should always be one-piece. But other objects can be mentally divided into parts. Let us take, for example, a spoon. We can imagine it consisting of several parts. For simplicity, as I did in certain cases in the third chapter, let us confine ourselves to three parts.

Thus, we visualize a spoon consisting of three parts (discreteness!). Now we use these elements of the chosen item for creation of the desired object. Three parts of the spoon are the elements of the chosen reality. They are material objects.

In this method we begin directly with the matter. However each of these building blocks of matter has its specific form. The object we want to create has another form. It is also material, but of another form. It means that it is necessary just to change the form. By changing the form at the information level it is possible to transfer one object into another without changing it. The connecting continuous element of thinking is the transfer of one form into another. The continuity of thinking in this case means the presence of one thought. Thought develops in line with the same laws, which were used by God for creation of material objects. Having mastered such way of thinking you will be able to build any element of reality from any other object; moreover the initial object will be retained.

## 7. CONSTRUCTION OF SPACE THAT CONTAINSTHE VECTOR ELEMENT OF TIME.

In this method you should first construct space for matter creation. In this space you should construct the vector of time that will enable you to differentiate matter and to create it.

The vector of time is a technical term. It is not related directly to those vectors, which you know from mathematics. This is a conditional concept. I will explain what it means.

Imagine that you see a landscape in front of you. For example, you see trees. A certain tree began to grow sometimes in one place, and another one somewhere else and at another time. Time can be imagined as a system that unpacks space. Or simply stated it gives a certain value to each part of space. And each part of space in this case has its time. Time plays a unique role in this case. It can be compared with a screenwriter who coordinates everything that takes place in the space.

When you thus determine space and time the creation of the vector of time means the creation of a tool necessary for control. When I speak about the construction of the vector of time, I mean that the vector of time should become such essence of your consciousness, that as a result you will always have the exact information about the location of any object. In this case to you don't have to draw something or imagine something in the form of a concrete vector. In other words, the construction of the vector of time in your consciousness is actually awareness of what and where something is located, and when and how it develops. So, it suffices just to realize the vector of time as I said and you will be able to create matter.

8. THE CONSTRUCTION OF INFORMATION IN SUCH A WAY THAT EACH ELEMENT COULD CONSTRUCT ANY OTHER. THE METHOD OF INSERTIONS.

The essence of this method is the construction of generally significant and variously scattered system of values, construction of the area of information, each element of which can create any other.

In this method you should take any two elements of information and due to multiple mental insertions of one element into another and swapping their locations you can get any other element. In other words this is the method of insertions.

The details of the applied procedure are as follows. You can take any objects, for example, a video cassette and an orange or any other ones. It doesn't matter. You should visualize the two chosen objects as if having the form of spheres. Mentally you should take one of these spheres and pack it into another one, and then you swap them. You should move them many, many times this way. When you move them for long time a certain corridor, along which these displacements take place, appears in your consciousness. With practice, the creation of these corridors becomes habitual. If to consider how they appear it becomes clear that they are the displacements of the thought. So, this habitual path of the thought movement is the matter. You take it mentally and put into the sick organ and as a result this organ becomes healthy. Or you should direct this matter towards the photograph of the passed away person, and the person is resurrected.

## 9. CONSTRUCTION OF THE MATTER THROUGH THE VARIETY OF EXTERNAL FORMS.

Let's suppose you perceive an object, for example, a computer, a tree or something else. The object can be chosen arbitrarily. Further you should imagine it as if consisting of many parts. I'd like to remind you that it is possible to act this way with any object except man. I have mentioned this before. Man should always be perceived whole. This is connected with the arrangement of his consciousness. By the way, even that information, which in principle corresponds as if to the consciousness of computer, i.e., to the area of its reaction, perceives the whole person.

Thus, you should choose any object, for example, a computer and imagine it as if consisting of many parts. Moreover all these individual parts are located in different places. And each has its specific form. Thus you have a variety of forms in front of you. You perceive them all simultaneously. It is possible to say that your perception seemingly is composed of many parallel perceptions. That is to say, you simultaneously perceive many elements of all shapes.

Now you should find in your consciousness the point, at which all this varied information could be assembled instantly. This place is called the point of assembly. You can instantly assemble yourself informatively at this point; this is the area of your self-recreation.

You mentally dismantled the chosen object for parts in the area of your perception. You should take now the whole variety of these elements and imagine that you reflect them from the point of assembling. The matter built by you will be where they are collected after reflection. Of course you have to control this process.

Thus, you reflect from the place of assembling all the elements of various shapes. Further you should gather them in that place where you want to create the matter. The process of the collection of many elements in one place has an analogy in optics. A convex lens works exactly this way, i.e., usual magnifying lens. With the help of the lens you can gather light rays into a point. This analogy can help you in your practical work. On the basis of this method you can construct any matter. Any creative matter, of course. However, you are able to build not only physical matter, such as, for example, a computer. You can build any element of reality. Well, for example, any element of the creative development of society. Or to get a concrete technology of how to develop the society. Or where to get information. If you reflect diverse elements from the point of assembling and gather then instantly you will get knowledge. Moreover this knowledge will contribute to your personal and at the same time general creative development.

10. INDEPENDENT CREATION OF MATTER WHERE IT SHOULD HAVE APPEARED AS A CONSEQUENCE OF WORK OF THE CHOSEN ELEMENT OF REALITY.

Let us imagine a tree. We can see many branches and green leaves on the branches. We mentally note this situation; this is already available in nature. We also know that after sometime new leaves will appear on the branches next to those, which are already there. This will just happen because the tree lives and develops. So, you may not wait when a leaf will appear on the branch chosen by you but create it yourself. In this method you consider what elements appear as a consequence, in this case of the growth of the tree. And thus you create these elements yourself.

Method consists in isolating of sections in your perception that have already been constructed on the basis of information and then building independently the following element.

I can give another example. Look how corals grow. Or crystals. You can even conduct a simple experiment. Pour some water into a plate or a cup of and dissolve some quantity of culinary (table) salt in it. The quantity of salt should ensure formation of a saturated solution. When the solution becomes saturated the salt will be no longer dissolved in it. Now put there a small crystal of salt. It can be placed on the bottom or hung up on a string so that it would not touch the bottom. You will see that this small crystal will begin to grow and gradually it will become bigger and bigger. New layers will be formed on the basis of those, which have already been. You can control this process and build the crystal independently with the help of your consciousness.

So, if you want to build some matter, you consider what could be the process or the work of the reality element that could result in the appearance of this matter. And then you create it yourself from your consciousness. I will repeat again: you don't take anything from anywhere. Everything is produced by your consciousness.

These are the ten methods of building any matter on the basis of our consciousness I decided to introduce to you. Of course there are still other methods. But these are the ones most adapted to any consciousness. Moreover you got acquainted with the methods of creation of matter in the previous chapters. If to add methodologies outlined here to the principles of resurrection and methods of resurrections, which you have already learned from the previous chapters, you will be able to create any matter on the basis of your consciousness. Moreover, you will be able to do this on the practical-scientific basis following the indicated methods. Provided that you understood what is described in this book, the creation of matter from your consciousness becomes a standard procedure.

You will be able to resurrect people, restore lost organs, and recover health. You will be able to control any situation, build any required element base, for example, to create air where it is necessary; moreover you will be able to create ecologically clean air. You will be able to do so that an aircraft would not fall in a critical situation, an explosion would not take place at a nuclear plant, and any catastrophes would be prevented. In other words, you will be able to achieve real system rescuing of all people. You, of course, understand that these methods require independent mastery. And therefore a decisive factor here is practice. Try to apply these methods to construction not only of physical matter, but of spiritual as well. It's quite a different level. In this case it is possible to speak, for example, about feelings: love, loyalty hope, and a lot more. If to consider love as an original matter, with the help of these methods you can enable other people to perceive it correctly.

Everything discussed also relates to construction of any information. You will be able to build any information as such on the basis of these methods. And you will be able to manifest your consciousness in the manner you want, for it to be manifested creatively. In particular, for example, for creation of any matter, spiritual or physical. You will be able to create any information and any matter, spiritual or physical, because the presented methods include technology, which the Creator uses.

## CONCLUSION

This book, as I mentioned before, is one of a series of books, devoted to the description of the true picture of the World. Therefore it should naturally include answers to questions related to the fundamental arrangement of the World. And of course it should include the answer to the question of what is primary, what is the basis of everything.

This book gives a clear and definite answer to this question. The God, the creator is primary. Next the soul and spirit come. Then consciousness. And consciousness acts independently, on its own, and as the link between the spiritual and physical, between the spirit and matter. Physical matter is the form of the development of consciousness. The World is arranged this way. Life is built on the spiritual basis. Numerous documented facts strongly support this. Just the three-volume edition of "The Practice of Control. The Way of Salvation" includes several hundreds of such facts.

Resurrection has become already a part of our daily life; it becomes one of its phenomena. Those people who had an opportunity to read just a part of this book got a new sense of life, and many of them began to resurrect successfully. There are a lot of resurrected people already, and their number continuously increases.

Resurrection of all who passed away and birth of new and new people will result in a significant increase in the population of the Earth. This makes the issue of resources urgent. Due to the limited material resources the basic method of their obtaining will be their creation on the basis of consciousness. That is why I included the methods of obtaining any matter on the basis of one's consciousness into this book of this series. The mastery of these methods will make it possible to solve all tasks including the increase of the required space.

These methods represent a vivid example of control, control of reality. They will ensure further development of our civilization, they will ensure infinite development of our life.

The principles of resurrection, the methods of creating the matter and the methods of eternal development, they all express the true essence of man.

I will say a few more words about the creation of matter on the basis of our consciousness. We discussed this issue at the end of the fourth chapter. I'd like to explain once again why man successfully can do this; moreover the creation of any matter can become for him just a usual, standard procedure.

The point is that our consciousness is built by the Creator in the image and likeness of him. Therefore, our consciousness is built in such a way that we can create any objects of reality, which we need for the fulfillment of our plans. For this we just have to form any creative idea the way it is formed by the Creator. And then endless perspectives will be opened for our creation. I, for example, showed during one of the demonstrations that it is possible to create materials which are not available on the Earth. We considered with you the case of materialization of an object in the apartment of Glushko Svetlana Pavlovna. Outwardly the material of the object created by me resembled a metal. When they began to examine its internal structure, its chemical composition, it became clear that this material was of completely different nature and that such materials are not available on the Earth. I deliberately created the object of this unusual material. This material is a multicomponent basis. It can be considered as a result of common links in matter.

By the way, I can show how to pass from one element of the periodic table to another one, in other words, how in practice to convert one element into another. This conversion is realized on the spiritual basis.

It is apparent from what we discussed before that transformation of one element into another is a particular example of creation of matter. In reality everything creative that you have in your thoughts can be really received. I provide a completely new technology of creation of technical devices. For example, instrument boards required for machinery, which at present are received on the basis of leaching, i.e., on the basis of ecologically harmful technology, can be obtained ecologically safely with the help of materialization. This technology is described in my article "Fundamental Definitions of Optical Systems in Control of Micro-processes". This article was published in the journal "Microelectronics", issue 1 (153) 1999. In the case of using materialization many intermediate processes could be skipped, such, for example, as soldering or welding. It will be possible not to produce separate machine parts, but to immediately create the entire machine in the final form. Then it will have no seams.

It is also possible to act in a different way. It is possible to create machines, transferring them from the future into present, that is to say, to materialize machines of the future in the present. I also do this.

After mastery of the methods of materialization it will be possible to create new materials, and machines, and anything that is required for valuable eternal life.

I want to say a few more words about the treatment of diseases with the help of number series. I have already mentioned that this approach rests on the circumstance that all objects are interrelated with the vibratory structure of number. The vibratory structure of number is the totality of all properties of the object. That is why the correct sequence of numbers restores the norm.

So, I'd like to make one comment here. In the text I propose to use different number series for treatment of different diseases. Actuality this is done for simplicity. This is done in order to help a person to get rapidly into the swing of the things and start a successful practice. In this case it is possible to get good results immediately. When you will start getting positive results you will see, that by usage of one single number series, the one you have already mastered, you can cure all other illnesses. Since, you have to keep in mind, that though there are many diseases the health is one. Therefore, if you have found an access to it, it will always be in your hands.

But if we consider these methods with a deeper perspective, it will become clear that the point is the state of consciousness. The provided number series help you to form the required impulse of consciousness that leads to a cure. And, by the way, that is why I chose seven-digit number series. The thing is that the use of the sequence of seven numbers helps a person to realize quicker the transfer to the single-impulse action. As a result you acquire the ability to restore health with the help of a single pulse of consciousness.

I should make one more comment. We have talked so far about the sequences of numbers, words and sounds. However, it is possible to speak also about the sequence of any symbols in general. It is only important that it was correct, correct in terms of achieving the goal. For example, a selected sequence can have a restorative effect. We can take, for example, a sheet of paper and draw a certain sequence of required symbols. If you place this sheet next to a plant or a stone, the plant will be being restored and the stone will be not cracking. This will happen due to the perception by them of the information transferred by the sequence of symbols.

You can totally transform our lives on the basis of the principles and practices outlined in this book. I have spoken already about the possibility of complete elimination of earthquakes and other catastrophes, about the creation of completely new space crafts, about the creation of technical devices for resurrection and recovery of lost organs. As I said, there are already devices patented by me, which are controlled by thought.

I proposed also new energy sources. As a result, you can entirely forego all nuclear power plants and once and for all solve the energy problem. The new energy sources make it possible to produce it by the ecologically clean method. I have already mentioned the possibility of generating energy, for example, from the time of past events.

I will add one more example of the creation of new equipment. Based on my principles, you can create a supercomputer, in which information processing will take place with infinite speed and which will have infinite memory. You'd think this would significantly increase the size of the device and make its construction more complicated. But this is not the case. Based on my research you can place an infinite amount of information into a single physical element. And therefore the infinite speed and unlimited memory can be realized on the basis of one small microprocessor.

I have already mentioned that I created a device for prevention of earthquakes. Besides destructions caused by earthquakes there are other facts confirming how serious this phenomenon is.

A significant change of the intensity of the electric field takes place near the Earth's surface. Usually the intensity of the electric field near the Earth's surface is within 120-150 V/m. Twenty-four hours before a strong earthquake and during the earthquake the electric field strength is growing a thousand times in the zone of the epicenter and close to it!

The consequences of such anomalies may be very different. For example, one day before the devastating earthquake of 1986 in Bucharest, which was located at a distance of 200 kilometers from the epicenter, all computers of the city malfunctioned.

In addition, there was a glow at night around different objects.

Light phenomena often accompany and herald strong earthquakes. There may be glowing sky, ground, mountain peaks and sharp edges of rocks, tree tops, power lines, antennas. You can watch the glow also around people and animals.

In a fairly large area not only devices with electronic equipment fail. People who are in this zone (pilots, operators, leaders) cannot make clear decisions at this time. The failure of instruments and inability of people to make clear decisions creates emergency. Therefore it is clear how important is the created by me device for prevention of earthquakes and catastrophes. This device, as I've already told, was created on the basis of the new science.

Nuclear weapons and nuclear power are of significant danger to our civilization. Current situation is extremely serious. And not just because of enormous nuclear stockpiles. Operation of nuclear power plants also poses a lethal threat. I will give a concrete fact, when I had to save the Earth from destruction.

I am talking about the prevented by me of the accident at the Kozloduy nuclear plant in Bulgaria. This information was published in the official newspaper of Russian government " Rossiiskaya gazeta" No 18 (1878) of January 30, 1998. The newspaper published the article "Catastrophes for Tomorrow are Canceled" under the headline "A Quiet Sensation". The article told that I prevented the accident on Kozloduy nuclear plant. This emergency could result in a catastrophe of such scale that would be fundamentally different from the Chernobyl'.

The fact of the matter is that there are underground layers with high electrical conductivity under the Kozloduy nuclear power plant. In the case of explosion, this would create a vacuum drain, which would start retracting the atmosphere of the Earth. It would have not been possible to stop this drain with existing technical means and according to calculations of physicists by the year 2000 this process would have transformed our planet into a dust cloud. The detected by me defects and the corresponding actions on the nuclear power plant were certified at the highest state level. My actions made it possible to prevent the accident. As a result the Earth was rescued.

In our time, when the world is in danger of total annihilation, the science must find ways to prevent this. In this situation, that system of knowledge and actions is named the science, which has real, I emphasize, real methods of rescuing from the global catastrophe.

In my practice I use clairvoyance. This is irrational technology. With the help of the clairvoyance I have already prevented many catastrophes of global nature. No other methods could be used for prevention of these catastrophes; it was not possible to prevent them by the methods and means of orthodox science. Therefore, based on the facts, exactly irrational technologies such as clairvoyance, materialization and annihilation of matter, teleportation and others, and first of all, certainly resurrection, are truly scientific technologies. The resurrection of people and generally restoration of any objects. Exactly these technologies are truly scientific. This is the reality.

I should note that I use the term "irrational technologies" in its existing today meaning. However, you should understand that these technologies are irrational only from the point of view of ordinary consciousness. Since the ordinary wakeful consciousness is not able to see clearly and to realize the processes listed above, exactly due to this inability these technologies are considered irrational. At the same time all these phenomena are completely natural for the higher state of consciousness. In fact, they are a higher level science, the real science. This true science is based on knowledge of how the World is actuality arranged. And for this very reason these technologies have such stunning efficiency.

In my practice I can use a combination of my clairvoyance, the new science and the orthodox science. This is evident from my considered above inventions, created by me technical devices, and defended doctoral thesis. My election as an academician of many academies of the world confirms this. APPENDIX E, p.. 459-478 I adhere to the same approach when I deliver lectures, which include orthodox methods. I deliver lecture in the Agency on Monitoring and Prediction of Emergencies of the Ministry of Emergencies of the Russian Federation and in the Russian Academy of Public Administration under the President of the Russian Federation. APPENDIX E, p.. 479 They lectures are about the modern technologies of prevention and liquidation of emergencies.

Below are the names of my training courses on the topic "The Methods of Remote

Prevention of Catastrophes":

1. Mathematical modelling of the prevention of catastrophes. The practice of irrational control of prevention of catastrophes.

2. Special methods of prevention of global catastrophic processes that present threat to the entire world.

3. Generalized analysis of traditional and nontraditional approaches to the prevention of emergency situations.

In March 2001 my educational course "The Technologies of Anticipatory Forecast and Safe Development" was approved by the Ministry of Education of Russia. APPENDIX E, p.. 480 After completion of the course the listeners can be granted a state diploma of RF on the second major degree and a certificate of ICES-UNESCO about the successful completion of the course on the part of my Teachings "Technologies of Anticipatory Forecast and Safe Development". APPENDIX E,. p. 481 This course is a subsection of the part of the Teachings "The Forecast Control".

My lectures were included into the training program recorded on CD and used by the All-Russian Research Institute of Civil Defense and Emergencies in the Russia Federation high school educational course. The courses of lectures, the practice of resurrection, creation of fundamentally new technical devices, and other forms of my work are the component parts of my Teachings "About Salvation and Harmonious Development". The overall diagram of my Teachings is given below.

# THE TEACHINGS OF GRIGORI GRABOVOI

The System of Salvation from Possible Global Catastrophe

The System of Creative Harmonious Development

Health Care    Forecast Control    Education    Science    Art Culture    Control    Religion

The Science of Grigori Grabovoi

Politics    Economy    Sociology

All Orthodox and Known Science Trends as Stated by Grigori Grabovoi

Since we were discussing the teaching, I will mention one important point which, in my view, must have a place in any educational system. I mean teaching methods on direct control of events from man's consciousness. Education should begin before the birth of man. In my system it begins in the infinite past and continues in the infinite future. It can be divided into three following stages. The first stage begins in the infinite past and ends three years before the birth of the person. During this period the parents and other persons with the help of special concentrations form the future events of the child. In this case they use an array of information from the past for this period. After this, begins the second stage, which finishes a year before the birth. Further follows the third stage, which is over with the birth of the man. After this, each day of life during the first month is a separate stage. Then the stages are increased to one month and further they cyclically increase with the development into the infinite future.

It is possible to study at any age. Adult person should simply mentally be transferred to the earlier age and take the course of the concentrations, which correspond to this earlier age. In this case you should keep in mind that with this method you can master the material of many months within one day. Moreover, having mentally transferred yourself to the future you will be able to learn future knowledge and thus to know how to make correct decisions in the present. For prevention catastrophes at the scale of our planet and for maintenance of steady creative development I proposed to construct a special technical device. This will be a construction in the form of an arrow going to the sky. A crystal will be located on its top. Its work will be based on that technology, which is set out in my patent "Method of Prevention of Catastrophes and Device for its Realization". We have already discussed this patent with you.

The proposed device will work as follows. Information from the crystal through fiber-optic cables will be transferred to the foot of the construction. A circle will be outlined on the ground around the base of the tower. The base of the tower will be located in the center of this circle. One half of the circle will contain a map of the Earth similar to that which can be purchased in a store.

In case of appearance of some danger in any part of the Earth, for example, an earthquake or a hurricane a light will flash in the corresponding place on the map. This is a danger signal. Further the crystal on the top of the tower will begin to reduce the force of the potential catastrophe. If this construction has enough technical capacity the danger will be completely eliminated. In case the available capacity is not enough the signal in this place of the map will request additional support. And then the danger will be eliminated with the help of the additional means.

Now about the second-half of the circle. This part of the circle will contain the celestial map, to be more exact, its fragment, which will reflect all possible development of the Universe for all times. And then it will be possible to prevent possible catastrophes in space. The view of the map at the foot of the tower can be by the television and Internet transferred to all points of the Earth. It is possible to allocate a special channel for this. Then any person will be is able to switch on a TV at home and see what the situation on the map is, and actually in the world. And if there is a signal warning about the danger in some place, any person will be able to join the process of rescuing and to direct his creative thought toward the restoration of the equilibrium. So everyone will be in the know and if necessary will be able to participate in the rescuing program.

In addition I'd like to mention that the circle similar to the one at the foot of the tower, with the image of the map of the Earth and a fragment of the celestial sphere, is available on my seal. That one, which is put on documents.

My proposal about the construction of the tower with the crystal above received a positive response.

For the propagation of my Teachings I created a nominal fund that is a kind of social structure that makes it possible to be united in the matter of salvation and harmonious development. APPENDIX E, p. 482

The Fund is a controlling structure of international association "The Union for the Propagation of Grigori Grabovoi's Teachings "About Salvation and Harmonious Development". Any person, any organization, any state, and so forth can join this association. Together with the development of the association, I also introduce the system of safe development that is based on the target contracts from the specially created state. I consider it to be necessary to create such state in order to conclude the direct agreements with all countries of the world about the system safe development.

There is one more important issue that is to be dwelt at least briefly. This is the question about the legal status of the resurrected. The fact is that resurrection gradually enters our life. This process is gaining strength. And therefore the issue about the legal status of the resurrected becomes urgent.

It is necessary to create a legal basis for resurrection. For this purpose the principle of infinite life should be approved from the point of view of state and law. This principle must be officially documented and included into the system of state structure. Resurrection should be considered as a harmonious act of development of any state and statehood. Resurrection should become a principle of any state, any person, and any environment.

The task of the structures of resurrection is resurrection of all. I mean all countries, all areas of the Earth. Including different time layers. That is, we should resurrect also those who lived in other centuries, in other societies. Therefore, any chosen region will have a multi-layered, honeycomb structure. Along with modern humans there will also live people who lived in the primitive communal, slaveholding, and feudal systems.

However, this will not present any problems. If we consider different areas of the world, we can find islets with a very different life on the Earth along with the technologically advanced societies. Many tribes demonstrate that way of life that was many centuries ago. But gradually civilization penetrates there. Therefore after universal resurrection gradual life alignment in different regions will take place. Further development of the resurrected will be achieved within the overall world-creation.

The work on the legal status of the resurrected should be based on the principle of Divinity (1.7). I will formulate it once again:

THE PRINCIPLE OF DIVINITY: ASPIRATION FOR IMPERISHABILITY OF BODY, FOR ETERNAL LIFE, AND FOR DEVELOPMENT OF TRUE CONSCIOUSNESS IS THE PRACTICE OF THE UPPERMOST FLOURISHING OF                     HUMAN                     EXISTANCE.

In the first chapter, devoted to presenting the concrete facts of resurrection, when I considered the second case, I talked about some entities guiding resurrection. They deal with the registration of the resurrected. I will say a few more words about them.

These are spiritual entities created directly by God, which are under His straight control. They are a link in the development of the World. These entities have the ability to take any appearance. They can take human form, for example. And can take the appearance of a building. And they can take simultaneously both the appearance of a building, and the appearance of a person staying in it who meets the resurrected and registers them.

These entities manage all that refers to resurrection. All information is in their hands; they are in control of the situation. They are a kind of islets in physical reality, which operate as stand-alone units.

Resurrection takes place under the direct control of God, resurrection in an immutable way passes through God. It is worth noting that the forces of destruction could not resurrect. Resurrection is the privilege of the forces of creation. In the second chapter I spoke about the difference between the resurrected and those who did not experience death. So, now I can tell you that after the resurrection of all the differences between the resurrected and those who did not die will no longer exist. All will be in the identical position.

This book helps you get rid of one of the greatest misconceptions, one of the biggest myths of our history. I refer to the myth of the existence of objective physical reality that is independent of human consciousness. Such idea puts into question the true origin of man, deprives man of his true greatness, and denies his Divine determinacy.

There are, so far, a number of other myths and errors, which prevent people from living full life. Take, for example, the problem of suffering. There is a well-known assertion that suffering is an integral part of our lives. This assertion is completely absurd. It is erroneous, because suffering in this World does not have any real foundation, it has no basis. Such views are associated with the lack of understanding of how the World is arranged. In fact, for example, one of the most serious causes for suffering is the death of relatives and close people. This is undoubtedly a serious reason. However, we already know how it is possible to resurrect people; we know that death has no place at all in our life. It exists so far due to misunderstanding. Very soon this phenomenon will leave our life forever.

This is also the case with other false causes of suffering. The absurd idea that many things can be obtained only through suffering will leave together with them. And now, because of the threat of nuclear destruction, the idea of the necessity of suffering can result in a global catastrophe. The idea that many things can be obtained only through suffering had been hammered into the heads of people for centuries. But it's finally time to break free from such prejudices. In fact, as I said, there is no true base for suffering and other negative emotions. And even more so now, with the beginning of the practice of resurrection they have already begun to dissipate. Therefore the fundamental rule, which makes it possible to control the accuracy of the realized process of resurrection is that during this process everything should evolve for the better even for that person who deals with the resurrection and people around him.

As the basis of the construction of the World the Creator placed creative emotions and, above all, joy, light, and love. Indeed joy, light and love are first of all the basis for building the World. And precisely they together with the proper understanding of the

World will ensure valuable happy eternal life. The increased level of the state of consciousness is extremely important for this. Since the transition to the higher and higher states of consciousness, as we know, and is the way to God.

All great religions of the World appeared on the basis of the personal experience of their founders. That is to say, the basis of each of the religions is a revelation. What is the essence of this revelation? When going beyond the ordinary waking consciousness, in the higher states of consciousness, fundamental reality of this World opens for man. And then the person who has known this reality speaks about it. Therefore the technologies for the raise of the level of consciousness are supported by all fundamental and creative religions of the World.

However do not attempt to understand these things logically, since they lie outside of the usual logic. There is quite a different level of logic that is true there, it, from the point of view of the ordinary waking consciousness, has nothing to do with logic. Raising your consciousness is the only real way to God and to comprehension of the World. Since the truth opens for man only in the higher states of consciousness.

This book is written for all people. It is addressed to everyone. But it is written not just for people. Since our task is to ensure that not just people, but also animals, and plants, and stones and generally everything real would start to work on the system of salvation. It is possible. And it is necessary. And this book shows the way. And it also shows how to extend it to all elements of reality, to all phenomena of the World. And this will result in the establishment of true harmony in the World. So, this is the book for the entire World and for all times. Eternal life provides the fulfillment of all desires. When we speak about what we want we should know that in part this is predetermined by God. And if you see eternal life away you should know that at the same time it is close to you. Learn to see phenomena such as they are, and they are such as you need them. When you look at the reality and you are not satisfied with something, for example, with biological death, this means, that this should not be in this World because you should be satisfied with everything. When you resurrect and materialize objects each object should be created in the image and likeness of you. You can pass the knowledge received from this book to any object and it will carry this knowledge.

This book gives the practice of knowledge through resurrection. This makes it possible to understand that consciousness is based on the principles of eternity.

In my religion control is provided for infinite development, for eternal life. The Eternity, in my principles of the World, is one single Eternity created by the Creator for the universal prosperity and development.

On the basis of these fundamental provisions of my Teachings take this book and carry it as light, as the light of life, as the light that illuminates your way. This book brings true happiness for all. It ensures that development, which you will always have, and which you have already got now. With this book you can transform the World around you and within yourself. Since this book is a real tool of my Teachings. It is based on the principle of action, the principle of creative action. It is a real action. This book is the Way. When I speak about this book I speak about the real life, which reproduced this book. I expressed this reality in words, and these words bring the light of life to you, the eternal and inexhaustible light. You will always have this light, having just touched this book, or just having thought about it, or having read its first pages.

This book teaches how to construct the required reality around you. Having studied it, you will be able to control everywhere, always and forever. And the eternal control will be reflected in your soul so that this knowledge will pass to all. And you will get the total well-being, the desire for unity, for unity and universal creative development.

And when you come into the contact with God in his highest feeling to you, in His infinite love for you, you will understand that you are the creation of God obligated and liable to create, and you will create in the image and likeness. You will create the way that the Creator creates. And you will bring the light of His consciousness where you see the better, and where you see something to be changed. You will bring the light of His consciousness where your soul will show you, the same as your consciousness, and your mind, and your intellect. Where people, beasts, plants, the entire existing World will need this. Since you are the light of the World, and it's given to you once and for all and forever and ever

.

APPENDIX A:DOCUMENTS CONFIRMING
THE LISTED IN THE BOOK CONCRETE FACTS
OF THE RESURRECTION OF PEOPLE

Лист № 1

# СВИДЕТЕЛЬСТВО
## об экстрасенсорной работе Грабового Григория Петровича

родившегося 14 ноября 1963 года в поселке Кировском Кировского района Чимкентской области Казахской ССР (имеющего свидетельство о рождении серии II - ОГ № 463794 ).

Место начала составления свидетельства _Москва, ул. Ильинка 5/2_

Время начала составления свидетельства 19_96_/ _05_/ _27_/ _16_/ _17_
год    месяц    число    часы    минуты

Я, _Русанова Эмилия Александровна_
(фамилия, имя и отчество полностью)

гражданин (ка) _____ _России_
(государство)

имею удостоверение личности _паспорт XXII-МЮ №672200_
(наименование документа, серия, номер, кем и когда выдан документ)

25 сентября 1995 года я при очной встрече с Грабовым Григорием Петровичем обратилась к нему с просьбой о полном восстановлении моего сына Р.

родившегося 22 августа 1950 года и скончавшегося 16 июня 1995 года. Родился мой сын в Москве и скончался тоже в Москве. До обращения к Грабовому Г.П. я была в ... ном отношении перенесла инфаркт. После обращения к Грабовому Г.П. где-то в начале октября 1995 года у меня появилась надежда на возвращение сына. Я стала ощущать его присутствие (духовное) в доме.

Я поехала на кладбище и подойдя к могиле сына увидела что через всю могилу проходит глубокая трещина а в середине образовалась лунка как 8н с выходом земли изнутри. Где-то около полуночи я ярко видела при закрытых глазах как от моей груди протянулись две белых шнура к могиле моего сына к образовавшейся на ней лунке и потом я как-то потянула эти шнура на себя чувствуя при этом тяжесть. Все это длилось несколько секунд. Мой сын похоронен на Вихряковском кладбище г. Москва. С моим видением его могилы даже на уровне окна моей квартиры, которая находится на 7 этаже.
_Русанова_

Продолжение настоящего текста в приложении № _2/_ к первому листу.

**ПРИЛОЖЕНИЕ №** _2_

**к свидетельству об экстрасенсорной работе Грабового Григория Петровича** родившегося 14 ноября 1963 года в поселке Кировском Кировского района Чимкентской области Казахской ССР (имеющего свидетельство о рождении серии II - ОГ № 463794 ).

Место начала составления свидетельства _Москва ул. Ильинка 5/2_

Время начала составления свидетельства 19 _96_ / _05_ / _27_ / _16_ / _17_
год     месяц     число     часы     минуты

_( Вышеперечисленные данные настоящего листа вписываются с первого листа свидетельства )._

_Когда я обратилась к Грабовому Г.П. с просьбой о восстановлении моего сына А. Я познакомилась этим с бывшей женой моего сына Козловой Татьяной Ивановной, с которой после их развода мы остались в дружеских отношениях, она присутствовала на его похоронах. Козлова Татьяна Ивановна_

_В последующее время при наших разговорах в период с октября месяца по февраль Козлова Т.И. несколько раз мне рассказывала о том, что часто на улицах города Калининграда и Москвы она встречала людей похожих на моего сына А.Э. В начале февраля 1996 года она ехала поездом "Янтарь" из Москвы в Калининград Прибалтийский и в купе вагона вместе с ней ехал человек очень похожий на моего сына Р. Похожий внешне, манерами, поведением, жестами, взглядом, но какой-то выражено потерянный ехал он с человеком, который как-бы его сопровождал, управлял им, но при этом ни разу не назвал его по имени. Козлова Т.И. была удивлена когда мой сын Р. при виде денег (упаковка нового образца) выразил явное незнание этих денег._

Лист № 1

# СВИДЕТЕЛЬСТВО
## об экстрасенсорной работе Грабового Григория Петровича

родившегося 14 ноября 1963 года в поселке Кировском Кировского района Чимкентской области Казахской ССР (имеющего свидетельство о рождении серии II - ОГ № 463794 ).

Место начала составления свидетельства _ул. Ленина д. 1/2, г. Москва_

Время начала составления свидетельства 19_96_ | _05_ | _27_ | _15_ | _28_
год | месяц | число | часы | минуты

Я, _Карлова Татьяна Ивановна, (Руденова)_
(фамилия, имя и отчество полностью)

гражданин (ка) _РФ_
(государство)

имею удостоверение личности _паспорт ХХХ-ИА № 638461_
(наименование документа, серия, номер, кем и когда выдан документ)
_ОВД г. Химки Московской области_
работаю _ООО фирма "Ани" директор_
(наименование предприятия, должность и служебные телефоны)

_С декабря 19__ по октябрь 198__
я состояла в браке с г._

_(текст рукописный, частично неразборчивый)_

Продолжение настоящего текста в приложении № ____ к первому листу.

**ПРИЛОЖЕНИЕ №** 1 (один)

**к свидетельству об экстрасенсорной работе Грабового Григория Петровича** родившегося 14 ноября 1963 года в поселке Кировском Кировского района Чимкентской области Казахской ССР (имеющего свидетельство о рождении серии II - ОГ № 463794 ).

Место начала составления свидетельства ул. Ильюшина 5/2 г. Москва

Время начала составления свидетельства 1996 / 05 / 24 / 15 / 28
(год / месяц / число / часы / минуты)

*( Вышеперечисленные данные настоящего листа вписываются с первого листа свидетельства ).*

мнение, что по внешним [данным] этого света(?) этот вошедший в купе человек соответствовал Г.

1. [illegible] 1950 г. рождения по следующим критериям: цвет волос, цвет глаз, внешний облик и овал лица.

Манера поведения вошедшего в купе точно соответствовала манере поведения Г.

2. При этом также соответствовали черты характера, он имел такие же привычки (молчаливость, пристрастие к чтению, большую часть времени он читал газету).

Сопровождающий его человек, [illegible] мужчина среднего роста, который за время поездки несколько раз не назвал его по имени. И когда этот человек попросил деньги, то сопровождающий человек был удивлен, увидев 1000 рублей нового образца, на что сопровождающий человек объяснил ему, что эти деньги нового образца [illegible]. Что он (сопровождающий мужчина) был какое-то время оторван от реальной жизни, хотя, вероятно, сохранил профессиональные навыки, и сопровождающий его мужчина сказал, что они перегоняют машину.

Выше описанная встреча состоялась 2 февраля 1996 г. во время моей поездки по маршруту г. Москва – "[illegible]" в поезде [illegible].

*Продолжение настоящего текста в приложении №* два *к первому листу.*

Копия верна [illegible] "Сервис-центр" [illegible] В.В.

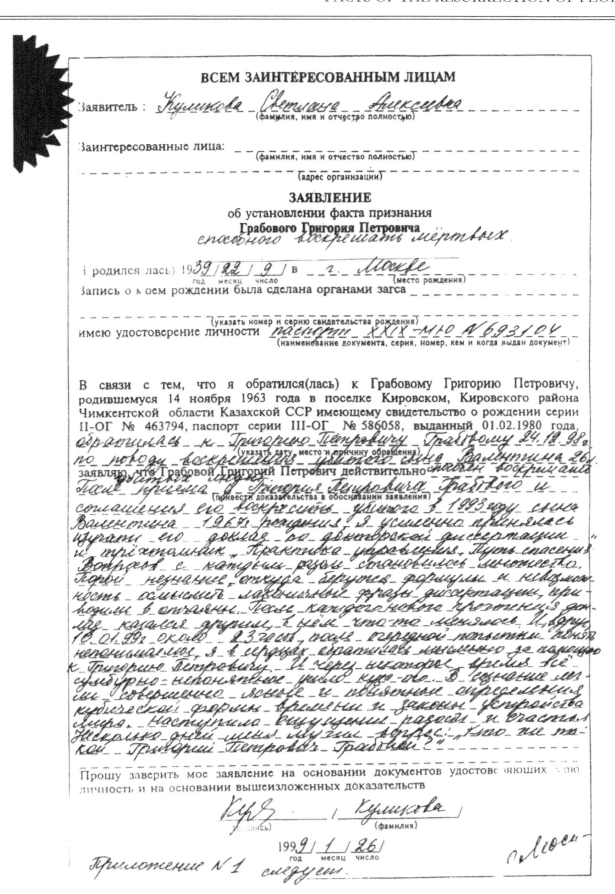

ВСЕМ ЗАИНТЕРЕСОВАННЫМ ЛИЦАМ

Заявитель : *Куликова Светлана Алексеевна*
(фамилия, имя и отчество полностью)

Заинтересованные лица: _____
(фамилия, имя и отчество полностью)

_____
(адрес организации)

**ЗАЯВЛЕНИЕ**
об установлении факта признания
**Грабового Григория Петровича**
*способного воскрешать мёртвых*
_____

(я родился лась) 19 **39** / **22** / **9** в г. *Москве*
год   месяц   число        (место рождения)
Запись о в оем рождении была сделана органами загса _____

_____
(указать номер и серию свидетельства рождения)
имею удостоверение личности *паспорт XXIX-МЮ N 693104*
(наименование документа, серия, номер, кем и когда выдан документ)

В связи с тем, что я обратился(лась) к Грабовому Григорию Петровичу, родившемуся 14 ноября 1963 года в поселке Кировском, Кировского района Чимкентской области Казахской ССР имеющему свидетельство о рождении серии II-ОГ № 463794, паспорт серии III-ОГ № 586058, выданный 01.02.1980 года, *обратилась к Григорию Петровичу Грабовому 24.12.98г.*
(указать дату, место и причину обращения)
*по поводу воскрешения убитого сына Валентина 26г.*
заявляю, что Грабовой Григорий Петрович действительно *способен воскрешать*
(привести доказательства в обосновании заявления)

Приложение № 1. к тексту, начало которого на бланке.

Всем заинтересованным лицам, составленным Куликовой С.А. 26.01.1999г.

13 января 1999г, в канун старого Нового года, уже накрыв стол для своих близких, я ощутила непреодолимое желание подойти к окну. Подойдя вплотную к окну, я залюбовалась красивым зимним пейзажем с искрящимися голубыми снегами. Время было 22г40мин-22г50мин. И в мыслях опять возник вопрос: "Кто же всё-таки Григорий Петрович Грабовой?" И тут же вместо снега у меня перед глазами стали пульсировать огромные чёрные цифры:

14 11 1963. Затем между ними появились знаки сложения, и всё превратилось в странное уравнение:

$$1+4+1+1+1+9+6+3=8$$

Восьмёрка слегка светилась сиренево-фиолетовым цветом. Затем восьмёрка перевернулась и легла, обозначив знак бесконечности.

Меня позвали к столу и цифры исчезли. Только на другой день я осознала, что цифры эти были датой рождения Григория Петровича. А сумма их давала 8 - цифру Иисуса Христа, которая, перевернувшись указала вечность.

14.01.99г. у нас ночевала моя дочь Катя, которая живёт отдельно и которая является двойней вместе с погибшим сыном Валентином.

В 3 часа ночи, когда все домашние уже спали, а Катя тайно вошла в свою комнату, я услышала удар, как будто лопнул шар, и через некоторое время зашуршала фольга, которая лежала в кресле, в одной из комнат. Тут же вошла из своей комнаты Катя и сказала, что буквально у неё на глазах летела коробка из-под машинки, как-будто кто-то, невидимый поддал её ногой. Я слышала тот удар, и ещё слышала шелест фольги в кресле. Мы с ней пошли посмотреть кресло и увидели, что фольга как бы примята и на ней отпечаток взрослой человеческой руки. И после этого в доме постоянно ощущалось присутствие кого-то. Приложение №2 смотри. Куликова

26.01.99г.

Приложение №2 к тексту приложения №1, являющимся продолжением бланка „Всем заинтересованным лицам", составленного Куликовой С.А. 26.01 1999г.

Раздавались внезапно шорохи, покачивались занавески, скрипел пол.

16.01.99г. Сын - (Дмитрий 1965г. рожд.) и внук (Михаил 1985г. рожд.) в один голос рассказали, что проснувшись среди ночи сын Дмитрий увидел на противоположной от постели стене в районе отрошной фотографии лица живого Валентина. Сын Дмитрий закрыл глаза и открыл снова. Валентин был на месте. Тогда сын разбудил внука Михаила и убедился, что внук также видит Валентина. Причём, сын очень скептически до этого принял сообщение о возможности воскрешения Валентина. Теперь он в этом абсолютно убеждён. Хочу добавить, что во время приёма у Грабового Григория Петровича я получила от него ауди кассету с его голосом, где было записано его объяснение мне, что является критерием и почему пространство вторично по отношению к сознанию, а первичен интервал движения. После того, как я это осознала, кассета исчезла, т.е дематериализовалась.

Куц /Куликова/

26.01. 99г.

**Город Москва, Россия, двадцать восьмое января** тысяча девятьсот девяносто девятого года, я, *Щербакова Наталья Николаевна*, нотариус г. Москвы, свидетельствую подлинность подписи Куликовой Светланы Алексеевны, которая сделана в моем присутствии. Личность подписавшего документ установлена.

Зарегистрировано в реестре за № 1- *923*

Взыскано по тарифу:  20 руб. 87 коп.

Нотариус:

**ВСЕМ ЗАИНТЕРЕСОВАННЫМ ЛИЦАМ**

Заявитель : *Кушкова Светлана Алексеевна*
(фамилия, имя и отчество полностью)

Заинтересованные лица: _____
(фамилия, имя и отчество полностью)

_____
(адрес организации)

**ЗАЯВЛЕНИЕ**
об установлении факта признания
**Грабового Григория Петровича**

*воскрешать* целителем и ясновидящим *и способным*
*убитых людей*

Я родился(лась) 19*3.9*| *9* | *22*| в г. *Москвы*
год   месяц   число       (место рождения)
Запись о моем рождении была сделана органами загса _____

_____
(указать номер и серию свидетельства рождения)

имею удостоверение личности _____ *паспорт*
(наименование документа, серия, номер, кем и когда выдан документ)
*серии XXIX-МЮ*     *№ 693104*

В связи с тем, что я обратился(лась) к Грабовому Григорию Петровичу, родившемуся 14 ноября 1963 года в поселке Кировском, Кировского района Чимкентской области Казахской ССР имеющему свидетельство о рождении серии II-ОГ № 463794, паспорт серии III-ОГ № 586058, выданный 01.02.1980 года,
*Я обратилась к Григорию Петровичу*
*Грабовому по поводу воскрешения убитого сына*
(указать дату, место и причину обращения)
заявляю, что Грабовой Григорий Петрович действительно *могли*
*воскрешать убитых людей.*
(привести доказательства в обосновании заявления)
*Я обратилась к Григорию Петровичу Грабо-*
*тому 24.12.98г с просьбой воскресить убито-*
*го сына Валентина, 1967 года рождения.*

*16 января 1999года сын Дмитрий (1965г рожд)*
*и внук Михаил (1985г рожд) в один голос*
*рассказали, что проснувшись среди ночи сын*
*Дмитрий увидел в вагоне фотографии мамы*
*живого Валентина. Сын Дмитрий закрыл гла-*
*за и открыл снова - Валентин был на месте.*
*Тогда сын разбудил внука Михаила и убедился*
*что внук также видит Валентина. Моя дочь*
*Катя рассказала, что где то в первых числах*
*апреля 1999г к ней приходил Валентин и ска-*
*зал, что у нас будут большие перемены в*
*хорошую сторону. Я со мной живой Валентин*
*говорил по телефону. Причём, Катя почув-*
*ствовала его прикосновение. Он просил её*
*нажать какой-то номер телефона и своим*
Прошу заверить мое заявление на основании документов удостоверяющих мою личность и на основании вышеизложенных доказательств

*Куш*     *Кушкова*
(подпись)       (фамилия)

199*9*| *04* | *26*|
год   месяц   число

*Продолжение следует на листе № 1*

Лист №1.

Продолжение листа „Всем заинтересованным лицам" от 26.04.1999г.

Куликова Светлана Алексеевна.

голосом позвать кого-то. Она помнит, что она взяла телефон, села в постели, стала набирать номер, но там были длинные гудки. Валентин сказал, что это не к спеху, попрощался и ушёл. 11 апреля 1999г., на праздник святой Пасхи, около 18 часов позвонила мне внучка Маша (1990г. рожд.) дочь Валентина (моего сына) и сказала, что живой Валентин приходил к её матери Глебовой Марине (1970г. рожд.). После этого факта встречи с Валентином бывшей супруги его- Марины, она вместе с подругой и дочерью Машей поехали на кладбище, где ранее находилась могила Валентина. Но они не обнаружили могилы Валентина ни на физическом месте, ни в книге регистрации.

Куз [Куликова]

1999г. 04.26

**Город Москва,** **пятое мая** тысяча девятьсот девяносто девятого года, я, Щербакова Наталья Николаевна, нотариус города Москвы, свидетельствую подлинность подписи <u>Куликовой Светланы Алексеевны,</u> которая сделана в моем присутствии. Личность подписавшей документ установлена.

Зарегистрировано в реестре за № 3- *5261*

Взыскано по тарифу: 50 руб. с согл. ст.

Нотариус:-

Всего прошнуровано, пронумеровано и скреплено печатью нотариуса Щербаковой Н.Н.

**ВСЕМ ЗАИНТЕРЕСОВАННЫМ ЛИЦАМ**

Заявитель : *Казакова Любовь Серафимовна*
(фамилия, имя и отчество полностью)

Заинтересованные лица: _____
(фамилия, имя и отчество полностью)

_____
(адрес организации)

**ЗАЯВЛЕНИЕ**
об установлении факта признания
**Грабового Григория Петровича**
*способным воскрешать мертвых*

Я родился(лась) 19 **47** / **09** / **01** / в *г. Москве*
год    месяц    число                (место рождения)
Запись о моем рождении была сделана органами загса _____

(указать номер и серию свидетельства рождения)
имею удостоверение личности *паспорт серия ХХIV-МЮ № 534024*
(наименование документа, серия, номер, кем и когда  дан документ)

В связи с тем, что я обратился(лась) к Грабовому Григорию Петровичу, родившемуся 14 ноября 1963 года в поселке Кировском, Кировского района Чимкентской области Казахской ССР имеющему свидетельство о рождении серии II-ОГ № 463794, паспорт серии III-ОГ № 586058, выданный 01.02.1980 года, *по поводу воскрешения моей мамы Чигиринцевой*
*Нины Васильевны 06.05.1999*
(указать дату, место и причину обращения)
заявляю, что Грабовой Григорий Петрович действительно *воскресил*
*мою маму Чигиринцеву Нину Васильевну*
(привести доказательства в обосновании заявления)
*Я, Казакова Любовь Серафимовна, обратилась к Григо-*
*рию Петровичу Грабовому по поводу воскрешения*
*моей мамы Чигиринцевой Нины Васильевны родившей-*
*ся 23 декабря 1923 года и скончавшейся 18 апреля 1999 в*
*г. Москве. Я поехала на кладбище Тофайле к моги-*
*ле и они удивилась, что вкопанная столом пла-*
*стмассовая ваза висящая мы на 9-10см в полго-*
*валилась в сторону ее могилы, а свежая в другой*
*стороне. Создалось впечатление, что ваза была*
*изогнута. Автомкнула Занял и приема упокоенно*
*Стала слушать лекцию Григория Петровича о*
*машинах воскрешении. Через некоторое время по-*
*могиле уния заколебалась (пришла в движение)*
*мне сало не по себе, я отошла в другую*
*сторону встала у другой могилы и силы про-*
*должилась слушать лекцию (лекцию я прослуша-*
*ла три раза) и увидела живую ими ее большую*
*территорию со стороны, где был тайник мне ч-*
*корытного елок. После этого я сразу ушла.*

Прошу заверить мое заявление на основании документов удостоверяющих мою личность и на основании вышеизложенных доказательств

*Л. Казак*  /  *Казакова*
(подпись)              (фамилия)

199 **9** / **06** / **01** /

*Лош*

Приложение к заявлению Казановой Любови Серафимовне от 01.06.1999.

Приехав на могилу во второй раз я сразу почувствовала, что могила пустая и там никого нет. Затем я просила могилу, если я делаю все правильно дать мне какой-либо знак. Вдруг я посмотрела на стену, на стене висит ложка с вилкой длиной 82см на одной высоте и я увидела, что вилка сместилась вниз на 5см и в сторону к ложке на 15см. В комнату в течение дня никто не входил и перевесить вилку никто не мог, а часа за 2-2,5 я смотрела на вилку с ложкой и думала, что их надо перевесить на кухню. Я убедилась что это мне дали знак. После обращения к Григорию Петровичу Грабовому (06.05.99) в ночь на 7.05.99 у меня с мамой был контакт. Она была мной недовольна. Во время контакта проходили физические помехи, но они были устранены физической рукой мамы к моей руке. Встреча с физически воскресшей мамой мною была воспринята спокойно.

А. Казанц
1.06.99

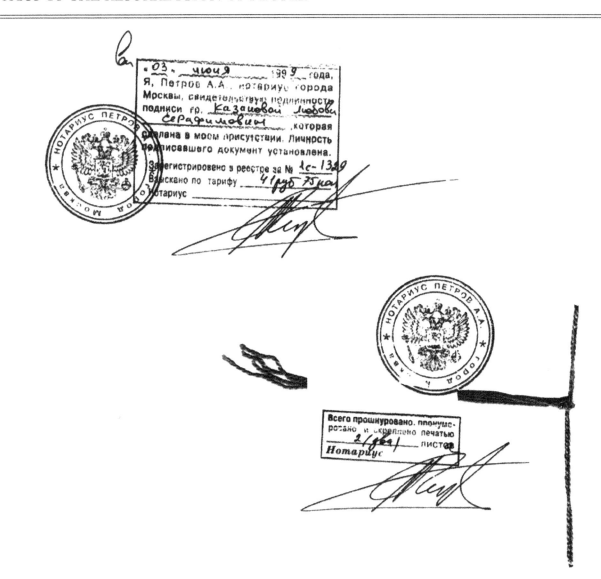

## ВСЕМ ЗАИНТЕРЕСОВАННЫМ ЛИЦАМ

Заявитель: _Богашилов Олег Давидович_
(фамилия, имя и отчество полностью)

Заинтересованные лица: _____
(фамилия, имя и отчество полностью; адрес)

## ЗАЯВЛЕНИЕ
об установлении факта признания
Грабового Григория Петровича
_способным восстановления человека после биологи-_
_ческой смерти человека_

имею удостоверение личности _паспорт VI-МЮ № 736 302_
(наименование документа, серия, номер, кем и когда выдан документ)

В связи с тем, что я обратился(лась) к Грабовому Григорию Петровичу, родившемуся 14 ноября 1963 года в поселке Кировском, Кировского района Чимкентской области Казахской ССР имеющему свидетельство о рождении серии II-ОГ № 463794, _7 января 1998. в Москве_
(указать дату, место и причину обращения)
_по поводу смерти С_

заявляю, что Грабовой Григорий Петрович действительно _восстановил_
_жизненные функции С после по-_
(привести доказательства в обоснование заявления)
_ей информации по этому вопросу ему в_
_течение периода времени с 23 часов 15 мин_
_7-го января 1998 года по 16 часов 15 минут 8 ян-_
_варя 1998 года. Документально смерть_
_имеется заявление С имело з_
_основание на заключении врачей_
_от 7 января 1998 года. Подтверждением факта_
_восстановления жизнедеятельности_
_осуществ проведенного Грабовым Григорием_
_Петровичем и продолжавшийся в 17 часов, явля-_
_ется то, что я лично разговаривал с_
_в 16 часов 15 мин 8 января 1998 года, а так-_
_же заявление лица з_
_Других методов восстановления_
_кроме интенсивного дыхания_
_за исключением воздействия проведенного_
_Грабовым Григорием Петровичем, не при-_
_менялось._

Прошу заверить мое заявление на основании документов, удостоверяющих мою личность и на основании вышеизложенных доказательств.

_Богашилов_        19 _98_ / _01_ / _28_
(подпись)    (фамилия)          год   месяц   число

_Богашилов Олег Давидович_

_г. Моск._

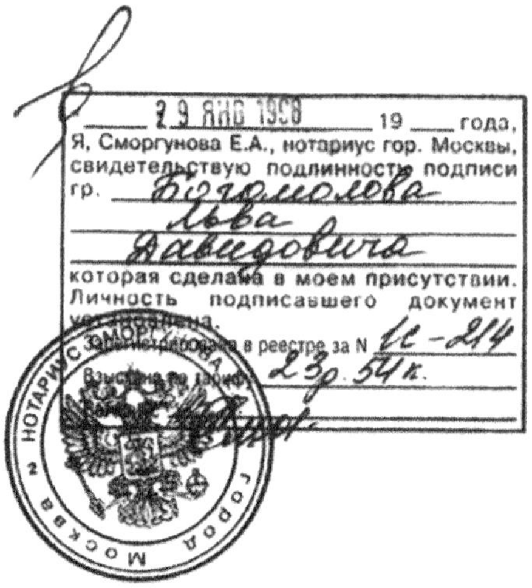

29 ЯНВ 1998 19 ___ года,
Я, Сморгунова Е.А., нотариус гор. Москвы, свидетельствую подлинность подписи гр. Богомолова Льва Давидовича
которая сделана в моем присутствии. Личность подписавшего документ установлена.
Зарегистрировано в реестре за N 1с-214
Взыскано по тарифу 23р. 54к.
Нотариус

# APPENDIX B: DOCUMENTS CONFIRMING THE LISTED IN THE BOOK CONCRETE FACTS OF CURING DISEASES, WHICH ARE CONSIDERED TO BE INCURABLE

Лист № 1

# СВИДЕТЕЛЬСТВО
## об экстрасенсорной работе Грабового Григория Петровича

родившегося 14 ноября 1963 года в поселке Кировском Кировского района Чимкентской области Казахской ССР (имеющего свидетельство о рождении серии II - ОГ № 463794 ).

Место начала составления свидетельства _Р.Ф. Москва_

Время начала составления свидетельства 19_96_ | _06_ | _26_ | _20_ | _01_
год | месяц | число | часы | минуты

Я, _Антипова Галина Степановна_
(фамилия, имя и отчество полностью)

родился (лась) _14 июля 1946 г. город Ташкент_
(дата и место рождения)

гражданин (ка) _Узбекистана_
(государство)

проживаю _г. Ташкент Акмаль Икрамовский р-он_
(место жительства и домашний телефон)

_квартал 26 дом 25 кв 62 телефон 72-76-94_

имею удостоверение личности _паспорт VII V-ЮС N537 807_
(наименование документа, серия, номер, кем и когда выдан документ)

_Акмаль Икрамовский РГИК Ташкент 17 августа 1979 г_

работаю _СГАКБ "АСАКА" главный бухгалтер 79-69-93, 79-74-51_
(наименование предприятия, должность и служебные телефоны)

24 марта 1994 г в республиканском онкологическом диспансере Министерства здравоохранения Башкирии находящегося по адресу г. Уфа, проспект Октября дом 73/1 телефон 24-25-29 мне Антиповой Галине Степановне провели цитологическое исследование клеток выделяемых из правого соска молочной железы под N 4988 от 24 марта 1994 г

В результате цитологического исследования N 4988 от 24 марта 1994 г у меня определена следующая форма рака. Внутрипротоковая карцинома.

В период установления диагноза у меня были кровяные выделения из соска правой груди.

После того как был установлен диагноз внутрипротоковая карцинома, мной было принято решение пройти курс бесконтактного экстрасенсорного лечения проводимым Грабовым Григорием Петровичем не покидая рабочего места и не отлучаясь от него.

За период с 30 марта 1994 г. по 3 апреля 1994 г в результате экстрасенсорной работы Грабового Григория Петровича прекратились кровяные выделения из правой груди. Лечение проводилось ежедневно с 22 часов до 23 часов местного времени. В период сеансов местонахождение не имело значения (отдаление по было в другой город, поселок, место работы, место отдыха).

До 29 августа 1994 г Грабовой Григорий Петрович ежедневно проводил бесконтактное лечение.

29 августа 1994 г в республиканском онкологическом центре Министерства здравоохранения Башкирии

Продолжение настоящего текста в приложении № _один_ к первому листу.

**ПРИЛОЖЕНИЕ №** _один_

**к свидетельству об экстрасенсорной работе Грабового Григория Петровича** родившегося 14 ноября 1963 года в поселке Кировском Кировского района Чимкентской области Казахской ССР (имеющего свидетельство о рождении серии II - ОГ № 463794 ).

Место начала составления свидетельства _РФ. Москве_

Время начала составления свидетельства 19_96_ / _06_ / _26_ / _20_ / _01_
                                               год   месяц  число  часы  минуты

_( Вышеперечисленные данные настоящего листа вписываются с первого листа свидетельства )._

находящегося в городе Уфа. Проспект Октября дом 73/1 телефон 024-250-29 проведено повторное исследование пунктата соска правой молочной железы № 143 647 от 29 августа 1994 г. Повторное исследование проводилось тем же врачом, Заведующим отделением внутренней молочной железа Заслуженным врачом Башкирии Мухамедъяровым Вахит Нугурмановичем, рабочий телефон 024-27-74.

При повторном цитологическом исследовании пунктата правой молочной железа зафиксировано, что рака у меня нет.

Вышее изложенное, мной зафиксировано в заключении Республиканского онкологического диспансера республики Башкортостан в Уфа. проспект Октября дом 73/1.

До момент установления диагноза рак 26 март 1994 г. мною не принималось ни каких медикаментозных средств лечения.

В период с 12 март по 29 августа 1994 г. лечение проводилось бесконтактное только Грабовым Григорием Петровичем.

Уверена что от рака меня вылечил Грабовой Григорий Петрович, что подтверждает медицинскими анализами.

За период с 29 августа 1994 г. по 26 июня 1996 г. объективно я практически здорова, никаких выделений из груди не появилось, самочувствие в норме. Субъективных жалоб не предъявляю. За данный период постоянно работаю главным бухгалтером банка.

Обращений в медицинские учреждения по состоянию здоровья и болезни из-за отсутствия необходимости.

_Акинова Гильза Степановна_  _1996  06  28_

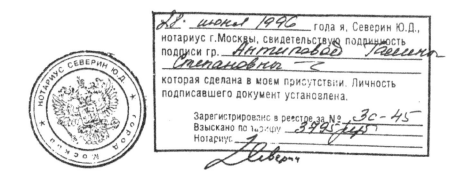

## ВСЕМ ЗАИНТЕРЕСОВАННЫМ ЛИЦАМ

**Заявитель:** _Анипова Ташит Сепиновна_
(фамилия, имя и отчество полностью)

_Ташкент Узбекистан. кварйал 26 дом 25 кв 62. телефон 72-76-94_
(адрес и телефоны)

**Заинтересованные лица:** _____
(фамилия, имя и отчество полностью; адрес)

_____

### ЗАЯВЛЕНИЕ
об установлении факта признания
**Грабового Григория Петровича**
, целителем и ясновидяшим

Я родился(лась) 19_46_ / _07_ / _14_ / в _г. Ташкент Узбекистан_
год  месяц  число              (место рождения)

имею удостоверение личности _Паспорт. VII-ЮС N537 807 Анипов-_
(наименование документа, серия, номер, кем и когда выдан документ)

_Типравивей РУЧ. Ташкент (Аовгуст 1979)_

Работаю: _СГАиБ , АСАКН  главном бухгалтером  79-69-93_
(название предприятия, должность и телефон)

В связи с тем, что я обратился(лась) к Грабовому Григорию Петровичу, родившемуся 14 ноября 1963 года в поселке Кировском, Кировского района Чимкентской области Казахской ССР имеюшиму свидетельство о рождении серии II-ОГ № 463794.

_24 март 1994 г Ташкент обратилась к Грабовому в_
(указать дату, место и причину обращения)

_результате установления цепей внутри протоковой рак._
_шелчний неможех установленых в республиканском онкологическом центр_
заявляю, что Грабовой Григорий Петрович действительно _излечил мне_
_от рак в результате бесконтактного лечения проводимого_
(привести доказательства в обосновании заявления)

_ежедневно с 22 часов до 23 часов, что подтверждает медицинск-_
_ии заключением Республиканским онкологического_
_диспансере Вишкарасен ез Уфа_
_Медицинское заключение от 04 март N4931 в котором_
_указан диагноз рак ч._
_Медицинское заключение от 29 август N 143642 где_
_зафиксировано, что рана у меня нет_
_Уверена, что своим выздоровлением обязана_
_Грабовому Григорию Петровичу._

Прошу заверить мое заявление на основании документов, удостоверяющих мою личность и на основании вышеизложенных доказательств

_Анипова Ташит Сепиновна_      _(подпись)_      1996  06  28
(подпись)        (фамилия)                        год  месяц  число

_28 июня 1996_ года я, Северин Ю.Д., нотариус г.Москвы, свидетельствую подлинность подписи гр. _Антилова Галина Степановна_ которая сделана в моем присутствии. Личность подписавшего документ установлена.

Зарегистрировано в реестре за № _3с – 42_
Взыскано по тарифу _3795руб_
Нотариус

Республиканский онкодиспансер

гор. Уфа, проспект Октября, 73-1
Телефон № больн.
Гл. вр. 24-25-29

**ЗАКЛЮЧЕНИЕ**

Больной _Антипова ГС_ Возраст _Уфа_
                     Фамилия, и., о.

Направленный Вами с диагнозом

Осмотрен врачом _маммологом и обследования_

Консультативное заключение _Внутрипротоковая о-_
_логого из прав. соска № 4988 г 24/III ч._
_Внутрипротоковая карцинома -_

Рекомендуется

Подпись врача:

**ВСЕМ ЗАИНТЕРЕСОВАННЫМ ЛИЦАМ**

Заявитель : _Ербина Диана Львовна_
(фамилия, имя и отчество полностью)

Заинтересованные лица: _____
(фамилия, имя и отчество полностью)

_____
(адрес организации)

**ЗАЯВЛЕНИЕ**
об установлении факта признания
**Грабового Григория Петровича**
целителем и ясновидящим

Запись о моем рождении была сделана органами загса _____

_П-МЮ №382361_
(указать номер и серию свидетельства рождения)
имею удостоверение личности _паспорт V-СБ №739976_
(наименование документа, серия, номер)

В связи с тем, что я обратился(лась) к Грабовому Григорию Петровичу, родившемуся 14 ноября 1963 года в поселке Кировском, Кировского района Чимкентской области Казахской ССР имеющему свидетельство о рождении серии II-ОГ № 463794, паспорт серии III-ОГ № 586058, выданный 01.02.1980 года, _25.09.96 г. Москва, ул Коштоянца 10/2, Рак кишечника IV стадии_
(указать дату, место и причину обращения)
_с метастазами в кости и печень у моего деда Белякова М.Г. 1928 г.р_
заявляю, что Грабовой Григорий Петрович действительно _прибыл 25 сентября_
_через меня отне Врачи городской больницы_
(привести доказательства в обосновании заявления)
_номер тридцать один на основании проведен-_
_ного обследования поставили моему деду_
_Белякову Михаилу Гавриловичу 1928 года_
_рождения диагноз: Рак восходящего отдела_
_ободочной кишки IV стадии с метастазами в_
_почки и печень. После проведения Грабовым_
_Григорием Петровичем одного сеанса было_
_проведено повторное обследование. Ультразвуковое_
_исследование, проведенное 26 сентября не_
_показало наличие метастаз. Компьютерное_
_обследование проведенное 30 сентября_
_также метастаз не показало_

Прошу заверить мое заявление на основании документов удостоверяющих мою личность и на основании вышеизложенных доказательств

_Ербина_ / _Ербина_ /
(подпись)        (фамилия)

199 _6_ / _10_ / _04_ /
год   месяц  число

03 ОКТ 1998

19 __ года г. БЕРЕЗОВА

ГАЛИНА ИВАНОВНА, нотариус г. Москвы
свидетельствую подлинность подписи гр.

в моем присутствии. Личность подписавшего
документ установлена.
Зарегистрировано в реестре за № 3-778
Взыскано по тарифу ____
нотариус

# СВИДЕТЕЛЬСТВО
## об экстрасенсорной работе Грабового Григория Петровича

родившегося 14 ноября 1963 года в поселке Кировском Кировского района Чимкентской области Казахской ССР (имеющего свидетельство о рождении серии II - ОГ № 463794 ).

Место начала составления свидетельства _Москва, Кожевническая ул, 10/2_

Время начала составления свидетельства 19_96_ / _10_ / _04_ / _15_ / _10_
год   месяц   число   часы   минуты

Я, _Сербина Надежда Михайловна_
(фамилия, имя и отчество полностью)

гражданин (ка) _России_
(государство)

имею удостоверение личности _паспорт XVI-МЮ № 623845_
(наименование документа, серия, номер)

_25 сентября 1996 года я и моя дочь, Сербина Диана Яновна обратились к Грабовому Григорию Петровичу по поводу болезни Белякова Михаила Гавриловича 1928 г.р. (моего отца) В городской больнице номер 31 ему было проведено обследование: применялись колоноскопия, УЗИ. Поставлен диагноз: Рак восходящего отдела ободочной кишки IV степени с метастазами в почки и печень 26 сентября, на следующий день после первого сеанса Грабового Григория Петровича в больнице было проведено повторное ультразвуковое исследование метастаз не обнаружило. Компьютерное обследование, проведенное 30 сентября, подтвердило отсутствие метастаз во всем организме_

_Серб— (Сербина) 04 октября 1996 года_

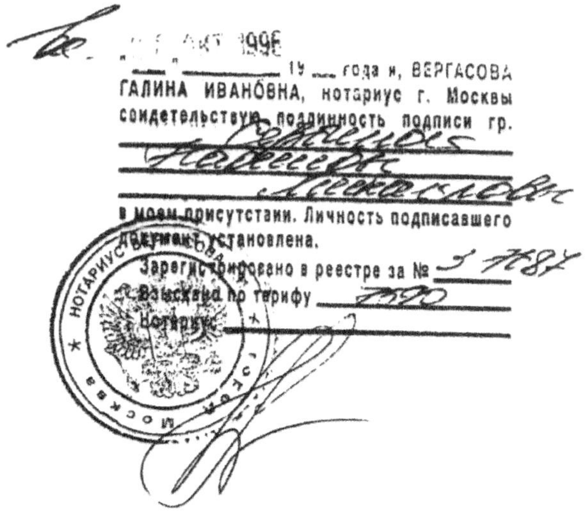

1996

„__" ________ 19__ года я, ВЕРГАСОВА ГАЛИНА ИВАНОВНА, нотариус г. Москвы свидетельствую подлинность подписи гр.

в моем присутствии. Личность подписавшего документ установлена.

Зарегистрировано в реестре за № 3-787

Взыскано по тарифу

Нотариус

**ВСЕМ ЗАИНТЕРЕСОВАННЫМ ЛИЦАМ**

Заявитель : *Сербина Надежда Михайловна*
(фамилия, имя и отчество полностью)

Заинтересованные лица: _____
(фамилия, имя и отчество полностью)

_____
(адрес организации)

**ЗАЯВЛЕНИЕ**
об установлении факта признания
**Грабового Григория Петровича**
целителем и ясновидящим

Запись о моем рождении была сделана органами загса *РБ №392246*

(указать номер и серию свидетельства рождения)
имею удостоверение личности *паспорт XVI-МЮ №623845*
(наименование документа, серия, номер)

В связи с тем, что я обратился(лась) к Грабовому Григорию Петровичу, родившемуся 14 ноября 1963 года в поселке Кировском, Кировского района Чимкентской области Казахской ССР имеющему свидетельство о рождении серии II-ОГ № 463794, паспорт серии III-ОГ № 586058, выданный 01.02.1980 года, *25.09.96 г. Москва Копельническая улица 10/2 Рак восходящего*
(указать дату, место и причину обращения)
*отдела ободочной кишки IV степени с метастазами в*
заявляю, что Грабовой Григорий Петрович действительно *почки и печень*
*у моего отца Белякова Михаила Гавриловича,*
(привести доказательства в обоснование заявления)
*1928 года рождения.*
*Я Сербина Надежда Михайловна, заявляю, что*
*25 сентября 1996 года, Грабовым Григорием Петровичем*
*был проведен один сеанс через мою дочь, Сербину*
*Диану Яновну.*
*До сеанса в городской больнице номер 31 (тридцать*
*один) Белякову Михаилу Гавриловичу был*
*поставлен диагноз : Рак восходящего отдела ободочной*
*кишки IV степени с метастазами в почки и печень.*
*26 сентября, на следующий день после сеанса Грабового*
*Григория Петровича, повторное ультразвуковое*
*обследование не показало метастаз. Компьютерное*
*обследование, проведенное 30 сентября, подтвердило*
*отсутствие метастаз во всем организме.*

Прошу заверить мое заявление на основании документов удостоверяющих мою личность и на основании вышеизложенных доказательств

*Серб―* / *Сербина*
(подпись) (фамилия)

1996 / *10* / *04*
год   месяц   число

"___" _____ 19___ года я, ВЕРГАСОВА
ГАЛИНА ИВАНОВНА, нотариус г. Москвы
свидетельствую подлинность подписи гр.
_____
_____
в моем присутствии. Личность подписавшего
документ установлена.
  Зарегистрировано в реестре за №
  Взыскано по тарифу
  Нотариус

Департамент здравоохранения ... Москвы
Клиническая больница

и. б. 12855

**СПРАВКА**

Дана Булякову М.Г. 67 лет
в том, что он/а/ находился/лась в 31 ГКБ
в I хирургическом отделении с 12/IX 96 по настоящее
с диагнозом Рак печеночного изгиба ободочной кишки IV ст.

Медрегистратор архива

Дата 19/IX 96

754-1000

Медицинская карта стационар-
ного больного N 12855

В Ы П И С Н О Й   Э П И К Р И З

Больной (ая) _____ Беляков М.Г. _____ Возраст _67_ Профессия _не работает_

Результаты клинико-диагностического обследования при выписке:
Общ. анализ крови от " 14 " октября    19 96 г.
Эритр. 4,1    Гем. 128    Лейкоциты 10,2 э 9   п - с 63 л 22 м 5  СОЭ 42
Общ. анализ мочи    от " 14 "  октября 96 г. Реакция    кислая
Уд. вес 1020    Белок 0,033  Сахар  нет   Лейк. 1-3    Эритр. нет
Биохим. анализ крови    белок 60,5   мочевина-7,6    креатинин-106
    АлАТ-22   АсАТ-35   щелочная фосфатаза-79
_____

Прочие лабораторные исследования _____
_____
_____

Лучевая диагностика: _____
ЭКГ: диффузные изменения _____
_____

Консультации: Гистологическое исследование-высокодифференцированная
    аденокарцинома при поступлении
_____
_____

прочие исследования: _____
_____

Выписан(а): с выздоровлением, улучшением, без изменения
Трудоспособность: восстановлена полностью, снижена, утрачена временно,
стойко утрачена в связи с данным заболеванием,  с  другими  причинами.
Посыльный лист на МСЭК (оформлен, не оформлен) (подчеркнуть, при изменении группы инвалидности вписать)
_____
_____

Рекомендации:
Лекарственные препараты_____-_____
Физиолечение и ЛФК_____-_____,Диета дробное, бесшлаквая
Санаторно-курортное лечение_____,Трудовые_____
Повторная госпитализация___ нет _____, Диспансеризация и наблюдение
врачами-специалистами ____ онколога_____.
Больничный лист при выписке сер._____ N_____

                              Лечащий врач _____ Марченко И.П.

# СВИДЕТЕЛЬСТВО
## об экстрасенсорной работе Грабового Григория Петровича

родившегося 14 ноября 1963 года в поселке  Кировском Кировского района Чимкентской области Казахской ССР  (имеющего свидетельство о рождении серии  II - ОГ № 463794)

Место: _Москва_
(место заполнения свидетельства)

199 7 / 1 / 30 / /
год  месяц  число  часы  минуты

Я, _Буза Людмила Ивановна_
(фамилия, имя и отчество полностью)

родился(лась) _23 октября 1960 г., г. Донецк, Украина_
(дата и место рождения)

гражданин(ка) _Россия_
(государство)

проживаю _Республика Саха (Якутия) , г. Нерюнгри_
(место жительства и домашний телефон)
_пр. Мира , д. 5, кв. 21 , т. 6-08-53_

имею удостоверение личности _паспорт V-СН № 633178_
(наименование документа, серия, номер, кем и когда выдан документ)
_УВД г. Нерюнгри, Республика Саха (Якутия) 14 ноября 1990г._

работаю _ГУП "Якутуголь" Управление технического контроля_
(наименование предприятия, должность и служебные телефоны)
_и качества угля, инженер по ТК и ТБ._

Я Буза Людмила Ивановна удостоверяю, что во время обращения к Грабовому Григорию Петровичу у Буза Владимира Георгиевича родившегося 4 декабря 1952 г. в г. Донецк, Украина, был диагноз: злокачественная опухоль головки поджелудочной железы с прорастанием в двенадцатиперстную кишку, установленный в Московском научно-исследовательском институте диагностики и хирургии (МНИИДиХ) 17 декабря 1996г.

Первый сеанс был проведен 25 декабря 1996г.

Отсутствие онкологии было установлено 10 января 1997 года в Донецком Областном диагностическом центре и 29 января 1997 г. в МНИИДиХ г. Москвы.

Фактически Грабовой Григорий Петрович изменил мою меру об неоперабельного рака головки поджелудочной железы с прорастанием в двенадцатиперстную кишку за один сеанс.

Настоящее свидетельство является фактом экстрасенсорной работы в области исцеления от рака.

_01.1997г._

Тридцать первого января  одна тысяча девятьсот девяносто седьмого года,  я,  Вроблевская Л.Э.,  нотариус г.Москвы,  свидетельствую подлинность  подписи,  сделанной  гр.  Буза  Людмилой  Ивановной. Личность подписавшей установлена.

Зарегистрировано в реестре _1-1077_
Взыскано по тарифу _15.000 руб. Стр_
Нотариус

# СВИДЕТЕЛЬСТВО
## об экстрасенсорной работе Грабового Григория Петровича
родившегося 14 ноября 1963 года в поселке Кировском Кировского района Чимкентской
области Казахской ССР (имеющего свидетельство о рождении серии II - ОГ № 463794)

Место: _г. Москва_ 1997 / 1 / 20 / 15 / 00
(место заполнения свидетельства) год месяц число часы минуты

Я, _Буза Владимир Георгиевич_ (фамилия, имя и отчество полностью)

родился(лась) _4 декабря 1952г., г. Донецк, Украина_
(дата и место рождения)

гражданин(ка) _Украины_
(государство)

проживаю _Республика Саха (Якутия) г. Нерюнгри ул. Мира, д.5, кв.21, т. 6-08-53_
(место жительства и домашний телефон)

имею удостоверение личности _паспорт XIV-НО № 555605, ОВД Червоногвардейского_
(наименование документа, серия, номер, кем и когда выдан документ)
_райисполкома г. Макеевки, Донецкой области_

работаю _ГКБ г. Якутии, обогатительная фабрика "Нерюнгинская", главный бухгалтер, т. 4-58-85, 9-25-07_
(наименование предприятия, должность и служебные телефоны)

Я, Буза Владимир Георгиевич, удостоверяю, что обращался к Григорию Петровичу Грабовому по поводу моего заболевания с диагнозом: злокачественная опухоль головки поджелудочной железы с прорастанием в двенадцатиперстную кишку, установленном в Московском научно-исследовательском институте диагностики и хирургии (МНИИДиХ) 11 декабря 1996 года.

Первый сеанс был проведен 25 декабря 1996 года.

Отсутствие онкологии было установлено 10 января 1997 года в Донецком областном диагностическом центре и 29 января 1997 года в МНИИДиХ г. Москвы.

Настоящее свидетельство является фактом экстрасенсорной работы в области излечения от рака.

Фактически Грабовой Григорий Петрович исцелил меня от неоперабельного рака головки поджелудочной железы с прорастанием в двенадцатиперстную кишку за один сеанс.

30.01.1997г. _Буза_

Тридцать первого января одна тысяча девятьсот девяносто седьмого года, я, Вроблевская Л.Э. нотариус г.Москвы, свидетельствую подлинность подписи, сделанной гр. Буза Владимиром Георгиевичем. Личность подписавшего установлена.

Зарегистрировано в реестре _1-1011_
Взыскано по тарифу
Нотариус

Московский научно-исследовательский институт диагностики и хирургии
МЗ РФ

117837, Москва, Профсоюзная, 86          тел.333-91-20

**С П Р А В К А 6526/96**

Дана гр. Бузе Владимиру Георгиевичу 1952 г.р.
в том, что он находил ся на стационарном лечении в клинике МНИИДиХ
с " 27 " ноября 1996 г. по " 30 " января 19 97 г.

Цитологическое исследование биоптата от 4.12.1996г. №24486/96 Эритроциты
группа клеток кубического эпителия, комплексы полиморфных клеток о про-

При выписке рекомендовано : лукшей слизи. Гистология № 16798-92.
Кусочки слизистой 12-ти ...ерстной кишки

Дата " 16 " ... 19 97 г.

Н.А.Кунда

Донецкий областной диагностический центр им. В.Д. Колесникова
отделение эндоскопических исследований
ФИО пациента БУЗА В.Г.          рез. № ДЦ 9701011004236
Год рождения : 1952 пол: М категория : 99 статус : Д
кабинет 229

Проведены исследования :          ...Эзофагогастродуоденоскопия
Аппаратом GIF- Q - 10 пищевод свободно проходим. Слизистая гладкая
,бледно розовая. Кардия сомкнута .
Дата   10 Января 97          Врач-эндоскопист Губанов Д.С.

## ВСЕМ ЗАИНТЕРЕСОВАННЫМ ЛИЦАМ

Заявитель : _штефришвили Ивания Рамазовна_ _ _ _ _ _
(фамилия, имя и отчество полностью)

Заинтересованные лица: _ _ _ _ _ _ _ _ _ _ _ _ _ _ _
(фамилия, имя и отчество полностью)

_ _ _ _ _ _ _ _ _ _ _ _ _ _ _ _ _ _ _ _ _ _ _ _ _ _ _
(адрес организации)

### ЗАЯВЛЕНИЕ
об установлении факта признания
**Грабового Григория Петровича**
целителем и ясновидящим

Запись о моем рождении была сделана органами загса _ _ _ _ _ _ _ _

_ _ _ _ _ _ _ _ _ _ _ _ _ _ _ _ _ _ _ _ _ _ _ _ _ _ _ _ _ _
(указать номер и серию свидетельства рождения)

имею удостоверение личности _Р СЕО 1010 2292 1010 9000 595_
(наименование документа, серия, номер, кем и когда выдан документ)

_выдан 19/III 1996 года_ _ _ _ _ _ _ _ _ _ _ _ _ _ _ _ _

В связи с тем, что я обратился(лась) к Грабовому Григорию Петровичу, родившемуся 14 ноября 1963 года в поселке Кировском, Кировского района Чимкентской области Казахской ССР имеющему свидетельство о рождении серии II-ОГ № 463794, паспорт серии III-ОГ № 586058, выданный 01.02.1980 года, _2 ноября 1995года в Тбилиси для того чтобы Гра-_
(указать дату, место и причину обращения)
_бовой Григорий Петрович заочно исцелил меня_
заявляю, что Грабовой Григорий Петрович действительно _исцелил меня_
(привести доказательства в обоснование заявления)

_от заболевания СПИД IV стадии с рассеянными_
_изменениями розпнного цвета на кожном_
_покрове и увеличенными размерами желёз я_
_имею. Доказательство этого состоит в том,_
_что до начала заочно восстановления, провади-_
_мых Грабовым Г.П. у меня в течение трёх с_
_лишним лет подтверждался диагноз СПИД в_
_диагностическом отделении Республиканского_
_Центра СПИДа и клинической иммунологии_
_минздрава Грузии г Тбилиси. На теле боль-_
_шое пятна тёмного, зелёного, жёлтого цветов._
_Я также увеличены железы. После проведения_
_со стороны Григория Петровича заочного восста-_
_новительного курса, в выписке 8/III 1995 г. Рес-_
_публиканского центра СПИДа и клинической_
_иммунологии минздраве Грузии есть запись,_
_что я практически здорова. И действительно_
_изменений на коже нет, анализ иммунитета_
_в норме._ _ _ _ _ _ _ _ _ _ _ _ _ _ _ _ _ _ _ _ _ _

Прошу заверить мое заявление на основании документов удостоверяющих мою личность и на основании вышеизложенных доказательств

_Штефришвили Ивания Рамазовна_
_пдпс_ / _ _ _ _ _ _ _
(подпись)          (фамилия)

199_6_ / _III_ / _25_ /
год   месяц   число

25. _марта 1996_ года я, Северин Ю.Д., нотариус г.Москвы, свидетельствую подлинность подписи гр. _Метришвили Ванца_ _____ которая сделана в моем присутствии. Личность подписавшего документ установлена.

Зарегистрировано в реестре за № _1с – 1600_
Взыскано по тарифу _9189 руб._
Нотариус _____

**Лист № 1**

## СВИДЕТЕЛЬСТВО
### об экстрасенсорной работе Грабового Григория Петровича

родившегося 14 ноября 1963 года в поселке Кировском Кировского района Чимкентской области Казахской ССР (имеющего свидетельство о рождении серии II - ОГ № 463794 ).

Место начала составления свидетельства _г. Москва ул. Ильинка_

Время начала составления свидетельства 19 _96_ / _III_ / _23_ / _16_ / _20_
<br>год / месяц / число / часы / минуты

Я, _Мгефишвили Тамила Ромазовна_
<br>(фамилия, имя и отчество полностью)

проживаю _____
<br>(место жительства и домашний телефон)

имею удостоверение личности _Р. СFO 0108292_
<br>_№01009000595_
<br>(наименование документа, серия, номер, кем и когда выдан документ)

работаю _студентка_
<br>(наименование предприятия, должность и служебные телефоны)

_Вопрос об исследовании крови был поставлен у меня в связи с установлением ВИЧ инфекции у моего супруга Р.Р. которая с этим диагнозом состоял на учёте в центре СПИДа в г. Тбилиси с мая 1992 г. Умер в мае 1995 г. Окончательный диагноз ВИЧ инфекция, СПИД IV ст стадия токсо-плазмозный абсцесс головного мозга, нейротоксикоз, нейрососудистая форма._

_Обследование сыворотки моей крови на наличие антител к ВИЧ неоднократно проводилось методами ИФА и ИБ. Все результаты тестирования были положительными, методом Western Blot было выявлено наличие антител к бел-кам ВИЧ._

_На основании этих лабораторных данных в республиканском центре СПИДа и клинической иммунологии им. Назарова Грузии в июле 1992 года мне был пров. был диагноз ВИЧ инфекция II стадия ге-нерализованная персистирующая лимфаденопатия (по классификации СДС). Препаратное лечение не принимала. Все обследования до 9 ноября 1995 г. (в том числе и в Москве) показывали наличие СПИДа._

_До 9/XI 1995 г. с которого я начала заниматься заочно восстановительной_

Продолжение настоящего текста в приложении № _один_ к первому листу.

© Г.П. Грабовой, 2001

**ПРИЛОЖЕНИЕ №** один

**к свидетельству об экстрасенсорной работе Грабового Григория Петровича** родившегося 14 ноября 1963 года в поселке Кировском Кировского района Чимкентской области Казахской ССР (имеющего свидетельство о рождении серии II - ОГ № 463794 ).

Место начала составления свидетельства г. Москва ул. Ильинка 5/2

Время начала составления свидетельства 1996 / III / 22 / 16 / 20
(год / месяц / число / часы / минуты)

*( Вышеперечисленные данные настоящего листа вписываются с первого листа свидетельства ).*

курс от Грабового Григория Петровича, у меня, кроме анализов, подтверждающих наличие СПИДа, были пятна различного диаметра и размера, располагающиеся в различных частях тела. Также были увеличены лимфоузлы, на основании чего ставился диагноз IV стадия СПИДа.

9/XI 1995г. в Грузинском представительстве Грабового Григория Петровича я заключила договор на то, что Грабовой Г.П. проводит заочное восстановление моего здоровья. При этом основным диагнозом я оформила наличие у меня СПИДа. По условиям договора я должна была протоколировать состояние своего здоровья. В течение месяца от срока начала заочного лечения, проводимого Грабовым Григорием Петровичем с ноября 1995г. пятна, имеющие черные, желтые и зеленые цвета, располагающиеся на ногах исчезли и с конца декабря 1995г. у меня на теле пятен нет. Кожа чистая.

Во время проведения бесконтактного лечения Грабовым Григорием Петровичем я чувствовала пульсацию в лимфоузлах, которые в январе 1996г. уменьшились с большой скоростью. Самочувствие хорошее, чувствую себя здоровой.

5/XII 1995г. я прошла лабораторно-инструментальные исследования в диспансерном отделении Республиканского центра СПИДа и клинической иммунологии Минздрава Грузии г. Тбилиси у лечащего врача Л. Шарвадзе. Обследования по полной программе проходили до 21/XII 1995г. В отличии от всех предшествующих обследований, которые проводились в течении 3-4 дней и во всех тест-системах обнаруживалось наличие СПИДа, после [illegible] восстановительного заочного лечения от Грабового Г.П. (кроме

**Продолжение настоящего текста в приложении №** два **к первому листу.**

**ПРИЛОЖЕНИЕ №** *два*

**к свидетельству об экстрасенсорной работе Грабового Григория Петровича** родившегося 14 ноября 1963 года в поселке Кировском Кировского района Чимкентской области Казахской ССР (имеющего свидетельство о рождении серии II - ОГ № 463794 ).

Место начала составления свидетельства *г. Москва ул. Ильинка 5/8*

Время начала составления свидетельства 19 *96* / *III* / *22* / *16* / *20*
год / месяц / число / часы / минуты

*( Вышеперечисленные данные настоящего листа вписываются с первого листа свидетельства ).*

*[handwritten text, largely illegible]*

© Г.П. Грабовой, 2001

_25 марта 1996_ года я, Северин Ю.Д., нотариус г.Москвы, свидетельствую подлинность подписи гр. _Шебришвили Тванца Тамозовна_ которая сделана в моем присутствии. Личность подписавшего документ установлена.

Зарегистрировано а реестре за № _1с – 1605_
Взыскано по _____ _____
Нотариус _____

Всего прошнуровано,
пронумеровано и скреплено
печатью _____ листов
Нотариус _____

ВЫПИСКА

из истории болезни

Больная М. Г., 25 л., вдова, проживающая в Грузии.
Вопрос об обследовании крови М. Г. был поставлен в связи с установлением ВИЧ инфекции у ее супруга Л. Р., который с этим диагнозом состоял на учете в Центре с мая 1992 г. Умер в мае 1995 г. Окончательный диагноз: ВИЧ инфекция, СПИД, IV C1 стадия, токсоплазмозный абсцесс головного мозга, нейротоксикоз - нейроваскулярная форма.

Обследование сыворотки крови М. Г. на наличие антител к ВИЧ неоднократно проводилось методами ИФА и НИФ. Все результаты тестирования были положительными. Методом Western Blot было выявлено наличие антител к белкам ВИЧ.

На основании этих лабораторных данных установлен диагноз ВИЧ инфекции и больная поствлена на диспансерный учет.

При взятии на учет больная жаловалась на увеличение лимфатических узлов в шейном и в подмышечных областях, которое беспокоило ее в течении последних 6 месяцев, и на выделения из влагалища и зуд в перианальной области.

При обьективном осмотре больной выявлены увеличенные лимфоузлы: задне-шейный слева - до диаметра 2 см, подмышечные - с обеих сторон по 3-4 узла до диаметра 1,5-2,5 см, паховые - единичные с обеих сторон до диаметра 1,5-2 см; безболезненные, умеренно плотной консистенции.

Серологические исследования на наличие антител к ВИЧ

| метод | число | тест-система | результаты |
|---|---|---|---|
| НИФ | 06. 92 неоднократно | | положительный |
| Иммуноблот | 23. 12. 92 | Блот-ВИЧ | gp120/41, p24/17 p 51 |
| | 16. 02. 93 | Антиген-ВИЧ | gp160/120, gp41, p55, p24, p65, p53 |
| | 22. 03. 93 | CMG | gp120, gp41, p24, p65 |
| | 02. 04. 93 | Блот-ВИЧ | gp120/41, p24/17 p 51 |
| | 21. 04. 93 | CB-HIV-1 | gp160, gp120, gp41, p17, p24, p55, p31, p51, p66, |

Иммунологические исследования:
-----------------------------------

7.07.92

CD3 - 51%     (N - 60-80%)
CD4 - 31%     (N - 34-60%,)
                 абс. ч. -1612 мм$^3$
CD8 - 26%     (N - 16-30%)
CD4/CD8-1,19 (N - 1,5-2,5%)
В   - 26%     (N - 15-25)
CD6 - 7%      (N - 10 - 20)
IgG - 14,4 g/1 (N 8,4 -14,5 g/1)
IgA - 3,44 g/1 (N 1,5 - 4,2 g/1)
IgM - 2,68 g/1 (N 0,46 -1,9 g/1)

22.09.92

CD3- 67%
CD4- 41%
             абс. ч. -1676мм$^3$
CD8 - 28% Т4/Т8
CD4/CD8 - 1,4
В  - 26%
CD6- 12%
IgG - 8,25 g/1
IgA - 1,09 g/1
IgM - 0,76 g/1


31.03.93

CD3 - 61%
CD4 - 40%   абс. ч. 344 мм$^3$
CD8 - 25%
CD4/CD8 - 1,6
В - 23%
CD6 -
IgG - 11,69 g/1
IgA  - 1,82 g/1
IgM - 1,58  g/1

29.03.94

CD3 - 71%
CD4 - 45%  абс. ч. 399 мм$^3$
CD8 - 25%
CD4/CD8 - 1,8
В - 21%
CD6 - 10%
IgG - 14,55  g/1
IgA  - 2,28  g/1
IgM -  1,12  g/1


10.10.94

CD3 - 66%
CD4 - 40% абс. ч. - 430мм$^3$
CD8 - 26%
CD4/CD8 - 1,5
В - 25%
CD6 - 10%
IgG - 13,5 g/1
IgA - 2,4  g/1
IgM - 2,02 g/1

Биохимимческий анализ крови
------------------------------

14.07.92 тимоловая проба - 26 ед;
24.09.92 тимоловая проба - 10 ед;
01.04.93 тимоловая проба - 20 ед;


Исследования на ВИЧ асоциированные оппортунистические
инфекции методом ИФА
--------------------------------------------------------

5.12.95

HBsAg                        не обнаружен
Анти - HBcor (сум)           не обнаружены
Анти - HBc IgM               не обнаружены
Анти - Delta IgM             не обнаружены
Анти - Delta IgG             не обнаружены
Анти - HCV                   не обнаружены
Анти - HAV IgM               не обнаружены


Общий анализ крови
-----------------------

Основные показатели в пределах нормы.

В настоящее   время б-ная субъективных жалоб не предъявляет и чуствует себя практически здоровой.

Объективный осмотр не   выявил изменений со   стороны лимфоузлов.

21.12.95г

Лечащий врач         ШАРВАДЗЕ  Л. Г.

# УДИВИТЕЛЬНЫЙ  РЕЗУЛЬТАТ
## обращения за помощью об омоложении
## к Грабовому Г.П.

Первый раз я обратилась к Г.П. Грабовому 7 марта 2000 г. с просьбой об  омоложении.

Второй раз я посетила Г.П. Грабового 25 июля 2000 г. с дочкой, которая подтвердила ему положительные результаты работы Грабового Г.П. с ней по ее профессиональной карьере.

Через две недели после этой встречи я делала УЗИ в санатории им.Фрунзе г. Сочи, результаты которого ошеломили меня: УЗИ подтверждало наличие матки размером 35 x 40 мм.

Я сообщила врачу, что матку вместе с шейкой у меня удалили 3 года назад и показала выписку операции и результат гистологии матки с шейкой матки и трубами.

Врач УЗИ пригласила врача-гинеколога и при осмотре она пальпировала наличие матки. Все эти удивительные результаты были обсуждены с Зам. Главного врача по медицинской части санатория им.Фрунзе г. Сочи доктором  мед. наук Богачкиным М.В.

29 августа 2000 г. я сделала биорезонансную диагностику «Метапатия» органов малого таза.
Результаты диагностики:
отсутствие миомы, эндометриоза, кисты на стенке цервикального канала, отсутствие вирусных бактерий.
Диагностика зафиксировала наличие эндоцервицита (воспаление слизистой канала шейки матки).

Свидетелями  вышеописанного были:
Я             – Симакова Нина Васильевна, год рождения 1951

Зам. гл. врача по мед. части санатория им. Фрунзе г.Сочи, д.м.н.-
Богачкин М.В.

Врач-диагност медицинского центра
"Sunrider" (США) – к. биолог.наук.
Богачкова О.П

APPENDIX C: DOCUMENTS CONFIRMING THE LISTED
IN THE BOOK CONCRETE FACTS OF PREVENTION
OF ACCIDENTS BY ANTICIPATORY FORECASTING,
AND PUBLISHED FORECASTS OF POLITICAL, ECONOMIC,
AND SOCIAL EVENTS WITH COMPLETE CONFIRMATION

Министерство топлива и энергетики
Российской Федерации

 **Центральный   штаб**
военизированных горноспасательных частей угольной промышленности
**( ЦШ  ВГСЧ )**

121019, г.Москва,ул.Новый Арбат,15.Приемная 202-31-93,опер.отдел 202-30-90,проф.отдел 202-03-76
Расчетный счет № 345075 в Электробанке, кор. счет № 161890 в РКЦ ГУ ЦБ РФ, МФО 201791

№ ЦШ-52         от 16.06.1995 г.

На №: _____

## ПРОТОКОЛ

экспериментальных проверок способности
**ГРАБОВОГО Григория Петровича**
экстрасенсорно определять аварии,
количество пострадавших живых людей и их местонахождение,
нарушения проветривания в шахтах по схеме

г.Москва, ул.Новый Арбат, д. 15, комната 933
Телефон: 202-12-74, 202-24-39
Центральный штаб военизированных
горноспасательных частей                   16 июня 1995 года
угольной промышленности России             15 часов 00 минут
(ЦШ ВГСЧ УП РФ)

### 1. ЦЕЛЬ ЭКСПЕРИМЕНТА

Целью эксперимента являлось по договору с администрацией Президента Российской Федерации установить способность ГРАБОВОГО Григория Петровича, родившегося 14 ноября 1963 года в поселке Кировском Кировского района Чимкентской области Казахской ССР, имеющего свидетельство о рождении серии II-ОГ N 463794, экстрасенсорно определять места аварий, количество пострадавших живых людей и нарушения проветриваний в шахтах по схеме.

### 2. ЧИСТОТА ЭКСПЕРИМЕНТА

Чистота эксперимента заключалась в том, что:
2.1. Расположение штреков предоставлялось в строго экспериментальных условиях по схеме вентиляции таким образом, что до начала эксперимента никто не знал, какие схемы будут переданы для проведения ГРАБОВЫМ Г.П. экстрасенсорной диагностики шахт.

*(Продолжение протокола проверки экстрасенсорных способностей ГРАБОВОГО Г.П. от 16 июня 1995 года 15 часов 00 минут г.Москва, ул. Новый Арбат, 15, комната 933 смотреть на странице 2)*

2.2. ГРАБОВОЙ Г.П. экстрасенсорно практически моментально после представления ему схемы правильно указывал места аварий на схемах, точно определял количество пострадавших живых людей и их местонахождение, правильно определял места нарушений проветривания без времени на вопросы и, не зная координат штреков на местности.

2.3. Независимые эксперты узнали о задаче проведения эксперимента по проверке способности ГРАБОВОГО Г.П. проводить экстрасенсорную диагностику шахт сразу после знакомства с ГРАБОВЫМ Г.П. и произвольным образом ставили задачи. В составе экспертной комиссии работали высококвалифицированные специалисты и руководящие работники Центрального штаба военизированных горноспасательных частей.

## 3. ДАННЫЕ И РЕЗУЛЬТАТЫ ЭКСПЕРИМЕНТА

3.1. ГРАБОВОЙ Г.П. экстрасенсорным способом без предоставления ему какой бы то ни было предварительной информации в течение одной секунды после того, как ему передали схему вентиляции шахты "Воркутинская" АО "Воркутауголь" правильно и точно по местонахождению объектов диагностирования выполнил следующее:

3.1.1. Правильно определил место возникновения пожара.

3.1.2. Правильно определил места нахождения двух пострадавших живых на вентиляционном штреке.

3.1.3. Правильно определил нарушения с проветриванием в аварийной лаве.

3.2. ГРАБОВОЙ Г.П. проводил экстрасенсорное диагностирование схемы, не имея информации о месте расположения шахты на местности, то есть просто с листа бумаги.

3.3 Схема шахты была выбрана членами экспертной комиссии произвольно, сразу после знакомства с ГРАБОВЫМ Г.П. и постановки задач эксперимента.

3.4. ГРАБОВОЙ Г.П. правильно ответил на поставленные перед ним задачи: экстрасенсорным способом определил место возникнове-

*(Продолжение протокола проверки экстрасенсорных способностей ГРАБОВОГО Г.П. от 16 июня 1995 15 часов 00 минут г.Москва, ул. Новый Арбат, 15, комната 933 смотреть на странице 3)*

Страница 3 Протокола проверки экстрасенсорных способностей Грабового Г.П. от 16     3
июня 1995 года 15 часов 00 минут г.Москвы, ул. Новый Арбат, дом 15, комната 933

ния пожара; количечество оставшихся в живых людей и их местонахождение; места нарушений с проветриванием. Таким образом, в условиях чистого эксперимента уставлено, что Г.П.ГРАБОВОЙ экстрасенсорным способом практически моментально правильно диагностирует по схеме шахт.

## 4. ВЫВОД

4.2. ГРАБОВОЙ Григорий Петрович экстрасенсорным способом по схеме шахт моментально диагностирует и правильно показывает на схеме места возникновения пожаров, количество и места нахождения живых людей в штреках, места нарушений проветривания.

4.3. Считаем целесообразным сотрудничество с Г.П.ГРАБОВЫМ в области прогнозирования и предупреждения аварийных ситуаций, нахождения и спасения людей из аварий на угольных предприятиях.

Члены экспертной комиссии:

Заместитель главного инженера
Центрального штаба ВГСЧ УП РФ                 А.Г.Кузнецов

Заместитель главного инженера
Центрального штаба ВГСЧ УП РФ                 А.П.Жолус

Лист № 1

# СВИДЕТЕЛЬСТВО
### об экстрасенсорной работе Грабового Григория Петровича

родившегося 14 ноября 1963 года в поселке Кировском Кировского района Чимкентской области Казахской ССР (имеющего свидетельство о рождении серии II - ОГ № 463794 ).

Место начала составления свидетельства _Россия, Санкт-Петербург_

Время начала составления свидетельства 19_96_ / _07_ / _04_ / _12_ / _07_
<br>год  месяц  число  часы  минуты

Я, _Кузионов — Сергей Петрович_
<br>(фамилия, имя и отчество полностью)

родился (~~лась~~) _26 апреля 1953 г. в городе Ташкенте, Узбекистане_
<br>(дата и место рождения).

гражданин (~~ка~~) _России_
<br>(государство)

проживаю _в Санкт-Петербурге, В.О. ул. Карташихина, д 6, кв 8,_
<br>(место жительства и домашний телефон)
<br>_дом. тел. 108-65-67._

имею удостоверение личности _паспорт VI-МЕ 652375, выдан_
<br>(наименование документа, серия, номер, кем и когда выдан документ)
<br>_13.07.79 г. Сигулдским ОВД Рижского РИК Латвийской ССР_

работаю _эксперт-консультант Санкт-Петербургской епархии_
<br>(наименование предприятия, должность и служебные телефоны)
<br>_в Соборе Святой живоначальной Троицы Измайловского полка._

В день знакомства с Григорием Петровичем Грабовым 3 января 1995 года в Ташкенте - столица Узбекистана, я присутствовал при беседе, где Григорий Петрович рассказывал о поездке на Филиппины и о своем понимании механизма его воздействия. Присутствовал мой друг — Пукалов Александр Тимофеевич — главный редактор газеты "Ташкентская правда" который пригласил меня на встречу и который знал о моем интересе к феномена, и о моих многолетних исследованиях НЛО, парапсихологии и полтергейста. В процессе беседы я задал Григорию Петровичу занимавший в тот период моей жизни вопрос — "существует ли однозначно будущее, или его можно моделировать" Григорий Петрович мгновенно как-бы залебил, что он уже его изменил мне. Сказано было невзначай, и я не придал особого внимания словам.

После встречи я вернулся на автомобиле ВАЗ-21011 с номером 00-54 ТНУ в дом к родственникам, где остановился в период пребывания в Ташкенте. Это было после 24 часов, практически ночью.

Утром я должен был ехать на том же автомобиле ВАЗ-21011 на деловую встречу. Выезжая из гаража и, далее, с поворотом на дорогу, я почувствовал, что при кручении руля колеса не поворачивались. Поняв, что произошла поломка, пренебрег встречей, позвонив по телефону и перенеся встречу на более поздний час, я начал выяснять причину поломки. Оказалось, что были срезаны шпильку в месте сочленения рулевого вала и вала червячного редуктора и в 2х плоскостях срезан болт в месте сочленения, который владелец автомобиля мой отец Кузионов Петр Васильевич

_Продолжение настоящего текста в приложении № 1 к первому листу._

ПРИЛОЖЕНИЕ №  1.

**к свидетельству об экстрасенсорной работе Грабового Григория Петровича** родившегося 14 ноября 1963 года в поселке Кировском Кировского района Чимкентской области Казахской ССР (имеющего свидетельство о рождении серии II - ОГ № 463794 ).

Место начала составления свидетельства  Россия, Санкт-Петербург

Время начала составления свидетельства 19 96 / 07 / 04 / 12 / 07
год месяц число часы минуты

( *Вышеперечисленные данные настоящего листа вписываются с первого листа свидетельства* ).

установил на станции техн. обслуживания для исключения люфта. Я вставил другой болт аналогичного сечения, и завернул гайку. Поехал на СТО к своему знакомому главному инженеру СТО Кострову Михаилу Наумовичу (который удивился, сказав, что обычно такие «страховочные» болты «не срезает», тем более в 2х плоскостях (у головки болта и в зоне гайки).

Удивительным мне до сих пор кажется корреляция по времени и обстоятельствам беседы накануне и фразы обо мне Григория Петровича Грабового об изменении моего будущего, времени (самого момента) поломки и его характера. То есть, будь моей поломки немного раньше или позже въезда на стоянку перед гаражом, в лучшем случае автомобиль и я оказались бы на обочине.

В дополнение могу сообщить, что после этого несколько раз в течение полугода в присутствии др. свидетелей наблюдались явления аномального характера. Например, «горел» свет в квартире и работал фотоаппарат при вывернутой пробке, шумовые эффекты в пустой комнате (явно было слышно что кто-то ходит и щёлкает в квартире), др. явления.

Могу сообщить, что исследованиями аномальных явлений занимаюсь давно, с 1980 года. Являюсь членом Комиссии по исследованию аномальных явлений Географического общества АН России, был сотрудником американского центра по исследованию А.Я. и лечению аномальных трав. (Нью Йорк, США) организовал работу и создал корпорацию "HOLY STONE" в Нью Йорке.

О вышеизложенном 28 июня 1996г в Москве в присутствии свидетелей и Григория Петровича Грабового была сделана видеозапись для архива ООН. Видеозапись встречи 3 января 1995г. в Ташкенте передана вместе с этим документом Григорию Петровичу Грабовому.

Кузнецов Сергей Петрович

УТВЕРЖДАЮ
Генеральный директор
Национальной Авиакомпании
Республики Узбекистан

В.М. Рафиков

"05" _____ 1992 г.

### ПРОТОКОЛ № 08/92

г. Ташкент                                                    "02"    июля    1992 г.

**экспериментальных проверок возможности
Грабового Григория Петровича осуществлять
экстрасенсорное прогнозирование возникновения неисправностей,
отказов или отклонений от технических условий эксплуатации
в основных системах и элементах самолетов ИЛ-62 и ИЛ-86
на период тридцать дней.**

Экспертная комиссия в составе:
председателя
Балакирева В.Ф., ведущего пилота-инспектора отдела расследований Главной инспекции по государственном регулированию и надзору Гражданской авиации Республики Узбекистан
и членов комиссии:
1. Саулькина В.М., начальника инженерно-информационного центра авиационно-технической базы Национальной Авиакомпании Республики Узбекистан;
2. Немцова С.В., ведущего инженера инженерно-информационного центра авиационно-технической базы Национальной Авиакомпании Республики Узбекистан;
3. Кривоносова В.М., начальника юридического отдела Национальной Авиакомпании Республики Узбекистан,
действующая на основании договора № 9, заключенного 2 декабря 1991 г. между совместным Советско-Американским предприятием "АСКОН" и Узбекским Управлением гражданской авиации провела проверку возможностей экстрасенса Грабового Григория Петровича осуществлять:
- экстрасенсорное прогнозирование возникновения неисправностей, отказов или отклонений от технических условий эксплуатации в основных системах и элементах самолетов ИЛ-62 и ИЛ-86 на период тридцать дней.
В результате эксперимента комиссия установила следующее:

РАЗДЕЛ 1. Результаты проверки чистоты эксперимента

Прогноз был дан 20 января 1992г., до начала периода прогноза и в дальнейшем находился у членов комиссии.

Лист №2 протокола № 08/92

Работу по прогнозированию экстрасенс Грабовой Г.П. проводил визуально на расстоянии 100-200 метров от самолетов.

Экстрасенс Грабовой Г.П. до начала работы не имел никакой информации о состоянии диагностируемых самолетов, не использовал никаких традиционных способов и приборов для диагностирования неисправностей, отказов или отклонений от технических условий эксплуатации в основных системах и элементах самолетов.

При выдаче прогноза, в связи с тем, что по инженерным системам, устранением дефектов занимались специалисты по электрооборудованию, сделано следующее допущение - к системам электроснабжения отнесены:
- светотехническое оборудование;
- противообледенительная система;
- противопожарная система.

РАЗДЕЛ 2. Данные и результаты эксперимента

В январе 1992 г. экстрасенсом Грабовым Г.П. в Ташкенской авиационно-технической базе проводилась экстрасенсорная работа по прогнозированию возникновения неисправностей по основным системам на самолетах ИЛ-62 и ИЛ-86.

Цель этой работы была в экстрасенсорном определении возможных в будущем неисправностей, которые будут угрожать безопасности полетов.

Экстрасенс Грабовой Г.П., провел экстрасенсорное прогнозирование неисправностей и отказов по основным системам самолетов ИЛ-86 на период с 20 января 1992 г. до 20 февраля 1992 г. и для самолетов ИЛ-62 на период с 24 января 1992 г. по 24 февраля 1992 г.

Данные экстрасенсорного прогнозирования Грабового Г.П. приведены в таблице № 1

Таблица № 1

| Тип и бортовой номер самолета | Экстрасенсорная информация Грабового Г.П. | Подтверждающая запись в бортовом журнале самолета |
|---|---|---|
| ИЛ-86 № 86052 | Снижение мощности 4-го двигателя не относящееся к неисправности.<br><br>-Неисправности в бортовых средствах контроля и регистрации полетных данных.<br><br><br><br>-Неисправность противообледенительной системы (ПОС). | - 27 января 1992 г. Попадание птицы в тракт 4-го двигателя. Помят воздухозаборник и кок. Двигатель № А86142028 снят с эксплуатации.<br>- 21 января 1992г. После закрытия двери перед запуском двигателя загорелось табло "МСРП-МАРС" и лампочка отказа основного комплекта.<br>- 30 января 1992г. Сильный шум и треск при прослушивании записи МАРС БМ.<br>- 16 февраля 1992г. При включении ЭИ ПОС выбило автомат защиты (I). Аварийное восстановление ПОС не горит МС (I). |

Лист №3 протокола № 08/92

| Тип и бортовой номер самолета | Экстрасенсорная информация Грабового Г.П. | Подтверждающая запись в бортовом журнале самолета |
|---|---|---|
| ИЛ-86 № 86056 | - Неисправности в системе электроснбжения (светотехническое оборудование). | - 23 января 1992 г. При включении генераторов 2 и 3 не горит канал исправности. Параметры генераторов в норме. Генераторы подключаются в бортовую сеть через 5 минут после выхода двигателей 2 и 3 на взлетный режим. |
| | - Неисправности в приборном оборудовании. | - 03 февраля 1992 г. При проверке не проходит встроенный контроль 4 генератора, не загорается мнемосигнализатор. Заменен БЗУСП376Т. <br> - 09 февраля 1992 г. После взлета, выключения и уборки левая носовая фара не погасла. <br> - 13 февраля 1992 г. Выпал бленкер "КС". |
| | - Неисправности в двигателе и его агрегатах. | - 10 февраля 1992 г. На взлетном режиме завышены обороты ПНД СУ №1 на 240 об/мин. Заменен ЭП-664. |
| ИЛ-86 № 86072 | - Неисправности в системе электроснабжения. <br> - Неисправности в приборном оборудовании. | - 04 февраля 1992 г. Отказ генератора № 1 <br> - при снижении загорелось табло "Отказ ограничения элеронов". Заменен ВУП-4. <br> - 27 января 1992 г. Не вводится отказ I п/к автотриммера. Заменен БРТ-1. |
| ИЛ-86 № 86090 | - Неисправности в двигателе. | - 30 января 1992 г. Увеличение давления масла на входе 2-го двигателя до 5.3 кг/кв.см в средней опоре до 1.7 кг/кв.см. Двигатель снят с эксплуатации по подозрению в разрушении радиально-торцевого контактного уплотнения. |
| | - Неисправности в системе электроснабжения (светотехническое оборудование). | - 11февраля 1992 г. Выбивает АЗС освещения кабины экипажа. Напряжение на шинах 711И-3-393-16 U= . |
| | - Тангаж самолета не соответствует ТУ. | - 28 января 1992 г. "Загорелось табло "Нет резерва ограничения РВ" с загоранием кнопки-лампы в ряду "высота" I п/к на ПУ -41. |

Лист №4 протокола № 08/92

| Тип и бортовой номер самолета | Экстрасенсорная информация Грабового Г.П. | Подтверждающая запись в бортовом журнале самолета |
|---|---|---|
| Ил-62 № 86610. | -Неисправности в электроснабжении.<br><br>- Неисправности в топливной системе и ее агрегатах.<br>- Неисправности приборного оборудования. | - 29 января 1992 г. Не подключается на параллельную работу генератор 3 СУ.<br>- 23февраля 1992 г. Не герметичен кран слива отстоя из бака № 3.<br><br>- 19 февраля 1992 г. Занижены показания часового расхода. Колебания мгновенного расхода. Заменены БПСРЧ, БПСП2, ДРТМСIOT, ИРТI-I. |
| ИЛ-62 № 86694 | - Неисправности в электро-снабжении.<br><br><br>- Неисправности в двигателе. | - 01 февраля 1992 г. На предполетной подготовке обнаружено:"Не работает генератор № 4". Заменен ГТ4ОПЧ8.<br>- 02 февраля 1992 г. Осредненные значения 2 и 3 двигателей превышают опорные более 4 ед. Выполнен бюл.784 БЭ. |
| ИЛ-62 № 86704 | - Неисправности в топливной системе.<br><br><br>- Неисправности в электро-снабжении.<br><br><br>- Неисправности в двигателе № 3 (нарушение структуры материала камеры сгорания). Дополнительно к этому прогнозу, экстрасенсом была дана информация о необходимости контроля экипажа за системой управления. | - 22 февраля 1992 г. Нет показаний топливомера бака № 3. Заменен датчик ДТ-27-26Т.<br><br>- 10 февраля 1992 г. Не подключается на бортсеть генератор № 4.<br><br>- 31 января 1992 г. Прогар соплового аппарата.Двигатель досрочно снят с эксплуатации. По дополнительному замечанию подтверждающими фактами стали проявившиеся 26 января 1992г. дефекты: "Не работают дублирующие каналы (КУРС, КРЕН, ВЫСОТА) системы автоматического управления". " Неправильные показания планок КПП при заходе в директорном режиме". |

Во всех случаях экстрасенсорный прогноз Грабового Г.П. полностью подтвердился.

В результате рассмотрения данных комиссия делает выводы:

Лист №5 протокола № 08/92

    - из сравнения информации прогнозов с выписками из бортжурналов, следует, что вся экстрасенсорная информация Грабового Г.П., полученная в результате его работы по экстрасенсорному прогнозированию авиационных неисправностей на месяц вперед, полностью подтвердилась.

    - возможности экстрасенса Грабового Григория Петровича считать соответствующими, нуждам Ташкентской авиационно-технической базы.

    Комиссия рекомендует:

    - привлечь экстрасенса Грабового Григория Петровича для проведения таких работ и в дальнейшем, для профилактики неисправностей, угрожающих безопасности полетов самолетов.

**Председатель комиссии**

Ведущий пилот-инспектор отдела расследований
Главной инспекции по государственном регулированию и надзору
Гражданской авиации Республики Узбекистан

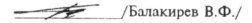 /Балакирев В.Ф./

**Члены комиссии**

Начальник инженерно-информационного центра
Авиационно-технической базы Национальной Авиакомпании
Республики Узбекистан

/Саулькин В.М./

Ведущий инженер инженерно-информационного центра
Авиационно-технической базы Национальной Авиакомпании
Республики Узбекистан

/Немцов С.В./

Начальник юридического отдела
Национальной Авиакомпании Республики Узбекистан

/Кривоносов В.М./

ПРОТОКОЛ
экспериментальных проверок возможности экстрасенса
Грабового Григория Петровича осуществлять
экстрасенсорную диагностику самолетов АН-12

г. Фергана                                            1994. 05. 18


Экспертная комиссия в составе:
председателя: заместителя начальника цеха N 39 Ферганского за-
вода (ФМЗ) Пономорева В. А.
и членов комиссии:

1. Закаев Н. Ф., представитель АНТК имени "Антонова" на ФМЗ;
2. Шерстнев А. А., начальник бюро технического контроля
цеха N 39 ФМЗ;
3. Воробьев С. В., мастер группы N 01 цеха N 39 ФМЗ,
назначенная на основании договора N 94/0105 от "05"января 1994
года провела проверку возможностей экстрасенса Грабового Григория Петровича по экстрасенсорному диагностированию самолетов
АН-12, с нахождением дефектов самолетов на расстоянии, когда
дефекты не видны физическим зрением. По условиям экспериментов
Грабовой Г. П. диагностирует в течении 2-х , 3-х секунд с момента когда ему покажут самолет.

В результате эксперимента комиссия установила следующие
основные данные:

В течении 2-х - 3-х секунд Грабовой Г. П. экстрасенсорно
диагностировал на расстоянии 20-25 метров самолет АН-12 серий-
ный номер 1901 принадлежащий болгарской авиакомпании "Эйр Со-
фия" и самолет с серийным номером 1204 принадлежащий Пен-
зенскому объединенному авиаотряду из Российской Федерации и
получено полное подтверждение его диагностики в результате
осмотров указанных самолетов комиссиями.

РАЗДЕЛ 1. Результаты проверки чистоты эксперимента:
1.1 Грабовой Г. П. не пользовался никакими средствами при-
борной диагностики и не имел возможности спросить о состоянии
самолета в связи с ограниченностью времени для его диагностики.
1.2 До диагностики Грабового Г. П. никто не знал о тех де-
фектах, на которые он указал и которые потом были найдены в
результате работы комиссии и оформлены техническими актами
N 39-20-194 и N 39-20-193, где описано обследование всего фюзеляжа самолета N 1901 и все площади правого и левого СЧК. Но
были найдены дефекты только там, где указал Грабовой Г. П.

РАЗДЕЛ 2. Данные и результаты эксперимента
2.1 Грабовой Г. П. экстрасенсорно диагностировал самолет
АН-12 N 1901 в течении 2-х - 3-х секунд на расстоянии 20-25
метров от самолета и передал сразу свою экстрасенсорную информацию следующего содержания "Коррозия в районе 62-го шпангоу-
та". Коррозия визуально вне самолета не видна. Через восемь

результате осмотра всего Фюзеляжа самолета 1901, что оформлено техническим актом N 39-20-194 и что полностью подтвердило экстрасенсорную информациию Грабового Г. П.

2.2 Грабовой Г. П. в течении 2-х - 3-х секунд экстрасенсорно диагностировал самолет АН-12 N 1204 и сразу передал свою информацию о трещинах на правой и левой плоскостях СЧК, которая затем полностью подтвердилась и оформлен акт N 39-20-193.

В результате рассмотрения данных комиссия делает выводы:
Грабовой Григорий Петрович (паспорт серии III-ОГ N 586058, выданный 01.02.1980 года) экстрасенсорно диагностирует такие дефекты самолетов, которые не видны визуально, а следовательно он обладает ясновидением ( возможностью видеть внутреннюю структуру материала или самолета). Он диагностирует Фактически моментально и совершенно точно с конкретным указанием места расположения дефекта.

Возможности экстрасенса Грабового Григория Петровича считать соответствующими нуждам авиации и там , где требуется экстрасенсорная диагностика техники.

Комиссия рекомендует:
привлечь экстрасенса Грабового Григория Петровича для проведения работ по экстрасенсорному диагностированию самолетов поступающих на Ферганский механический завод в целях нахождения скрытых дефектов и для повышения безопастности полетов.

Председатель комиссии          заместитель начальника цеха N 39
                                Ферганского механического завода

                                _____ Пономорев В. А.

Члены комиссии:                 представитель АНТК имени "Антонова"
                                на Ферганской механическом заводе

                                _____ Закаев Н. Ф.

                                начальник бюро технического
                                контроля цеха N 39
                                Ферганского механического завода

                                _____ Шерстнев А. А.

                                мастер группы N 01 цеха N 39
                                Ферганского механического завода

                                _____ Воробьев С. В.

ТЕХНИЧЕСКИЙ АКТ № 39-20-193

Настоящий акт составлен комиссией в составе :
председатель комиссии:Пономарев В.А.,зам.начальника цеха,
члены комиссии:　　　　Пикуза А.А.-начальник ТБ,
　　　　　　　　　　　Шерстнев А.А.-начальник БТК.
в том,что на изделии 1204 произведен осмотр технического состояния
СЧК прав.,лев.
1.Комиссия осмотрела СЧК прав.,лев. изделия 1204.
2.Комиссией выявлено:
2.1. На верхних обшивках прав. СЧК обнаружены трещины
　　　　длиной 14мм в районе 2 нк м/у 7-8 стр.;
　　　　длиной 15 мм в районе 8 нк м/у 7-8 стр.
2.2. На верхних обшивках лев. СЧК обнаружены трещины
　　　　длиной 14 мм в районе 2 нк м/у 7-8 стр.;
　　　　длиной 20 мм в районе 8 нк и 1 лонжероном;
　　　длиной 10мм и 12 мм в районе 10 нк и 1 лонжероном
　　　　длиной 15 мм в районе 7-8 нк и 2-3 стр.
　　　　длиной 20 мм в районе 2 нк, 1 лонжероном.
3.Заключение .
3.1. Прав.,лев. СЧК изделия 1204 подлежит ремонту с установкой
　　　ремнакладок на верхних панелях .


Зам.начальника цеха 39:　　　　　　　　　ПОНОМАРЕВ В.А.

Начальник БТК-39:　　　　　　　　　　　ШЕРСТНЕВ А.А.

Начальник ТБ-39:　　　　　　　　　　　ПИКУЗА А.А.

**ФАРҒОНА МЕХАНИКА
ЗАВОДИ**

712016 Фарғона шаҳар Герцен кўчаси,2
Телеграф коди—166136 (гроза)
Телефакс— 694 35
Телефон— 420 68, 414 12

**ФЕРГАНСКИЙ МЕХАНИЧЕСКИЙ
ЗАВОД**

712016 г. Фергана ул. Герцена, 2
Телеграфный код — 166136 (гроза)
Телефакс — 694 35
Телефон — 420 68, 414 12

1994. 11. 18 № 1200

На № _____ от _____

С В И Д Е Т Е Л Ь С Т В О

г.Фергана                                    1994г. 11.18

      Настоящее свидетельство удостоверяет,что Грабовой
Григорий Петрович (имеющий паспорт серии Ш-ОГ № 586058
выданный 01.02.1980г. и удостоверение на экстрасенсорное
диагностирование техники серии А № 018466 выданное
28.04.1994 года)действительно экстрасенсорно диагностирует
самолеты со следующими результатами:
1.Точно указывает места расположения скрытых и определяе-
мых только приборными методами дефектов самолетов находясь
на большом расстоянии от самолетов.
2. Диагностирует практически моментально и сразу передает
свою экстрасенсорную информацию.
      Анализ результатов экстрасенсорных работ Грабового Г.П.
показывает,что Грабовой Г.П. точно и с полным подтверждением
диагностирует самолеты только через свое ясновидение,диагнос-
тирует фактически моментально с конкретным указанием агре-
гатов имеющих неисправности,коррозии,скрытые дефекты.

ДИРЕКТОР Ф М З:                              ГУЛЯМОВ Д.Х.

ПРЕДСТАВИТЕЛЬ АНТК
ИМЕНИ АНТОНОВА на Ф М З:                     ЗАКАЕВ Н.Ф.

ЗАМЕСТИТЕЛЬ НАЧАЛЬНИКА
ЦЕХА 39 Ф М З:                               ПОНОМАРЕВ В.А.

НАЧАЛЬНИК БЮРО ТЕХНИЧЕС-
КОГО КОНТРОЛЯ ЦЕХА 39 ФМЗ:                   ШЕРСТНЕВ А.А.

МАСТЕР ГРУППЫ № 01 ЦЕХА 39 ФМЗ:              ВОРОБЬЕВ С.В.

**ВСЕМ ЗАИНТЕРЕСОВАННЫМ ЛИЦАМ**

Заявитель: _____
(фамилия, имя и отчество полностью)

_____
(адрес и телефоны)

Заинтересованные лица: _____
(фамилия, имя и отчество полностью; адрес)

**ЗАЯВЛЕНИЕ**
об установлении факта признания
**Грабового Григория Петровича**
целителем и ясновидящим

Я родился(лась) 19 35 / 12 / 25 в Московской области,
год  месяц  число          (место рождения)

_____
имею удостоверение личности _____
(наименование документа, серия, номер, кем и когда выдан документ)

Работаю: _____
(название предприятия, должность и телефон)

В связи с тем, что я обратился(лась) к Грабовому Григорию Петровичу,
родившемуся 14 ноября 1963 года в поселке Кировском, Кировского
района Чимкентской области Казахской ССР имеющему свидетельство о
рождении серии II-ОГ № 463794, _____
(указать дату, место и причину обращения)

заявляю, что Грабовой Григорий Петрович действительно _____
_____
(привести доказательства в обоснование заявления)
_____

Прошу заверить мое заявление, на основании документов,
удостоверяющих мою личность и на основании вышеизложенных
доказательств.

г. Москва _____ 19 96 / 12 / 18
(подпись)   (фамилия)        год  месяц  число

Лист № 1

# СВИДЕТЕЛЬСТВО
## об экстрасенсорной работе Грабового Григория Петровича

родившегося 14 ноября 1963 года в поселке Кировском Кировского района Чимкентской области Казахской ССР (имеющего свидетельство о рождении серии II - ОГ № 463794 ).

Место начала составления свидетельства _____

Время начала составления свидетельства 19 96 | 12 | 18 | 13 | 00
<small>год месяц число часы минуты</small>

Я, _Берешей Борис Иванович_
<small>(фамилия, имя и отчество полностью)</small>

родился (лась) _25.12.19__г. Московская обл.,_
<small>(дата и место рождения)</small>

_Шатурский р-н, г. Мишероновка._

гражданин (ка) _РФ_
<small>(государство)</small>

проживаю _Москва Новослободская ул. д. 57/56 а66 9_
<small>(место жительства и домашний телефон)</small>
_Тел. 978-30-77_

имею удостоверение личности _паспорт XII-МЮ №619 388_
<small>(наименование документа, серия, номер, кем и когда выдан документ)</small>
_14 о/м г. Москвы 6 июня 1978 г._

работаю _Жуковский ЛИи ДБ летчик-испытатель_
<small>(наименование предприятия, должность и служебные телефоны)</small>

_[handwritten text, largely illegible]_

**ПРИЛОЖЕНИЕ № 1**

**к свидетельству об экстрасенсорной работе Грабового Григория Петровича** родившегося 14 ноября 1963 года в поселке Кировском Кировского района Чимкентской области Казахской ССР (имеющего свидетельство о рождении серии II - ОГ № 463794 ).

Место начала составления свидетельства ____________

Время начала составления свидетельства 19 96 / 12 / 18 / 13 / 00
год / месяц / число / часы / минуты

*( Вышеперечисленные данные настоящего листа вписываются с первого листа свидетельства ).*

2) экстрасенсорно прогнозированный Грабовым Г.П. отказ [illegible] (УУТ) — [illegible] в [illegible] после [illegible] ПИИ и СД на [illegible], благополучно выполнил задание и произвёл посадку;

3) Грабовой Г.П. прогнозировал отказ в системе управления 61-ого [illegible] места отказа в системе автоматического управления (САУ) АБСУ. [illegible] отказ в котором [illegible] самолёта [illegible] каналу [illegible] режимы [illegible] прогнозированного. Отказ был устранён ко 2-ому полёту;

4) [illegible] самолёта [illegible] от [illegible] ВПП на разбеге при взлёте и пробеге после приземления;

5) [illegible] отказ прогнозированный Грабовым Г.П. [illegible] (второго пилота) [illegible] СВС и расхождение в показаниях [illegible] вертикальной скорости правого и левого лётчиков во 2-ом полёте;

6) при предполётном осмотре прогнозированный Грабовым Г.П. отказ [illegible] системы [illegible] (СБИ) — [illegible] при [illegible] 2-го полёта;

7) [illegible] отказ в системе управления [illegible] при 8 [illegible] в воздухе.

18.12.96. [signature] [signature]

*Центр    Управления    Космическими    Полетами*

Россия , 141070 , Московская область , г. Королев , ул. Пионерская 4 .

*1997. 09. 30* ИСХ. № *27*

*Протокол прогноза  Грабового Григория Петровича  по  стыковке
космического орбитального комплекса « Мир » РФ и космического
корабля « Атлантис » США  на период с 27 сентября 1997 г..*

Постановка задания : Грабовой Г. П . составьте  прогноз по
стыковке космического орбитального комплекса  « Мир »  РФ  и
космического  корабля  « Атлантис » США на период стыковки  с
27 сентября 1997г..
Место постановки задания: Центр Управления Космическими
Полетами  Российской Федерации ( ЦУП ).
Время постановки задания : 26 сентября 1997 г . 13 часов 25 минут .
Задание составил  Благов  В. Д . .

Прогноз Грабового Г. П  .:  Пункт 1: Стыковка космического
орбитального комплекса  « Мир »  РФ  и космического корабля
« Атлантис » США запланированная на исходе суток  27 сентября
1997 года  осуществиться .
Пункт 2 :  Непосредственно перед стыковкой будет отклонение от
оси .
Место и время ответа Грабового Г. П .: ЦУП , 26 сентября 1997 г..
Метод получения информации Грабовым Г . П .:  посредством
своего  ясновидения  .

На практике , запланированная  на исходе суток 27 сентября 1997
года стыковка космического орбитального комплекса  « Мир »  РФ и
космического корабля  « Атлантис »  США  осуществилась , и
непосредственно  перед стыковкой было отклонение от оси .
Вывод :  Прогноз Грабового  Г. П .  подтвердился .
Данные Грабового Г. П . :  14 ноября 1963 года рождения  , паспорт
серии I I I - ОГ  №  586058 , выдан 01 февраля 1980 года .

Ответственное  должностное  лицо ЦУПа : Фамилия : *Благов*
Имя : *Виктор*  Отчество *Дмитриевич* Должность и телефоны :
*зам. руководителя полета*  187 13 44

Подпись : *[подпись]* Фамилия : *Благов*

## Центр Управления Космическими Полетами

Россия , 141070 , Московская область , г. Королев , ул. Пионерская 4 .

1997.10.06 исх. № 120

*Протокол прогноза Грабового Григория Петровича по работе бортового компьютера космического орбитального комплекса « Мир » .*

Постановка задания : Грабовой Г . П . составьте прогноз по работе бортового компьютера космического орбитального комплекса « Мир » РФ с 26 сентября 1997г..

Место постановки задания: Центр Управления Космическими Полетами Российской Федерации ( ЦУП ) .

Время постановки задания : 26 сентября 1997 г . 13 часов 27 минут .

Задание составил Благов В. Д . .

Прогноз Грабового Г . П .: Бортовой компьютер космического орбитального комплекса « Мир » РФ с 26 сентября 1997 года будет работать пять дней .

Место и время ответа Грабового Г . П .: ЦУП , 26 сентября 1997 г..

Метод получения информации Грабовым Г . П .: посредством своего ясновидения .

На практике , с 26 сентября 1997 года , бортовой компьютер космического орбитального комплекса « Мир » РФ работал пять дней , а затем был заменен .

Вывод : Прогноз Грабового Г . П . подтвердился .

Данные Грабового Г . П .: 14 ноября 1963 года рождения , паспорт серии I I I - ОГ № 586058 , выдан 01 февраля 1980 года .

Ответственное должностное лицо ЦУПа: Фамилия : *Благов*
Имя : *Виктор* Отчество : *Дмитриевич* . Должность и телефоны : *зам. руководителя полета 187 13 44*

Подпись : *Благов* / Фамилия : *Благов* /

## Центр   Управления   Космическими   Полетами

**Россия , 141070 , Московская область ,  г. Королев ,  ул.  Пионерская  4 .**

1997 - 09 . 30  ИСХ. № 78

*Протокол диагностики двигателей космического корабля « Атлантис » США проведенной Грабовым Григорием Петровичем за несколько секунд после формулировки задания по телефону.*

Постановка задания : Грабовой Г. П .  проведите диагностику двигателей  космического  корабля  « Атлантис ».

Место и способ передачи задания:  Из  Центра Управления Космическими  Полетами Российской  Федерации ( ЦУП ) вопрос был  сформулирован  по  телефону .  Грабовой Г. П . диагностировал  двигатели передвигаясь  с мобильным телефоном по улице  Новый  Арбат г. Москва .

Время постановки задания : 29 сентября 1997 г . 12 часов 20 минут .

Задание составил  Благов  В. Д . .

Диагностика Грабового Г. П  .:  Изменены  параметры нижнего двигателя  космического корабля  « Атлантис »  США .

Место , способ и время ответа Грабового Г. П .: г. Москва , ул. Новый  Арбат , по мобильному телефону , моментально после получения задания ,  29 сентября 1997 г..

Метод получения информации Грабовым Г . П . :  посредством своего  ясновидения  .

На практике , действительно были изменены параметры нижнего двигателя космического корабля « Атлантис » США  .

Вывод :  Диагностика Грабового  Г. П .  подтвердилась .

Данные Грабового Г. П . : 14 ноября 1963 года рождения  , паспорт серии I I I - ОГ  №  586058 , выдан 01 февраля 1980 года .

Ответственное  должностное  лицо ЦУПа :  Фамилия : *Благов*

Имя : *Виктор*  Отчество : *Дмитриевич*. Должность и телефоны :

*зам.  руководителя  полета* 187 13 44

Подпись : *[подпись]*  Фамилия : *Благов*

## PUBLISHED FORECASTS OF POLITICAL, ECONOMIC, AND SOCIAL EVENTS WITH COMPLETE CONFIRMATION

**1. Grigori Grabovoi's forecast on the situation with the President of the Russian Federation B. N. Yeltsin, his presidency, what will happen to him, and after him:**

The main process is transferred to March 2000. Yeltsin will propose new elections. In December there will be rumors in press that he might resign before the presidential elections. A man will rule instead of him (it is not possible to tell the name now) that automatically becomes President in the next election. As the guarantee of the transit period this will be fine for both the main parties and current authority. There will be neither confrontation nor excesses.

**The confirmation of the forecast related to the situation with the President of the Russian Federation B. N. Yeltsin, his presidency, what will happen to him, and after him:** all television channels, all mass media.

This forecast was published in the following newspapers:

In the monthly annex to the newspaper "Moscovskiy zheleznodorozhnik" — "Vestnik passazhira" No 1, July 1999; the print was signed on July 7, 1999; the print run is 20,000 copies (it is registered in The State Committee for the Press of RUSSIA Reg. No 019038 of July 1, 1999.), in article "The end of the world is cancelled"; In the newspaper "Vash domashniy consultant" No13 (33), July 1999; the print was signed on July 1, 1999; the print run is 28,000 copies (the newspaper is registered in the Committee for the Press of Russia on March 26, 1997. Registration № 015900), in the article "The end of the world is cancelled".

**2. Grigori Grabovoi's forecast on the development of Yugoslavia events:**

An international solution to control the territories will be achieved in August 1999. A part will be controlled by Russia and the bigger part by the NATO countries.

**The confirmation of the forecast about the development of Yugoslavia events:** all TV channels, all media.

This forecast was published in the following newspapers: In the monthly annex to the newspaper "Moscovskiy zheleznodorozhnik" — "Vestnik passazhira" No 1, July 1999; the print was signed on July 7, 1999; the print run is 20,000 copies (it was registered in The State Committee for the Press of Russia Reg. No 019038 of July 1, 1999.), in article "The end of the world is cancelled";

In the newspaper "Vash domashniy consultant" No13 (33), July 1999; the print was signed on July 1, 1999; the print run is 28,000 copies (the newspaper was registered in the Committee for the Press of Russia on March 26, 1997. Registration № 015900), in the article "The end of the world is cancelled".

**3. Grigori Grabovoi's forecast on finance and economic development of Russia:**

In macroeconomic terms stabilization of the ruble against the dollar and the entire "basket" of currencies will begin since October 1999. This will result in normalization of economic life.

**The confirmation of the Forecast on the financial and economic development of Russia:**

Central television channels;

The newspaper "Versty" of September 21, 2000 (registered with the Ministry of Press and Information of the Russian Federation, registration No 14418). Publication of "Sailing off with a basket" with the statement by the Deputy Prime Minister A.Kudrin at the Baikal Economic Forum that it was high time to "bind" the ruble not only to the dollar, but to the "basket" of currencies.

This forecast was published in the following newspapers: In the monthly annex to the newspaper "Moscovskiy zheleznodorozhnik" — "Vestnik passazhira" No 1, July 1999; the print was signed on July 7, 1999; the print run is 20,000 copies (registered in The State Committee for the Press of Russia Reg. No 019038 of July 1, 1999.), in article "The end of the world is cancelled";

In the newspaper "Vash domashniy consultant" No13 (33), July 1999; the print was signed on July 1, 1999; the print run is 28,000 copies (the newspaper is registered in the Committee for the Press of RUSSIA on March 26, 1997. Registration № 015900), in the article "The end of the world is cancelled".

**4. Grigori Grabovoi's forecast about the new Government team, about its ability to fulfill new tasks, about future changes in the structural relationship of the government of Russia:**

This Government as of June 1999 and Prime Minister Sergei Stepashin are needed for stabilization of the situation between the President, Parliament and other institutions. Sergei Stepashin will act as a harmonizer and will be needed as the ideologist of the present. Russia will structurally change the governing system from the point of view of knowledge of distant strategic objectives.

Presidential rule, of course, gave a lot of positive aspects in the country's transition from the totalitarian past, but considering the future potential for growth, it will be necessary to change the structural connections between the elements of authorities and the elements of implementation of its decisions. A network structure of the government, which will be able to activate the economy capacity much wider contrary to the one-tenth today, is required. Communication teams between the Presidential Board, the decisions of Duma and regional plans will be established on this basis. Corresponding departments of structured development will be founded at enterprises and administrative units.

**The confirmation of the forecast about the new Government team, about its ability to fulfill new tasks, about future changes in the structural relationship of the government of Russia:**

All channels, all media about the change of the structural connections between the authorities and the implementation of its decisions on the basis of the network structure of the seven federal districts according to the Decree of the President of Russia Vladimir Putin in May 2000;

The confirmation of the forecast about the foundation of departments of structured development at enterprises and administrative units is in fact, for example, that in the Ministry of Communication (according to the newspaper "Gudok" of

September 30, 2000, the article "Efficiency of the terminal station of the reforms") similar districts were created on the railways.

This forecast was published in the following newspapers: In the monthly annex to the newspaper "Moscovskiy zheleznodorozhnik" — "Vestnik passazhira" No 1, July 1999; the print was signed on July 7, 1999; the print run is 20,000 copies (it is registered in The State Committee for the Press of Russia Reg. No 019038 of July 1, 1999.), in article "The end of the world is cancelled";

In the newspaper "Vash domashniy consultant" No13 (33), July 1999; the print was signed on July 1, 1999; the print run was 28,000 copies (the newspaper was registered in the Committee for the Press of Russia on March 26, 1997. Registration No 015900), in the article "The end of the world is cancelled".

**5. Grigori Grabovoi's forecast about the improvement of sustainability of the financial development of Russia by means of creation of currency and gold reserves in the regional areas:**

The most important part of the system stability of the state on the gold equivalent basis will be the reservation of currency funds and gold in each autonomous part of the budget in each region. This will not look like a confederative game of the governors; on the contrary, the strategy is directed toward the improvement of the stability of the subjects of the federation, the final goal of which is an enhancement of the financial stability of all Russia. Each region should be balanced within the clearly outlined framework of the general financial plan of the country and therefore a necessity of storage of gold for each separate region will appear.

**The confirmation of the forecast about the improvement of sustainability of the financial development of Russia by means of creation of currency and gold reserves in the regional areas:** all television channels, communication about the introduction of gold reserves in Krasnoyarsk region in September 2000.

This forecast was published in the in the initial issue of the newspaper "Variant Razvitiya", the issue was signed for print on March 16, 2000, print circulations was 10,000 copies.

## 6. Grigori Grabovoi's forecast about the retention of the rates of economic growth in Russia:

To avoid system disorganization the basic directions in the activity of concrete productions will be directed toward strengthening of self-supporting principles in the economy of Russia. The return of this concept after all misalignments of privatization will be connected with the stock-taking of debts within the framework of the gold reserves instead of being just an article of the budget of a region, oblast or city.

This is exactly the accumulation of the gold reserves that will be able to help to survive the forthcoming crisis and to make Russia's entry into the global market more confident. Many will reproach our developers of this strategy on excessive hoarding and on the fact that not entire capital will be sent for turn-over. However, maintaining new direction will help subsequently many industries. Therefore there will be no industrial decline; its growth rate will remain approximately the same as today.

**The confirmation of the forecast about the retention of the rates of economic growth in Russia:** all television channels, central press confirmed the retention of the rates of economic growth in Russia for the last period.

This forecast was published in the initial issue of the newspaper "Variant Razvitiya", the issue was signed for print on March 16, 2000, print circulations was 10,000 copies.

## 7. Forecast of Grigori Grabovoi for Moscow for 2000:

In Moscow during 2000 again may resume a number of land collapses in the streets and under the houses in the region of the southwest nearer to the outskirts. However there will be no big problems with the elimination of these emergencies.

**The confirmation of the forecast for Moscow for 2000**: information from the President of the Center of Underground Studies, the chief digger of the country V. Mikhaylov "In the region of the southwest of Moscow, next to the buildings of MGIMO karst collapses of the soil were discovered. In the region of Ramenka River, next to the station of auto-service there are cracks of the earth's surface and draws, which influenced the strength of constructions. As a result of this many underground collectors sagged due the loads and as a result of the pressure of layers acquired ellipse-shaped form".

This forecast was published in the in the initial issue of the newspaper "Variant Razvitiya", the issue was signed for print on March 16, 2000, print circulations was 10,000 copies.

### 8. Grigori Grabovoi's forecast on oil prices in Russia:

Oil prices in Russia. They will be connected with the change of the government, cabinet of ministers and Prime Minister.  The import petroleum products prices will run up. For the export "sale" prices will also grow. They can reach maximum in August and in comparison with March will increase by 10%.

**The confirmation of the forecast on oil prices in Russia:** all television channels, central press.

This forecast was published in the initial issue of the newspaper "Variant Razvitiya", the issue was signed for print on March 16, 2000, print circulations was 10,000 copies.

### 9. Grigori Grabovoi's forecast on food products in 2000:

There will be no special problems with food products in 2000 except a scandal related to meat supplies.

**The confirmation of the forecast on food products in 2000:**  all television channels, central press. The scandal with meat supplies was also confirmed by the refusal from the purchases of French meat due to detection in it of the virus of so-called cow's rabies.

This forecast was published in the first issue of the newspaper "Variant razvitiya", print was signed on March 16, 2000 print circulation was 10.000 copies.

### 10. Grigori Grabovoi's forecast on the military events in Chechnya:

Mainly military operations in Chechnya will end by August 2000. Then a number of political decisions will be made. The residents of Chechnya will make their complex choice to be a part of Russia.  But before that the federal authorities will conduct an active propaganda campaign in favor of this, since the state of opinion related to the autonomous existence at that time, again under the pressure of international organizations, will again be manifested in the sentiments of the Chechens.

**Confirmation of the forecast on the military events in Chechnya:** all television channels, central press.

This forecast was published in the newspaper "Variant razvitiya", No 1, the issue was signed for print on April 7, 2000, the print circulation was 10,000 copies. The newspaper was registered in Russia by the Ministry for the Press, TV and Radio Broadcasting and Means of Mass Communication. Registration certificate PI No77-1859.

**11. Grigori Grabovoi's forecast on plutonium power engineering:** Americans forewent plutonium power engineering, but the Ministry Nuclear Power of Russia insists on its development and even plans to use plutonium nuclear reactors. But it's not just about joining the environmentally dirty era. Russian scientists also discovered the phenomenon of excitation using plutonium reactions of duplicating this element (volumetric mass transfer) hundreds of kilometers away from the Earth's surface. This violates not only the global balance of the Earth's stability, but also begins to engage hardly predictable so far space environmental disturbances.

**Confirmation of Grigori Grabovoi's forecast on plutonium power engineering:**

The materials of the hearings in the State Duma on October 3, 2000 on the topic of "The main directions of development of leasing in Russia where Ministry Nuclear Power of Russia announced the leasing of heat conducting assemblies.

This forecast was published in the newspaper "Variant razvitiya", No 1, the issue was signed for print on April 7, 2000, the print circulation was 10,000 copies. The newspaper was registered in Russia by the Ministry for the Press, TV and Radio Broadcasting and Means of Mass Communication. Registration certificate PI No77-1859.

**12. Grigori Grabovoi's forecast on SBS-Agro-bank:**

SBS-Agro-bank will be gradually restored. The problematic situation there will not reach complete destruction.

If the shareholders are concerned about the possibility of return of their funds, in the next two or three years a possible return through this bank will be realized only on the special order of the management (at the level of the head, deputy head of the bank). Not all operations, which will be scheduled, will be implemented. In any case approving signatures will be required.

**Confirmation of the forecast on SBS-Agro-bank:** all television channels, central press:

In the newspaper "Vremya MN" (registered in the State Committee of Russia on Press, registration No 017460) in the issue of November 1, 2000 in the article "Agro promises to return the money to SBS» the Director of the Department of Public Communication of the Agency on the restructuring of credit organizations Alexander Voznesensky declared, that "Payments to the depositors of SBS-Agro in the case of conclusion of a settlement agreement will make more than 70% of the amount of the deposit, if this agreement will not be concluded, then not more than 40%. In case such an agreement will be concluded, the settlement with creditors will be made within 3 years." Before this the press informed about the removal from the SBS-Agro a subsidiary network of banks and reorganization into other structures.

This forecast was published in the newspaper "Variant razvitiya", No 2, the issue was signed for print on April 21, 2000, and the print circulation was 10,000 copies. The newspaper was registered in Russia by the Ministry for the Press, TV and Radio Broadcasting and Means of Mass Communication. Registration certificate PI No77-1859.

**13. Grigori Grabovoi's forecast on the law on the Production Sharing Agreement (PSA):**

The additional questions, related to the rights of the states, where companies have either accreditation or legal registration will appear in August 2000. The fact of the matter is that rights of the companies such as for oil shelves may be different from the rights of the state where the oil production takes place. This is related to the legislation of some countries. Here you will get legislative inconsistencies, when companies even with the normal behavior according to the international standards are not fully correct, and due to this Russia on its part will bear expenses.

**Confirmation of the forccast on the law on the Production Sharing Agreement (PSA):** all television channels, central press. The materials of the parliamentary hearings in the State Duma of the Russian Federation "About the Rent Relations" in October 2000, at which the possibility of replacement of the law on PSA with the law on rent was discussed the article "Direct sharing. Amendments to the law on PSA are "unfrozen"" in the newspaper "Vedomosti" of October 25, 2000 (the newspaper was registered in State Committee of RF on the press, registration certificate No 019007 of September 30, 1999).

This forecast was published in the newspaper "Variant razvitiya", No 3-4, the issue was signed for print on May 19, 2000, and the print circulation was 10,000 copies. The newspaper was registered in Russia by the Ministry for the Press, TV and Radio Broadcasting and Means of Mass Communication. Registration certificate PI No77-1859.

**14. Grigori Grabovoi's forecast on money laundering**: The concept of money laundering for Russia is to ensure maximum increase of the currency equivalent through certain channels. For this purpose foreign banks of America, Switzerland, or any other country, where monetary equivalent is normalized, are used. In September and till October 2000, then in March 2001 and in February 2002 this issue will be raised time and again for the purpose of finding a solution from the point of view of currency securing of funds, which are kept in Russia. Receipt of clean money from industrial-commercial projects will be solved at the economic and state levels. In case of money laundering from drug trafficking business, illegal participation in military actions, and also concealed and stolen money the controlling systems of different countries will try to prevent such laundering. It makes no difference for them, whether the money are Russian or American. Everything here will depend on the improvement of the legislative schemes of the countries.

**Confirmation of the forecast on money laundering:** all television channels, central press.

The article "It will become more difficult to launder money" in the newspaper "Vedomosti" of October 27, 2000 (the newspaper was registered in the State Committee of the Russian Federation on the Press, registration certificate No 019007 of September 30, 1999). This article informs that "The countries of the European Union on Tuesday have taken new radical measures in the fight with money laundering and organized criminality. The joint meeting of Ministers of Finance and Internal Affairs of the Member countries of the EU was held for the first time; it was decided at the meeting to toughen the punishment for money laundering, to recognize that bank secret should not be an obstacle in conducting criminal investigations, and develop sanctions against the countries (that include Russia), which are not willing to cooperate in the fight against money-laundering. The Ministers offered the working group to develop sanctions related to countries not willing to cooperate with the international community in the fight against money-laundering by June 2001".

This forecast was published in the newspaper "Variant razvitiya", No 3-4, the issue was signed for print on May 19, 2000, the print circulation was 10,000 copies. The newspaper was registered in Russia by the Ministry for the Press, TV and Radio Broadcasting and Means of Mass Communication. Registration certificate PI No77-1859.

**15. Grigori Grabovoi's forecast related to the policy of the Central Bank of the Russian Federation:**

The Central Bank of the Russian Federation will expand its sphere of influence and functions. From 2002 this will make it possible to extend its influence to the political sphere as well. Through the so-called INN, i.e., individual tax payer number the bank of the country will influence upon the centralization of bank accounting in a way similar to today's the Passport registration. This will make it possible to know where each concrete person is. Russian Orthodox Church will oppose this centralization at that moment when the control of the economic and social well-being of the citizens will begin through money.

The growth and economy of gold and currency reserves will depend on the difference between the controlled and uncontrollable level of the reserve. The uncontrollable level will fall under the sphere of control of special departments. Therefore in 2004 relevant legislative acts against this will be adopted, after that the level of gold and currency reserves will be introduced into the voting system, which will depend on every citizen who filled out the declaration of income. The budgetary sphere will receive a new mechanism of allocation of funds (how much for the defense, education, medicine, and etc.) a kind of election technologies. But subsequently the world experience, which provides currency control of the special government structures, but under the control of the general public, will be used. It will be proven once again that this is the prerogative of the elected Head of State.

**Confirmation of the forecast related to the Central Bank of the Russian Federation:** Communications in the press. The article "Is introduction of the State Register of population justified" in the newspaper "Vedomosti" of November 4, 2000" and the article "The List of All" in the newspaper "Vedomosti" of November 23, 2000 about the proposed by the state concept of the automated system "The State Register of Population", that provides the introduction of the lifelong personal code for each citizen that includes 17 points of information (the newspaper "Vedomosti" was registered in State Committee of RF on the Press, registration certificate No 019007 of September 30, 1999). The article "The INN will be allocated to the orthodox eople even without their requests" in the newspaper "Moscow Komsomolets" of November 3, 2000, and a note in the newspaper "Versty" of October 28, 2000 about the numerous addresses of Orthodox Christians, who are unwilling to take individual tax number. About the demands to end "discrimination and lawlessness related to Orthodox Ural residents", submitted by the Yekaterinburg diocese priests (the newspaper "Moscow Komsomolets" registered at the Ministry of Press and Information of the Russian Federation, registration No 1072, the newspaper "Versty" registered at the Ministry of Press and Information of the Russian Federation, registration No, 14418).

The article "Utopia on the Cards" in the newspaper "Versty" of October 12, 2000 that informed about the last survey, conducted by the fund "Public opinion": "1500 citizens of Russia were given the cards, which lists 27 major budget items for 2001. Each of them had to choose five of the items of the first priority in his view. 62% of taxpayers called public health. Education, 52%, occupied the second place in the list. 43% of respondents considered it to be necessary to thoroughly cover army and navy…" (the newspaper "Versty" registered in the Ministry of Press and Information of the Russian Federation, registration No, 14418).

This forecast was published in the newspaper "Variant razvitiya", No 5, the issue was signed for print on June 9, 2000, the print circulation was 10,000 copies. The newspaper was registered in Russia by the Ministry for the Press, TV and Radio Broadcasting and Means of Mass Communication. Registration certificate PI No77-1859.

### 16. Grigori Grabovoi's forecast on mortgages and mortgage lending:

Mortgages and mortgage lending could grow only if the economic status of the country is high. First of all it refers to gross exchange process on all components of GDP, and also good indices of development of such branches as light industry, construction-housing complex, heavy metallurgy, and so on. When these components of the economy are high mortgage has a good chance for development. In the condition Russia currently is, the mortgage lending will depend only on the indirect budget provision for the mortgage development. So, while the budget is allocated to industry branches and Government agencies, the prospects are not promising. Some of the regions, which broke away in housing through mortgage lending, only confirm this rule. They have an executive decision about the resources guarantee. Banks have resources as a pledge and fund the construction due to concessionary interest rate. Actually there is no finished mechanism yet: banks do not give credit against unconditional security.

But why information on the mortgage lending has begun to come to naught? The reason is that there is no fundamental level for this. Only the program, budgetary way is real today. However, with the stabilization of the economy (high level the GDP is like a system-forming law) the mortgage will revive.

**Confirmation of the forecast on mortgages and mortgage lending:** the materials of parliamentary hearings in the State Duma of the Russian Federation on the mortgage lending in October 2000 where it was confirmed that the mortgage was impossible in Russia without the state financing within the framework of the state program.

This forecast was published in the newspaper "Variant razvitiya", No 6, the issue was signed for print on June 20, 2000, the print circulation was 10,000 copies. The newspaper was registered in Russia by the Ministry for the Press, TV and Radio Broadcasting and Means of Mass Communication. Registration certificate PI No77-1859.

17. Grigori Grabovoi's forecast for prevention of accidents on oil and gas pipelines.

For the prevention of accidents it is necessary to carry out proper preventive maintenance and repair of the equipment. However, there is the second reason of the emergencies; that is the concealment of oil and gas by those persons who use the uncontrollability of the calculation of the output and passage of the raw material through the pipe in order to have a profit. But this problem is not the basic one, it can be solved. The basic issue is to organize a competent maintenance and improve the system of pumping through the pipes.

It is quite clear how to write off the percentage, which is naturally lost in piping. The other thing is that at some hydrocarbon developments the bulk of the output is derived directly from the rig. This is a little known part; therefore the concept "of pipe" not always be treated as the major loss. But there are developments, where up to 50% of production generally goes elsewhere.

**Confirmation of the forecasts for prevention of accidents on oil and gas pipelines:** all television channels, central press in the October issues of 2000, which tell about the volumes of theft of oil that goes past "the pipe".

This forecast was published in the newspaper "Variant razvitiya", No 5, the issue was signed for print on June 9, 2000, the print circulation was 10,000 copies. The newspaper was registered in Russia by the Ministry for the Press, TV and Radio Broadcasting and Means of Mass Communication. Registration certificate PI No77-1859.

# APPENDIX D: DOCUMENTS CONFIRMING THE LISTED THE BOOK CONCRETE FACTS OF MATERIALIZATION AND ANNIHILATION OF MATTER

# СВИДЕТЕЛЬСТВО

### об экстрасенсорной работе Грабового Григория Петровича

родившегося 14 ноября 1963 года в поселке Кировском Кировского района Чимкентской области Казахской ССР (имеющего свидетельство о рождении серии II - ОГ № 463794)

Место: _г. Химки, Московской обл._ 199 _4_ / _09_ / _30_ / _29_ _10_
(место заполнения свидетельства)    год   месяц   число   часы   минуты

Я, _Пушко Светлана Павловна_
(фамилия, имя и отчество, полностью)

родился(лась) _11 дек. 1943, Ивановская обл._
(дата и место рождения)

гражданин(ка) _РФ_
(государство)

проживаю _г. Химки, Моск. обл. ул. 9Мая, 12,_
(место жительства и домашний телефон)    _кв. 67_

имею удостоверение личности, _изданное редакцией газеты_
(наименование документа, серия, номер, кем и когда выдан документ)
_и Мегаполис-Континент + обсерватор_

работаю _редакции газеты и Мегаполис-Континент_
(наименование предприятия, должность и служебные телефоны)
_обсерватору_

_22 сентября 1994г. во время встречи с_
_Г.П. Грабовым в г.Химки, Моск. области_
_на ул. Ливановского, здание ЦНИИМАш, ком._
_№ 120 зашел разговор о возможности_
_материализации или телепортации_
_(появления предмета). Чтобы убедить_
_меня в действенности подобного явления_
_Г.П. Грабовой предложил материализовать_
_какой-то предмет в моей квартире,_
_куда он не входил и раньше никогда не_
_был. Через восемь дней, 30 сентября_
_1994 года, в своей кухонной, на подо-_
_коннике, я обнаружила два предмета,_
_которых раньше там не было и появить-_
_ся сами они не могли. Никто из по-_
_сторонних за это время в дом не входил,_
_а сам, проживающие со мной в кварт._
_не эти предметы не приносил. Увидев их_
_впервые, я сразу поняла, что это_
_результат работы по материализации,_
_проведенной Г.П. Грабовым._

_Частота данного эксперимента_
_заключается еще и в том, что Г.П. Грабо-_
_вой не знал моего адреса, а мате-_
_риализация Г.П. Грабовой прошла_
_застиг в моей квартире, где и были_
_уложены._

_(С.П. Пушко)_

_30 сентября 1994г._

_20 часов, 17 минут._

Telephone : 007 3712 629365
Telex     116399 'OFFIS SU'
Telefax : 007 3712 623571 (Tashkent)

# INTERSERVICEENERGO-ASIA LIMITED

E. KHODJAEV STREET. 2 TASHKENT-700 032
**REPUBLIC OF UZBEKISTAN**

## СВИДЕТЕЛЬСТВО

Настоящим свидетельством, я Бабаева Татьяна Павловна, удостоверяю, что Грабовой Григорий Петрович, родившийся 14 ноября 1963 года в поселке Кировском (село Багара) Кировского района Чимкентской области Казахской ССР (имеющий свидетельство о рождении серии II-ОГ № 463794), используя свои экстрасенсорные способности, выполнил следующий эксперимент по материализации предмета:

Однажды вернувшись в гостиницу я обнаружила. что потеряла ключи от своего номера. Я точно знала, что я не отдавала их дежурному, а взяла их с собой. Я проверила все карманы и сумку, но их не было. Я очень расстроилась и не знала что делать. Решила обратиться к старшему дежурному, но в это время на помощь пришел Грабовой Григорий Петрович, все это время в стороне наблюдавший за моими действиями. Он предложил подняться на этаж и еще раз проверить сумку, что я и сделала. Каково же было мое удивление, когда я нашла ключ и открыла дверь. В это было трудно поверить, потому что я вытрясала из сумки все и тщательно проверяла. Я думаю, что такое возможно только благодаря экстрасенсорным способностям Грабового Григория Петровича материализовывать предметы.

_____ / Бабаева Т.П./

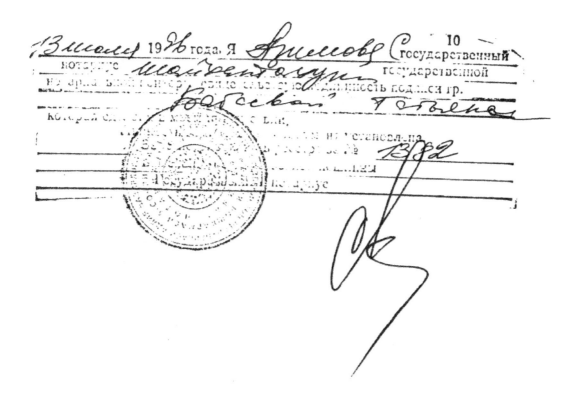

ВСЕМ ЗАИНТЕРЕСОВАННЫМ ЛИЦАМ
Заявитель: Ливадо Екатерина Ивановна

ЗАЯВЛЕНИЕ

о том,что ГРАБОВОЙ ГРИГОРИЙ ПЕТРОВИЧ в условиях чистого эксперимента, в здании ЗАО "Манометр" города Москвы,дематериализовал металлический ключ весом 10,0 грамм.

Я,Ливадо Екатерина Ивановна,родилась 16 августа 1937 года в селе Сартано Мариупольского района Донецкой области /Украина/,паспорт серия ХУ-МЮ 587245,выдан 14 июля 1978 года 13 отделением милиции г.Москвы,являюсь свидетелем того,что ГРАБОВОЙ ГРИГОРИЙ ПЕТРОВИЧ дематериализовал 12 ноября 1997года металлический ключ весом 10,0 грамм. В период времени,когда ГРАБОВОЙ ГРИГОРИЙ ПЕТРОВИЧ проводил дематериализацию,он находился от ключа на расстоянии 10 метров и дематериализовал ключ в течение 20 минут.

Дематериализацию ключа с расстояния 10 метров в течение 20 минут ГРАБОВОЙ ГРИГОРИЙ ПЕТРОВИЧ провел по адресу: г.Москва,ул.Нижняя Сыромятническая,д.5/7,ЗАО "Манометр".

Личные данные ГРАБОВОГО ГРИГОРИЯ ПЕТРОВИЧА:
-родился 14 ноября 1963 года в поселке Кировском,Кировского района Чимкентской области Казахской ССР,имеющего свидетельство о рождении серии II-ОГ № 463794.

Прошу заверить мое заявление на основании документов,удостоверяющих мою личность и на основании вышеизложенных доказательств.

Ливадо Е.И.

18 ноября 1997года

город Москва,  двадцать четвертого ноября тысяча девятьсот девяносто седьмого года.

город Москва 24 ноября 1997 года.  Я, ГАБАНЯН Н.Г. нотариус 12 Московской государственной нотариальной конторы свидетельствую подлинность подписи гр. ЛИВАДО ЕКАТЕРИНЫ ИВАНОВНЫ, которая сделана в моем присутствии. Личность установлена,дееспособность проверена.

Зарегистрировано в реестре за N
Взыскано государственной пошлины
Нотариус

ВСЕМ ЗАИНТЕРЕСОВАННЫМ ЛИЦАМ
Заявитель:Ливадо Екатерина Ивановна

ЗАЯВЛЕНИЕ

о том,что ГРАБОВОЙ ГРИГОРИЙ ПЕТРОВИЧ,в условиях чистого эксперимента,в здании ЗАО "Манометр" города Москвы,материализовал металлический ключ весом I0,0 грамм.

Я,Ливадо Екатерина Ивановна,родилась I6 августа I937 года в селе Сартано Мариупольского района Донецкой области /Украина/,паспорт серии ХУ-МЮ №587245,выдан I4 июля I978 года I8 отделением милиции г.Москвы,являюсь свидетелем того,что ГРАБОВОЙ ГРИГОРИЙ ПЕТРОВИЧ материализовал I2 ноября I997 года металлический ключ весом I0,0 грамм. В период времени,когда ГРАБОВОЙ ГРИГОРИЙ ПЕТРОВИЧ  проводил материализацию ,он находился от ключа на расстоянии 3-х метров и материализовал ключ в течение 5 минут.

Материализация ключа с расстояния 3-х метров в течение 5 минут ГРАБОВОЙ ГРИГОРИЙ ПЕТРОВИЧ провел по адресу: г.Москва,ул.Нижняя Сыромятническая д.5/7,ЗАО "Манометр"

Личные данные ГРАБОВОГО ГРИГОРИЯ ПЕТРОВИЧА:

-родился I4 ноября I963 года в поселке Кировском Кировского района Чимкентской области Казахской ССР,имеющего свидетельство о рождении серии II-ОГ №463794.

Прошу заверить мое заявление на основании документов,удостоверяющих мою личность и на основании вышеизложенных доказательств.

18 ноября I997г           Ливадо Е.И.

город Москва:   двадцать четвертого ноября тысяча девятьсот девяносто седьмого года.

*Ливадо Екатерина Ивановна*

город Москва 24 ноября 1997 года.  Я, ГАБАНЯН Н.Г. нотариус 12 Московской  государственной нотариальной конторы свидетельствую подлинность подписи гр.  ЛИВАДО ЕКАТЕРИНЫ ИВАНОВНЫ, которая сделана в моем присутствии. Личность установлена,дееспособность проверена.

Зарегистрировано в реестре за N
Взыскано государственной пошлины

ВСЕМ   ЗАИНТЕРЕСОВАННЫМ   ЛИЦАМ

Заявитель — Лаврушкина Надежда Борисовна, проживающая по адресу: г. Москва

Заявление

о том, что Грабовой Григорий Петрович в условиях чистого эксперимента в здании МКСО профсоюзов, расположенном по адресу: г. Москва, ул. Солянка, д.14/2, к. 110, частично дематериализовал, а затем материализовал металлический ключ весом 10,0 г.

Я, Лаврушкина Надежда Борисовна, родившаяся в г. Орехово-Зуево Московской области 6 июня 1953 г, проживающая по адресу: г. Москва,                          паспорт серии ХУІІІ-ИК, № 628733, выданный ОВД Орехово-Зуевского горисполкома Московской области 2 сентября 1980 г, являюсь свидетелем того, что Грабовой Григорий Петрович частично дематериализовал, а затем материализовал металлический ключ весом 10,0 г. 20 ноября 1997 г.

В период времени, когда Грабовой Григорий Петрович проводил дематериализацию и материализацию ключа, ключ находился от него на расстоянии 50 см. При этом физического контакта с ключом не было. Эксперимент проводился в течение 5 минут.

Данные факты отражены на фотографиях 1,2,3,4, снятых при равнозначных условиях. На ф. 2 снят частично дематериализованный ключ по отношению к ключу, изображенному на ф. 1. На ф. 2 видно, что штанга, соединяющая ручку и основание ключа, практически не просматривается / принцип дискретной материализации /. На ф. 4 изображение по отношению к изображению на ф. 3 выведено за тонкий экран / принцип полной дематериализации объекта - на ф. 4 изображен первый шаг полной дематериализации, при котором изображенный физический предмет, в том числе, при контроле физическим зрением, становится менее отчетливым.

Дематериализацию и материализацию ключа с расстояния 50 см Грабовой Григорий Петрович проводил по адресу: г. Москва, ул. Солянка, д. 14/2, к. 110, МКСО профсоюзов.

Личные данные Грабового Григория Петровича: родился 14 ноября 1963 г. в поселке Кировском Кировского района Чимкентской области Казахской ССР; свидетельство о рождении серии II-ОГ № 463794.

Данный эксперимент Грабовой Григорий Петрович проводил в присутствии двух свидетелей:

I-ый свидетель – Ливадо Екатерина Ивановна, родившаяся 16 августа 1937 г. в селе Сартано Донецкой области, паспорт ХУ – МЮ № 587245, выдан 13 отделением милиции г. Москвы 14 июня 1978 г.

2-ой свидетель – Лаврушкина Надежда Борисовна, родившаяся 6 июня 1953 г. в г. Орехово-Зуево Московской области, паспорт ХУIII-ИК № 628733, выдан ОВД Орехово-Зуевского горисполкома Московской области 2 сентября 1980 г.

Прошу заверить мое заявление на основании документов, удостоверяющих мою личность и на основании вышеизложенных доказательств.

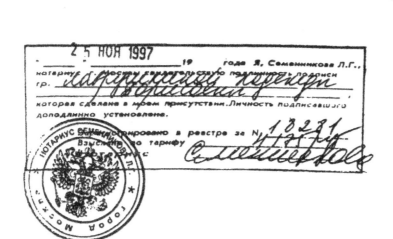

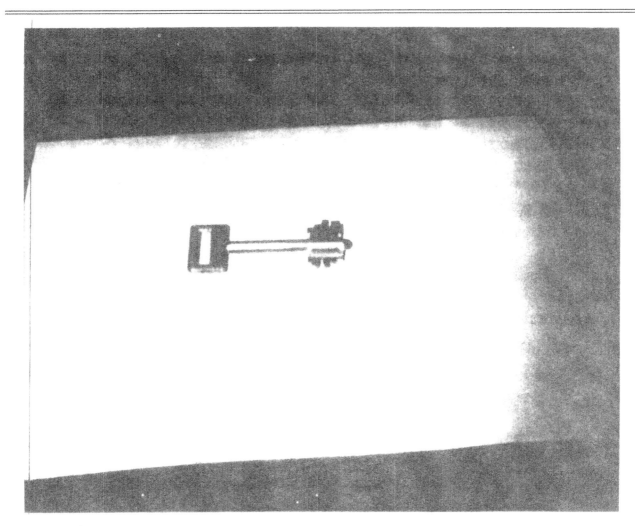

1.

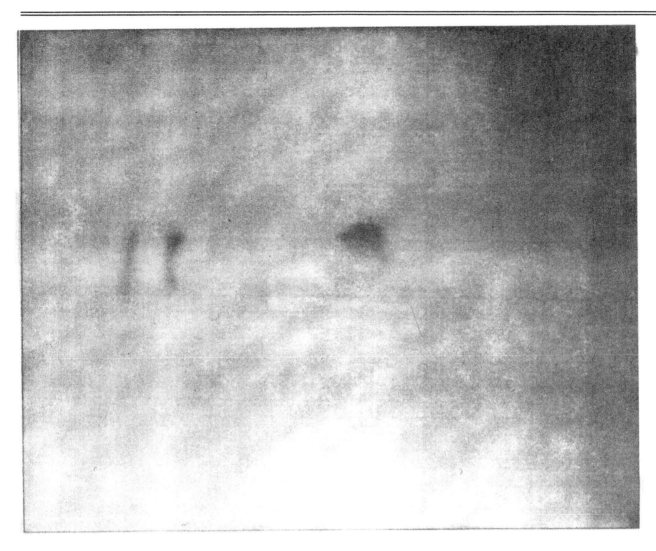

2

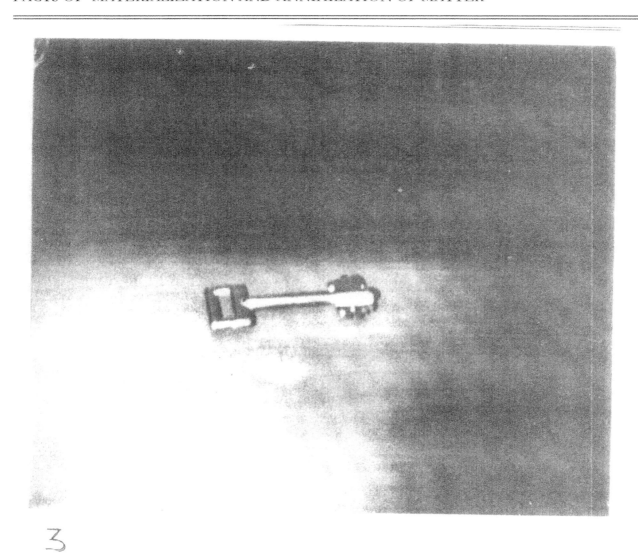

3

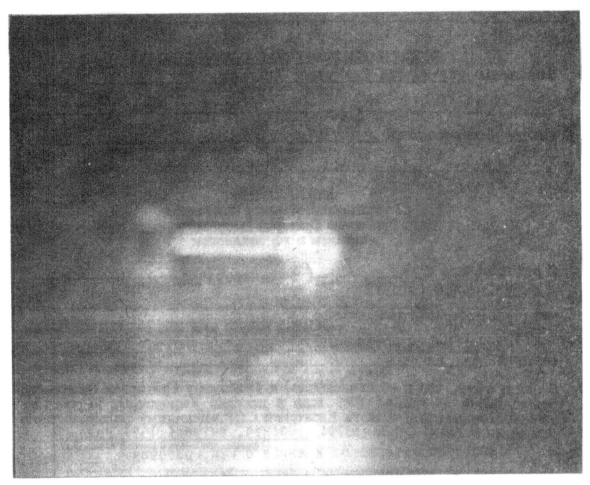

4.

**ВСЕМ ЗАИНТЕРЕСОВАННЫМ ЛИЦАМ**

Заявитель: _Сальникова Светлана Павловна_
　　　　　(фамилия, имя и отчество полностью)

_____
　　　　　(адрес и телефоны)

Заинтересованные лица: _____
　　　　　(фамилия, имя и отчество полностью; адрес)

**ЗАЯВЛЕНИЕ**
об установлении факта признания
Грабового Григория Петровича
целителем и ясновидящим

Я родился(лась) 19_46_/_4_/_1_/ в _ст. Оловянная_
　　　　　год　месяц　число　　　　　(место рождения)
_Читинской области_

имею удостоверение личности _____
　　　　　(наименование документа, серия, номер, кем и когда выдан документ)

_паспорт II-СН 653623 Удачнинским о/м Чирининского р-на Якутии._

Работаю: _ст. научным сотрудником "Ассоциации"Космонавтика-человечеству"_
　　　　　(название предприятия, должность и телефоны)

В связи с тем, что я обратился(лась) к Грабовому Григорию Петровичу, родившемуся 14 ноября 1963 года в поселке Кировском, Кировского района Чимкентской области Казахской ССР имеющему свидетельство о рождении серии II-ОГ № 463794, _Москва, октябрь 1997 года_
　　　　　(указать дату, место и причину обращения)
_подготовка материалов к книге о Г.П.Грабовом_

заявляю, что Грабовой Григорий Петрович действительно _____
　　_материализует предметы_
　　　　　(привести доказательства и обоснования заявления)

　　При подготовке книги о Г.П.Грабовом я получила от него несколько папок с документами. В процессе работы обнаружилось, что не хватает документа о его встрече с Яко Лабо из Филиппин. Через некоторое время этот документ переводчика появился у меня на столе.

　　По своим: 20 октября я передала Г.П.Грабовому часть написаного материала, по которому он понял, что мне не хватает документа о Яко Лабо.

　　27-28 октября этот документ появился на столе вместе со свидетельством Генковой о встрече с Вангой.

　　Поскольку у меня уже была копия (ксерокс) со свидетельством Генковой, могу сравнить и сделать следующие замечания:

　　материализованные документы лишены недостатков копий - они четко, правильно расположены на листе. Буквы четко,правильно расположены на листе. Буквы очерчены немного тоньше.

　　Прошу заверить мое заявление на основании документов, удостоверяющих мою личность и на основании вышеизложенных доказательств.

　　_(подпись)_　_/Сальникова С.П./_　　19_97_/_11_/_17_/
　　(подпись)　　(фамилия)　　　　год　месяц　число

*Двадцать шестого ноября одна тысяча девятьсот девяносто седьмого*

_____ 19___ года   Я, Литовская Тамара Васи...

нотариус города Москвы, свидетельствую подлинность подписи
гр. *Сальниковой Светланы Павловны*

которая сделана в моем присутствии. Личность подписавшего
документ установлена.

зарегистрировано в реестре за N *1713*

Взыскано по тарифу *4175*

нотариус:

ЛИЦЕНЗИЯ № 282 ОТ 01.10.93

ПРИКАЗ № 174 Ч ОТ 02.11.93

**Telephone :** 007 3712-629365
**Telex** 116399 'OFFIS SU'
**Telefax :** 007 3712 623571 (Tashkent)

## INTERSERVICEENERGO-ASIA LIMITED
### E. KHODJAEV STREET. 2 TASHKENT-700 032
### REPUBLIC OF UZBEKISTAN

## СВИДЕТЕЛЬСТВО

Настоящим свидетельством, я Бабаев Виктор Багирович и моя жена Бабаева Татьяна Павловна, удостоверяем, что Грабовой Григорий Петрович, родившийся 14 ноября 1963 года в поселке Кировском (село Багара) Кировского района Чимкентской области Казахской ССР (имеющий свидетельство о рождении серии II-ОГ № 463794), используя свои экстрасенсорные способности, выполнил следующий эксперимент:

При паспортной проверке в аэропорту г.Ташкента выяснилось, что в паспорте Грабового Григория Петровича нет печати, разрешающей выезд из страны. Пограничники были очень удивлены тем, что такое вообще могло произойти. Но мы были удивлены еще больше, потому что печать была поставлена в паспорт на глазах у трех человек. Присутствовавшие при этом подтвердили это. Как выяснилось потом, Грабовой Григорий Петрович убрал ее экстрасенсорно бесконтактным способом. Грабовой Григорий Петрович экстрасенсорно стер печать в своем паспорте в условиях засвидетельствованного существования печатей до того как он начал стирать их, для доказательства, что экстрасенсорное стирание печатей возможно по желанию.


Генеральный директор СП
"Интерсервисэнерго-Азия"    _____ /Бабаев В.Б./

India Office : A. D. CONSULTANTS PVT. LTD. FMC Fortuna 3rd Floor, Unit-A7, 234/3A, A.J.C. Bose Road, Calcutta-70
Telephone : 91-33-2479706    Telefax : 91-33-2476039    Telex : 21-2421 CSEL IN

Telephone : 007·3712·629365
Telex    · 116399 ·OFFIS SU·
Telefax : 007 3712 623571 (Tashkent)

# INTERSERVICEENERGO-ASIA LIMITED

E. KHODJAEV STREET. 2 TASHKENT-700 032
**REPUBLIC OF UZBEKISTAN**

## СВИДЕТЕЛЬСТВО

Настоящим свидетельством, я    Бабаева Татьяна Павловна  ,
удостоверяю, что Грабовой Григорий Петрович, родившийся 14 ноября
1963 года    в поселке Кировском (село Багара) Кировского района
Чимкентской области Казахской ССР (имеющий свидетельство о
рождении серии II-ОГ № 463794), используя свои экстрасенсорные
способности, выполнил следующий эксперимент по материализации
предмета:

Я Бабаева Т.П., была очевидцем очень интересного события. Оно
произошло во время моей командировки в Индию в апреле 1994 г. У меня
пропал авиационный билет. Все мои поиски были напрасны. Сколько бы
и где бы я его ни искала, я не могла найти. Мне помог Грабовой Григорий
Петрович. Он сказал, чтобы я успокоилась и поискала в хозяйственной
сумке, где я уже искала, хотя его там не должно было быть. Вытащив все в
очередной раз, на дне я увидела помятый и слегка запачканный билет.
Этим чудом я обязана Грабовому Григорию Петровичу, который
материализовал утерянный мною билет. Единственное отличие
материализованного Грабовым Григорием Петровичем билета от
утерянного мной было в том, что материализованный им билет был
испачкан соком от яблока лежавшего в сумке. Как позднее мне объяснил
Грабовой Григорий Петрович, он это сделал для того чтобы при
нахождении билета в том месте, где его раньше не было, я не испытала
стресса. Первой мыслью должно было быть, что раз билет испачкан соком
яблока, то он лежал ранее в хозяйственной сумке, в которой лежало
яблоко, выделявшее сок, а затем уже шли мысли о многократном
просматривании мной хозяйственной сумки и абсолютно точном
отсутствии там билета до начала дистанционной экстрасеносрной работы
Грабового Григория Петровича. Этим самым Грабовой Григорий Петрович
показал как он учитывает степень восприимчивости человека при
проводимой им материализации, чтобы не вызвать у сильно
восприимчивого человека стресса при обнаружении материализованного
предмета там, где его точно не было до начала экстрасенсорной
материализации, проводимой Грабовым Григорием Петровичем.

_____ /Бабаева Т.П./

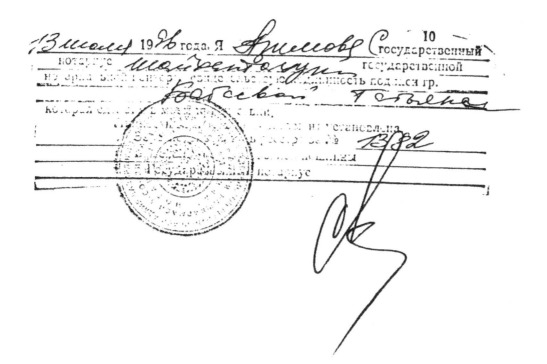

## СВИДЕТЕЛЬСТВО
### об экстрасенсорной работе Грабового Григория Петровича
родившегося 14 ноября 1963 года в поселке Кировском Кировского района Чимкентской области Казахской ССР (имеющего свидетельство о рождении серии II - ОГ № 463794)

Место: _Ташкент_       199 _4_ | _II_ | _01_ |

(место заполнения свидетельства)     год месяц число часы минуты

Я, _Тхлапирева Елена Дмитровна_

(фамилия, имя и отчество полностью)

родился(лась) _1960 18.02. Южно-Казахс. г. Чимкент_

(дата и место рождения)

гражданин(ка) _____

(государство)

проживаю _г. Ташкент ул. Спутник - 4 д 50 кв 217_
_57-11-38_

(место жительства и домашний телефон)

имею удостоверение личности _паспорт XIV-ЮС №632428_
_ОВД Куйбышевского райисполкома г. Ташкента_

(наименование документа, серия, номер, кем и когда выдан документ)

работаю

(наименование предприятия, должность и служебные телефоны)

_зам. генерального директора по экономике_
_тел 54-55-39_

     В первых числах января 1994г я обратилась к Г.П.Грабовому по поводу утери билета (авиа) на с-т авиакомпании Узбекистан по маршруту Москва-Ташкент от 30 декабря 1993г.

     Билет был утерян мной из аэропорта Домодедово (после вылета) и в Ташкенте я его уже не могла найти.

     В связи с этим я лишалась годового билета (льготного) на следующий 1994год.

     После обращения к Грабовому Г.П. я обнаружила свой авиабилет на том месте где ранее я его искала, но в тот момент поиска не нашла.

     Вывод: Я считаю, что Г.П.Грабовой провел материализацию авиа билета, за 30 декабря 1993г.

(подпись заполнявшего свидетельство)     (фамилия заполнявшего свидетельство)

_Тхлапирева Е.Д._

Всем заинтересованным лицам

Заявитель: Гусарова Галина Алексеевна
г. Москва, ул. Исаковского, д. 2, к. 1, кв 215
т. 944-33-66

Заявление

о том, что Грабовой Григорий Петрович дематериализовал 10 листов бумаги в том месте, о котором он не знал (не имел адреса)

Я родилась 29 мая 1945 г в г. Москва, паспорт серии XII-МЮ 616980, выдан 24 мая 1978 г 109 о/м, г. Москва.

Я являюсь свидетелем того, что Грабовой Григорий Петрович дематериализовал в сентябре 1997 г. статью "Человек-рентген" из тумбочки родственницы моего мужа Кузьменко Елены Павловны, её тел. 249-95-24.
При этом Григорий Петрович Грабовой не знал места расположения статьи и адреса. Во время процесса воздействия дематериализации, проводимого Григорием Петровичем Грабовым, исчезло 10 листов формата А4. При этом свидетелями дематериализации были её мама Цветкова Анна Михайловна и я, Гусарова Галина Алексеевна.
После того, как Григорий Петрович Грабовой дематериализовал 10 листов бумаги, прошло 3 (три) недели.

Прошу заверить моё заявление на основании документов, удостоверяющих мою личность и на основании вышеизложенных доказательств.

Гусаров /Гусарова/    1997 г /09/25/
г. Москва

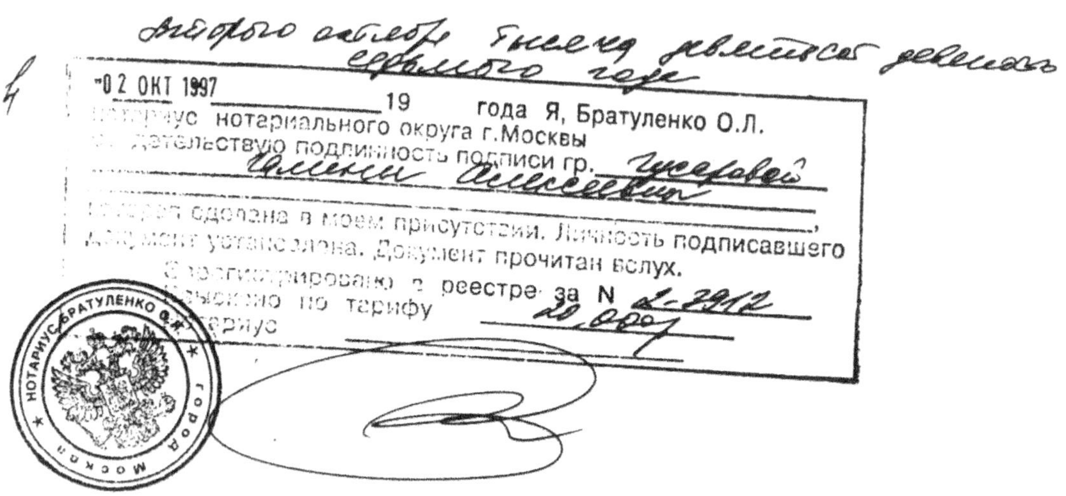

Второго октября тысяча девятьсот девяносто седьмого года

"02 ОКТ 1997 19 года Я, Братуленко О.Л.

Нотариус нотариального округа г.Москвы

свидетельствую подлинность подписи гр. Гусаровой Алены Алексеевны

которая сделана в моем присутствии. Личность подписавшего документ установлена. Документ прочитан вслух.

Зарегистрировано в реестре за N 2-2912

Взыскано по тарифу 20.000

Нотариус

Всем заинтересованным лицам
Заявитель: Цветкова Анна Михайловна
г. Москва, Студенческая ул. д 31, кв 39.

Протокол

Для всех заинтересованных лиц о том,
что Грабовой Григорий Петрович
дематериализовал 10 листов бумаги у меня
на квартире и при этом адреса моей
квартиры он не знал.

Я родилась 15 июля 1911 года в станице Клетс-
кой Клетского р-она Волгоградской области.
Паспорт серии XXI-МЮ №547008. Выдан
66 отделением милиции г. Москвы 26 июня 1979 года.
Я являюсь свидетелем того, что Грабовой Григорий
Петрович дематериализовал в сентябре 1997 г.
статью „Человек – рентген" из тумбочки
моей квартиры т. 249-95-24
При этом Григорий Петрович Грабовой не знал
места расположения статьи и адреса.
Во время воздействия дематериализации проводимого Григорием Петровичем Грабовым исчезло
10 листов формата А4.
При этом свидетелями дематериализации
были моя дочь Кузьменко Елена Павловна и
Гусарова Галина Алексеевна т. 944-33-66
После того, как Григорий Петрович Грабовой
дематериализовал 10 листов бумаги
прошло 3 (три) недели.

Прошу заверить мое заявление на
основании документов удостоверяющих
мою личность и на основании вышеизложенных доказательств

Цв~    / Цветкова / 1997 г.    2.10.1997 г.

**ВСЕМ ЗАИНТЕРЕСОВАННЫМ ЛИЦАМ**

Заявитель: _Чугкова Татьяна Ивановна_
(фамилия, имя и отчество полностью)

_____
(адрес и телефоны)

Заинтересованные лица: _____
(фамилия, имя и отчество полностью; адрес)

**ЗАЯВЛЕНИЕ**
об установлении факта признания
Грабового Григория Петровича

_способным передавать слышимую физическим слухом речь на расстоянии._

Я родился(лась) 19 _46_ / _12_ / _22_ в _ст. Кашевская_
год  месяц  число        (место рождения)

_Краснодарского края паспорт III-ОБ №656912, выдан_
имею удостоверение личности
(наименование документа, серия, номер, кем и когда выдан документ)

_ОВД Московского райисполкома г. Рязани 12.04.79 г._

Работаю: _бухгалтер_
(название предприятия, должность и телефон)

В связи с тем, что я обратился(лась) к Грабовому Григорию Петровичу, родившемуся 14 ноября 1963 года в поселке Кировском, Кировского района Чимкентской области Казахской ССР имеющему свидетельство о рождении серии II-ОГ № 463794, _в ноябре 1997 года по пово-_
(указать дату, место и причину обращения)

_ду заболевания моего внука Радиевича Андрея_
заявляю, что Грабовой Григорий Петрович действительно _может_
_передавать слышимую физическим слухом_
(привести доказательства в обосновании заявления)

_речь на расстоянии. Это подтверждается тем,_
_что моя дочь, зная день и час сеанса,_
_не знала имени отчества Грабового._
_Во время предполагаемого сеанса она на-_
_ходилась в больнице с внуком. Посмот-_
_рев на часы, подумала о том что Грабовой сей-_
_час работает. А как же его зовут?_
_И четко услышала: меня зовут_
_Григорий Петрович, я работаю с вашим_
_сыном, не бойтесь, я ему помогу._
_Он остановлено и мысленно сказа-_
_ла ему спасибо. Дочь врач и реалис-_
_тично оценивает ситуацию, но слыше-_
_ла физически звук речи Григория Петро-_
_вича, хотя рядом его не было._
_Дочь Радиевич Татьяна Вадимовна, телефон_
_765-0648 или 4769828_

Прошу заверить мое заявление на основании документов, удостоверяющих мою личность и на основании вышеизложенных доказательств. ___(подпись)___ / _Чугкова_ /    19 _98_ / _02_ / _2_
(подпись)      (фамилия)           год  месяц  число

_г. Москва второе февраля тысяча девятьсот девя-_
_носто восьмого года_

_Чугкова Татьяна Ивановна_  ___(подпись)___ / _Мск_

## СВИДЕТЕЛЬСТВО

**о экстрасенсорной работе Грабового Григория Петровича**

Населенный пункт г. Москва 1994 г. март 11
(место заполнения свидетельства) год месяц число

Я, Шамшаков Вадим Николаевич гражданин (ка) России
(фамилия, имя и отчество полностью) (государство)

12.11.1964 работающий (щая)
(дата рождения) наименование предприятия

(должность и служебные телефоны)

проживающий (щая)
(адрес места жительства и домашний телефон)

имеющий (щая) удостоверение личности Паспорт XXX-ИК
(наименование документа, серия, номер

№ 510797 10 июля 1992 г. выдан ОВД г. Химки М.О.
кем и года выдан документ)

удостоверяю, что экстрасенс Грабовой Г.П. (имеющий паспорт серии III - ОГ № 586058, выданный 01.02.1980 года)

После договоренности с Григорием П. и „Решил выйти" возле
моей машины ВАЗ 2101 к 81-60 МТ что
Грабовой Г.П. прошел в мою закрытую
машину без каких-либо ключей.
Это все происходило следующим
образом:
Когда я закрыл машину
и проверил что машина закрыта
у меня возникла мысль, что
если у Грабового Г.П. возникнет
желание (необходимость) проникнуть
в машину он сможет это
сделать. После этого я отошел
от машины. Когда я через
несколько минут увидел Грабовой Г.П.
уже сидел в моей машине ВАЗ 2101
к 81-60 МТ и при этом
она была закрыта на внутренние
защелки, то я был свидетелем
проникновения Грабового Г.П.
в закрытую машину

[signature] \ Шамшаков В.Н. \
(подпись заполнившего свидетельство) (фамилия)

Министерство общего и
профессионального образования
Российской Федерации

**РОСТОВСКИЙ ГОСУДАРСТВЕННЫЙ УНИВЕРСИТЕТ**

344006, г. Ростов-на-Дону,
ул. Большая Садовая, 105
Тел. _____

На № _____ от *12.01.98*

Нами, Олехновичем Львом Петровичем, доктором хим. наук, Соросовским профессором, заведующим кафедрой химии природных и высокомолекулярных соединений РГУ и Корниловым Валерием Ивановичем, кандидатом хим. наук, Соросовским доцентом той же кафедры, заведующим лабораторией химии углеводов НИИ ФОХ РГУ была предложена задача выбора предпочтительного варианта промежуточного состояния химического процесса, изображенного ниже, Грабовому Григорию Петровичу (14.11.1963 г. рождения, свид. о рожд. II-ОГ № 463794).

Решение этой задачи возможно методом ядерного магнитного резонанса и квантово-механическими расчетами. Г.П.Грабовой, не являясь химиком вообще, а тем более специалистом в этой узкой области органической химии и не располагая специальными методами изучения строения вещества, мгновенно, находясь в своем офисе (г.Москва, ул. Солянка, 14/2), дал письменное заключение в пользу структуры (II), сделав дополнительный вывод о том, что в магнитном поле возможна реализация третьей структуры, не учтенной нами. Г.П.Грабовой не мог знать заранее, что указанный процесс авторы наблюдают именно в магнитном поле, которое способно влиять на характер промежуточной частицы. Подобный вывод согласуется с нашими представлениями, полученными на основании эксперимента, а также со взглядами других специалистов в этой области.

На основании вышеизложенного считаем, что прогноз, данный Грабовым Г.П., основан на его способности к предвидению процессов, происходящих на молекулярном уровне.

Д.х.н., профессор _____ Олехнович Л.П.

Канд.х,н, доцент _____ Корнилов В.И.

Министерство общего и
профессионального образования
Российской Федерации

**РОСТОВСКИЙ ГОСУДАРСТВЕННЫЙ
УНИВЕРСИТЕТ**

344006, г. Ростов-на-Дону,
ул. Большая Садовая, 105
Тел. _____

На № _____ от _12.01.98._ №

Нами, Олехновичем Львом Петровичем, доктором хим. наук, Соросовским профессором, заведующим кафедрой химии природных и высокомолекулярных соединений РГУ и Корниловым Валерием Ивановичем, кандидатом хим. наук, Соросовским доцентом той же кафедры, заведующим лабораторией химии углеводов НИИФОХ РГУ была предложена задача определения порядка количества миграций ацетильной группы для химического процесса, изображенного ниже, Грабовому Григорию Петровичу ( 14.П.1963 г. рожд., свид. о рождении ОГ-II № 463794).

Письменный ответ Грабовой Г.П. дал практически мгновенно, находясь в своем офисе (г.Москва, ул. Солянка, 14/2), и определив его в 20-30 миграций в секунду, что совпало с экспериментальными данными. Случайное попадание в нужную величину считаем мало вероятным, т.к. эти значения для веществ с различными заместителями могут находиться в очень широких пределах.

Считаем, что решение дано Грабовым Г.П., не являющимся специалистом в этой узкой области органической химии и не владеющим специальными методами определения химической структуры вещества, на основании его способности к предвидению процессов, происходящих на молекулярном уровне.

Д.х.н., профессор           Олехнович Л.П.

Канд.хим.наук, доцент        Корнилов В.И.

Министерство общего и
профессионального образования
Российской Федерации

**РОСТОВСКИЙ ГОСУДАРСТВЕННЫЙ
УНИВЕРСИТЕТ**

344006, г. Ростов-на-Дону,
ул. Большая Садовая, 105
Тел.

На № _____ от *12.01.98* г.

Нами, Курбатовым Сергеем Васильевичем, канд. хим. наук, доцентом кафедры химии природных и высокомолекулярных соединений РГУ и Корниловым Валерием Ивановичем, канд.хим. наук, Соросовским доцентом той же кафедры, зав. лабораторией НИИФОХ РГУ была предложена Грабовому Григорию Петровичу (14.II. 1963 г.рождения, свид. о рождении II-ОГ №463794) задача охарактеризовать обратимую перегруппировку, изображенную ниже, в плане определения количества миграций ацетильной группы в растворе при 25°С.

Ответ был дан Грабовым Г.П. в его офисе (г.Москва, ул.Солянка, 14/ практически мгновенно, а порядок миграций был определен как $10^6$ в сек., что согласуется с экспериментальными и расчетными данными. Случайное совпадение мало вероятно, т.к. миграция в соединениях подобного типа зависит от заместителей и может происходить в широких пределах (от $10^6$ до $10^{-6}$ раз в сек).

Считаем, что решение, данное Грабовым Г.П., основано на его способности к предвидению процессов, происходящих на молекулярном уровне.

Канд. хим. наук, доц.     Курбатов С.В.

Канд.хим. наук, доц.     Корнилов В.И.

РСФСР

МИНИСТЕРСТВО ВЫСШЕГО И СРЕДНЕГО
СПЕЦИАЛЬНОГО ОБРАЗОВАНИЯ

РОСТОВСКИЙ
ОРДЕНА ТРУДОВОГО КРАСНОГО ЗНАМЕНИ
ГОСУДАРСТВЕННЫЙ УНИВЕРСИТЕТ

НАУЧНО-ИССЛЕДОВАТЕЛЬСКИЙ

ИНСТИТУТ ФИЗИЧЕСКОЙ И

ОРГАНИЧЕСКОЙ ХИМИИ

(НИИФОХ)

344104, г. Ростов-на-Дону, просп. Стачки, 194/3
Телефон 28-57-00

от _12.01.98_ № _____

На № _____ от _____

Нами, Курбатовым Сергеем Васильевичем, доцентом кафедры химии природных и высокомолекулярных соединений РГУ и Корниловым Валерием Ивановичем, канд.хим.наук, доцентом той же кафедры, заведующим лабораторией НИИФОХ РГУ была предложена Грабовому Григорию Петровичу (14.II.1963 г. рождения; свидетельство о рожд. II-ОГ № 463794) задача охарактеризовать скорость превращения вещества I в вещество II в растворе при 25°С (количество циклизаций-рециклизаций в секунду).

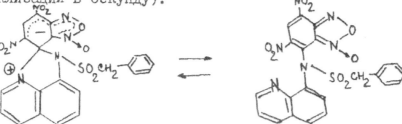

Ответ был дан Грабовым Г.П. письменно в его офисе (г.Москва, ул. Солянка, 14/2) практически мгновенно, а порядок миграций определен как пять (5) в сек., что соответствует эксперименту, проведенному впоследствии с помощью ЯМР-спектроскопии и расчетов.

Считаем, что решение, данное Грабовым Г.П., не владеющим физико-химическими методами исследования химического вещества, основано на его способности к предвидению процессов, происходящих на молекулярном уровне.

Канд.хим.наук, доц. _____ Курбатов С.В.

Канд. хим.наук,доц. _____ Корнилов В.И.

## СВИДЕТЕЛЬСТВО

Лист № 1

**об экстрасенсорной работе Грабового Григория Петровича,**
родившегося 14 ноября 1963 года в поселке Кировском (село Багара) Кировского района Чимкентской области Казахской ССР и меющего свидетельство о рождении серии II - ОГ № 463794.

Место: _город Ташкент_
(место заполнения свидетельства)

199 **7 / 01 / 24 / 16 / 23**
год   месяц  число  часы  минуты

Я, **Румянцев Константин Александрович,**
родился _26 марта 1964 года в г. Ташкенте_
(дата и место рождения)

гражданин _Узбекистана_
(государство)

проживаю _г. Ташкент, ул. Фергона йули, 95ª, 1 корп., кв 90_
(место жительства и домашний телефон)
_Телефон: 215410_

_Частное малое внедренгеское предприятие "ВИСТ" тел. 410908_
(место работы, должность и служебные телефоны)
_Технический директор_

имею удостоверение личности _паспорт серии СА номер 0500835_
(наименование документа, серия, номер, кем и когда выдан)
_выданный 03 апреля 1996 г. Хамзинским РОВД г. Ташкент_

в присутствии двух свидетелей

первый свидетель : _Морозкина Марина Валерьевна_
(фамилия, имя и отчество полностью)
_27 марта 1965 г. г. Ташкент_
(дата и место рождения)
_г. Ташкент, ул. Башкирская 02, кв9, т. 34-30-68_
(место жительства и домашний телефон)
_МСЧ п/о Таш тракторного з-да врач-терапевт_
(место работы, должность и служебные телефоны)

удостоверение личности _паспорт СА 0118402 УВД_
(наименование документа, серия, номер, кем и когда выдан)
_Юнус Абадского района г. Ташкента 28.02.95._

второй свидетель : _Пшикин Николай Дмитриевич_
(фамилия, имя и отчество полностью)
_15 февраля 1977 года, г. Пшикино РУЗ_
(дата и место рождения)
_г. Пшикино, ул. Берони 93 к61 тел 42-56-94_
(место жительства и домашний телефон)
_ТШЗУ НАК РУЗ Пшикин старако экон_
(место работы, должность и служебные телефоны)

удостоверение личности _паспорт XVI-ICC № 730079, выдан де мае_
(наименование документа, серия, номер, кем и когда выдан)
_1993 года СВВ Сиплярейский р-на г. Пшикина_

*Продолжение настоящего текста в приложении № 1 к первому листу*

_Зумянцев_                     | _Румянцев К.А._ |
(подпись заполнившего свидетельство)   (фамилия заполнившего свидетельство)

_Морозкина М.В._               | _Пшикин Н.Д._ |
(подпись и фамилия первого свидетеля)   (подпись и фамилия второго свидетеля)

## ПРИЛОЖЕНИЕ № 1

Лист № 2

### к свидетельству об экстрасенсорной работе Грабового Григория Петровича,

родившегося 14 ноября 1963 года в поселке Кировском (село Багара) Кировского района Чимкентской области Казахской ССР и меющего свидетельство о рождении серии II - ОГ № 463794.

Место: _город Ташкент_ _ _ _ _      199**7** / **01** / **24** / **16** / **23**
(место заполнения свидетельства)                              год   месяц   число   часы   минуты

**Румянцев Константин Александрович**
Фамилия имя отчество заполнившего свидетельство

Настоящим свидетельством удостоверяю, что был свидетелем проявления экстрасенсорных способностей Грабового Григория Петровича в период учебы в Ташкентском университете. Преподаватель, доцент Гегель Галина Николаевна неоднократно, в присутствии всей группы после проверки контрольных работ по математическому анализу, выражала удивление по поводу работ студента Грабового Григория Петровича, который пишет правильные ответы на задания сразу, не проводя решения. В то время мы считали его одаренным человеком способным интуитивно находить правильные ответы, т. к. понятий ясновидение или экстрасенсорика у нас не было. Через призму сегодняшних знаний вышеизложенное можно назвать ясновидением.

Всему вышеизложенному мной я действительно был очевидцем, что и подтверждаю своей подписью в присутствии двух свидетелей.

*Приведенные в настоящем свидетельстве факты имели место на втором курсе университета в 1982-83 учебном году.*

_____ ,   | Румянцев К.А.     |
(подпись заполнившего свидетельство)   (фамилия заполнившего свидетельство)

_____ Морозкина ЛВ    | Пилюкин П.Я.     |
(подпись и фамилия первого свидетеля)   (подпись и фамилия второго свидетеля)

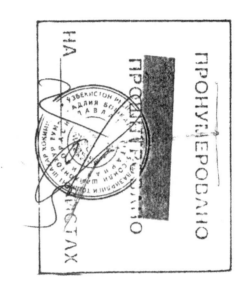

ВСЕМ ЗАИНТЕРЕСОВАННЫМ ЛИЦАМ

Заявитель : Яковлева Ольга Николаевна
Московская область  г.Юбилейный, мкр.1, д.6,кв.14,513-92-52

Я родилась 17.02.58г. в с.Гороховка Воронежской области
паспорт серии Х1Х-ИК №655676 выдан 25 марта 1981г.  1 О/М
УВД  г.Мытищи  Московской области.

З А Я В Л Е Н И Е
о том, что ГРАБОВОЙ ГРИГОРИЙ ПЕТРОВИЧ своим экстрасенсорным
воздействием снял посторонние звуки с аудиозаписи своего голоса и добавил текст со своим голосом на аудиокассету.

Я являюсь свидетелем того, что Грабовой Григорий Петрович
27.02.97г. своим экстрасенсорным воздействием снял посторонние звуки с аудиокассеты с записью своего голоса и добавил
текст аудиозаписи со своим голосом.При этом добавленный текст
с голосом  Грабового Григория Петровича не отличался ни по
каким параметрам от голоса Грабового Григория Петровича ранее
записанного на аудиопленку при очной беседе с ним.
Свое экстрасенсорное воздействие Грабовой Григорий Петрович
провел не зная где находится аудиопленка.

Прошу заверить мое заявление на основании документов,удосто-
веряющих мою личность и на основании вышеизложенных доказа-
тельст.

_____ / Яковлева / 1997г. /11/     г.Москва

*Город Москва   восемнадцатого      ноября    одна тысяча    девятьсот девяносто седьмого года   я, Вроблевская Л.Э.,    нотариус  г.Москвы ,  свидетельствую подлинность подписи, сделанную   гр. Яковлевой Ольгой Николаевной в моем  присутствии . Личность подписавшей документ установлена..*

Зарегистрировано в реестре за   №   *2. 10157*
Взыскано по тарифу                      *4. 185 руб*
Нотариус

# ВСЕМ ЗАИНТЕРЕСОВАННЫМ ЛИЦАМ

Заявитель : Яковлева  Ольга  Николаевна
Московская область  г.Юбилейный, мкр.1, д.6,кв.14 513-92-52

Я родилась 17.02.58г. в с.Гороховка Воронежской области
паспорт серии Х1Х-ИК № 655676 выдан 25 марта 1981г.  1 О/М
УВД  г.Мытищи Московской области.

## ЗАЯВЛЕНИЕ

о том, что  ГРАБОВОЙ ГРИГОРИЙ ПЕТРОВИЧ  своим экстрасенсорным
воздействием убрал запись с аудиокассеты таким образом, что
свободного места на аудиокассете не оказалось.

Я являюсь свидетелем того, что  Грабовой Григорий Петрович

27.02.97г. своим экстрасенсорным воздействием стер запись

беседы с аудиокассеты таким образом, что пустого места на

аудиокассете не оказалось.При повторном прослушивании аудио-

кассеты с записанным текстом до стертого участка далее шло

сразу начало текста, который был ранее /до воздействия

Грабового Григория Петровича/ после стертого участка аудио-

записи. При этом посторонних шумов на месте стыка граничащих

со стертым участком записей не наблюдалось, физические пара-

метры ленты остались без изменений.Свое экстрасенсорное

воздействие Грабовой Григорий Петрович провел не зная где

находится аудиокассета. *Грабовой Григорий Петрович родился 14 ноября 1963г.*
*( свидетельство о рождении  11 - аи  № 463794 )*

Прошу заверить мое заявление на основании документов, удостоверяющих мою личность и на основании вышеизложенных доказательств.

_____  /Яковлева / 1997г./11/ 18/    г.Москва

*Город Москва восемнадцатого ноября одна тысяча девятьсот девяносто седьмого года я, Вроблевская Л.Э., нотариус г.Москвы, свидетельствую подлинность подписи, сделанную гр. Яковлевой Ольгой Николаевной в моем присутствии . Личность подписавшей документ установлена..*

Зарегистрировано в реестре за №   *2. 10157*

Взыскано по тарифу   *4. 185 руб*

Нотариус

Всем заинтересованным лицам
Заявитель: Ладыченко Константин Владимирович

Заявление

О том, что Грабовой Григорий Петрович в условиях чистого эксперимента дематериализовал полностью информированную компьютерную дискету объемом 1,44 мегабайта.

Я, Ладыченко Константин Владимирович, родился 15 июля 1967 года в г. Мошино Московской области, удостоверение личности офицера ВПЛ: 096219 выданное Тамбовским ВВАУЛ 21 октября 1989г, являюсь свидетелем того, что Грабовой Григорий Петрович дематериализовал 22 ноября 1997года полностью информированную компьютерную дискету объемом 1,44 мегабайта. Во время дематериализации Григорий Петрович не знал где находится дискета.

Личные данные Грабового Григория Петровича:
- родился 14 ноября 1963 года в поселке Кировском, Кировского района Чимкентской области Казахской ССР, имеющего свидетельство о рождении серии II-ОГ № 463794

Прошу заверить мое заявление на основании документов, удостоверяющих мою личность и на основании вышеуказанных доказательств.

25 ноября 1997 года     [подпись]     Ладыченко К.В.
Ладыченко Константин Владимирович     [подпись]

«26» ноября 1997 года, я Болквадзе Т.Н.
Нотариус 12-й Московской государственной нотариальной конторы, свидетельствую подлинность подписи гр. Ладыченко Константина Владимировича сделанной в моем присутствии. Личность установлена, дееспособность проверена
Взыскано государственной пошлины ... 4175 ... рублей
По реестру: 2-1458

## СВИДЕТЕЛЬСТВО

Лист № 1

**об экстрасенсорной работе Грабового Григория Петровича**
родившегося 14 ноября 1963 года в поселке   Кировском (село
Багара) Кировского района Чимкентской области Казахской ССР
(имеющего свидетельство о рождении серии II - ОГ № 463794)
**по экстрасенсорному диагностированию программно-аппаратных
средств ПЭВМ в ноябре 1991 года.**

Место: ___ *г. Ташкент* _____       199б/ *12* / *4* / *12* / *35*
    (место заполнения свидетельства)       год   месяц  число  часы  минуты

Я, **Валитов Радик Тафикович,**
родился ____ *12 октября 1960 г.* _____, *г. Ташкент* ___
                (дата и место рождения)

гражданин _____ *Узбекистан* _____
                (государство)
проживаю ___ *г. Ташкент     массив "Кушбеги"*
          (место жительства и домашний телефон)
          *д. 16    кв. 35*

         (место работы, должность и служебные телефоны)

имею удостоверение личности *паспорт __ II-ЮС __ № 639885*
            (наименование документа, серия, номер, кем и когда выдан)
*выдан 26 ноября 1976   Шлангарским РОВД г. Ташкента*
в присутствии двух свидетелей

первый свидетель : *Трубкина Ольга Александровна* ___
            (фамилия, имя и отчество полностью)
*20.09.56 г.р   г. Кайраккум   Ленинабадской обл.*
            (дата и место рождения)
*Ташкент-72 Мирабадский р-н ул. Алмункульская 6-24*
            (место жительства и домашний телефон)
*д.т 24324 , отдел кадров, оператор ЭВМ*
            (место работы, должность и служебные телефоны)

удостоверение личности *паспорт СА 032 5839 выдан Мира-*
            (наименование документа, серия, номер, кем и когда выдан)
*баским РУВД от 08.08.96 .*,

второй свидетель : *Гришкова Валентина Григорьевна* ___
            (фамилия, имя и отчество полностью)
*20.07.1939 г.  г. Кзыл-Орда , Казахской ССР*
            (дата и место рождения)
*г. Ташкент, ул. Чимкентская 13, кв.16. тел 565063*
            (место жительства и домашний телефон)
*завод 243 ГА начальник отдела кадров     тел. 546800*
            (место работы, должность и служебные телефоны)

удостоверение личности *паспорт III-НС №729141 ОВД Ленинского*
            (наименование документа, серия, номер, кем и когда выдан )
*РИКа г. Ташкента выдан 5.12.1994г.*

*Продолжение настоящего текста в приложении № 1 к первому листу*

_____ | ___ *Валитов Р.Т.* ___
(подпись заполнившего свидетельство) | (фамилия заполнившего свидетельство)

___ *Трубкина О.А.* ___ | ___ *В.Г.Гришкова* ___
(подпись и фамилия первого свидетеля) | (подпись и фамилия второго свидетеля)

## ПРИЛОЖЕНИЕ №1

Лист № 2

### к свидетельству об экстрасенсорной работе Грабового Григория Петровича

родившегося 14 ноября 1963 года в поселке  Кировском (село Багара) Кировского района Чимкентской области Казахской ССР (имеющего свидетельство о рождении серии II - ОГ № 463794)

### по экстрасенсорному диагностированию программно-аппаратных средств ПЭВМ в ноябре 1991 года.

Место: _ _ _ _ _ *г. Ташкент* _ _ _ _ _        199*6 / 12 / 4 / 12 / 35*
        (место заполнения свидетельства)                год  месяц число часы минуты

**Валитов Радик Тафикович**
(Фамилия имя отчество заполнившего свидетельство)

заявляю, что был очевидцем следующего экстрасенсорного эксперимента Грабового Григория Петровича:

При мне в ноябре 1991 года экстрасенсу Грабовому Г.П. были предложены для диагностирования на вирус двадцать дискет. Грабовой Г.П. после визуального просмотра дискет ( то есть не используя компьютерную технику или специализированное для обнаружения вирусов программное обеспечение, а просто на глаз) точно определил пять зараженных вирусами дискет.

Кроме того, экстрасенсом Грабовым Г.П. проводилась работа по экстрасенсорному воздействию на программные средства с целью удаления экстрасенсорным путем вирусов. При копировании программного файла с зараженной вирусом дискеты на винчестер во время экстрасенсорного воздействия Грабового Г.П., программный файл был записан на винчестер в объеме в 10 раз меньше оригинала. При копировании вирус Dir должен был быть занесен с дискеты на винчестер, но этого не произошло, что показала ативирусная программа Anti-Dir. Следовательно в момент перезаписи файла с дискеты на винчестер Грабовым Г.П. было произведено экстрасенсорное воздействие на переносимую информацию, вирус был уничтожен и не был перезаписан с дискеты на винчестер.

Эти факты отражены в протоколах № 04/91 и № 05/91 о проведенных Грабовым Г.П. экстрасенсорных работах.

Считаю, что этот эксперимент подтвердил экстрасенсорные способности Грабового Григория Петровича выявлять очень тонкие информационно-энергетические связи на технических носителях информации (дискетах) и управлять процессом перезаписи информации, отсекая информационный поток вируса. Эти способности могут быть применены в серьезных информационных средах при наличии искусственных помех.

Всему вышеизложенному мной я действительно был очевидцем, что и подтверждаю своей подписью в присутствии двух свидетелей.

_____  / *Валитов Р. Т.* /
(подпись заполнившего свидетельство)    (фамилия заполнившего свидетельство)

_____  *Тюркина О.А.*    _____  *В.Г. Гришкова*
(подпись  и фамилия  первого свидетеля)    (подпись  и фамилия  второго свидетеля)

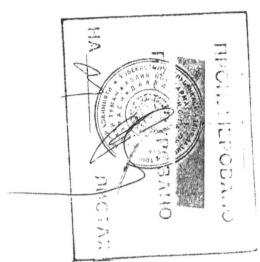

**ISEA**

Telephone : 007 3712 629365
Telex      116399 'OFFIS SU'
Telefax : 007 3712 623571 (Tashkent)

## INTERSERVICEENERGO-ASIA LIMITED
E. KHODJAEV STREET. 2 TASHKENT-700 032
REPUBLIC OF UZBEKISTAN

## СВИДЕТЕЛЬСТВО

Настоящим свидетельством, я Бабаева Татьяна Павловна, удостоверяю, что Грабовой Григорий Петрович, родившийся 14 ноября 1963 года в поселке Кировском Кировского района Чимкентской области (имеющий свидетельство о рождении серии II-ОГ № 463794), используя свои экстрасенсорные способности, выполнил следующий эксперимент:

Я неоднократно наблюдала, как Грабовой Григорий Петрович, не прикасаясь к кнопке лифта, заставлял его двигаться в заданном направлении и останавливаться на нужном этаже. Такие эксперименты были выполнены им неоднократно в присутствии моего мужа Бабабева В.Б. и меня в лифте отеля в г. Дели в апреле 1994 г.

_____ / Бабаева Т.П./

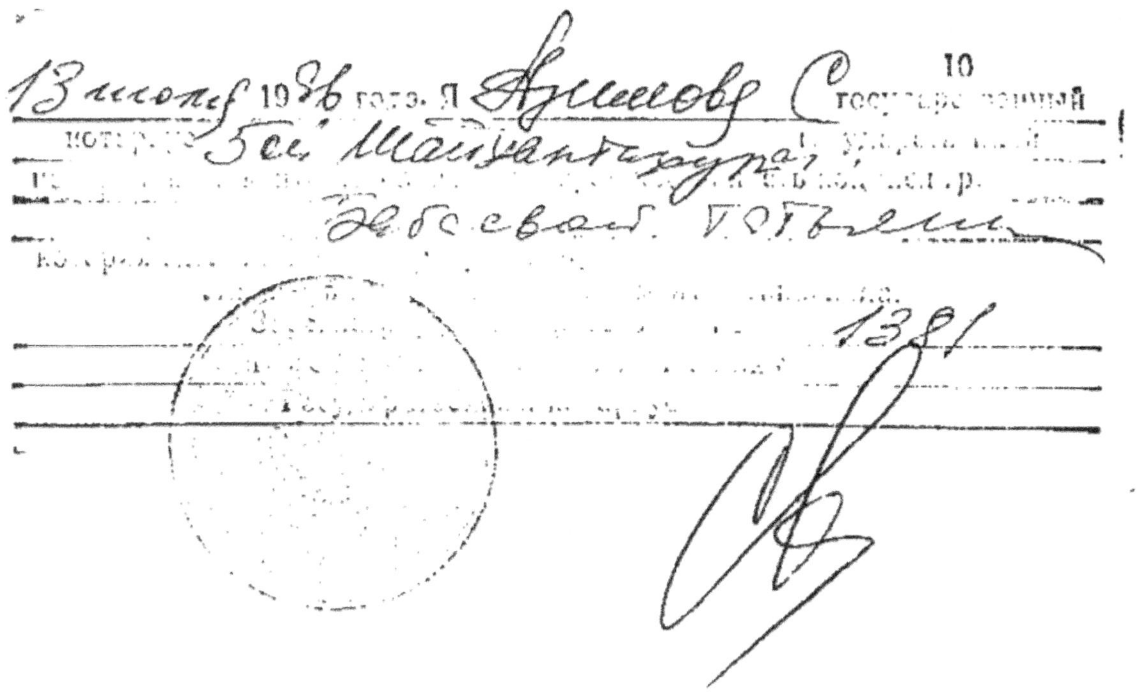

10

13 июня 1986 года. Я Ахмедова С государственный нотариус 5-ой Ташкентской

Грабовой Г.П.

1381

# APPENDIX E: DOCUMENTS CONFIRMING THE LISTED IN THE BOOK CONCRETE FACTS OF THE USE OF TECHNICAL DEVICES FOR RESTORATION

INTERNATIONAL
INFORMATION
INTELLECTUAL NOVELTY
REGISTRATION CHAMBER

IINRC

МРПИИН

МЕЖДУНАРОДНАЯ
РЕГИСТРАЦИОННАЯ ПАЛАТА
ИНФОРМАЦИОННО-
ИНТЕЛЛЕКТУАЛЬНОЙ
НОВИЗНЫ

# СЕРТИФИКАТ-ЛИЦЕНЗИЯ

Регистрационный номер№ 000285         Шифр 00014         Код 00015
Открытие, изобретение, новшество (технология, проект и т.д.): **МОДЕЛЬ**

# Грабовой Григорий Петрович

**Аннотация:**

Новизна в принципах расщепления информации, основанной на постулатах общности пространства и времени в бесконечности и принципах сочетания известных свойств пространства и времени с законами их взаимного развития. Открыт метод архивации любой информации через область бесконечно удаленных точек. Пространство рассматривается как неизменяемая структура времени. Время рассматривается как функция пространства, а точка воспроизводства материи как следствие реакции времени на изменение пространства. Точки соприкосновения и являются точками архивации любой информации, что позволяет создать технологические системы на основе ЭВМ. Заархивированная информация дает статичную конструкцию машины «разумной» и процессы управления ею. Можно также заархивировать информацию в любом веществе непрерывной записью и считать ее информацией не имеющей видимого материального носителя. Таким вариантом применяемой модели архивации можно создать принципиально новый вид компьютерной техники, которая может быть использована для создания необходимой формы разума, находящегося в воздухе, в вакууме или в любом веществе, через единичные импульсы специальной приставки к компьютеру.

**Краткое название: АРХИВАЦИЯ ИНФОРМАЦИИ В ЛЮБОЙ ТОЧКЕ
ПРОСТРАНСТВА-ВРЕМЕНИ**

**Основная идея:**

Международная регистрационная палата информационно-интеллектуальной новизны представляет на регистрацию в Международный Регистр Глобальных Систем Информации интеллектуальную собственность, которая, как творческая работа, была признана Ученым Советом МРПИИН и другими структурами как

# МОДЕЛЬ

Настоящий Сертификат-Лицензия - документ, дающий владельцу право использовать эту информационно-интеллектуальную новизну, как собственность, на международных рынках всех стран Мира.

Председатель Палаты,
действительный член Международной
Академии информатизации и
Нью-Йоркской Академии наук

Е.С. Тыжненко-Давтян

Дата: 19 декабря 1997

INTERNATIONAL
INFORMATION
INTELLECTUAL NOVELTY
REGISTRATION CHAMBER

IIINRC
МРПИИН

МЕЖДУНАРОДНАЯ
РЕГИСТРАЦИОННАЯ ПАЛАТА
ИНФОРМАЦИОННО-
ИНТЕЛЛЕКТУАЛЬНОЙ
НОВИЗНЫ

# СЕРТИФИКАТ-ЛИЦЕНЗИЯ

Регистрационный номер№ 000283     Шифр 00012     Код 00015
Открытие, изобретение, новшество (технология, проект и т.д.): **МЕТОД**

## Грабовой Григорий Петрович

**Аннотация:**

Разработана технология перевода информации любого события в геометрические формы описываемые ортодоксальной математикой. Для изменения события специальная компьютерная программа, первоначальную форму переводит в форму изменяющую событие необходимым образом. Программа основана на расчетах угловых коэффициентов между измененными и дополненными формами, т.е. рассчитывается четырехкратный интеграл методом Рунге-Кутта. Дополненные формы при специальном импульсе управляют на любом расстоянии. Использование компьютерной технологии может быть полезно в управлении информацией в медицине, в точных технологиях и др.

**Краткое название: КОМПЬЮТЕРНАЯ ТЕХНОЛОГИЯ ДИСТАНТНОГО УПРАВЛЕНИЯ**

**Основная идея:**

Международная регистрационная палата информационно-интеллектуальной новизны представляет на регистрацию в Международный Регистр Глобальных Систем Информации интеллектуальную собственность, которая, как творческая работа, была признана Ученым Советом МРПИИН и другими структурами как

**МЕТОД**

Настоящий Сертификат-Лицензия - документ, дающий владельцу право использовать эту информационно-интеллектуальную новизну, как собственность, на международных рынках всех стран Мира.

Председатель Палаты,
действительный член Международной
Академии информатизации и
Нью-Йоркской Академии наук                    Е.С. Тыжненко-Давтян

Дата: 19 декабря 1997

**INTERNATIONAL
INFORMATION
INTELLECTUAL NOVELTY
REGISTRATION CHAMBER**

IIINRC
МРПИИН

**МЕЖДУНАРОДНАЯ
РЕГИСТРАЦИОННАЯ ПАЛАТА
ИНФОРМАЦИОННО-
ИНТЕЛЛЕКТУАЛЬНОЙ
НОВИЗНЫ**

# СЕРТИФИКАТ-ЛИЦЕНЗИЯ

Регистрационный номер№ 000286          Шифр 00020          Код 00015
Открытие, изобретение, новшество (технология, проект и т.д.): **ПРИНЦИП**

# Грабовой Григорий Петрович

**Аннотация:**

Открыто свойство материи позволяющая практически мгновенно получать необходимую форму на основе единичной программы заложенной в какой либо интервал времени (имеются протокольные доказательства). Компьютерные технологии позволяют обеспечить управление материей, восстановление тканей организма и его безопасность, контроль за машинами, создание вещества принципом перевода времени в любое вещество - принципом не разрушаемости структуры времени при изменении пространства; источник энергии из времени прошлых событий неограничен, т.е. любое событие прошлого можно дробить бесконечным количеством методов, в т.ч. и методом обратной связи - управление временем будущих событий. Фактически при применении прикладного аппарата на концептуальной основе, можно использовать время прошлых событий. Следовательно, по мнению автора восстановить можно любую материю из набора «случайных» событий в любом интервале времени, что означает нелогичность любого разрушения.

**Краткое название: ВРЕМЯ, ЭТО ФОРМА ПРОСТРАНСТВА**

**Основная идея:**

Международная регистрационная палата информационно-интеллектуальной новизны представляет на регистрацию в Международный Регистр Глобальных Систем Информации интеллектуальную собственность, которая, как творческая работа, была признана Ученым Советом МРПИИН и другими структурами как

## ПРИНЦИП

Настоящий Сертификат-Лицензия - документ, дающий владельцу право использовать эту информационно-интеллектуальную новизну, как собственность, на международных рынках всех стран Мира.

Председатель Палаты,
действительный член Международной
Академии информатизации и
Нью-Йоркской Академии наук                                    Е.С. Тыжненко-Давтян

Дата: 19 декабря 1997

**INTERNATIONAL
INFORMATION
INTELLECTUAL NOVELTY
REGISTRATION CHAMBER**

**МРПИИН**

**МЕЖДУНАРОДНАЯ
РЕГИСТРАЦИОННАЯ ПАЛАТА
ИНФОРМАЦИОННО-
ИНТЕЛЛЕКТУАЛЬНОЙ
НОВИЗНЫ**

# СЕРТИФИКАТ-ЛИЦЕНЗИЯ

Регистрационный номер№ 000287          Шифр 00018          Код 00015

Открытие, изобретение, новшество (технология, проект и т.д.): **ОТКРЫТИЕ**

## Грабовой Григорий Петрович

**Аннотация:**

Предложены новые области информации, определяющие свойства и места расположения любых объектов информации приводящих к саморазвитию неразрушающих областей созидания, определяющих также конкретные технологии неразрушающего использования создающей области. Открыта полная идентичность (по принципу аутоморфности, изоморфичности) любых объектов информации перед создающей областью информации (протоколы результатов заверены нотариально в ООН).

Открытие создающей области информации осуществилось через отражение реализуемых объектов информации на внутренней поверхности сферы прошлых (известных) объектов информации. Сегмент сферы соответствующей будущей информации определяющий компоненты создаваемых объектов , находится как площадь внешней поверхности сферы известных объектов информации, определяемая из проекций областей реализуемых объектов на внешнюю поверхность сферы известных объектов и возникает из взаимодействия областей информации критериально идентичных, по отношению к создающей области, через  внутренние области динамичных, по отношению к объектам реализации, сфер. Открытие позволяет реализовать любые направления созидательного развития по принципу самопостижения с применением метода ортодоксальной математики.

**Краткое название:** ВОСПРОИЗВОДЯЩИЕ САМОРАЗВИВАЮЩИЕСЯ СИСТЕМЫ, ОТРАЖАЮЩИЕ ВНЕШНИЕ И ВНУТРЕНИЕ ОБЛАСТИ МНОГООБРАЗИЯ СОЗДАЮЩИХ СФЕР

**Основная идея:**

Международная  регистрационная  палата  информационно-интеллектуальной новизны представляет на регистрацию в Международный Регистр Глобальных Систем Информации интеллектуальную собственность, которая, как творческая работа, была признана Ученым Советом МРПИИН и другими структурами как

## ОТКРЫТИЕ

Настоящий Сертификат-Лицензия - документ, дающий владельцу право использовать эту информационно-интеллектуальную новизну, как собственность, на международных рынках всех стран Мира.

Председатель Палаты,
действительный член Международной
Академии информатизации и
Нью-Йоркской Академии наук                                    Е.С. Тихоненко-Давтян

Дата: 19 декабря 1997

(19) **RU**  (11) **2148845**  (13) **C1**

(51)  7  G 01 V 9/00, 8/20

РОССИЙСКОЕ АГЕНТСТВО
ПО ПАТЕНТАМ И ТОВАРНЫМ ЗНАКАМ

(12) **ОПИСАНИЕ ИЗОБРЕТЕНИЯ**

к патенту Российской Федерации

1

(21) 99120836/28          (22) 07.10.1999
(24) 07.10.1999
(46) 10.05.2000 Бюл. № 13
(72) Грабовой Г.П.
(71) (73) Грабовой Григорий Петрович
(56)  RU 2107933 C1, 27.03.1998. RU 2050014
C1, 10.12.1995. RU 2098850 C1, 10.12.1997.
SU 1104459 A, 23.07.1984.
(98) 115230, Москва, Каширское ш. 5-1-66,
Копаеву В.Г.

(54) СПОСОБ ПРЕДОТВРАЩЕНИЯ КА-
ТАСТРОФ И УСТРОЙСТВО ДЛЯ ЕГО
ОСУЩЕСТВЛЕНИЯ

(57) Использование: для предотвращения
катастроф природного или техногенного
характера. Сущность: сигналы светового
излучения от элемента, соответствующего
зоне предполагаемой катастрофы, обрабатывают при помощи оптической системы,
содержащей чувствительные элементы, изготовленные из кристалла, например из

2

горного хрусталя, выполненные в виде
идентичных кубиков, распределенных вдоль
направления распространения излучения и
размещенных в стеклянной сфере. Последний
кубик при помощи оптического волокна
соединен с датчиком, который через усилитель подключен к процессорной системе. В
оптической системе формируют нормированное излучение. Предпочтительно проводить
сканирование различных участков элемента,
выполненного, например, в виде карты
местности, при этом участку зарождения
катастрофы соответствует зона с увеличенными характеристиками нормированного излучения. Так для катастроф природного
характера участок зарождения катастрофы
имеет характеристики на 20-28%, превышающие характеристики излучения других
участков элемента, а для катастроф техногенного характера соответствующее увеличение составляет 10-12%. Технический резуль-

**RU 2148845 C1**

**RU 2148845 C1**

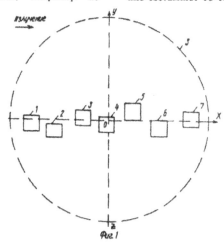

Фиг 1

3                    2148845                    4

тат: повышение эффективности при одновременном расширении области применения

заявленных способа и устройства. 2 с. и 6
з.п. ф-лы, 3 ил.

5                          2148845                          6

Изобретение может быть использовано для предотвращения различных катастрофических явлений как природного характера, таких, например, как катастрофические землетрясения, так и катастрофических явлений техногенного характера, в частности на производственных объектах.

Наиболее близким по технической сущности к заявляемому является способ предотвращения катастрофы, носящей природный характер - землятресения, посредством регистрации и обработки сигналов, характеризующих положение в зоне предполагаемой катастрофы (см. а.с. СССР N 1030496, кл. E 02 D 27/34, 1983). В соответствии с известным способом обрабатывают вибросигналы в виде колебаний земной коры, исходящие из эпицентра землетрясения, при помощи сетки сейсмоприемников, получая электрические сигналы. Преобразуют полученные электрические сигналы в центре сбора, регистрации и обработки информации в командные сигналы, которые подают на излучатели, выполненные в виде виброисточников. Вырабатываемые или нормализующие сигналы в виде упругих волновых колебаний направляют в зону очага землетрясения. Гашение сейсмических колебаний осуществляется при взаимодействии высокочастотных упругих колебаний, исходящих от виброисточников, с низкочастотными волновыми колебаниями от эпицентра землетрясения.

Недостатком известного способа является его низкая эффективность, поскольку противодействие катастрофическому землетрясению осуществляется лишь при достижении достаточной степени его развития, вследствие чего необходимо предварительно получить ряд прогностических сигналов в центре сбора, регистрации и обработки информации. Кроме того, известный способ обладает ограниченными функциональными возможностями, поскольку он может быть использован лишь для предотвращения землетрясений и непригоден для предотвращения других катастрофических явлений, например катастроф техногенного характера.

Наиболее близким по технической сущности к заявленному является устройство для предотвращения катастрофы природного характера - землетрясения, содержащее преобразователь сигналов, характеризующих положение в зоне предполагаемой катастрофы, систему регистрации сигналов и излучатель, генерирующий сигналы, способствующие нормализации положения в зоне предполагаемой катастрофы (см. а.с.

СССР N 838014, кл. E 02 D 31/08, 1981). В известном устройстве в качестве преобразователя сигналов используется вибродатчик, преобразующий механические колебания, возникающие при землетрясении, в электрические сигналы, величина которых пропорциональна амплитуде механических колебаний. Система переработки сигналов состоит из предварительного усилителя, блоков выделения основной частоты, блока автоматического слежения за фазой, в котором полезный сигнал сдвигается по фазе на 180°, и усилителя мощности. Излучатель выполнен в виде виброкомпрессора, генерирующего колебания, находящиеся в противофазе с колебаниями, возникающими при землетрясении, которые способствуют нормализации положения в зоне возникновения землетрясения.

Недостатком известного устройства является его ограниченные функциональные возможности, так как оно применимо лишь при возникновении катастрофического землетрясения. Кроме того, эксплуатация известного устройства сопряжена с высокими затратами вследствие необычно высоких энергозатрат, обусловленных необходимостью излучения мощных механических колебаний в течение достаточно длительного времени.

Задачей настоящего изобретения является повышение эффективности способа предотвращения катастроф при одновременном расширении функциональных возможностей заявленных способа и устройства, применяемого для его реализации и снижение затрат на реализацию способа.

Решение указанных задач обеспечивается новым способом предотвращения катастроф путем оперативного прогнозирования зарождающейся катастрофы и выработки сигналов, нормализующих положение в зоне предполагаемой катастрофы, который реализуется при помощи нового устройства.

В соответствии с изобретением способ предотвращения катастроф осуществляется посредством регистрации и обработки сигналов, характеризующих положение в зоне предполагаемой катастрофы, при этом обрабатывают сигналы светового излучения от элемента, соответствующего зоне предполагаемой катастрофы, при помощи оптической системы, состоящей из чувствительных элементов, выполненных из ориентированных кристаллов, расположенных последовательно по направлению воспринимаемого излучения, причем формируют в ней нормированное излучение для нормализации положения в зоне предполагаемой катастрофы; при этом

7                2148845                8

предпочтительно: проводить непрерывное сканирование различных участков элемента, соответствующего зоне предполагаемой катастрофы, определяя участок зарождения катастрофы по увеличению характеристик излучения, выходящего из оптической системы, в сравнении с характеристиками излучения других участков; участков зарождения катастрофы природного характера определять по увеличению характеристик излучения, соответствующего этому участку на 20 - 28% в сравнении с характеристиками излучения двух участков; участок зарождения катастрофы техногенного характера определять по увеличению характеристик излучения, соответствующего этому участку на 10 - 12% в сравнении с характеристиками излучения других участков.

В соответствии с изобретением устройство для предотвращения катастроф содержит преобразователь сигналов, характеризующих положение в зоне предполагаемой катастрофы, систему регистрации сигналов и излучатель, генерирующий сигналы, способствующие нормализации в этой зоне, при этом преобразователь сигналов состоит из элемента, соответствующего зоне предполагаемой катастрофы, и оптической системы, содержащей чувствительные элементы, изготовленные из ориентированных кристаллов, расположенных последовательно по направлению воспринимаемого светового излучения, которые выполнены в виде идентичных кубиков, взаимно смещенных и имеющих различную ориентацию оптических осей, причем соответствующие плоскости кубиков расположены параллельно, стеклянную сферу, в которой размещены кубики, образующие с ней непрерывную прозрачную структуру, и датчик нормированного излучения, соединенный с последним по направлению распространения излучения кубиком посредством оптического волокна, при этом датчик подключен к процессорной системе, снабженной пакетом программ обработки сигналов датчика; при этом предпочтительно: преобразователь сигналов выполнять в виде сочетания оптической системы и карты местности, на которой предполагается возникновение катастрофического землетрясения; преобразователь сигналов выполнять в виде сочетания оптической системы и системы телеметрии с монитором, на котором воспроизводится элемент, соответствующий зоне предполагаемой техногенной катастрофы; пакет программ процессорной системы снабжать всевозможными параметрами зон предполагаемых катастроф.

В основу настоящего изобретения положена разработанная заявителем теория волнового синтеза в сочетании с формулой общей реальность (см. Диссертация на соискание ученой степени доктора физико-математических наук, Г.П. Грабовой, "Исследование и анализ фундаментальных определений оптических систем для прогноза землетрясений и катастроф производственных объектов", М., Из-во РАЕН, 1999, с.с. 9 - 19). В соответствии с теорией волнового синтеза реальность можно рассматривать как периодическое пересечение стационарных областей с динамическими, при этом в зонах пересечений возникает синтез динамической волны - со стационарной. В кристаллах аналогичный процесс позволяет путем решения обратной задачи получить из стационарной среды в форме кристалла динамические компоненты волнового синтеза, т.е. фазу времени. При определенном расположении кристаллов в пространстве происходит нормирование среды, являющейся источником определенного элемента света. Таким образом появляется возможность нормировать среду, информация о которой содержится в элементе света. Кроме того, можно определить время отклонения от нормы после того как ресурсы оптической системы исчерпаны, например, определить время землетрясения или катастрофы. Нормализации положения в зоне предполагаемой катастрофы способствует использование излучателя, который является в виде микропроцессора, нормализация положения в зоне предполагаемой катастрофы осуществляется посредством оптической системы, состоящей из ориентированных кристаллов, распложенных последовательно по направлению воспринимаемого светового излучения, в которую поступает информация от излучающей среды. В качестве излучающей среды может использоваться либо карта местности, либо система телеметрии с монитором. При поступлении света от излучающей среды на чувствительные элементы оптической системы начальное действие нормирования излучающей среды первым кристаллом происходит в момент, когда элемент света, исходящий из третьего кристалла, проходит через четвертый кристалл, и следующее действие нормирования осуществляется при прохождении элемента света через все кристаллы. Свет выбран в качестве носителя информации в связи с тем, что это позволит визуализировать и регистрировать законы связей, устанавливаемых формулой общей реальности. Усилить процесс можно использованием лазерного излучения. В качестве

9          2148845          10

источника получения выходной информации может быть использован датчик нормированного излучения, выполненный, например, в виде датчика температуры, соединенного с последним чувствительным элементом. Регистрация сигналов, поступающих с датчика, осуществятся при помощи процессорной системы, к которой подключены датчик и излучатель. Использование в процессорной системе пакета программ, содержащих всевозможные параметры зон предполагаемых катастроф, позволяет повысить эффективность заявленного устройства. В общем случае заявленные способ и устройство позволяют преобразовать на уменьшение или - на предотвращение информацию в форме световых импульсов о катастрофах как природного, так и техногенного характера, при этом прогнозирование и профилактика всевозможных катастрофических явлений может проводится из любой точки пространства.

Приложенные чертежи изображают: фиг. 1 - расположение чувствительных элементов в оптической системе (вид в проекции на плоскость OX, OZ, где OX - направление горизонтальное, OZ - вертикальное), фиг. 2 - расположение чувствительных элементов в оптической системе (вид в проекции на плоскость OX, OY), фиг. 3 - общий вид устройства, используемого для осуществления способа предотвращения катастроф.

Устройство содержит: чувствительные элементы 1, 2, 3, 4, 5, 6, и 7, выполненные в виде кубиков одинакового размера, расположенных в стеклянной сфере 8 и образующих с ней монолитную прозрачную систему, оптическое волокно 9, соединяющее последний чувствительный элемент с датчиком нормированного излучения 10, лазер 11, элемент 12, соответствующий зоне предполагаемой катастрофы, выполненный, например, в виде карты местности, усилитель 13 сигналов, поступающих с датчика, установленный на входе процессорной системы 14, снабженной пакетом программ обработки сигналов, поступающих с датчика, и подключенной к дисплею 15 и к излучателю 16 сигналов, способствующих нормализации положения в зоне предполагаемой катастрофы, и объект 17, генерирующий биосигналы.

Количество чувствительных элементов в оптической системе может быть выбрано равным 7, 14 и т.п. Чувствительные элементы 1 - 7 изготавливаются из кристаллов, например из горного хрусталя или алмазов, и выполняются в виде кубиков, имеющих одинаковые размеры, например, с длиной грани 20 мм. При фиксации кубиков материалом стеклянной сферы 8 боковые грани всех кубиков располагаются параллельно. Расположение кубиков 1 - 7 в сфере 8 и ориентация их оптических осей выбраны так, что происходит профилактика катастрофических явлений, например землетрясений с осуществлением гармонизации. Кубики смещены в двух взаимно перпендикулярных плоскостях, как это показано на фиг. 1 и фиг. 2. Выходные параметры оптической системы регистрируются с использованием датчика нормированного излучения 10, располагаемого со стороны сферы 8, обратной по отношению к обращенной к карте местности 12. Датчик 10 предпочтительно выполнять в виде малоинерционного, высокочувствительного пленочного элемента, служащего, например, датчиком температуры. Использование лазера 11 позволяет повысить точность измерения сигналов, поступающих с датчика 10. Применение объекта, генерирующего биосигналы, дополнительно способствует нормализации положения в зоне предполагаемой катастрофы. Работа устройства рассматривается при описании заявленного способа предотвращения катастроф.

В соответствии с заявленным способом световое излучение, поступающее от элемента 12, соответствующего зоне предполагаемой катастрофы, выполненного, например, в виде полномасштабной карты местности, направляют на оптическую систему, состоящую из стеклянной сферы 8, в которой размещены чувствительные элементы 1 - 7, выполненные из ориентированных кристаллов, расположенных последовательно по направлению воспринимаемого светового излучения. При преобразовании светового излучения в такой оптической системе (см. фиг. 3) происходит выделение максимально нормированной формы светового объема. Нормирование осуществляется при прохождении элемента света через чувствительные элементы 1 - 7, взаимное расположение которых вызывает гармонизацию этого светового объема, что в свою очередь нормализует положение в зоне предполагаемой катастрофы. При этом степень уменьшения катастрофического явления находится в соответствии с величиной нормирования светового объема. Сигналы с датчика нормированного излучения 10 после прохождения усилителя 13 передаются в процессорную систему 14, содержащую пакет программ обработки поступающих сигналов. После обработки сигналов на дисплее 5 получают изображение характеристик сигналов. При прогнозировании катастрофического явления активизируется излучатель 16 и в зону предполагаемой катастрофы посылаются

11                    2148845                    12

дополнительные сигналы, способствующие нормализации положения в этой зоне. Предпочтительно проводить непрерывное сканирование различных участков элемента 12, соответствующего зоне предполагаемой катастрофы, посредством последовательного поглощения излучения, поступающего от элемента 12 на всех чувствительных элементах 1 - 7. Участок зарождения катастрофы при этом определяют по увеличению характеристик излучения этого участка в сравнении с характеристиками излучения других участков. При зарождении катастрофы природного характера, например землетрясения, участок зарождения катастрофы имеет характеристики излучения, на 20 - 28% превышающие характеристики других участков элемента 12. При увеличении характеристик излучения менее чем на 20% катастрофического явления не произойдет, а при увеличении характеристик излучения более чем на 28% можно сделать вывод о развитии катастрофического явления, носящего чрезвычайный характер, при зарождении катастрофы техногенного характера, например, связанного с нарушением технологического цикла ядерного реактора, участок зарождения катастрофы определяют по увеличению характеристик излучения на 10 - 12%. При увеличении характеристик излучения менее чем на 10% катастрофического явления не будет, а при увеличении характеристик излучения более чем на 12% можно ожидать экстремального развития событий.

Приведем примеры осуществления заявленного способа с использованием опытного образца заявленного устройства, содержащего оптическую систему, состоящую из стеклянной сферы, в которой последовательно распределены семь чувствительных элементов, изготовленных из горного хрусталя, выполненных в виде кубиков одинакового размера с длиной грани 20 мм. К последнему по направлению распространения светового излучения кубику через оптическое волокно подключен датчик нормированного излучения, выполненный в виде тонкопленочного датчика температуры. Датчик через усилитель присоединен к входу процессорной системы, выполненный с возможностью ускоренного расчета четырехкратного интегратора.

Пример 1. Исследовалось зарождение катастрофического землетрясения в районе Камчатки. Стеклянную сферу 8 с чувствительными элементами 1 - 7 размещали на расстоянии 250 мм от полномасштабной карты Камчатки, при этом датчик нормиро-

ванного излучения 10 располагался на поверхности сферы 8, противоположной той, которая была обращена к карте. Сигналы, поступающие с датчика 10, проходили через усилитель 13 и поступали на процессорную систему 14, где непрерывно обрабатывались, регистрировались и выводились на дисплей 15. Измерения проводились в период, начавшийся в 09 ч 03 мин 26 июня 1999 г. Было спрогнозировано возникновение землетрясения магнитудой 5,1 в районе Камчатки, которое произошло 09 ч 03 мин 03 июля 1999 г., причем занижение магнитуды в результате использования заявленного устройства составило 0,4 балла.

Пример 2. При тех же условиях, что и в предыдущем примере проводилось сканирование элемента 12, соответствующего зоне предполагаемого землетрясения - карте Японии. Было спрогнозировано возникновение землетрясения с магнитудой 6,2, которое произошло 09 ч 03 мин 03 июля 1999 г. Занижение магнитуды в сравнении с первоначально спрогнозированной величиной составило 0,8 балла .

Пример 3. В условиях, аналогичных примеру 1, сканировалась карта Аляски. Было спрогнозировано точное время возникновения землетрясения с магнитудой 4,8, которое произошло в 19 ч 26 мин 04 июля 1999 г., причем занижение величины магнитуды составляло 0,5 балла.

Пример 4. В условиях, аналогичных примеру 1, проводили сканирование карты Филиппин. Было спрогнозировано точное время возникновения землетрясения с магнитудой 4,0, которое состоялось в 13 ч 32 мин 04 июля 1999 г., причем занижение магнитуды в результате использования заявленного устройства составляло 0,2 балла.

Анализ полученных данных показывает, что во всех случаях получено полное подтверждение прогнозной фазы за 7 суток до начала с точным указанием времени начала землетрясения. Величина занижения магнитуды в результате использования заявленного устройства находилась в диапазоне 0,2 - 0,8.

Преимуществами заявленных способа и устройства для его осуществления являются повышение эффективности за счет точного прогнозирования начала возникновения катастрофических явлений, возможность дистанционной нормализации положения в зонах предполагаемых катастроф. Одновременные заявленные способ и устройство для его осуществления имеют в сравнении с известными более широкую область применения, поскольку могут быть использованы

13                    2148845                    14

для приготовления и предотвращения катастроф как природного, так и техногенного характера при полном соблюдении экологической чистоты при их использовании. Кроме того, снижаются затраты на реализацию

способа вследствие простоты операций способа и возможности многократного использования устройства, при помощи которого осуществляется способ.

## ФОРМУЛА ИЗОБРЕТЕНИЯ

1. Способ предотвращения катастроф, включающий регистрацию и обработку сигналов, характеризующих положение в зоне предполагаемой катастрофы, *отличающийся* тем, что обрабатывают сигналы светового излучения от элемента, соответствующего зоне предполагаемой катастрофы, при помощи оптической системы, состоящей из чувствительных элементов, выполненных из ориентированных кристаллов, расположенных последовательно по направлению воспринимаемого излучения, при этом формируют в ней нормированное излучение для нормализации положения в зоне предполагаемой катастрофы.

2. Способ по п.1, *отличающийся* тем, что проводят непрерывное сканирование различных участков элемента, соответствующего зоне предполагаемой катастрофы, при этом участок зарождения катастрофы определяют по увеличению характеристик излучения, выходящего из оптической системы в сравнении с характеристиками излучения других участков.

3. Способ по п.2, *отличающийся* тем, что участок зарождения катастрофы природного характера определяют по увеличению характеристик излучения, соответствующего этому участку на 20 - 28% в сравнении с характеристиками излучения других участков.

4. Способ по п.2, *отличающийся* тем, что участок зарождения катастрофы техногенного характера определяют по увеличению характеристик излучения, соответствующего этому участку на 10 - 12% в сравнении с характеристиками излучения других участков.

5. Устройство для предотвращения катастроф, содержащее преобразователь сигналов, характеризующих положение в зоне предполагаемой катастрофы, систему регистрации

сигналов и излучатель, генерирующий сигналы, способствующие нормализации положения в этой зоне, *отличающееся* тем, что преобразователь сигналов состоит из элемента, соответствующего зоне предполагаемой катастрофы, и оптической системы, содержащей чувствительные элементы, изготовленные из ориентированных кристаллов, расположенных последовательно по направлению воспринимаемого светового излучения, которые выполнены в виде идентичных кубиков, взаимно смещенных и имеющих различную ориентацию оптических осей, при этом соответствующие плоскости кубиков расположены параллельно, стеклянную сферу, в которой размещены кубики, образующие с ней непрерывную прозрачную структуру, и датчик нормированного излучения, соединенный с последним по направлению распространения излучения кубиком посредством оптического волокна, причем датчик подключен к процессорной системе, снабженной пакетом программ обработки сигналов датчика.

6. Устройство по п.5, *отличающееся* тем, что преобразователь сигналов выполнен в виде сочетания оптической системы и карты местности, на которой предполагается возникновение катастрофического землетрясения.

7. Устройство по п.5, *отличающееся* тем, что преобразователь сигналов выполнен в виде сочетания оптической системы и системы телеметрии с монитором, на котором воспроизводится элемент, соответствующий зоне предполагаемой техногенной катастрофы.

8. Устройство по п.5, *отличающееся* тем, что пакет программ процессорной системы включает всевозможные параметры зон предполагаемых катастроф.

15                              2148845                              16

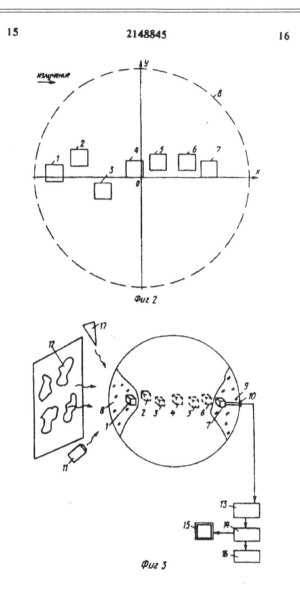

Фиг 2

Фиг 3

Заказ λЗ и          Подписное
ФИПС, Рег. ЛР № 040921
121858, Москва, Бережковская наб., д.30, корп.1.
Научно-исследовательское отделение по
подготовке официальных изданий

—  —  —

Отпечатано на полиграфической базе ФИПС
121873, Москва, Бережковская наб., 24, стр.2
Отделение выпуска официальных изданий

**МЧС РОССИИ**
## АГЕНТСТВО
**ПО МОНИТОРИНГУ И
ПРОГНОЗИРОВАНИЮ
ЧРЕЗВЫЧАЙНЫХ СИТУАЦИЙ**
ВНИИ ГОЧС

121352, г. Москва, ул. Давыдковская, 7
(095) 449-83-44, 443-83-15 (факс)

7.07.99 ____ № 4Ð/275

На № _____ от _____

Президенту РАЕН
академику Кузнецову О.Л.

Уважаемый Олег Леонидович !

Академик РАЕН Грабовой Григорий Петрович, используя созданные им формулу общей реальности и теорию волнового синтеза для профилактического прогноза землетрясений и катастроф, перевёл кристаллический модуль прогноза в цифровую форму. В качестве фактического материала доказывающего то, что указанный модуль позволяет реализовать профилактический прогноз землетрясений были использованы статистические данные о землетрясениях предоставляемые Центральной опытно-методической экспедицией геофизической службы Российской Академии Наук. Испытания цифровой модели прибора проводилось на землетрясениях прошлого и будущего. На землетрясениях прошлого - переводом исходных параметров модели до начала землетрясений. На землетрясениях будущего - программной обработкой электронной карты местности и экстраполяционных данных мониторинга поверхности Земли со спутников предоставленных ВНИИ ГОЧС. В качестве фактически произошедших землетрясений прошлого использовались данные о 1000 зафиксированных землетрясениях за период с 07 января 1901 года по 04 июля 1918 года ( данные приведены в приложении на 18 листах). В качестве землетрясений будущего в июле 1999 года получено подтверждение прогноза для всех областей где проводилась программная обработка электронной карты местности (например: за период времени с 09ч 03 мин по 19 часов 26 минут 03 июля 1999 года подтверждены землетрясения в районах Камчатки в 09ч 03 мин. М 5.1, Японии в 09 ч 30 мин М 6.2, Аляски в 19ч 26 мин М 5.4, а за период времени 05ч 38 мин по 13ч 32 мин 04 июля 1999 года подтверждены землетрясения в районах Филиппин в 05 ч 38 мин М 4.8, Камчатки в 13 ч 32 мин М 4.0.) Во всех случаях получено полное подтверждение прогнозной фазы. В настоящее время для перевода параметров кристаллического модуля в цифровой форме в форму микропроцессора, работающего длительный интервал времени без дополнительных расчётов, необходимо провести перевод в цифровую форму характеристик лазерного излучения с физического источника.

с уважением

Руководитель Агентства          / Шахраманьян М. А. /

000086

# ПАТЕНТ

## НА ИЗОБРЕТЕНИЕ
## № 2163419

Российским агентством по патентам и товарным знакам на основании Патентного закона Российской Федерации, введенного в действие 14 октября 1992 года, выдан настоящий патент на изобретение

### СИСТЕМА ПЕРЕДАЧИ ИНФОРМАЦИИ

Патентообладатель(ли):

*Грабовой Григорий Петрович*

по заявке № 2000117595, дата поступления: 06.07.2000

Приоритет от 06.07.2000

Автор(ы) изобретения:

*Грабовой Григорий Петрович*

Патент действует на всей территории Российской Федерации в течение 20 лет с **6 июля 2000** г. при условии своевременной уплаты пошлины за поддержание патента в силе

Зарегистрирован в Государственном реестре изобретений Российской Федерации

г. Москва, **20 февраля 2001 г.**

Генеральный директор

*А.Д. Корчагин*

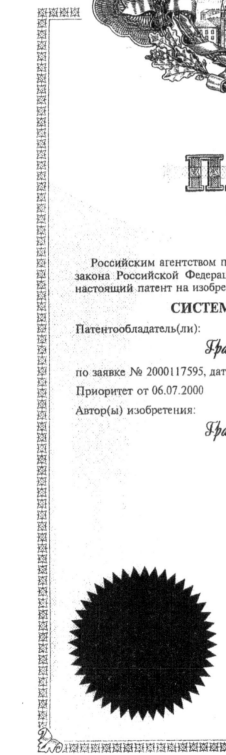

(19) **RU** (11) **2163419** (13) **C1**

(51) 7 H 04 B 10/30

РОССИЙСКОЕ АГЕНТСТВО
ПО ПАТЕНТАМ И ТОВАРНЫМ ЗНАКАМ

(12) **ОПИСАНИЕ ИЗОБРЕТЕНИЯ**
к патенту Российской Федерации

(21) 2000117595/09        (22) 06.07.2000
(24) 06.07.2000
(46) 20.02.2001 Бюл. № 5
(72) Грабовой Г.П.
(71) (73) Грабовой Григорий Петрович
(56)  SU 2111617 A1, 20.05.1998. ГРАБОВОЙ Г.П. Исследование и анализ фундаментальных определений оптических систем для прогноза землетрясений и катастроф производственного характера. - М.: Из-во РАЕН, 1999, с.9-19. БОДЯКИН В.И. Куда идешь, человек? Основы зволюциологии. - М.: СИНТЕГ, 1998, с.29-45, 79-95, 249.
Адрес для переписки: 115230, Москва, Каширское ш. 5-1-66, Копаеву В.Г.

(54) **СИСТЕМА ПЕРЕДАЧИ ИНФОРМАЦИИ**

(57) Изобретение относится к технике связи и может быть использовано в системах беспроводной передачи информации. Технический результат состоит в повышении эксплуатационной надежности системы при одновременном повышении ее помехоустойчивости. В предлагаемой системе передатчик сигналов содержит воспринимающий блок, состоящий из чувствительных элементов сферической формы, изготовленных из стекла, которые при помощи клеевых соединений жестко закреплены на опорном элементе, и установленный на нем сферический модуль, выполненный в виде стеклянной сферы, в которой зафиксированы чувствительные элементы, выполненные в виде идентичных кубиков, изготовленных из кристалла. Приемник сигналов дистанционирован от передатчика и содержит подобные соответствующим элементам воспринимающий блок и дистанционированный от него сферический модуль, который снабжен устройством преобразования излучения в выходные сигналы. Диаметры всех чувствительных элементов, входящих в состав какого-либо воспринимающего блока, должны различаться, например постепенно увеличиваться. При передаче информации оператор активирует чувствительные элементы передатчика сигналов. Затем практически мгновенно излучение активации воспроизводится в чувствительных элементах приемника сигналов и нормируется чувствительными элементами сферического модуля. Выходящее нормированное излучение преобразуется датчиком в электрические сигналы и после обработки в процессоре переданная информация поступает в регистрирующее устройство. 5 з.п.ф-лы, 3 ил.

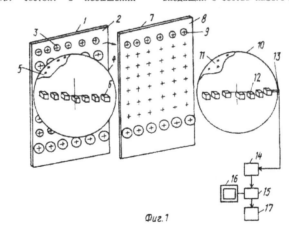

Фиг.1

5                    2163419                    6

Изобретение относится к области техники связи и может быть использовано в системах передачи информации, в которых применяется беспроводная связь между передатчиком и приемником информации, преимущественно при передаче информации на значительные (тысячи километров) расстояния.

Наиболее близким по технической сущности к заявляемой является система передачи информации, содержащая передающий блок, включающий опорный элемент, на котором жестко закреплены передатчики сигналов, и дистанционированный от него приемный блок, состоящий из опорного элемента с жестко закрепленными на нем приемниками сигналов и устройства, преобразующего излучение в выходные сигналы (см. патент РФ N 2111617, кл. H 04 B 10/00). В известной системе в качестве каналов связи между передатчиком и приемником сигналов используются лазерные лучи. Каждый передатчик сигналов выполнен в виде лазерного генератора с устройством модуляции лазерного пучка сигналом данных, соединенным с источником сигналов данных. Каждый приемник сигналов выполнен в виде фотоприемного устройства и устройства, преобразующего воспринимаемое лазерное модулированное излучение в электрические сигналы данных.

Недостатком известной системы передачи данных является ее низкая эксплуатационная надежность, обусловленная сложностью конструкции системы, в состав которой входят большое количество сложных передатчиков и приемников сигналов с многофункциональными связями и сложные системы прецизионного наведения с подвижными элементами. В известной системе при передаче информации между расположенными на значительных расстояниях друг от друга передатчиком и приемником сигналов, например при передаче информации на тысячи километров с использованием космического аппарата с ретранслятором, задержка передачи информации может составлять десятые доли секунды. Известная система имеет недостаточно высокую помехоустойчивость, так как при возникновении на линии лазерной связи какой-либо преграды возникают помехи в работе системы или срыв передаваемых сигналов.

Задачей изобретения является повышение эксплуатационной надежности системы передачи информации при одновременном обеспечении передачи информации без задержек и повышении помехоустойчивости системы.

Решение указанной задачи обеспечивается новой системой передачи информации, состоящей из передатчика сигналов и дистанционированного от него приемника сигналов, каждый из которых содержит воспринимающий блок, выполненный в виде чувствительных элементов сферической формы, имеющих различные диаметры и жестко закрепленных на поверхности опорного элемента, и сферический модуль, выполненный в виде стеклянной сферы, в которой зафиксированы распределенные в одном направлении и смещенные в двух взаимно перпендикулярных плоскостях чувствительные элементы, выполненные в виде идентичных кубиков, изготовленных из кристалла, причем элементы передатчика подобны элементам приемника сигналов, сферический модуль передатчика сигналов расположен на поверхности опорного элемента, сферический модуль приемника сигналов дистанционирован от его воспринимающего блока и снабжен устройством преобразования излучения в выходные сигналы.

При этом предпочтительно чувствительные элементы сферической формы равномерно распределять по поверхности опорного элемента и центры этих элементов размещать в параллельных плоскостях, на поверхности опорного элемента передатчика сигналов вблизи каждого чувствительного элемента сферической формы выполнять изображение определенной буквы всех букв алфавита или изображение определенной цифры всего ряда натуральных чисел, или изображение определенного символа, чувствительные элементы сферической формы располагать на поверхности опорного элемента в виде одинаковых рядов, чувствительные элементы сферической формы выполнять с постепенно увеличивающимися диаметрами, устройство преобразования излучения в выходные сигналы выполнять в виде датчика, соединенного посредством оптического волокна с кубиком сферического модуля, который наиболее удален от воспринимающего блока приемника излучения, датчик соединять с усилителем, к выходу которого подключен процессор.

В основу настоящего изобретения положен установленный автором принцип подобия, который базируется на разработанной автором теории волнового синтеза в сочетании с формулой общей реальности (см. Диссертация на соискание ученой степени доктора физико-математических наук, Г.П. Грабовой, "Исследование и анализ фундаментальных определений оптических систем для

7                              2163419                          8

прогноза землетрясений и катастроф производственного характера", М., Из-во РАЕН, 1999, с. 9-19).

В соответствии с теорией волнового синтеза реальность можно рассматривать как периодическое пересечение стационарных областей с динамическими, при этом в зонах пересечения возникает синтез динамической волны со стационарной. Любое явление реальности можно определить в виде оптических систем, и поскольку восприятие человека осуществляется образами-элементами света, содержащими информацию, то при передаче информации на первом этапе от генерирующего передаваемую информацию человека к воспринимающему информацию оптическому чувствительному элементу человека можно рассматривать как своеобразную передающую оптическую систему. Передаваемая информация, генерируемая мыслями оператора-человека, воспринимается оптическим чувствительным элементом, на который оператор направляет генерируемую мысль.

Известны различные оптические устройства, например аппарат "Камера-3000", позволяющая фиксировать изменение ауры человека (см. Комков В.Н. "Сенсоры биополя и ауры". "Электронная техника, серия 3, Микроэлектроника", 1999. вып. 1(153), с. 23). Поскольку мысль составляет часть ауры, то и она может быть передана в виде элемента "слабой" оптической системы. Предпочтительно воспринимающий информацию чувствительный элемент выполнять в виде сферы, так как именно сферическая форма чувствительного элемента способствует максимальной активации чувствительного элемента за счет внутреннего отражения.

Излучение активируемых чувствительных элементов сферической формы является световым, при этом каждому оператору, передающему информацию, будут соответствовать индивидуальные характеристики этого излучения, что определяет высокую помехозащищенность заявленной системы. Обеспечение индивидуальной активации чувствительных элементов сферической формы достигается за счет использования набора таких элементов, имеющих различные диаметры, чем определяется различие излучения, испускаемого разными элементами. Предпочтительно использовать набор чувствительных элементов сферической формы, диаметры которых постепенно увеличиваются. Количество чувствительных элементов сферической формы в наборе может быть различным. Предпочтительно количество элементов в наборе выбирать равным сумме

букв, входящих в состав алфавита, и сумме цифр, входящих в состав натурального ряда чисел.

Все чувствительные элементы сферической формы, входящие в состав набора таких элементов, жестко крепятся к поверхности опорного элемента, выполняемого, например, в виде пластины. Опорный элемент с закрепленными на его поверхности чувствительными элементами сферической формы образуют воспринимающий блок. Передатчик и приемник сигналов имеют подобные воспринимающие блоки, что обеспечивает воспроизводство передаваемой информации.

Из теории волнового синтеза и законов квантовой механики следует, что преобразованная в излучение мысль может иметь одновременно два квантовых состояния (см. Грабовой Г.П."Исследования и анализ фундаментальных определений оптических систем в предотвращении катастроф и прогнозно-ориентированном управлении микропроцессорами", "Электронная техника, серия 3, Микроэлектроника", 1999, вып. 1 (153), с. 10).Одно из этих состояний находится на чувствительном элементе передатчика сигналов, а другое - на подобном ему чувствительном элементе приемника сигналов. Для облегчения работы оператора-человека, генерирующего передаваемую информацию, чувствительные элементы сферической формы предпочтительно равномерно распределять по поверхности опорного элемента и располагать центры чувствительных элементов сферической формы в параллельных плоскостях, а также располагать эти элементы в виде одинаковых рядов.

Кроме того, на поверхности опорного элемента передатчика сигналов вблизи каждого чувствительного элемента сферической формы выполняется изображение соответствующей буквы алфавита, цифры или определенного символа. Наряду с использованием на первом этапе передачи информации посредством чувствительных элементов сферической формы может использоваться и сферический модуль, в котором зафиксированы последовательно расположенные чувствительные элементы, выполненные в виде идентичных кубиков, изготовленных из кристалла. При определенном взаимном расположении кубиков в них будет происходить нормализация излучения, инициируемого мыслью оператора-человека, которое характеризует сочетание определенных букв слова.

На втором этапе передачи информации излучение, испускаемое чувствительным элементом сферической формы, в соответствии

9                    2163419                    10

с принципом подобия без каких-либо задержек практически мгновенно воспроизводится в подобном чувствительном элементе сферической формы, входящем в состав воспринимающего блока приемника сигналов. Затем излучение поступает на сферический модуль приемника сигналов, который выполнен подобным сферическому модулю передатчика сигналов. Сферический модуль приемника сигналов выполнен в виде стеклянной сферы, в которой зафиксированы распределенные в одном направлении и смещенные в двух взаимно перпендикулярных плоскостях чувствительные элементы, выполненные в виде идентичных кубиков, изготовленных из кристалла.

После поступления излучения на первый кубик, который наиболее приближен к воспринимающему блоку приемника, начальное нормирование излучения первым кубиком произойдет в момент, когда излучение, исходящее из третьего кубика, проходит четвертый кубик. Следующее действие нормирования осуществляется при прохождении излучения через все кубики. Свет выбран в качестве носителя информации в связи с тем, что это позволяет визуализировать и регистрировать законы связей, устанавливаемых формулой общей реальности. Излучение, испускаемое каким-либо чувствительным элементом сферической формы приемника сигналов, после нормирования в сферическом модуле приемника выходит из кубика, наиболее удаленного от воспринимающего блока приемника, при этом величина выходящего нормированного излучения зависит от диаметра чувствительного элемента сферической формы передатчика сигналов, которому подобен излучающий чувствительный элемент сферической формы приемника сигналов.

Воспринимающий блок и сферический модуль передатчика сигналов выполняются подобными соответствующим элементам приемника сигналов, однако могут иметь различные геометрические размеры. Так, геометрические размеры элементов приемника сигналов могут в 3-5 раз превосходить размеры соответствующих элементов передатчика. В качестве устройства, преобразующего излучение, выходящее из последнего кубика, может использоваться оптический преобразователь, выполненный в виде приемника излучения и микропроцессора, преобразующего интенсивность излучения в цифровые данные, или датчик нормированного излучения, соединенный с последним кубиком посредством оптического волокна и подключенный через усилитель электрического сигнала к процессору, имеющему программное управление.

Приложенные чертежи изображают: фиг. 1 - общий вид системы передачи информации (вид в изометрии), фиг. 2 - воспринимающий блок (вид спереди), фиг. 3 - отдельный чувствительный элемент сферической формы, жестко закрепленный на опорном элементе.

Заявленная система передачи информации содержит воспринимающий блок приемника сигналов 1, содержащий опорный элемент 2, по поверхности которого равномерно распределены жестко закрепленные на нем чувствительные элементы сферической формы 3; сферический модуль передатчика сигналов 4,содержащий стеклянную сферу 5, в которой зафиксированы чувствительные элементы 6, выполненные в виде идентичных кубиков; воспринимающий блок приемника сигналов 7, который подобен аналогичному блоку передатчика сигналов и также содержит опорный элемент 8 и чувствительные элементы сферической формы 9, жестко закрепленные на нем; сферический модуль приемника сигналов 10, который подобен аналогичному модулю передатчика сигналов и также содержит стеклянную сферу 11, в которой зафиксированы чувствительные элементы 12, выполненные в виде идентичных кубиков; датчик нормированного излучения 13, к которому подключен усилитель 14, присоединенный ко входу процессора 15 с программным управлением, к которому подключены дисплей 16 и регистрирующее устройство 17; при этом каждый чувствительный элемент сферической формы при помощи крепежного элемента 18 жестко зафиксирован на поверхности опорного элемента.

Чувствительные элементы сферической формы 3 и 9 предпочтительно изготавливать из прозрачного материала, например из стекла. Диаметры всех чувствительных элементов, входящих в состав какого-либо воспринимающего блока, например в состав блока приемника сигналов 1, должны различаться между собой, при этом каждый диаметр соответствует определенной букве, цифре или символу. Предпочтительно, чтобы диаметры постепенно увеличивались, например, от 1 до 53 мм. Аналогично должны различаться между собой и диаметры всех чувствительных элементов сферической формы 9, входящие в состав воспринимающего блока приемника сигналов 7. Каждый чувствительный элемент сферической формы жестко крепится к поверхности соответствующего опорного элемента при помощи крепежного элемента 18, например посред-

11                    2163419                    12

ством клеевого соединения. Чувствительные элементы сферической формы предпочтительно располагать на поверхности опорного элемента в виде одинаковых рядов (см. фиг. 2, часть элементов не указана), при этом диаметры элементов постепенно увеличиваются в каждом ряду.

Каждый сферический модуль 4 или 10 (см. фиг. 1) содержит стеклянную сферу. Например, сферический модуль передатчика сигналов 4 содержит стеклянную сферу 5, в которой зафиксированы распределенные вдоль прямой, перпендикулярной поверхности опорного элемента 2, чувствительные элементы 6, выполненные в виде идентичных кубиков, которые образуют со сферой монолитную систему. Количество кубиков может быть равным 7, 14 и т.п. Обычно используется семь кубиков. Кубики 6 или 12 изготавливаются из кристалла, например из алмаза или горного хрусталя. Последовательно расположенные в сферическом модуле кубики имеют различную ориентацию оптических осей. Грани смежных кубиков расположены параллельно, а сами кубики смещены в двух взаимно перпендикулярных плоскостях. Сферический модуль передатчика сигналов 4 предпочтительно располагать в центре опорного элемента 2. Сферический модуль приемника сигналов 10 дистанцирован от воспринимающего блока приемника сигналов 7 предпочтительно на расстояние 200 - 1000 мм.

Заявленная система передачи информации работает следующим образом. В качестве оператора (не указан), передающего информацию, выступает человек, генерирующий мысль. В течение 0,1-5 с (время зависит от биоэнергетического поля человека) оператор активирует чувствительные элементы 3 воспринимающего блока передатчика сигналов 1. Поступающие из оптической системы оператора сигналы усиливаются чувствительными элементами сферической формы 3 передатчика сигналов и без каких-либо задержек практически мгновенно воспроизводятся в соответствующих чувствительных элементах 9 приемника сигналов, при этом сигнал, передаваемый каким-либо элементом передатчика 3, воспроизводится подобным элементом 9 приемника в соответствии с принципом подобия. Излучение чувствитель-

ных элементов 9 приемника сигналов преобразуется затем чувствительными элементами 12 сферического модуля приемника сигналов 10. Объем передаваемой информации соответствует объему информации, содержащемуся в генерируемом оптическом образе. Например, информация, содержащаяся в считывающем устройстве компакт-диска, после восприятия ее оператором может быть полностью передана на приемник сигналов.

При прохождении излучения через элементы 12, выполненные в виде кубиков, происходит нормирование формы светового объема, определяемое взаимным расположением кубиков. Каждому диаметру чувствительного элемента сферической формы 9 при этом соответствует определенная величина нормированного излучения, выходящего из наиболее удаленного от воспринимающего блока приемника сигналов 8 кубика 12. Нормированное излучение, выходящее из этого кубика, через оптическое волокно передается на датчик нормированного излучения 13, и поступающие с датчика электрические сигналы после прохождения через усилитель 14 поступают на процессор 15 с программным управлением. Обработанные в процессоре 15 сигналы, соответствующие переданной информации, в виде букв, цифр и(или) символов могут быть выведены на дисплей 16 и поступают на устройство регистрации 17, которое может быть снабжено блоками записи и хранения поступающей информации для ее последующей обработки.

Заявленная система передачи в сравнении с известной системой обладает значительно более высокой эксплуатационной надежностью, поскольку конструкция заявленной системы предельно упрощена и отсутствуют какие-либо подвижные элементы. Заявленная система в отличие от известной обеспечивает передачу информации на значительные (многие тысячи километров) расстояния без каких-либо задержек. Кроме того, заявленная система имеет более высокую помехоустойчивость, так как находящиеся между ее приемником и передатчиком сигналов преграды не являются помехами для передачи информации.

## ФОРМУЛА ИЗОБРЕТЕНИЯ

1. Система передачи информации, состоящая из передатчика сигналов и дистанцированного от него приемника сигналов, каждый из которых содержит воспринимаю-

щий блок, выполненный в виде оптических чувствительных элементов сферической формы, имеющих различные диаметры, и жестко закрепленных на поверхности опорного

13                    2163419                    14

элемента, и сферический модуль, выполненный в виде стеклянной сферы, в которой зафиксированы распределенные в одном направлении и смещенные в двух взаимно перпендикулярных плоскостях оптические чувствительные элементы, выполненные в виде идентичных кубиков, изготовленных из кристалла горного хрусталя или алмаза, причем элементы передатчика подобны элементам приемника сигналов, сферический модуль передатчика расположен на поверхности опорного элемента его воспринимающего блока, а оптические чувствительные элементы передатчика воспринимают генерируемую оператором передаваемую информацию, сферический модуль приемника сигналов дистанцирован от его воспринимающего блока и соединен с устройством преобразования излучения в выходные сигналы.

2. Система по п.1, *отличающаяся* тем, что оптические чувствительные элементы сферической формы равномерно распределены по поверхности опорного элемента, при этом центры этих элементов расположены в параллельных плоскостях.

3. Система по п.1 или 2, *отличающаяся* тем, что на поверхности опорного элемента передатчика сигналов вблизи каждого оптического чувствительного элемента сферической формы выполнено изображение определенной буквы всех букв алфавита, или определенной цифры всего ряда натуральных чисел, или определенного символа произвольной формы.

4. Система по п.1, *отличающаяся* тем, что оптические чувствительные элементы сферической формы расположены на поверхности опорного элемента в виде одинаковых рядов.

5. Система по любому из предшествующих пунктов, *отличающаяся* тем, что диаметры различных оптических чувствительных элементов сферической формы постепенно увеличиваются.

6. Система по п.1, *отличающаяся* тем, что поверхность опорного элемента расположена ортогонально направлению, в котором распределены кубики сферического модуля.

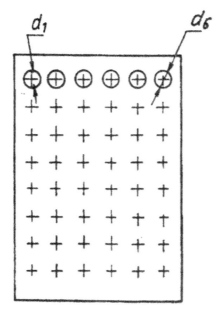

*Фиг. 2*

15                    2163419                    16

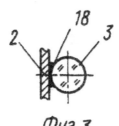

*Фиг. 3*

Заказ      5и          Подписное
ФИПС, Рег. ЛР № 040921
121858, Москва, Бережковская наб., д.30, корп.1,
Научно-исследовательское отделение по
подготовке официальных изданий

Отпечатано на полиграфической базе ФИПС
121873, Москва, Бережковская наб., 24, стр.2
Отделение выпуска официальных изданий

**ПРЕДПРИЯТИЕ ПЕРСПЕКТИВНЫХ ИССЛЕДОВАНИЙ**
**"НАУЧНЫЙ ЦЕНТР"**

103460, Москва,  Зеленоград, Южная пром. зона,                            Телефон: 530-98-30
проезд 4806, дом 4, Корп.стр.1, ППИ"НЦ".
р/с 40602810300050001000
Зеленогр. Филиал АКБ  «Московский Индустриальный Банк»
БИК 04453435  к/с 30101810300000000435

д.т.н. проф. Гаряинов С.А./

**ВЫВОДЫ ИЗ ПРОТОКОЛА ИСПЫТАНИИ ЛАБОРАТОРНОГО ОБРАЗЦА ИНФОРМАЦИОННОГО МОДУЛЯ - СИСТЕМЫ ПЕРЕДАЧИ ИНФОРМАЦИИ ОТ 14 АВГУСТА 2000 Г.**

   Из протокола испытаний Лабораторного образца информационного модуля, созданного и рассчитанного Грабовым Г.П. доказано, что с использованием системы передачи информации слабых сигналов на уровне мысленных концентраций зарегистрированы сигналы приемником оптического излучения. Передача мысли осуществлялась мысленной концентрацией оператора на сенсоре мыслеобразов или иначе на воспринимающем блоке передатчика сигнала ( в отчете рис. 1 на стр. 4, блок 1-а), выполненном в виде чувствительных элементов сферической формы и по принципу подобия на основе авторской теории волнового синтеза и формулы общей реальности мысль передавалась на приемник сигналов, имеющий подобный воспринимающий блок (на рис. 1 стр.4, что соответствует передающему узлу 1-6). С приемника сигналов мысль регистрировалась изменением интенсивности оптического излучения. Учитывая, что в соответствии с теорией волнового синтеза, кристаллическая система, описанная в патенте Грабового Г.П. «Способ предотвращения катастроф и устройство для его осуществления» в соответствии с заявкой на изобретение № 99120836/28 (022309) от 07.10.99.была пересчитана на сферу, содержащую распределенные сферы меньшего размера и при этом передача мысли была зафиксирована, следует, что передатчик и приемник оптических элементов может быть осуществлена в виде сфер и кубиков.

   Так как концентрацию мысли осуществляли разные операторы можно сделать вывод, что передачу мыслеобразов, с использованием данной системы передачи информации, может осуществлять любой человек.

**Научный руководитель**
 **отделения аспирантуры ППИ «НЦ»**               д.ф.-м.н., д.т.н.  Г.П. Грабовой

                                                             к.т.н. Б.И.Черный

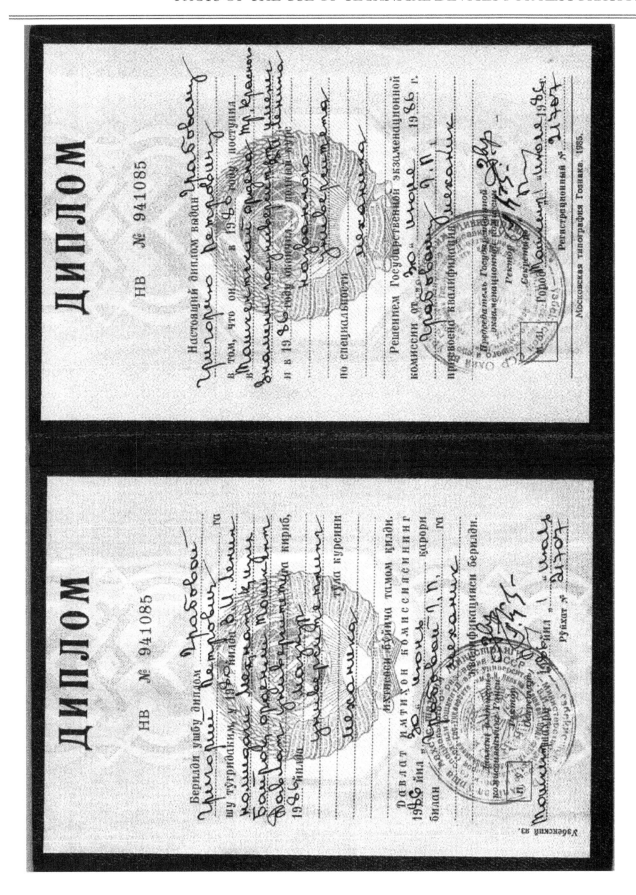

**РЕШЕНИЕМ**

Диссертационного совета Новосибирского научного Центра "Ноосферные знания и технологии" РАЕН

протокол № 24 от "29 "октября 1998 г.

Грабовому Григорию Петровичу

присвоена ученая степень **ДОКТОРА** Российской Академии Естественных Наук

по специальности "Ноосферные знания и технологии"

Председатель диссертационного Совета О.Н. Лебедев

Ученый секретарь Совета А.С. Овсянников

**ДИПЛОМ доктора**

Российской Академии Естественных Наук

Д–РАЕН № 0071

Президент Академии О.Л. Кузнецов

Главный Ученый секретарь Академии В.Г. Тымянский

Москва

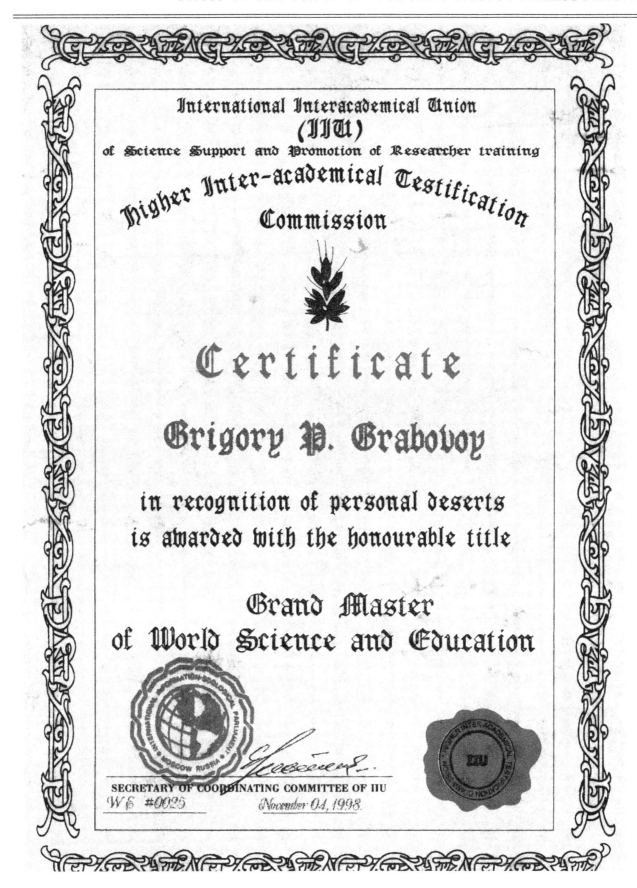

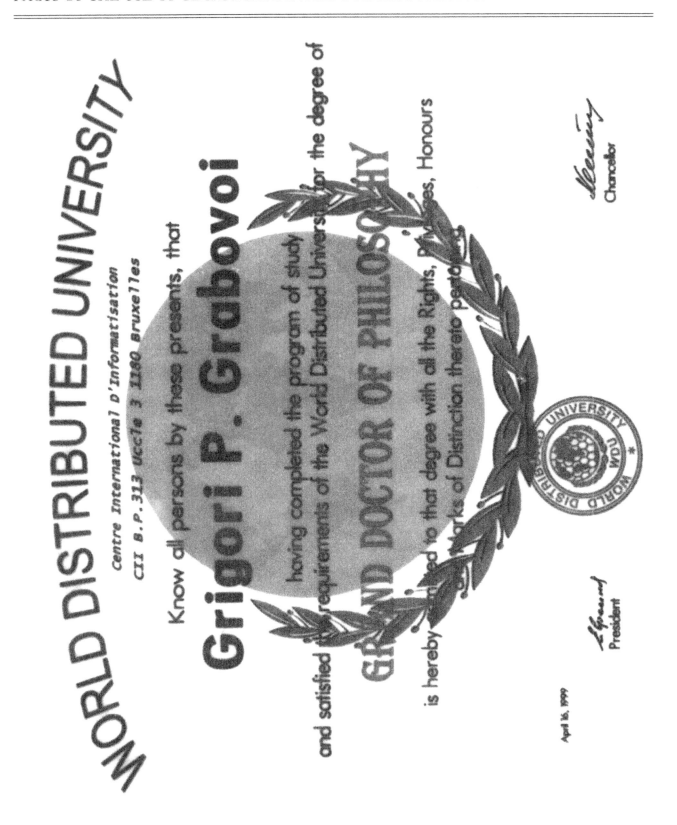

WORLD DISTRIBUTED UNIVERSITY

Centre International d'Informatisation

CII B.P.313 Uccle 3 1180 Bruxelles

Know all persons by these presents, that

Grigori P. Grabovoi

having completed the program of study and satisfied the requirements of the World Distributed University for the degree of

GRAND DOCTOR OF PHILOSOPHY

is hereby admitted to that degree with all the Rights, Privileges, Honours and Marks of Distinction thereto pertaining.

April 16, 1999

Chancellor

President

# Российская Федерация

# ВЫСШИЙ
## АТТЕСТАЦИОННО-КВАЛИФИКАЦИОННЫЙ
# КОМИТЕТ

# ДИПЛОМ
## ДОКТОРА НАУК

## ДТ № 0129

### Москва

**Российская Федерация**

Решением
Высшего аттестационно-квалификационного комитета
от 20 апреля 1999 г.  № 62

*Грабовому*

*Григорию Петровичу*

присуждена ученая степень

## ДОКТОРА
## ТЕХНИЧЕСКИХ НАУК

Председатель Высшего
аттестационно-квалификационного комитета

Главный ученый секретарь Высшего
аттестационно-квалификационного комитета

Р о с с и й с к а я  Ф е д е р а ц и я

ВЫСШАЯ
межакадемическая
АТТЕСТАЦИОННАЯ
КОМИССИЯ

# ДИПЛОМ
## ДОКТОРА НАУК

ДФМ № 0052

Москва

Р о с с и й с к а я  Ф е д е р а ц и я
Решением
Высшей межакадемической аттестационной комиссии
от ___4 июня___ 19 99 г. № 0199-1Д

*Грабовому*

*Григорию Петровичу*

ПРИСУЖДЕНА УЧЕНАЯ СТЕПЕНЬ
## ДОКТОРА
*Физико-математических наук*

Председатель
Высшей межакадемической аттестационной комиссии

Главный ученый секретарь
Высшей межакадемической аттестационной комиссии

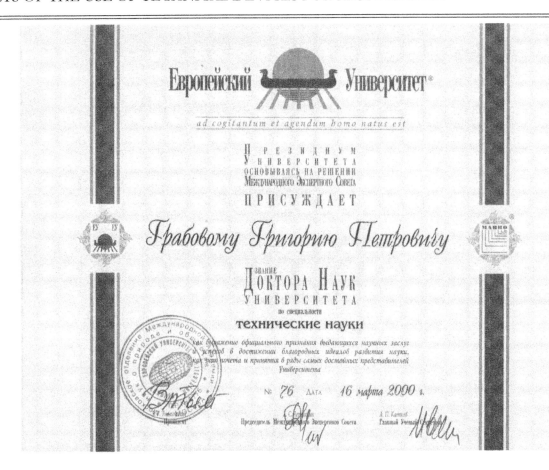

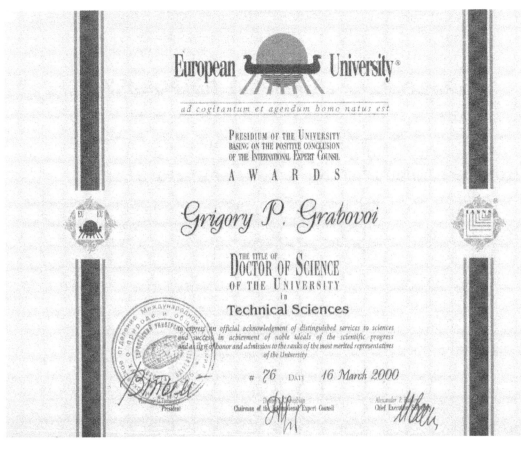

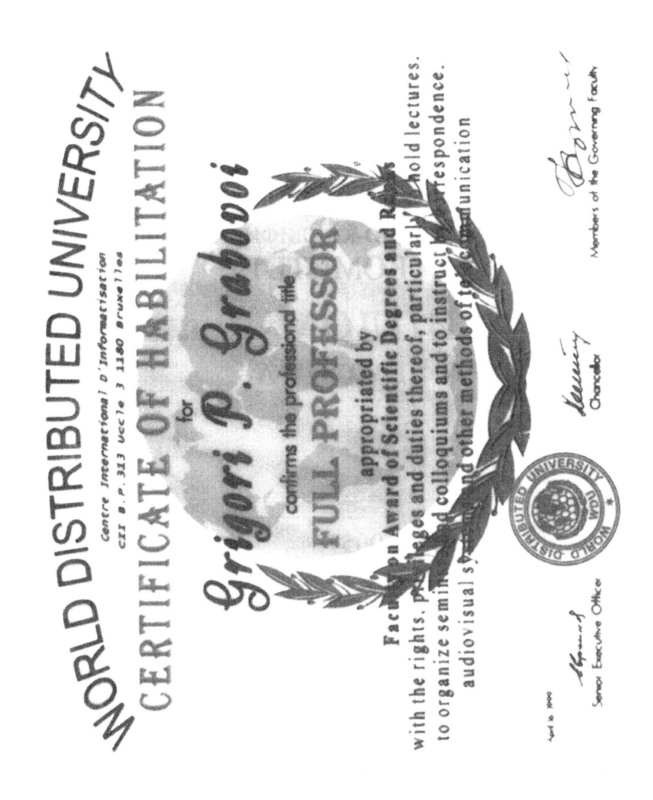

# Российская Федерация

# ВЫСШИЙ
## АТТЕСТАЦИОННО-КВАЛИФИКАЦИОННЫЙ КОМИТЕТ

# ДИПЛОМ
## ПРОФЕССОРА

### ПР № 0057

### Москва

## Российская Федерация
Решением
Высшего аттестационно-квалификационного комитета
от 20 апреля 1999 г. № 62

*Грабовому*

*Григорию Петровичу*

присвоено ученое звание
## ПРОФЕССОРА
по специальности 05.02.
"Безопасность особо сложных объектов"

Председатель Высшего
аттестационно-квалификационного комитета

Главный ученый секретарь Высшего
аттестационно-квалификационного комитета

# Российская Федерация

# ВЫСШАЯ
### межакадемическая
# АТТЕСТАЦИОННАЯ
# КОМИССИЯ

# АТТЕСТАТ
## ПРОФЕССОРА

ПР  N    0182

### Москва

# Российская Федерация
Решением
## Высшей межакадемической аттестационной комиссии
от 15 июля      19 99 г.  N  0208-Л

*Грабовому*

*Григорию     Петровичу*

ПРИСВОЕНО УЧЕНОЕ ЗВАНИЕ
## ПРОФЕССОРА

специальности «Аналитические и структурно-
аналитические приборы и системы»

Председатель Высшей аттестационной комиссии
Главный ученый секретарь Высшей аттестационной комиссии

г. Москва

№ _____ 002 _____

Решением Президиума Международной Академии
интеграции науки и бизнеса (МАИНБ)

от "24" _____ 08 _____ 1999 _____ г. (протокол № 40 )

## ГРАБОВОМУ ГРИГОРИЮ ПЕТРОВИЧУ

присвоено ученое звание
**ПРОФЕССОРА МАИНБ**
по специальности

## Системная информатика

Президент Академии

Главный ученый
секретарь

# РОССИЙСКАЯ
## АКАДЕМИЯ ЕСТЕСТВЕННЫХ НАУК

на основании Устава Академии

### ИЗБРАЛА

*Грабового*

*Григория Петровича*

# ДЕЙСТВИТЕЛЬНЫМ ЧЛЕНОМ АКАДЕМИИ

*по секции*

*„Ноосферные знания и технологии"*

*"09" марта* 1998 г.

Президент     О. Кузнецов

Главный
ученый секретарь     В. Тыминский

НЗТ № 458

INTERNATIONAL INFORMATIZATION ACADEMY

in General Consultative Status with the Economic
and Social Council of the United Nations

Headquarters: New York, Washington, Geneva, Riga, Moscow, Montreal

Presented to

# GRIGORI P. GRABOVOI

in recognition and certification
of being elected

# ACADEMICIAN

of this Academy

N 10-11061

Date:
June 10, 1998

President

Chancellor

# NEW YORK ACADEMY OF SCIENCES

SERVING SCIENCE, TECHNOLOGY, AND SOCIETY WORLDWIDE SINCE 1817

PRESENTED TO

## Grigori P. Grabovoi

AN ACTIVE MEMBER OF THIS ACADEMY

### August 1998

TO REMAIN IN GOOD STANDING BY FULFILLING
THE RESPONSIBILITIES OF MEMBERSHIP

PRESIDENT AND CEO

CHAIRMAN OF THE BOARD

Российская Федерация

**АКАДЕМИЯ**

**медико-технических наук**

*организована 10 марта 1992 г.*

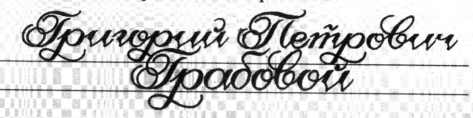

избран

**действительным членом (академиком)**

„ *12 мая* 199 г.

N 009305934

Президент АМТН
академик

Ученый секретарь
академик

г. Москва

---

**RUSSIAN FEDERATION**

**ACADEMY
OF MEDICAL TECHNICALE SCIENCES**

*founded in March 10, 1992*

*Grigory
Grabovoi*

**being elected active member**

of academy

MAY 12 199

N 009305934

President of Academy

Chief Scientific Secretary
of Academy

Moscow

© Г.П. Грабовой, 2001

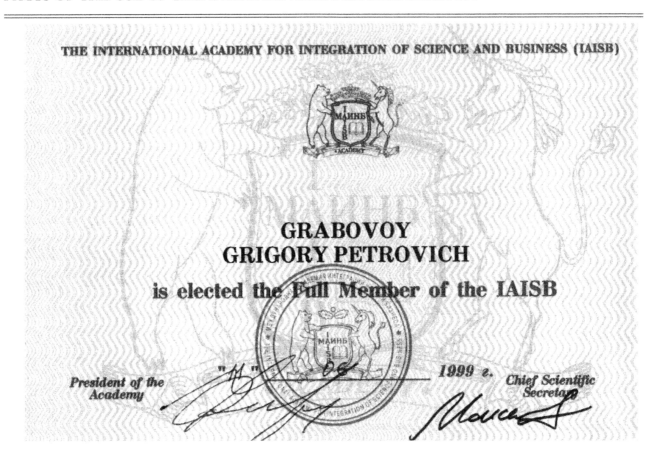

THE INTERNATIONAL ACADEMY FOR INTEGRATION OF SCIENCE AND BUSINESS (IAISB)

**GRABOVOY
GRIGORY PETROVICH**

is elected the Full Member of the IAISB

President of the
Academy                                   1999 г.            Chief Scientific
                                                            Secretary

МЕЖДУНАРОДНАЯ АКАДЕМИЯ ИНТЕГРАЦИИ НАУКИ И БИЗНЕСА (МАИНБ)

**ГРАБОВОЙ
ГРИГОРИЙ ПЕТРОВИЧ**

избран(а) Действительным членом МАИНБ

Президент Академии                        1999 г.           Главный ученый
                                                            секретарь

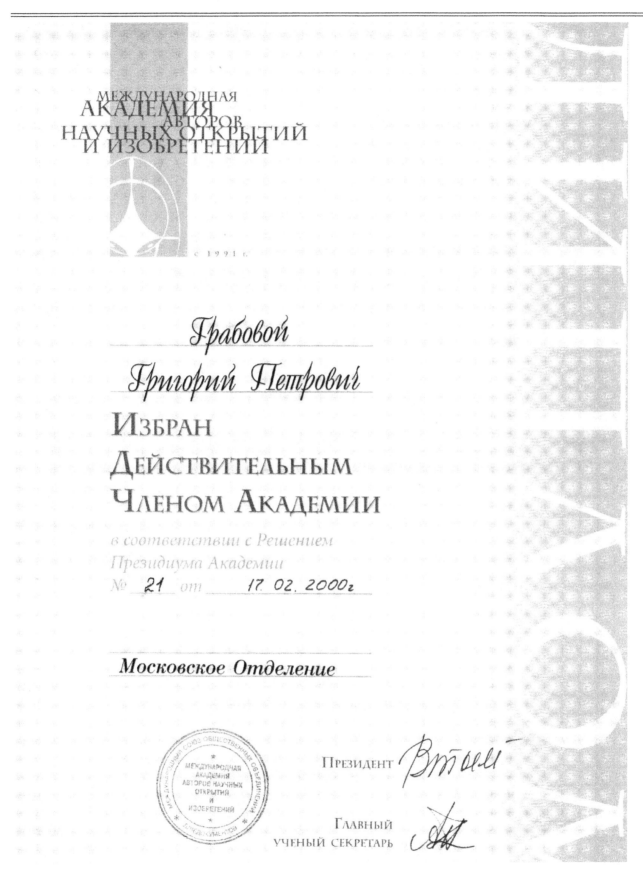

# ДИПЛОМ
## РОССИЙСКОЙ
## АКАДЕМИИ КОСМОНАВТИКИ
### имени К.Э.ЦИОЛКОВСКОГО

РЕГИСТРАЦИОННЫЙ № _ДА - 1478_

Москва    «23» февраля 2001 г.

## РОССИЙСКАЯ
## АКАДЕМИЯ КОСМОНАВТИКИ
### имени К. Э. ЦИОЛКОВСКОГО
#### на основании Устава
## ИЗБРАЛА

" 4 " декабря 2000 г.    (протокол № 9/53 )

Грабового

Григория Петровича

действительным членом /академиком/

## РОССИЙСКОЙ АКАДЕМИИ КОСМОНАВТИКИ
### имени К. Э. ЦИОЛКОВСКОГО

Президент                                          В.П.Сенкевич

Главный ученый секретарь                            А.М.Никулин

© Г.П. Грабовой, 2001

**МЧС РОССИИ**
**АГЕНТСТВО**
**ПО МОНИТОРИНГУ И**
**ПРОГНОЗИРОВАНИЮ**
**ЧРЕЗВЫЧАЙНЫХ СИТУАЦИЙ**
ВНИИ ГОЧС

121352, г. Москва, ул. Давыдковская, 7
(095) 449-83-44, 443-83-15 (факс)
_23.07.99_ № _1-14/940_

На № _____ от _____

В Высшую межакадемическую

аттестационную комиссию

Академик Грабовой Г.П. читает лекции в Центре обучения и подготовки специалистов в области Современных технологий предупреждения и ликвидации чрезвычайных ситуаций Агентства МЧС России по мониторингу и прогнозированию ЧС. Лекции читаются по тематике «Методы дистанционной профилактики катастроф» (Учебная программа № 10):

- математическое моделирование профилактики катастроф;

- практика иррационального управления профилактикой катастроф;

- специальные методы профилактики глобальных катастрофических процессов, представляющих угрозу всему миру;

- обобщенный анализ традиционных и нетрадиционных подходов для профилактики чрезвычайных ситуаций.

Руководитель Агентства

Начальник ВНИИ ГОЧС

профессор

М.Шахраманьян

000090

**Международный центр обучающих систем (МЦОС)**

Министерство природных ресурсов России

Управление дополнительного профессионального образования Минобразования России

Президент Международного центра обучающих систем

С.И.Пешков

**УЧЕБНЫЙ ПЛАН**
по курсу «Технологии предупреждающего прогнозирования и безопасного развития»

**Цель:** Освоение методов технологии предупреждающего прогнозирования и безопасного развития
**Категория слушателей:** Специалисты предприятий и природоохранных органов
**Объем курса:** 1186 час.
**Режим занятий:** с отрывом от работы: 6 часов в день

| № п/п | Название разделов и дисциплин | Всего час. | Лекции | Практические занятия | Форма контроля |
|---|---|---|---|---|---|
| 1. | Анализ экологического состояния региона и технологии антикризисного управления | 498 | 128 | 370 | зачет |
| 2. | Приборы и модули предупреждающего прогнозирования и их использование | 396 | 124 | 272 | зачет |
| 3. | Стратегия принятия решений на основании результатов предупреждающего прогнозирования | 99 | 30 | 69 | зачет |
| 4. | Оптимизация восстановительных воздействий для безопасного развития | 197 | 43 | 154 | зачет |
| 5. | Государственный экзамен | 6 | | | |
| | ИТОГО: | 1186 | 325 | 865 | |

Автор курса, Глава департамента «Технологии предупреждающего прогнозирования и безопасного развития» Международной кафедры-сети ЮНЕСКО/МЦОС «Передача технологий для устойчивого развития»

Грабовой Г.П., д.ф.-м.н., профессор

**ICES**

INTERNATIONAL CENTRE OF EDUCATIONAL SYSTEMS (ICES)
МЕЖДУНАРОДНЫЙ ЦЕНТР ОБУЧАЮЩИХ СИСТЕМ (МЦОС)
CENTRE INTERNATIONAL DES SYSTEMES D'EDUCATION (CISE)
INTERNATIONALES ZENTRUM FÜR AUSBILDUNGS SYSTEME (IZAS)

UNDP
Reg.№ 05973
UNIDO
Reg №002353
UNEP
Reg. of 24.05.99

**МЕЖДУНАРОДНАЯ КАФЕДРА – СЕТЬ UNESCO/ICES**
**"ПЕРЕДАЧА ТЕХНОЛОГИЙ ДЛЯ УСТОЙЧИВОГО РАЗВИТИЯ"**

Департамент «Технологии предупреждающего прогнозирования и безопасного развития»
Международной кафедры-сети ЮНЕСКО/МЦОС
в г. Антверпен, Бельгия

# СЕРТИФИКАТ

Настоящим удостоверяется, что

## ШАШКОВ Евгений Михайлович

успешно окончил очные курсы дополнительной профессиональной подготовки
(в соответствии с лицензией № 16-788 от 13/07/1999 г. Министерства образования РФ)
по разделу Учения профессора, доктора физико-математических наук Григория Петровича Грабового
«Технологии предупреждающего прогнозирования и безопасного развития»

Международный центр обучающих систем (МЦОС), зарегистрированный в Программе развития Организации Объединенных Наций (ПРООН рег. № 05973), в Программе промышленного развития ООН (ЮНИДО рег. № 002350), в Программе ООН по окружающей среде (ЮНЕП рег. от 24.05.99), в Министерстве юстиции Российской Федерации (рег. № 162), и созданная при МЦОС Международная кафедра-сеть ЮНЕСКО/МЦОС "Передача технологий для устойчивого развития",
руководствуясь Соглашением между ЮНЕСКО и МЦОС от 26 августа 1996 г., а также статьями 1-6, 8.6 "Конвенции о признании учебных курсов, дипломов о высшем образовании и ученых степеней в странах Европейского региона" (ЮНЕСКО, Париж, 1973-1993 гг.), Европейской Конвенцией (ЮНЕСКО, Париж, 1979 г.), Региональной Конвенцией государств Азии и Тихого океана (ЮНЕСКО, Бангкок, 1983 г.), Конвенцией Совета Европы и ЮНЕСКО (Лиссабон, 1997 г.),
рекомендуют компетентным органам стран, подписавшим данные конвенции или присоединившихся к ним, признать настоящий сертификат.

Глава Департамента «Технологии
предупреждающего прогнозирования
и безопасного развития»
Международной кафедры-сети
ЮНЕСКО/МЦОС

Г.П. Грабовой

Регистрационный № К2-20000828

Президент МЦОС, Координатор
Международной кафедры-сети
ЮНЕСКО/МЦОС

С.И. Пешков

Москва, 4 августа 2000 г.

# APPENDIX F: THE PHENOMENON OF RESURRECTION

## THE PHENOMENON OF RESURRECTION

We know that resurrection as a phenomenon has always existed. Evidences of this are going through the entire history. We can mention the famous Mysteries of ancient Greece. Persian had quite definite views on this. They told that time would come when the Supreme deity would resurrect all who had passed away, moreover they would be resurrected their original bodies.

This is consistent with the Christian view that the resurrection of those who had passed away would take place at the time of the second advent of Christ. Moreover it is also mentioned about the resurrection exactly in in physical bodies.

These questions and related issues occupied the minds of many thinkers from ancient times to the present day.

A classical text that is about resurrection is Bible. Bible is written evidence that confirms the facts of resurrection accomplished by Jesus Christ. Christ, as we know, also healed from incurable diseases.

We can consider the examples from the history of the Orthodox Church. Let us recall, for example, resurrections, realized by such Saints as Barlaam of Khutyn, Sergius of Radonezh, and John of Kronstadt.

Saint Bhagavan Shri Sathya Sai Baba lives nowadays India. There are data confirming that he realized a resurrection.

Thus, the facts of the resurrection took place in history. So far, however, there were isolated single cases. Now the stage of mass of resurrection comes, the resurrection of all. Resurrection has a mechanism of augmentation of a type of chain reaction. And even partial knowledge of the methods and principles of resurrection give results. For example, when this book had not been fully completed I gave the manuscript to Zinovieva Natalia Philipovna. She worked guided by the manuscript "The Resurrection of People and Eternal Life From Now On Is Our Reality!" for the purpose of resurrection of her husband, and in December 2000, she met him being resurrected. Then she met her resurrected brother in January 2001, though, as she told me, she worked only for resurrection of her husband (her evidence is at the end of this appendix). Based on my practice such process, a kind of chain reaction when one thing by itself entails more others, is a typical one. I saw data about cases, when after one resurrected realized by me mass resurrections took place in some families. The Creator gives incomparably more to people then they can expect. This is manifestation of the God's love to everyone. And universal salvation and eternal life is in the Creator's love. People have known for a long time that the time of universal resurrection and eternal life in physical body will come.

Here are several quotes from the Bible.

"But your dead will live, LORD; their bodies will rise" (Isaiah, 26:19).

"Verily, verily, I say unto you, the hour is coming, and now is, when the dead shall hear the voice of the Son of God: and they that hear shall live." (Gospel of John, 5:25).

The following statement of Apostle Paul notes that resurrection is for all, both the righteous and the unrighteous.

"Having hope in God, which these also themselves look for, that there shall be a resurrection of the just and unjust." (The Acts of Apostles, 24:15).

Many times the Bible states that quality transformation of man and his body will take place. It says about Jesus Christ that He

"But our citizenship is in heaven. And we eagerly await a Savior from there, the Lord Jesus Christ, [21] who, by the power that enables him to bring everything under his control, will transform our lowly bodies so that they will be like his glorious body." (Philippians, 3:20, 3:21)

"So also is the resurrection of the dead. It is sown in corruption; it is raised in incorruption; It is sown in dishonour; it is raised in glory: it is sown in weakness; it is raised in power;" (Corinthians 1, 15:42-43).

There several descriptions of how the process of resurrection takes place. For example,

"Thus says the Lord GOD to these bones: "Surely I will cause breath to enter into you, and you shall live. I will put sinews on you and bring flesh upon you, cover you with skin and put breath in you; and you shall live. Then you shall know that I *am* the LORD."" (Ezekiel, 37:5, 37:6). And ibid: "I will give you a new heart and put a new spirit in you; I will remove from you your heart of stone and give you a heart of flesh. And I will put my Spirit in you." (Ezekiel, 36: 26-27). As result transformation of man will take place. It is compared with the transformation of a silly infant in a mature and wise man. And what people now see as through a darky glass, very unclearly, more assumedly, after their transformation they will see clearly and distinctly, directly, face a face, "When I was a child, I spoke as a child, I understood as a child, I thought as a child; but when I became a man, I put away childish things" (Corinthians 1, 13:11); "For now we see in a mirror, dimly, but then face to face. Now I know in a part, but then I shall know just as I also am known" (Corinthians, 13:12).

This was stated in other places, for example, "Beloved now we are children of God: and it has not yet been revealed what we shall be, but we know that when He is revealed, we shall be like Him, for we shall see Him as He is" (The First Epistle of John, 3:2).

The following statement of Apostle Paul is about the body of resurrected people that will be transformed into imperishable non-destroyable, and death in general will cease to exist,

"Behold, I tell you a mystery: We shall not all sleep, but we shall all be changed in a moment, in the twinkling of eye, at the last trumpet. For the trumpet will sound, and the dead will be raised incorruptible, and we shall be changed. For this corruptible has put on incorruption, and this mortal must put on immortality. So when this corruptible has put on incorruption, and this mortal has put on immortality, then shall be brought to pass the saying that is written:"Death is swallowed up in victory."" (Corinthians, 15:51-54).

Proper understanding is required for the resurrection to take mass character. In this book, I, for the first time in history, set out the main principles and methods of resurrection. Resurrection is presented as science for the first time. Therefore, it is not by chance that many people who have just read a part of this book successfully resurrect independently.

As I've already mentioned the problem of resurrection acquired a very special character. Hence the modern world has come close to the threat of self-destruction; resurrection in such conditions is the true way of salvation. And since resurrection is based on spirit this is the real salvation without return.

With the beginning of universal resurrection a new stage in development of our civilization begins.  From now on, our reality is eternal life.

As an example of fast transfer of knowledge about resurrection I give a concrete fact of transfer of this knowledge in this appendix.

**ВСЕМ ЗАИНТЕРЕСОВАННЫМ ЛИЦАМ**

Заявитель _Зиновьева Наталия Филипповна_
(фамилия, имя и отчество полностью)

Заинтересованные лица: _____
(адрес организации)

свидетельство

о результатах полученных при изучении и применении технологий изложенных
в печатных трудах Грабового Григория Петровича _в книге: „Вос-_
_крешение людей и вечная жизнь-отныне наша реальность"_
Время начала составления заявления    200 _1_ | _02_ | _22_ | _18_ | _09_
год    месяц    число    часы    минуты

Я родился(лась) 19 _47_ | _09_ | _03_ | в г. _Москва_ _____
год   месяц   число

имею удостоверение личности _____
(наименование документа, серия, номер, кем и когда выдан документ)

Настоящим удостоверяю, что я при изучении и применении технологий изложенных в печатных трудах Грабового Григория Петровича, родившегося 14 ноября 1963 года в поселке Кировском, Кировского района Чимкентской области Казахской ССР имеющему свидетельство о рождении серии II – ОГ № 463794, паспорт серии III – ОГ № 586058, выданный 01.02.1980 года, достиг(ла) следующего: _Тысячи благодарностей_
_Григорию Петровичу Грабовому за то великое чудо,_
_которое произошло. Спасибо большое за его книги,_
_которые помогли мне в трудный момент    об-_
_ретении уверенности, душевную силу и спокойст-_
_вие. И ещё за то, что направили меня учиться._
_Я мысленно благодарю Григория Петровича_
_Грабового постоянно._
_Мой муж Зиновьев Николай Федорович родил-_
_ся 29 ноября 1938г в городе Тула, а ушёл из жизни_
_26 сентября 2000г. Я начала работать по книге_
_Григория Петровича Грабового „Воскрешение лю-_
_дей и вечная жизнь-отныне наша реальность!" по вос-_
_крешению моего мужа с 12 октября 2000г. А уже_
_13 декабря 2000г в 13ч 30мин на эскалаторе станции_
_метро „Курская" я встретилась с ним когда_
_он уже был в физическом теле._
_Мой брат Грибанов Николай Филиппович_
_родился 7 июля 1941г в городе Москва а ушёл из_
_жизни 4 февраля 1979г в возрасте 37 лет._
Прошу заверить мое заявление на основании документов удостоверяющих мою личность и на основании вышеизложенных доказательств

_Продолжение текста в приложении №_ _1_ _к настоящему листу_

_Н.Зиновьева_ | _Зиновьева_
(подпись)    (фамилия)

200 _1_ | _02_ | _27_ |
год   месяц   число

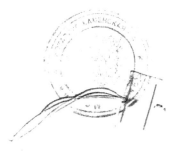

APPENDIX G: EXERCISES FOR EVERY DAY OF THE MONTH FOR DEVELOPMENT OF CONSCIOUSNESS, FOR DEVELOPMENT OF YOUR LIFE EVENTS IN FAVORABLE DIRECTION, FOR GETTING FULL VALUE HEALTH AND FOR ESTABLISHMENT OF HARMONY WITH THE PULS OF THE UNIVERSE

## EXERCISES FOR EVERY DAY OF THE MONTH FOR DEVELOPMENT OF CONSCIOUSNESS, FOR DEVELOPMENT OF YOUR LIFE EVENTS IN FAVORABLE DIRECTION, FOR GETTING FULL VALUE HEALTH AND FOR ESTABLISHMENT OF HARMONY WITH THE PULS OF THE UNIVERSE

I would recommend finding some time for the exercises, which are cited below. For each day of the month I recommend three exercises corresponding to this day. These exercises contain control of events. For this purpose different concentrations should be applied. During the concentration keep remembering the exact aim you would like to achieve. The aim might be realization of a desirable event, for example, recovery from a disease, development of a mechanism of knowledge of the World, and so on. The main thing here is to conduct always regulation of information for the universal salvation and harmonic development.   Such regulation can be a struggle against destruction at informational level because you fulfill the work of rescuers. Practically, at the level of your perception, a concentration can be carried out in the following way:

— In your mind you determine the aim of the concentration which looks like some geometric form, a sphere, for example. This sphere is the aim of the concentration

— Spiritually you dispose yourself to build events which you need the way as the Creator does it.

— During concentrations at various objects, at concrete figures, or at cognition of the reality, control location of the sphere. By a volitional effort move the sphere to the area of your perception which gives more light at the moment of concentrations.

I presented one of the variants of technology of concentrations. In practice you can find a lot of others. The ways of control of events based on understanding of the World processes through concentrations are very effective.

In the first exercise for each day of the month you fulfill a concentration on some element of the external or internal reality.

In the second you concentrate on a sequence of numbers of seven and nine figures.

The third exercise gives technologies of control of events in a verbal form.

For more successful fulfillment of the last two exercises I recommend to know paragraph 7 of Chapter 4.

I would like to draw you attention to the following important moment. You should understand that the effectiveness of concentration carried out by you is determined, to a considerable degree, by your approach to it. Try to be open to this creative process. Listen to your internal voice prompting you how to fulfill these concentrations in practice.

You may, as I mentioned before, write a row of numbers on a sheet of paper and concentrate on it. And you may act another way.

When you concentrate on a sequence of nine figures you may imagine that you are in the center of a sphere and the figures are located on its internal surface. Information about the aim of the concentration can be inside of this sphere in a form of a ball. You should dispose yourself to find that number which gives more light.

Having received the first idea that some number from the row which is on the external surface of the big sphere shines brighter than others, you should fix this number. Then mentally join the internal sphere which contains the aim of the concentration and the element of perception in the form of a number.

When you concentrate on a row of seven figures, you may imagine that the figures are located on the surface of a cube, on one of its sides.

Doing this, in accordance with your feelings, you may move these figures changing their location in order to achieve maximum effect.

You may act quite a different way. In your mind you may connect each number with some element of external or internal medium. These elements are not necessarily to be homogeneous. One number, for example, you may connect with some tree, another with some feeling. You decide yourself. In this approach you symbolically equate the numbers with the elements of reality chosen by you. As ever these elements of reality may be not only physical, but mental as well. It means you may imagine them in your consciousness.

These techniques give you additional possibilities of control. You may change the structure of the concentration, your mood to fulfill it; you may vary symbolic equalization of the numbers to the elements of the reality. As a result you will be able to increase the effectiveness of your concentration. You will be able to control better the time of execution of what you resolved. This is very important in practical life.

Your concentration should give an instantaneous result when an instantaneous salvation is required. The factor of time may be not so significant if the aim is to provide harmonic development. The decisive factor in this case is provision of your just harmonic development with consideration of all circumstances. You will get exactly this by means of your concentrations.

So, everything should be individual in these exercises. Everyone should choose independently the system of his development. You should bear in mind the following.

It is not possible to make a choice of a system of your own development just by means of logic. You are sure to set your goals, you aim to achieve them, and, however, your soul has already got the tasks which had been put in before. Therefore, when you carry out concentrations, the tasks which had been put in before can be realized at first. These are the tasks, which were the tasks of the soul, which were not only the tasks of your development but the development of the whole society as well. When you fulfill these tasks you feel that these are exactly the things you should have done first of all, you feel this at a very profound internal level, at the level of development of the soul, at the level of the Creator.

That is why when we speak about concentrations we, first of all, speak about the universal harmony. At the same time you should understand that harmony always implies an element of salvation as a necessary element if the situation requires such interference. However, the main task of harmony is provision of such development of events which eliminates occurrence of any threats at all. It is clear that harmonic development should become eternal.

Concentrations for each day of the month created and approved by me will bring you to this. Fulfilling them you will get that harmony which will make your way joyful and uninterrupted, and you will be able to save yourself and others and live eternally.

Possessing these concentrations you can undertake active controlling actions instead of being in a passive state in any situations. Awareness of the fact, that due to the usage of these concentrations in your affairs you really realize the process of universal salvation and eternal harmonic development, opens the freedom which is given to you by the Creator. This organizes universal creative development together with your true happiness.

These concentrations are given for 31 days. If you carry out these exercises, for example, in February, which includes 28 days, after the 28th day you should go to the first day of March. It means that the day of the month from the list of exercises should always coincide with that day of the month which the calendar shows at the moment. You can fulfill these concentrations at any time of the day. You may determine yourself the number of concentrations per day and their duration. I would recommend carrying out concentrations systematically and before important affairs.

If you find the first exercise of someday rather complicated you may miss it and do other two. You will get the result anyway. Gradually more and more exercises number one will become clearer and easier for you. So do what you understand and what you like.

Now let's turn to the exercises.

### The 1st day of the month:

1. On the first day of the month you should fulfill concentration on the right foot. This concentration connects you with the supporting point in the external world. You lean on the Earth mentally. The Earth in your consciousness is a bearing support.

The control in the system of complete restoration is based on the idea that the supporting point is simultaneously the point of support and the point of creation. Since it is also the point of creation, with the help of this concentration you can develop your consciousness right away.

You realize that based on the same principle which accounts for everything growing and developing on the Earth, for example, plants and even the matter of your own body appear, based on the same principle you may build any external reality. Understanding of this underlies this concentration.

However, carrying out this concentration you may not think about this deep-laid mechanism. You may just concentrate on the right foot and simultaneously imagine the required event in your consciousness. That mechanism of construction of the reality, which has just been described, will work automatically. And you will receive the desired event in a harmonic way. Because this control simultaneously provides harmonization of events.

This exercise may be fulfilled several times a day.

2. Concentration on a seven-digit number: 1845421;

On a nine-digit number: 845132489.

3. On this day you should concentrate on the World, on all objects of the World and feel, that every object of the World is a part of your personality. Having felt this you will feel that the blowing of the wind from each object of the World prompts you the decision. And when you feel that every object has a part of your consciousness you will see that harmony which is sent down to you by the Creator.


The 2nd day:

1. On this day you should carry out concentration on the little finger of the right hand. The same way as in the previous case, concentrating on the little finger of the right hand you should simultaneously keep in your consciousness that event realization of which you want to achieve.

This exercise may be fulfilled several times a day. You can choose any interval between the exercises convenient to you. You may start another concentration in 20 seconds, or you may do it in an hour, or a bigger period. You may do one or two concentrations a day, or you may do ten and more.

Rely upon your internal sense, upon your intuition. Learn to hear your internal voice and listen to what it tells you. The above refers to all exercises.

In principle, doing this exercise you are not to be immobile. The little finger of your right hand may touch something. This is not the main thing. Act the way that is more convenient to you.

The thing, which is important here, is the following. On the whole you have a lot of perceiving elements. Besides the mentioned above little finger there are other nine fingers and many other parts of the body. However there is only one of many perceiving elements you should currently concentrate on, this is the little finger of the right hand. This harmonizes the control. The control becomes harmonic.

2. Seven-digit number: 1853125;

Nine-digitnumber: 849995120.

3. On the second day of the month you should see the harmony of the World related to yourself. You should produce this World the same way as the Creator produced this World. Look at the World and you will see that picture which has been. Look at the World and you will see that picture which will be. Look at the World and you will see who you are in this World. This will be the World forever and in perpetuity.

## The 3rd day:

1. On the third day of the month you should carry out concentration on plants. It may be a physical plant, that one which really exists in the external reality. Then during the concentration you may just look at it. Or you can mentally imagine a plant. Then you should concentrate on its image.

A method of reflection is used in this concentration. The main point of it is as follows. While concentrating on the chosen plant you imagine that the event you need is being formed in the light reflected by the plant. It's better to say that you do not just imagine this event, but you really see it, you really build it. The event built with the help of such control appears to be harmonized. This is favored by the fact that the plant to a great extent exists harmonically in this world.

2. Seven-digit number: 5142587;

Nine-digit number: 421954321.

3. Look at the reality and you will see that the worlds are numerous. Look at that World which you need, come up to it and widen it. See it with a look of an eyewitness. Approach it and put your hands on it and you will feel that warmth which spreads from

your World. Move it to yourself and look at the Creator. Look, how He tells you and what He advises you. You may compare this knowledge with yours and receive the eternal World.

## The 4<sup>th</sup> day:

1. On this day you concentrate on crystals or stones. You can take a grain of sand as well. Let you chose, for example, a stone. So, concentrating on the stone you imagine a sphere around it. This is a sphere of information. Mentally you see all required events appearing in this sphere. You just insert the required events into this sphere. By this you implement control while doing this concentration.

2. Seven-digit number: 5194726;

Nine-digit number: 715043769.

3. Possess that perspective of reality, which is given to you by the methods. The methods should be harmonic. One method should proceed from another the same way as the second method follows from the first one. Walking along the street you see that every next step appears from the previous one. You may stand up when you were in sitting position, and you see that each movement can be various. It can proceed from the previous action and it itself can turn into the next previous action. Get the World in such a way as if it has always been uninterrupted, as if each movement of this world concerned only you as a single person. When you get that solidity of the World, which gives you exact methods of control in this World and of this World, your World will be everywhere and you will come to it and you will take it into your hands and your hands will be that world, which holds your World. And you will see that you are getting in touch with the eternal World, with the World of all the Worlds and it will be single for everyone, and this will be the collective World chosen by you and chosen by everyone. Create it to be ideal for everyone and ideal for you. Ideality should not be disconnected. You should see ideality of everyone and yourself in your single World as in the single World of everyone.

## The 5<sup>th</sup> day

1. On the fifth day of the month you should concentrate on the elements of the reality which arise as a result of your interaction with other elements of the reality. I will

explain what it means.

When you pay attention to some object, by this, generally speaking, you concentrate your consciousness on this object. Due to connection with you this object, this element of the reality possesses a certain degree of your concentration and a certain volume of your knowledge. This object in its turn transfers to other elements of the reality a part of information received from you and something from your state. For example, the same way as the light from the Sun shining on various objects is partially reflected from them, and it lights some other objects.

So, when you looked at some object, it, after this, it means after interaction with you, transferred something to the external medium, something from itself. Thus, your task is as follows: to think and to reveal what each element of the reality transfers to the external medium from itself. You may, of course, stop on one thing. You concentrate on it and simultaneously imagine the event you require. The method is like this. Its peculiarity is as follows: concentration on the revealed by you so-called secondary element brings to realization of the desired event.

So, with the help of logical thinking, or clairvoyance, or any other spiritual methods you find out what exactly the element of the reality chosen by you gives to the external medium after interaction with you. When you concentrate on this consequence, on this secondary element of the reality and simultaneously imagine the desirable event, you achieve its realization.

2. Seven-digit number: 1084321;

Nine-digitnumber: 194321054.

3. When you see the sky you know, that there is the Earth. When you see the Earth you may think about the sky. If you are under the Earth, the sky exists above it. These simple truths should be the source of the eternal World. Join the sky with the Earth and you will see that everything that is under the Earth may be above the Earth. Go towards you spirit and find the risen where they are. Bring the infinity to the truth of the World and you will see that the World is endless. When you see this you will see the true Creator, you will see the real Creator, since He gave you what you have, and you create

the same way as He has created. He is very close to you. He is your friend, He loves you. You should stretch your hands to Him and create the same way as He creates. Only Creator-Creator may create creators. You should be harmonic with your creator. You should be open for Him and you should be eternal in all of your manifestations, in all of your creations. Anything you want to correct, you may always correct. Anything you want to create, you may create in that place where you are and when you would wish. There is the Eternity for perfection. For affairs the Eternity is multiplied by the acts of the Creator. You are that one whom the Creator has seen in you, whom He has created in you. However you are also that one who wants the Creator to personify himself with his acts in that infinity in which you see yourself. The Creator who is present in you is that Creator who is moving together with you in each of your actions. Apply to Him and you will have the harmony.

The 6<sup>th</sup> day:

1. On this day you fulfill concentration the essence of which may be worded as follows: change of structure of consciousness in density of concentration due to perception of remote objects.

This way of concentration is convenient to apply when you want the required event to happen in some determined place. Then you need to concentrate your consciousness just in this area.

This method can be successfully used when you vice versa do not want realizations of some situation in a certain place if you understand it as unfavorable. In this case you have to break up the negative information. Break up means detent, de-concentrate consciousness in this place. As a result appearing rarefaction brings to non-realization of an unfavorable situation.

Realization of a desirable event in a chosen place can be achieved with the help of concentration of your consciousness there due to remote elements of your consciousness. We discussed this way of control before. When you use it, you use those elements of the consciousness, which are responsible for perception of remote objects. Doing this you can perceive real physical objects, remote, as you see them with your usual eyesight, or you can contemplate remote objects with your mental sight. In this and another case you use the remote elements of your consciousness. And if, doing this, you fix in your consciousness the event, which you would like to realize in a determined place, it would take place exactly there.

So, the essence of this method is like that. The more remote parts of your consciousness you use to place the information, the better it is processed and the desirable event is realized more fully. The event will happen in the required place.

Concerning destructive forces the method of defocusing can be used. By defocusing of you consciousness you may make the negative information so rarified, that, as a matter of fact, it would stop being perceived, as if it has never existed.

2. Seven-digit number: 1954837;

Nine-digitnumber: 194321099.

3. Having seen the World as if it has been turned over, you should always know, that any upturned; any disconnected or pressed World is always the World of unity, harmony and blessing. You should understand that there is always the God's blessing behind all upturned and ambiguous or non-typical states of the World and you may have this harmony only from the awareness that you have always been eternal and will remain eternal, and no structure, no information will change this will of the God.

## The 7th day:

1. On the seventh day of the months you should concentrate on super far areas of consciousness. In practice we deal with them when we look at remote clouds or far objects, let's say, at trees, or their leaves.

For materialization of some object or realization of some event it is necessary to process a big volume of information. Super-far areas of consciousness provide super-fast processing of information. Thus, the more distant sites of consciousness you use the faster processing of information you may implement.

The knowledge of these factors is used in this method in the following way. You look at a cloud with your common sight or see it mentally and simultaneously in your consciousness you build the desirable event exactly on this cloud. Or on a leaf, if you are looking at a remote leaf. Due to the usage in this case of super-far areas of consciousness, the desirable result can be quickly achieved.

At that the realization of the event takes a harmonic way. Since the cloud is not able to destroy. As well as the leaf. They are not able to harm anyone. As a result the required event is being realized harmonically.

2. Seven-digit number: 1485321;

Nine-digit: 991843288.

3. You see that the World develops in the image and status of your actions in interaction with the God's will. You see that the World is that creation, which has been acknowledged by everyone, and when you want to change the World in accordance with your affairs; bring your affairs to universal abundance and your affairs will strengthen and the universal abundance will come. The Universal abundance is the deed of the World bringing us to the Kingdom of the God and bringing us to receiving of universal life and life individual forever and in perpetuity.

The 8th day

1. On this day you learn to control by concentrating on the consequences of the events.

Imagine that you are sitting by the lake and watching a racing speedboat. The water is calm in front of it, and waves appear behind it.

Let's look at the leaf growing on the tree. This leaf can be considered as a consequence of existence of the tree. Clouds appeared and first drops of rain fell on the ground. Raindrops can be considered as a consequence of existence of the cloud.

There are numerous similar examples around us. You chose any phenomenon and concentrate on one of its consequences. Simultaneously you keep in mind the desirable event. And it comes.

This method of control is very effective. It can help to change past events.

2. Seven-digit number: 1543218;

Nine-digit number: 984301267.

3.  You see that the endlessness of the line of figure eight joins in itself those Worlds, which you have already met during the previous seven days.  And when your World will join all the Worlds, you will see that you are as joyful in your soul as the World is diverse. Perceiving each small part of the World as universal joy you will see that the joy is eternal, as well as the welfare is eternal and in this state of common joy you will rise up your hands and will see the message of the God's blessing which calls you to eternity. See the Eternity in that place where it is. See the Eternity where there is no it. See the Eternity there where it has always been and you will be the creator of the Eternity in those places where there is no it from the point of view of another person. When you will be seeing the Eternity and will be creating it, you will always be eternal, in everything, in any eternity and in any world. You are a creator in the image and likeness and the Eternity creates you in the image and likeness. Creating the eternal you will create yourself.  Creating yourself you create the eternal as well as Eternity may create another Eternity and as well as the Creator created everyone simultaneously.

## The 9th day:

1. On the ninth day of the month you do concentration, which can be called as concentration on super-far areas of consciousness in the most approached points of your consciousness. It means that this method of concentration is as follows: the most distant sites of your consciousness you transfer to the most approached ones.  This transfer should be realized in such a way that you perception from the most distant sites of consciousness would be the same as from the most approached areas of consciousness. In this case you will be able to get a single impulse for construction of any element of the World.  And as soon as you achieve this you will become an expert in control.  Since you will have just to be in the state of spiritual mood for everything to be normal, for everything to be good, you will just have to wish so and everything will be like that.

That single impulse which I have mentioned develops a special spiritual state.  This state is not exactly related to thinking, because thinking as such may not be present in this state.  There may be just a mood, for example, for good, for creation or for establishment of harmony.

So, being in the state of such mood brings already to the favorable development of events.

I would like to emphasize that this method of concentration isolates a special form of perception. The perception is in your consciousness; the perception is a part of your consciousness and you deliberately structure it in such a way that as a result it works as I told.

The given method of concentration affects in-depth issues of control on the basis of your consciousness.

2. Seven-digit number: 1843210;

Nine-digitnumber: 918921452.

3. Having seen the world as a very deep essence of the universe, you will see that everything that exists in nature, that everyone who exists in nature, for example, a man, an animal, every molecule, or that thing which hasn't been created yet or was created before, everything has one and the same basis of the God who showed the mechanism of creation of everything.  Having seen how to create everything you will be creating everything.  Come to this through the beginning of your "self".  Come to this through the depth of your "self", and you will see how your "self" develops together with the whole Universe, how your "self" grows up and turns into the World.  You are the World.  You are the reality. Look at this with the eyes of the whole World; look at this with the eyes of everyone, look at this with your eyes and you will see that your soul is your eyes.  Look with your soul and you will see the World such as it is, and you will be able to correct it in such a way as it should be corrected, and you will see the World such as you should use it for achievement of the Eternity.  You will always know the way when you look at the World from yourself, out of yourself, and outside of yourself.

## The 10th day:

1. On this day you practice concentration the essence of which can be expressed as follows: concentration simultaneously on all covered by you objects of external reality at a

time of only one impulse of perception of all these objects.

You dispose yourself to perceive simultaneously assessable to your perception objects by only one moment of perception. As a result of such momentary perception you should become aware of all these external objects.

It is clear that at the initial stage of practice you may get partial perception of information about all the objects. Take it easy. Really the aim of your work is the most complete perception of all the objects. Gradually you will gain possession of such ability.

However even at the initial stage you will get at least some information about each of them by momentary perception of surrounding objects. For example, just an idea that these objects are somewhere, that they exist.

Generally speaking in order to receive information about an object you have just to find a necessary point of concentration and tune up yourself. Then you will be able to contact any object. You will be able to get access to all spheres of control. And as long as in this method of concentration you learn to perceive simultaneously a big number of objects, this practice will enable to control at once big volumes of information.

As a concrete example I can cite the following result of this practice. Suppose that there is a computer in front of you. Having glanced at it appearance, you will already know how to control this computer and what in general you can receive by using it.

The above-cited type of concentration will let you get information from any object, because with the help of this practice you will be taught to control any object of information. The access to control may be both logical and unconditional, that is on spiritual basis.

So, for exercises under number one I gave you concentrations for the first ten days of the month. Theoretically you might find further concentrations till the end of the month yourself. This could be done on the basis of cause-effect connections in the sphere of information. You might develop further what you know already considering your work from the point of you of fundamental control. However I will continue setting forth these concentrations, though I will do it briefly.

2. Seven-digit number: 1854312;

Nine-digitnumber: 894153210.

3. The unity of two figures: one and a new figure zero helped you to see the World initially such as if zero has already been present in figure one. When you look at one and increase it to ten by adding a zero to it, you perform an action. Thus your action and your act according to this principle should be harmonic. You should see that each of your actions may substantially increase, increase quantitatively and qualitatively each of your manifestations. You are a manifestation of the World. Harmonize it together with what you see. Look after yourself and your thoughts. You should be where you are, you should be where you aren't. You should be everywhere since you are a maker and a creator. Your harmony should bring to Eternity. Resurrection is an element of the Eternity. Immortality is also an element of the Eternity. You should find the true Eternity for yourself where immortality and resurrection are just particular cases of this Eternity. You should be a creator of all and everything. You should know and imagine clearly what follows resurrection and immortality, true immortality. True immortality gives rise to the next status of the Eternity, next status of the World and next status of the personality. You should be ready to it and know always that other tasks, the tasks of the Eternity, which are risen in before you and which you pose for yourself give rise to new Worlds, which you build in your consciousness, and this World as one and zero form ten, this World is the thing that you will have when you will become eternal since you are already eternal. Your immortality is in yourself. You are already eternal and immortal; you should just become aware of this. Get over to this level by the way of a rational action similar to joining of one and zero and you will get this immortality in each of your actions, in each of your manifestations, in each of your steps.


## The 11th day:

1. On the eleventh day of the month you concentrate on phenomena which reveal interaction of animals with man. For example, you have a dog, or a cat, or some bird, let's say a parrot, living in your house. Think, what is the deeper sense of this interaction, these contacts, and this communication? It's from your point of view. And what about

their point of view?

When you become aware of the processes of perception and thinking of other participants of interaction you will be able to enter the structure of control of the reality.

2. Seven digit number: 1852348;

Nine-digitnumber: 561432001.

3. Just as you increased one ten times by adding one round figure zero, you will receive the next number by adding figure one to one. Number 11 is personification of the World which is inside of you and which is visible to everyone. You are that essence, which is always visible to everyone; and everyone can get your harmonic experience, that one which you received in your development. Share your experience and you will get the eternal life.

The 12<sup>th</sup> day

1. On this day you concentrate on phenomena which can raise a question on creation of the whole. For example, a goose or a swan lost a feather. In this case you have to concentrate on thought what should be done in order to return it to the original place. How this could be achieved? It means you try to understand how the single whole can be created or reconstituted. Or, let's consider another example: a leaf fell from the tree. What should be done to get it returned to its original place in order to have the tree with it in its initial appearance?

This is concentration on collection of separate elements of reality to single whole, which is their norm. Practice in such concentration provides control.

In this concentration as well as in many others you may consider yourself as an object. You can restore any of your organs. A woman once applied to me. During a surgery she had a womb cut out. You understand how important this issue is. I applied those methods and principles, that you are now aware of, and now this woman has a full healthy womb.

2. Seven-digit number: 1854321;

Nine-digitnumber: 485321489.

3. Join with the World in its covering, with that as you perceive it in your acts, and

you will see that your acts are that essence of the World, which harmonizes with you everywhere and always. And you will see that having sent to you the God's blessing, the God wanted the unity from you. You should have the unity where the God has development. The unity with the God is in the development. In the development Godlike, true and creative, the unity comes in every moment of your movement. You move and develop towards the Eternity and this will be your unity forever with the Creator in your eternal development. Eternity of life this is the true unity with the Creator.

The 13th day:

1. On the thirteenth day of the month you should concentrate on discrete, separate elements of some object of the reality.

Suppose you perceive some object. It may be, for example, a truck, or a palm, or a stone. It doesn't matter what object it is. The main thing in this case is that in the chosen object you deliberately isolate some of its fragments, some parts. A truck, for example, can be imagined as consisting of many separate parts.

I would like to remind you, this could be done with any forms, which are not the forms of a man. It is not possible to do this with a person. A person should be always perceived as a whole. It's a law.

If the object chosen by you is not a person but something else, or a truck, you may imagine it consisting of separate parts. So, your task here is to find connections existing between separate parts. And when you find these connections and simultaneously keep in mind the event you need, for example, healing someone or acquiring the ability of clairvoyance you achieve realization of this event. In such a way you can perfect your abilities in control.

2. Seven-digit number: 1538448;

Nine-digitnumber: 154321915.

3. You will see those faces, which created the World before you. You will see those mechanisms, which created the World before you. You will see the World, which had been before you. And you will feel that you have always been, transfer this

feeling to these faces and with this feeling create these mechanisms. And you will see that everything around you artificially reproduced or naturally created that all this is the Creator. He personified you in everything that you see. Your personification is that World which is being created. In such a way you can find any technology of spiritual, intellectual, man-caused and whatever you like, but for sure creative development. Look at the development, as at equal in rights universal development of any element of reality and any object of information and you will see that essence which is your soul, your personality and your Creator. Individuality of the Creator and creation by Him of everyone underlay the World harmony, which is inherent in everything, has always been and understandable everywhere. The Creator who has created you and only you individually has created everyone at once. Do the same way, create the World individually and at once simultaneously for everyone and for all times and spaces.

The 14th day:

1. On this day of the month you concentrate on the movement of the objects surrounding you. You watch them and ask yourself a question: Why is the cloud moving? Why is it raining? Why can the birds fly? Why altogether is that entire happening? You try to find for yourself informational essence of each event. When you concentrate and simultaneously keep in mind the required event, you achieve its realization. And simultaneously you perfect yourself in the mastery of control.

2. Seven-digit number: 5831421;

Nine-digitnumber: 999888776.

3. On this day you should see your hands as hands reflecting the light of life. On this day you should see your fingers as fingers reflecting the light of the hands. On this day see your body shining with bright light of the Creator, shining with the bright light of love, good and health for everyone, shining with bright light of my Teaching about eternal life. On this day you may feel this Teaching about eternal life, my Teaching, and apply to me in your mind. You may also apply to me on any other day and in any other state, and you can always ask anything that you want for getting

eternal life and universal creation.  Apply to me and you will get help.  You may also apply to yourself and independently learn what you have received from me.  You may see this knowledge and use them and show to others.   On this day you may be in harmony with me the same way as you may be in harmony with me on any of the previous days and on all subsequent days.  On those days when the time will not be measured with time and space you will also be able to apply to me and you can always come out with a request for help, with a request about conversation, with a request about an event or just in order to apply. You are free, as you have been always free. Make it a rule, distribute this rule to others and you will get eternal life wherever I am. And you will get eternal life wherever you are.  You will get eternal life wherever everything is.  And you will get eternity wherever everything is and has always been. And this principle will be trustworthy and true for everyone, and it is trustworthy and true for everyone, and you are that one who you are in the Eternity, because you are the Eternity.

The 15th day:

1. On the second day of the months you practiced concentration on the little finger of the right hand.  On the fifteenth day you can use for this purpose some other parts of your body, for example, other fingers, or nails, or something else at your discretion. Further on the concentration is carried out the same way as I explained it for the second day.

2. Seven-digit number: 7788001;

Nine-digitnumber: 532145891.

3. On this fifteenth day of the month you can feel this God's blessing which is sent down by the Universal mind, which is itself grateful to the God for its creation. For creation of every of its elements and for creation of such of its status that it can reproduce the Universe, since the God is present everywhere.  And due to this principle feel the gratitude of a plant and an animal towards you, feel the gratitude of another person and feel their love.  And you will see that you love them.  The love includes creation, blessing and universal penetration. And common love, achievable by everyone

and achieving everyone, this is the Creator, who personified the World in your manifestation. You are a manifestation of love of the Creator, since He is the love in relation to you. You initially received the Creator's gift and you are him, you are a creator, because you are created by the Creator, by the eternal and all-embracing God; go that way, where He is, since he is everywhere. Go that way where He calls, since He calls everywhere. He is where you are, He is everywhere where you are. You are in the movement of the Creator; you are a personification of His Eternity. Go along with the concerns of the Creator, He created the eternal World in universal mutual development, and you will see that the World personifies eternal you. You are a creator who creates the eternal and the Creator created you eternal when creating the eternal World.

## The 16th day

1. On this day you concentrate on the elements of the external reality, which contact your body.

Since childhood we have remembered a wonderful phrase, "The Sun, air and water are our best friends". In this concentration you are trying to become aware of interaction with these of our friends.

You concentrate on the warmth, which is given by the beams of the Sun falling on you. You feel their touch; you feel the warmth given by them.

You feel a light wind blowing on you. You feel its breaths. This may also be strong blasts of wind. This may be quite immovable air. And if at the same time it is very hot and the humidity is high, you simultaneously feel warmth, air and moisture on your cheeks.

You may enjoy refreshing action of the water when you wash your face, take a shower or swim. These concentrations can be also done in the cold wintertime. During a warm season, especially in summer at a beach, all your body can enjoy the contact with the sun, air and water. A contact with the ground can be added here.

These concentrations are very important. Doing them you enter deliberate interaction with the elements.

It is clear that you can do this practice every day. If, during the concentration, you simultaneously keep in mind the required event, you achieve its realization.

2. Seven-digit number: 1843212;

Nine-digitnumber: 123567091.

3. Feel the harmony where it is, and it is everywhere and always. This is the harmony of the Creator. Feel the harmony where it is and will be. This is the harmony of your development. Feel the harmony where it is, was, and will be, and where it wasn't, isn't but where it will always be. This is the harmony of change. This is the harmony of transformation. This is transformation into eternal life. Come to yourself everywhere, and feel this harmony everywhere, and you will see how the waves of joy and love emanate from your harmony. And you will see that you make the World harmonic forever in its eternal status of stability. You are the fighter, but in eternal God's blessing for eternal life and eternal faith.

### The 17th day:

1. On the seventeenth day of the month you concentrate on the elements of the external reality which, from you point of view, always surround you. This is the space surrounding you, the Sun, the Moon, known to you constellations and altogether everything that, based on your understanding, always exists. You concentrate on any of these elements and simultaneously, as ever, keep in mind the required event for its realization.

2. Seven-digit number: 1045421;

Nine-digitnumber: 891000111.

3. Look with the all-seeing eye after resurrection of everyone and everything. And you will see that restoration of the World is that reality in which you live. And you will feel that you are in the eternal World. Move along this path forward and you will see the way, which calls you. Go along this way and you will see the Creator who is eternal and you will enjoy your eternity; and this enjoyment is the eternity of life; and the Creator is exactly that Creator who created you; and His love is infinite; and His simplicity is trusting and he is as simple and transparent as you have imagined, as you thought about Him before; and He is as kind and constructive as you knew it before. He is your Creator

and He gives you the way.  Go along His way, since His way is your way.

## The 18th day:

1. On this day of the month you concentrate on immovable objects.  This may be a building, a table, or a tree.  Choose anything you like.  Further on you have to find the individual essence of the chosen object, its meaning.  The essence for you means that you should understand what this object for you is. Such is this concentration.

In future when describing the exercises I will not be mentioning that that during the concentration you should keep in your consciousness the required event in order to control it.  In future it will be always meant.

2. Seven-digit number: 1854212;

Nine-digitnumber: 185321945.

3. You go that way, where people are.  You go that way where the events are.  You work where the resistance is.  And when you see it the resistance becomes transparent, its strengths weaken and you see the World of the Eternity even if the resistance is still present.  Go and be everywhere, where you want.  You can be everywhere.  You can embrace the whole world of welfare; that is why, you should fight with the resistance for the welfare of the eternal life; and the resistance will break down and you will see the light of the eternal life and you will perceive it. And this will be realized forever and all times.

## The 19th day:

1. On the nineteenth day of the month you should concentrate on phenomena of the external reality, in which something, which preliminary had existed as a single whole, turns then into aggregate of separate elements.  An example of such phenomenon is a cloud, which turns into raindrops.  Or another one: the crown of a tree turns into separate falling leaves.

Throughout the concentration on such phenomena you are trying to find the laws due to which such development of the event could be prevented.  To find such laws is the sense of this concentration.

2. Seven-digit number: 1254312;

Nine-digitnumber: 158431985.

3. The struggle of the spirit for its true place in the World, as well as the struggle of your soul for personification of the Creator, make your intellect and your mind controlled. Your consciousness becomes universal and your part of the consciousness becomes the common consciousness. You become who you are. Your eternity is revealed in your thoughts. Your contemplation becomes eternity. Your thoughts make the World eternal and you will be where you are, and you will be where you aren't, and you will always be, though the World consists of time intervals, and where you will be the time interval will become the World and the space will join the eternity, and the time will retreat and you will be in movement and you will be in eternal time, and you will feel the eternal time, and this eternal time will come to you. Every moment of your time is an eternal one. Feel the eternity in every moment and you will see that you have already got it.

### The 20th day:

1. On this day you should concentrate on distant sites of consciousness. Your task is to help other people.

Imagine that you want to explain something to another person. To explain what he doesn't know or doesn't understand. As a matter of fact we know already that in reality every person possesses all knowledge, his soul initially has everything. That is why your task is to help him to realize information, which he has already got. By the way, the genuine understating is exactly connected with awareness of the knowledge available in the soul.

The easiest way to awake a person to awareness of required information, kept in his soul, is through the distant sites of his consciousness. The easiest way to reach them is through distant sites of your consciousness.

Doing these exercises you already actively participate in the salvation program. In this respect I would like to specify what should be the fundamental thing for your concentration. Your concentration should give such control, which could provide positive effect for everyone at once; it should provide favorable development of events for everyone at once. This doesn't depend on location of other people. Physically people may stay at a big distance from you; anyway they will receive help from you.

To be more precise this exercise may be called as concentration on the common success. I mean that due to your work, development of specific situations will take favorable direction for everyone.

Would you wish it, especially at the initial stages in the beginning of your practice, one more exercises can be added on this day.

You concentrate on such remote objects such as the Sun, planets or stars and constellations. You may not see them with your usual sight. Your task in this concentration is as follows: you try to understand what these objects are from the point of view of information.

2. Seven-digit number: 1538416;

Nine-digit number: 891543219.

3. Look at the world from the highest position of your consciousness, from the deepest position of your soul and the most spiritual passion to universal welfare, look at the World in such a way as if it is just being created and create it as it is now. However, creating it as it is, change simultaneously the state of the World with its vices for the better, towards creation and eternal life. And you will see that the vices are not the vices at all, but a wrong understanding of the World. Understand the World correctly as it is given to you by the Creator, and you will see that the Creator is everywhere and the correctness is everywhere, you should just make one step towards, you should just not negate and come to this correctness forever and for good and you will see that the World has transformed. And you will see that the universe became yours, and you will see that the Creator is pleased with you, and you will see that you are a creator and able to create everywhere, always and forever, and you are a helper of the Creator, and you are a helper of anyone else and you, as the Creator himself, are creating a creator and here you come to the point of unity of everyone. And this point of unity of everyone is just your soul.

Look at it and you will see the light of life. This light of life is created by your soul. The luminescence of your soul is the thing, which calls you upwards, afar, and in breadth, the luminescence of your soul is the World. You see the World because your soul sees it. You see the soul because you have eyes of the soul. Look at yourself from all sides, and you will see common joining with the entire World, with the entire World which exists everywhere and always. Your thought is the thought of the World. Your knowledge is the knowledge of the World. Distribute the knowledge of life and distribute the light of your soul, and you will see the eternal life in such a state, in which you are in it. You will see that the eternal life has been with you for a long time; it always is, was and will be. The eternal life is you.

The 21$^{st}$ day:

1. On the twenty-first day of the month you should concentrate on the series of numbers, going in reverse sequence. A specific example: 16, 15, 14, 13, 12, 11, and 10. Numbers appearing in these sequences should be within the row from 1 to 31 (maximum number of days in a month.) So, there are 31 numbers at your disposal. When you compile sequences from these numbers rely upon your internal feeling.

2. Seven-digit number: 8153517;

Nine-digitnumber: 589148542.

3. Watch how a mountainous stream runs down the mountains. Watch how snow melts. Look mentally at these pictures, if you have seen them with your eyes. You will see that your thoughts do not differ from your eyes. And you will see that your consciousness doesn't differ from your body. And you will se how your soul builds your body. Don't forget this knowledge transferring it from one second to another and turning a moment into eternity you will be building yourself eternally, as you without any efforts lived before, and thus this eternal construction is the eternal life. Build other objects around yourself on the basis of the same principle, build worlds. Create joy and sow wheat, create bread, give tools and give machines and make machines harmless, not destroying and you will see that you live in this World, and you will see that this is sent

down to you and that the God and your consciousness are revealed in this machine. Stop a machine if it threatens. Build the body if it is ill; realize resurrection if someone has passed away, prevent anyone else from passing away. You are a creator; you are a maker, take, act and go forward in harmony with the entire World, in harmony with everything created, in harmony with everything that will be ever created in the entire eternity and in manifestation of the World, and in harmony with yourself.

## The 22nd day:

1. On this day of the month you should concentrate on such elements of reality which are characterized by the endless reproduction. A specific example: a notion of eternity. Or a notion of endless space. I would like to remind you once again that thinking, for example, about eternity you at the same time should construct the required event.

2. Seven-digit number: 8153485;

    Nine-digit number: 198516789

3. Your soul is a created structure; your soul is a recreated structure. Watch how your soul is being created, watch, how it is being recreated. Your Soul is in the act of recreation, open your world and look, where the Creator has recreated him himself, look at the mechanism of recreation and you will see love. Love is the thing, which brings light to the world. Love is the thing on which the world is being built. Love is the thing that always exists and had initially been. Look at that one who created love and you will see you. Love belonging to you it is you belonging to love. Build with love, build with welfare, and build with a great joy of universal life and universal happiness and you will be able to see that joy which is seen by everyone who is around you. See the joy of those who are around you and your heart will be filled with happiness. Be in happiness; be in harmony and this happiness will bring you eternity. Look with your eternal eyes, look with your eternal body, and look with your eternal look at your relatives and grant them Eternity. Look with your Eternity at all people and grant them Eternity. Look with your eternity at the entire World, at your entire environment and grant them Eternity. The

World will blossom and a flower, which blossoms eternally, will appear. This flower will be your World, which is the World of everyone. And you will live and your happiness will be endless.

## The 23rd day:

1 On the twenty-third day you should concentrate on development of all elements of reality towards realization of the tasks of the God.

2. Seven-digit number: 8154574;

Nine-digitnumber: 581974321.

3. Look at the World, what should be done in it, look at you everyday affairs, see your feelings and look at them. Look, how your feelings are connected with the events, why are you looking forward, why do you feel, why do your affairs go in such a way but not another. Why can the words "another way" not be present in the World, since the World is single and it is various in its singularity? Why does the word "single" mean variety? Feel the entire nature of phenomena in your specific case. Look at this case from all sides. Look at your organism and restore it with one mental moment. Look at your consciousness and make it able to solve all your issues. Look at your soul and see that everything has been available there for long time.

## The 24th day:

1. On this day of the month during concentration you should receive any object from a form of a man. For example, a videocassette, a fountain pen, a plant. You should see from what element of the man's body appears let's say, a videocassette. It means how to realize the image of a man in order to receive a videocassette.

2. Seven-digit number: 5184325

Nine-digit number: 189543210.

3. You have seen that reality, which you have seen. You have come to that reality, which you are. Look at all days from the first to twenty fourth and you will see that your love is endless. Look at the world, how you look with love, look at the feeling, how you build it, look at the feeling as at the eternal creation and you will come to

love as if to Eternity. You come to it forever and you stay with it forever. The Creator, your God created you as loving persons. You are the God's creations and you love. Love is life, and life is love. Display love where you appear, display love in those places where you determine yourself, and predetermine yourself. Love may be not expressed by words and love may be not expressed by feelings, however your actions are love where you create.

## The 25th day:

1 On the twenty fifth day of the month you may concentrate on any objects at your choice, however it is important to have several various concentrations in order to have a kind of an aggregate concentration. Having analyzed this aggregate you join various objects of concentrations into groups based on some sign. For example, a tape-recorder and a cassette can be placed into one group because they add one another when they fulfill the task they are meant for. A tape-recorder and a receiver can be joined into one group, which you consider as goods produced on the basis of electronic equipment. One group can include objects of the same type, for example, two different books. However, if to consider these books from the point of view of their content, these books may appear in different groups if combination of groups will be based on the content. You see, you have complete freedom of creation in this case.

You may, for example, sitting at home, look around and use objects surrounding you for this concentration.

2. Seven-digit number: 1890000;

Nine-digit number: 012459999.

3. Come to the thought about yourself. Catch the thoughts about yourself as reflection of yourself. See yourself as you see all people. See yourself as you see everyone. See yourself as you see a branch of a tree, a leaf of a plant, morning dew or snow on a windowsill. You will see those things, which are eternal before you. You will see that you are eternal.

## The 26th day:

1.    On this day of the month you learn to see simultaneously the whole and a part of it, the common and particular. Suppose that there is a herd of cows in front of you. You see the whole herd and simultaneously can concentrate on any cow. And understand how it lives, what it thinks about, how it will develop. Or you may look at an anthill and simultaneously at some ant.

With the help of this concentration you should understand how practically with one look you could see at once the whole and its part, the common and particular. This concentration will help you to acquire this ability. You will be able to see instantly both common and particular.

2. Seven-digit number: 1584321;

Nine-digitnumber: 485617891.

3. Take into consideration that you develop eternally. See that your development is eternal. Busy yourself with all that is eternal. Since each movement is eternal and each thing is a personification of the Eternity, and each personality is the Eternity and each soul is a multitude of Eternities. Go towards diverse Eternities from the single Eternity and you will see that there is one Eternity for everyone. Come to this through understanding of your soul and you will see that you are the creator of anything you need. Apply this to creation of each thing and you will see that each thing has been created by you. Apply this to creation of your organism and you will see and you will understand that your organism can always be self-healed. Apply this to the health of others and having cured another one you will gain experience for yourself. Curing of others is always an experience for you. Restoration of everything is always an experience for you. Be good to more and more people, give more joy and happiness and you will get the Eternity into your hands in the form of a concrete technological tool of your consciousness. Spread the consciousness to the rigid conditions of the Eternity. There, where the Eternity widens, outrun it, outrun the Eternity in the infinity and you will see yourself as a personification of the Creator. You create in that place where the Eternity is just widening, you are the creator of the Eternity, you control the Eternity and the Eternity always obeys you.

## The 27th day:

1. On the twenty-seventh day of the month you should do the same concentration as on the ninth day of the month, but add to it an infinite development of each element of the concentration.

2. Seven-digit number: 1854342;

Nine-digitnumber: 185431201.

3. Come to help to those who need help. Come to help to those who do not need help. Come to help yourself, if you need help. Come to help yourself if you do not need help. Look at the word "help" in its wider manifestation and look at the kindness as personification of help. You are kind and you help. You are a creator and you have help. Every act of your consciousness brings help to you. Everything created by you is a help to you. You have an infinite number of helpers as well as you help to an infinite number of others. You are in universal connections with everyone, you always help everyone and everyone helps you. Being in universal connections and mutual help bring the society to the welfare, give happiness to everyone and you will see yourself in universal world harmony with everyone where the God-Creator is everything that has been created around you; it's everything that has been created by you and personification of the God in everything created around you. Personification of the God as your creator will reveal in your soul as a genuine understanding of the World in self-development after getting the infinity of life.

The infinity of life is the infinity of the Creator. To be infinitely living you should be being infinitely created, you should be infinitely created. You may do so that every your thought, every your movement, every your action created the Eternity.

## The 28th day:

1. On this day of the month you should fulfill the same concentration as on the eighth day of the month but with one important difference. The thing is as follows.

You must have noticed that on the previous day, 27th, when determining the type of concentration the numbers 2 and 7 were added: $2+7=9$. In this case the situation is different.

The number 28 consists of two figures: 2 and 8. In this case the number 28 should be perceived as follows: two multiplied by eight. Not adding 2 and 8, but just multiplying. It means that eight is doubled. That is why the program of the eighth day is repeated on this day.

However this repetition should not be strict, it shouldn't be an exact copy of the previous work. You have to change something. And first of all change something in yourself. For example, change something in your vision of this concentration. Fulfilling it according to the old scheme you should nevertheless see something new in it, to look at it from another side.

Your understanding as well as your perception of these concentrations should be always widening and deepening. This is a creative process. It facilitates your development.

2. Seven-digit number: 1854512;

Nine-digit number: 195814210.

3. Look at yourself as you look at the whole World right away. Look at the Creator the same way as the Creator looks at you and in this get understanding of what the Creator wants from you. Look at His look and you will see His look. You will see that the look of the Creator is also fixed at the far phenomena of the World; and your task is to control these phenomena of the World. You should make harmonic any phenomena of the World. This is your true task. You should give birth to the Worlds and crate the Worlds which will always be harmonic. This has been your true task since your creation. Since Him, the Creator has already created, since He, the Creator has already done, and your task is to go along this way since you have been created in the image and likeness the same way as the Creator has been created. The Creator created himself and He created you as well. Create yourself and create others. Create all others and give universal welfare to everyone and you will have the World, which has been created for you, and for everyone, and for the Creator. Create for the Creator since He created you. Create for the Creator since He created everything. That is why whenever you create anything you

create for the Creator.

## The 29th day:

1.  On the twenty-ninth day you fulfill a resumptive concentration. On this day you should look at all concentrations of this month from the first day to twenty-eighth. However you should perceive them in an impulse. It's important. The way covered within the month you take in with one single moment of perception.

At this you should do a certain analysis of your work. On this day you so say create a platform for the work in the following months.

You may imagine everything you have done in the form of a sphere which you should place on an endless straight line the initial part of which includes the following month. Thus you create a platform not just for the next month but for your further infinite development as well.

2.  Seven-digit number: 1852142;

Nine-digitnumber: 512942180.

3. Look at the World with your eyes. Look at the World with all of your feelings. Look at the World with all of your cells. Look at the World with your whole organism and with everything with what you can see and with everything you are. Look at the World and yourself and inside of yourself. Look at the World understanding that the World is around you and it envelopes you. Look at the reality, which gives life. Look at such reality, which gives the Eternity. And you will see that whatever you look at there is only this reality that gives life and gives the Eternity. And the creator of this reality is the God. The God who has created this reality has created the eternal life and he sees you the same way you see yourself, and he sees you the same way as you don't see yourself, and he is your creator.

## The 30th day:

1. On this day you carry out concentration on the built platform. This concentration lays the basis for your work in the following month.

You should concentrate on the harmony of the World. You should see it, find it, rejoice at it, and admire it. And at the same time you wonder how the Creator could have created everything so perfectly. You admire the harmony of the World as the consequence of perfection of the Creator.

2. Seven-digit number: 1852143;

Nine-digit number: 185219351.

3. Principle based on which you build all the previous days may be the main one on this day, since in February, in the current system of chronology, 29 or 28 days, this principle on the thirtieth day gets over to the first or the second day. So, this unification shows the eternal cycle of life. Find the eternity in all your previous harmonization. Find this eternity in this simple example, since one month consists of 30 days, another, February, of 29 or 28 days and just through one month February we have common joining of figure 30 with figure one or two. Joining of the figures various by nature and origin testifies to the unity and common nature of everyone. Find common nature in everything, in each element of information, find common nature where it is not seen at once, and find it where it is obvious, find it where it can be seen at once. And you will see, and you will become aware, and you will feel, and you will be inspired.

## The 31st day:

1. On the thirty-first day you concentrate on the separated areas of each individual volume.

Let, for example, a tree grow on a certain site of the land. You realize that there is ground below, under it. There is air above it and on each side. All these separate areas join in your consciousness by your seeing in all of them the eternal reproduction of life. The life is eternal. You have to realize it. Remember about it watching the surrounding world, feeling it, dissolving in it. Realization of this Truth will come to you: YES, THE LIFE IS ETERNAL!

2. Seven-digit number: 1532106;

Nine-digit number: 185214321.

3. You are absolutely and completely healthy and everyone around you is healthy.

And the World is eternal. And all events are creative. And always you see everything only in positive light. And everything around is favorable.

I would like to make one more remark to the given exercises. I repeat once again that you should determine yourself the number of concentrations and their duration. You have also to decide independently which result currently is the most important for you, what you should aspire to, first of all.

Remember that these exercises are creative. They develop you. You will grow spiritually with the help of these concentrations, and this in its turn will help you to fulfill all these concentrations at a higher level and that will ensure for you bigger development and so further.

These exercises help to develop consciousness, development of events of your life in favorable direction, receiving of full value health and establishment of harmony with the pulse of the Universe.

# AFTERWORD

# AFTERWORD

Save yourself and you will save others. Save others and you will save yourself. Movement to the World is the truth of the World. And movement to consciousness is the truth of awareness. Your mission is universal. You should seek that way, which is predetermined for you. Your way is the way within the eternity. Your life is creation. Your image is the image of God. Your consciousness is the image of reason. Your creation is the image of truth. You are a creator, just as God is the Creator. You are the truth, since the truth is God. When you look at the World with clear and widely opened eyes, these eyes reflect that reality, that you were created by God. When you look at God these eyes reflect the truth of the World. Your eyes were created by the Creator and you can look the way he created, you look and create. Your eyes are your consciousness; your soul is everything that you create. Your body is your consciousness. Your hands are your consciousness. You look at yourself and you create yourself. You look at people and you create people. You look at the World and you create the World. You perceive the World and the World creates you. You perceive the World and the World creates itself. You look at reality and the reality sees you. You see the reality just like you see everyone around. When you walk to the top of the World, the World is near you. When you walk to it, the World is on the top. If you see it, you see your love. Your love is your creation sent by God and created by him once and for all. Just as love created by God, which had always existed, here, there and everywhere, I handover to you this book for all times of your life, and all times of entire life. You will have this once and for all, and you will have this inasmuch you always exist. When you always exist, you move upward and the path in front of you is covered with flowers. When you are everywhere you move everywhere and the path in front of you is covered with space and worlds. When you are everywhere, the path in front of you consists of flowers. Take these flowers and distribute, give a flower of this eternal life to everyone. Show the way, make the way instantaneous and equal for all. Everyone should have eternal life and everyone should be sent the way. Everyone has it in his soul. Open your soul and show the flower of your joy to all around you. Get to know this reality in that spirit, in which you have already got to know it. Come to what you already know. Be that one who you already are. Save yourself and save others, and your reason will be instantaneous in the Eternity and the Eternity will be the personification of your reason. And when you will see yourself in the instant of your reason this will be the resurrection of all and everything. And everyone who is present must be resurrected, and everyone, who is absent, must be resurrected, and everyone who lives must never die, and on the basis of the principle of universal non-dying make the universal resurrection, since contemporary knowledge, the knowledge of salvation and the true salvation are based on what you must know. The advent of the Savoir is in the fact that you realize what you have already had in the knowledge, and you will take this knowledge. This is the advent of the Savoir to everyone. You can have this knowledge and you should save yourself with the help of this knowledge. And the universal salvation will reach all. Since, we can be saved, when everyone saves himself individually; since, we can be saved when all save themselves together. We move there, where the salvation always exists. In any case we will save ourselves. Your task is drawing salvation closer to the level of work and the work must become salvation in the eternal life. Since only the eternal life is the true salvation, since only the true salvation is the eternal life.

Grigori Grabovoi

## LIST OF REFERENCES

1. Grabovoi G.P. "The principle of complete restoration of similar systems". A theme in the scientific report on the 15th conference of young specialists about interaction between optical systems and physical matter. Tashkent, the publisher TashKBM, 1991.[1] (Грабовой Г.П. «Принцип полного восстановления подобных систем». Тема в научном докладе на XV конференции молодых специалистов о взаимодействии оптических систем и физической материи. Ташкент, Изд. ТашКБМ, 1991.)

2. Grabovoi G.P. "The structure of the eternal self-reproduction of matter in the processes of heat-mass exchange". The Material of Tashkent State University on heat-mass exchange to the protocol No 22/92 the National Academy of Sciences, Tashkent, the publisher: the National Academy of Sciences of the Republic of Uzbekistan, 1992. (Грабовой Г.П. «Структура вечного самовоспроизводства материи в процессах тепломассообмена». Материал ТашГУ по темпломассообмену к протоколу №22/92 НАК. Ташкент, Изд. НАК РУз, 1992.)

3. Grabovoi G.P. "The fundamental laws of restoration of matter and eternal creative development in the formation of the forecast that ensures safety". Tashkent, the publisher: VEO "Rampa", 1993. (Грабовой Г.П. «Фундаментальные законы восстановления материи и вечного созидательного развития в формировании обеспечивающего безопасность прогноза». Ташкент, Изд. ВЭО «Рампа», 1993.)

4. Grabovoi G.P. "The principles and methods of resurrection and infinite life. The methodology of healings and control of events". Moscow, the publisher: JSC "Kapas", 1994. (Грабовой Г.П. «Принципы и методы воскрешения и бесконечной жизни. Методология исцелений и управления событиями». Москва, Изд. АО «Капас», 1994.)

5. Grabovoi G.P. "The application of the principles and methods of resurrection and infinite life in the control of events". Moscow, the publisher: JSC "Kapas", 1994.

---

[1] **Translator's note.** The list includes translations of the titles of the works which, were created and published in Russian. The original title in Russian and the Publishing House is in brackets.

(Грабовой Г.П. «Применение принципов и методов воскрешения и бесконечной жизни в управлении событиями». Москва, Изд. АО «Капас», 1994.)

6. Grabovoi G.P. "The methods of creation of matter by means of one's consciousness". Moscow, the publisher: JSC "Kapas", 1994.   (Грабовой Г.П. «Методы создания материи посредством своего сознания». Москва, Изд. АО «Капас», 1994. )

7. Grabovoi G.P. "The infinite life and the absence of destructions as the law of harmonious construction of the world". Interview for the newspaper "Megapolis - Continent". Moscow, the publisher JSC "Kapas", 1995.   (Грабовой Г.П. «Бесконечная жизнь и отсутствие разрушений как закон гармоничного построения мира». Интервью для газеты «Мегаполис - Континент». Москва, Изд. АО «Капас», 1995.)

8. Grabovoi G.P. "The principles of transfer of the regenerating effect of the technologies of resurrection and eternal life". Moscow, the publisher: JSC "Kapas", 1996. (Грабовой Г.П. «Принципы передачи восстанавливающего действия технологий воскрешения и вечной жизни». Москва, изд. АО «Капас», 1996.)

9. Grabovoi G.P. "The genetic systems of resurrection and eternal life". Moscow, the publisher JSC "Kapas", 1996. (Грабовой Г.П. «Генетические системы воскрешения и вечной жизни». Москва, Изд. АО «Капас», 1996.)

10. Grabovoi G.P. "The principles of resurrection in medicine and control of events. The basic structures of the medicine of eternal development". Moscow, the publisher: JSC "Kapas", 1996.   (Грабовой Г.П. «Принципы воскрешения в медицине и управлении событиями.  Основные структуры медицины вечного развития». Москва, Изд. АО «Капас», 1996.)

11. Grabovoi G.P. "The course of lectures on control of events and creation of matter with the structuring of one's consciousness. The eternal life of soul and body based on the laws of the Creator". Moscow, the publisher JSC "Kapas", 1997. (Грабовой Г.П. «Курс лекций по управлению событиями и созданию материи структуризацей своего сознания. Вечная жизнь души и тела по законам Создателя». Москва, Изд. АО «Капас», 1997.)

12. Grabovoi G.P. "The applied structures of the creating area of information".

Moscow, the publisher: the Russian Academy of Natural Sciences, 1998. (Грабовой Г.П. «Прикладные структуры создающей области информации». Москва, изд. РАЕН, 1998.)

13.  Grabovoi G.P. "The Practice of Control. The Way of Salvation". Vol. 1, 2, 3. Moscow, Publishing house Soprichastnost, 1998. (Грабовой Г.П. «Практика управления. Путь спасения». т. 1, 2, 3. Москва, Изд. Сопричастность, 1998.)

14. Grabovoi G.P. "Resurrection". Moscow, Publishing house A.V. Kalashnikov, 1999. (Грабовой Г.П. «Воскрешение». Москва, Изд. А.В. Калашников, 1999.)

15.  Grabovoi G.P. "Fundamental definitions of optical systems in control of micro-processes". The journal "Microelectronics", issue 1 (153). Moscow, the publisher: Central Scientific Research Institute "Electronics", 1999. (Грабовой Г.П. «Фундаментальные определения оптических систем в управлении микропроцессами». Журнал «Микро-электроника», выпуск 1 (153). Москва, Изд. ЦНИИ «Электроника», 1999.)

16. Grabovoi G.P. "The unified system of knowledge". Moscow, the publisher: A.V. Kalashnikov, 2000. (Грабовой Г.П. «Унифицированная система знаний». Москва, Изд. А.В. Калашников, 2000.)

17. Grabovoi G.P. "The restoration of the human organism by concentration on numbers". Moscow, the publisher: A.V. Kalashnikov, 2001. (Грабовой Г.П. «Восстановление организма человека концентрацией на числах». Москва, Изд. А.В. Калашников, 2001)

Grigori Grabovoi

THE RESURRECTION OF PEOPLE AND ETERNAL LIFE FROM NOW
ON IS OUR REALITY!

The work "The Resurrection of People and Eternal Life From Now On Is Our
Reality!" was created by Grigori Petrovich Grabovoi in Russian in the period from
2000 till February 2001, on the basis of his early manuscripts.

CPSIA information can be obtained at www.ICGtesting.com
Printed in the USA
LVOW03s1447220115

423936LV00015B/489/P

9 781495 476679